LIFE AND LETTERS

IN THE

FOURTH CENTURY

LIFE AND LETTERS

IN

THE FOURTH CENTURY

BY

TERROT REAVELEY GLOVER M.A.

CLASSICAL LECTURER AND FORMERLY FELLOW OF ST JOHN'S COLLEGE CAMBRIDGE
LATE PROFESSOR OF LATIN IN QUEEN'S UNIVERSITY CANADA

NEW YORK / RUSSELL & RUSSELL

FIRST PUBLISHED IN 1901
REISSUED, 1968, BY RUSSELL & RUSSELL
A DIVISION OF ATHENEUM HOUSE, INC.
BY PERMISSION OF THE CAMBRIDGE UNIVERSITY PRESS
L. C. CATALOG CARD NO: 68-10923
PRINTED IN THE UNITED STATES OF AMERICA

TO

JOHN WATSON

JOHN MACNAUGHTON

AND

JAMES CAPPON

IN MEMORY OF

FIVE WINTERS IN CANADA

PREFACE

WHEN studying the history of the early Roman Empire the reader has at call a thousand impressions of the writers of the day, whom he has read from boyhood, and who have helped to form the mind and the temper with which he reads. But the same does not hold of the period of the Gothic invasions and the fall of Paganism. The literature is extensive, but it is not known, it is hardly read. No one who has given it a sympathetic study can call it wanting in pathos or power, but the traditions of scholarship point in another direction. An age that can boast an Augustine and a Synesius in prose, a Claudian and a Prudentius in poetry, is nevertheless in general ignored, except by scholars engaged in some special research, who use them as sources.

My endeavour has been, by reading (if I may use the expression) across the period, to gain a truer knowledge because a wider. Then, bearing in mind its general air and character, I have tried to give the period to my reader, not in a series of generalizations but in a group of portraits. I have tried to present the men in their own way, carefully and sympathetically; to shew their several attempts, successful or unsuccessful, to realize and solve the problems common to them all; and to illustrate these attempts from their environment, literary, religious and political. As far as possible, I have tried to let them tell their own tale, to display themselves in their weakness and their strength.

I have deliberately avoided the writers, whose work may be strictly called technical or special, for those whose concern was more with what is fitly called literature, but I have at the same time not forgotten the former. For instance, to have treated the theological writings of Athanasius or Augustine at all adequately would have gone far beyond my present limits. And indeed it was less necessary to attempt this, as it has been done fully and ably by others. Rather my concern has been with the world in which the philosopher and the theologian found themselves, and I trust that some who study them may find help in my effort to picture this world. For such students I am only supplying background. Still I hope this background may have for those who are interested in the refraction of light as well as in light itself, a value and an interest as a presentment of an important and even pathetic moment in the history of our race.

As my course has been across the period, I have had again and again to explore a fresh stream upward and toward its source. Every writer has his own antecedents, and some consideration of these has been in every case necessary. No stream however lacks tributaries, and some have many. I suppose that of all of these I should have had some personal knowledge, but as this would have meant a constantly widening and never-ending series of independent researches, I have done the human thing in accepting the work of other men in outlying regions, while surveying as far as I could myself the lands adjacent to my particular subject in each instance. In such cases I have generally given my authority. It may very well occur that specialists will find blunders in detail in my work. I have found them myself in places where I felt secure. But I trust that no blunders will be found of such dimensions as to un-focus any of my portraits or at least to affect at all materially my general picture.

I have made constant use of the works of Gibbon, of M. Boissier, of Dr Hodgkin and Professor Bury. Other books

which I have consulted are mentioned in the various notes.
Professor Dill's interesting book, *Roman Society in the last
Century of the Western Empire*, I did not see till some seven
of my chapters were written. As in one or two places his work
and mine have overlapped, I felt I had less freedom to use
his book, but in general it will be found that our periods and
provinces have been quite distinct. My table of dates is based
chiefly on Goyau, *Chronologie de l'Empire Romain*. Dr Sandys
has been kind enough to read some of my proofs.

Most of my work on this volume has been done in Canada.
Those who know the difficulties with which young Universities
have to contend in "all the British dominions beyond the
seas," difficulties incident to young countries and as a rule
bravely faced and overcome, will not be surprised that the
Library at my disposal was small. But any one who knows
Queen's University will understand what compensations I have
had for a limited number of books in the friendship, the
criticism and the encouragement of the colleagues to whom
I have dedicated my work.

St John's College, Cambridge,
September, 1901.

CONTENTS

NOTE. Summaries of the contents of the chapters may be found by reference to the index under the names of the authors treated.

TABLE OF DATES

346 Sapor again besieges Nisibis, but after seventy-eight days abandons
the siege.

347 ? John Chrysostom born.

348 War with Persia.
Prudentius born. ·

349 Sapor for the third time besieges Nisibis in vain.

350 Magnentius, a German, declared Emperor in Gaul.
Death of Constans.
Vetranio proclaimed Emperor at Sirmium (1 March).
Magnentius master of Rome.
Conference of Constantius with Vetranio (25 Dec.).   Vetranio's sol-
diers desert him.   He is pardoned by Constantius.
Gallus recalled to Constantius' court, and made Caesar next year.

351 War between Constantius and Magnentius.

352 Magnentius loses Italy and falls back on Gaul.
Liberius bishop of Rome.

353 Constantius marries Eusebia.
Magnentius, defeated and deserted, kills himself.
Paulinus (afterwards bishop of Nola) born at Bordeaux.

354 Constantius at war against the Alamanni.
Fall of Gallus.
Augustine born (13 Nov.) at Thagaste.

355 Campaign of Constantius against Alamanni.
Julian at Milan, and afterwards at Athens.
Revolt of Silvanus.
Franks, Alamanni and Saxons invade Gaul.
Julian declared Caesar, and married to Helena.   He pronounces his
first panegyric on Constantius and goes to Gaul.

356 Julian retakes Cologne, held by Germans 10 months.

357 Julian, in supreme command in Gaul, crosses the Rhine and defeats
the Germans.
Constantius visits Rome.

359 Gratian born.
Sapor crosses the Euphrates.
Siege and fall of Amid.

360 Julian's second panegyric to Constantius.
Further operations of Sapor.   Constantius prepares to meet him.
Soldiers proclaim Julian Emperor.
The Empress Eusebia dies.
? Stilicho born (or earlier).

361 Constantius marries Faustina.
Julian crosses the Rhine and Constantius the Euphrates ; both successful in their foreign campaigns and march against each other.
Death of Constantius (Nov.).
Julian enters Constantinople (Dec.), and orders re-opening of temples, and proclaims toleration.
Bishop George murdered in Alexandria.

362 Julian goes to Antioch (midsummer).
Heathen revival.

363 Julian's Persian campaign.
Death of Julian (June).
Jovian, Emperor, surrenders Nisibis and five provinces to Sapor.

364 Death of Jovian (Feb.).
Valentinian and Valens, Emperors, in West and East respectively.
Saxons, Picts and Scots ravage Britain. Alamanni in Gaul.

365 Avianius Symmachus prefect of Rome.
Revolt of Procopius.
? Sulpicius Severus born.
? Synesius born (Volkmann).

366 Fall of Procopius.
Death of Liberius bishop of Rome. Fight of Ursinus and Damasus for see of Rome. Damasus bishop.

367 Valens crosses the Danube to meet the Goths.

368 The Count Theodosius in Britain. He takes London.

369 Campaign of Valentinian against Alamanni across the Rhine.
Symmachus and Ausonius follow the expedition.

370 Ausonius writes the *Mosella*.

371 Rising of Firmus in Africa.
Death of Patricius, Augustine's father.

372 Adeodatus, son of Augustine, born.

373 Death of Athanasius.

374 Ambrose bishop of Milan.

375 Death of Valentinian. Gratian succeeds him and refuses the title *Pontifex Maximus*. Valentinian II also Emperor, aged 5 years.

376 Count Theodosius beheaded at Carthage.

377 Arcadius born.

378 Paulinus consul.
Gothic war. Defeat and death of Valens at Adrianople.
The younger Theodosius (I) succeeds him as Emperor in the East (379).

379 Ausonius consul.

381 Council of Constantinople.

383 Maximus proclaimed Emperor by his soldiers in Britain. He crosses
    to Gaul. War with Gratian.
    Murder of Gratian. Peace between Maximus and Valentinian II.
    Augustine goes to Rome.

384 Honorius born.
    Death of bishop Damasus, who is succeeded by Siricius.

385 Stilicho's campaign in Britain against Picts, Scots and Saxons.
    Theophilus bishop of Alexandria.

387 Affair of the Statues at Antioch.
    Baptism of Augustine.
    Maximus invades Italy.

388 Defeat and death of Maximus.

390 Massacre at Thessalonica by Theodosius' orders. Ambrose forbids
    him the church.

391 Symmachus consul.
    Anti-pagan legislation by Theodosius.

392 Valentinian II murdered by order of Arbogast, who makes Eugenius
    Emperor, in Gaul.

393 Eugenius comes to Italy and issues decrees in favour of paganism.

394 Flavian reestablishes pagan rites in Italy. His soldiers desert
    him on approach of Theodosius, and he commits suicide.
    Battle of the Frigidus between Theodosius and Eugenius (5 Sept.).
    Theodosius defeats and kills Eugenius (6 Sept.).
    Theodosius visits Rome.

395 Death of Theodosius at Milan. The Empire is divided between his
    sons Honorius (West) and Arcadius (East).
    Probinus and Olybrius consuls.
    Alaric invades Greece.
    Fall of Rufinus, minister at Constantinople.
    Augustine bishop of Hippo.

396 Stilicho blockades Alaric at Pholoe. Alaric escapes somehow.

397 Synesius goes to Constantinople.
    Gildo the Moor transfers his allegiance from Rome to Constantinople,
    and stops the corn supply of Rome.
    Chrysostom bishop of Constantinople.

398 War with Gildo, who is defeated and killed.

CHAPTER I

INTRODUCTION

BEFORE proceeding to the study of the fourth century in the lives and writings of a series of typical men, it will be well to take a general survey of the period as a whole. Such a course, without the further study, is apt to be unfruitful and unsatisfactory, yet as a preface to it, it may help the student to a right orientation. The different phases of the century's life will be dealt with at more length in the various essays, in which many things set here will find fuller illustration. Here however in the meantime our concern is with general outlines and broad statements. For the sake of clearness certain main lines will be followed,—a plan which has the drawback, incidental to all such dissection, of failing to shew in the fullest way the interlacing of forces and tendencies which constantly react on one another. I shall try to shew something of this in my summary, but it is best felt when we read the period in flesh and blood.

Let us begin with the Roman Empire—difficult indeed to grasp in all its meanings, and apart from the Church the greatest factor in history. What it first meant to mankind was peace and law. We may be shocked to read here of a Roman governor in Spain or there of one in Asia burning men alive in the days of Cicero and Virgil, of endless crucifixions, of the extortions of a Verres, of venal rulers and infamous publicans. Yet there is another side to all this, for in the first place we know of all these things chiefly because they shocked the Roman conscience. There was a great deal more that should have shocked it but did not, because the world was not yet

I. The Empire. Its good side.

educated. In the next place, what did the Empire replace? We do not know this so well, but where we have any light we see that it was generally a change for the better. The sentimentalist may sigh for Greek freedom and for the national independence of other races, but in the great age of Greece liberty had meant the right of single cities to rule themselves, and what was now left of it was worse than worthless, while the other peoples had never (with one exception) been very clearly conscious of their nationality. The peoples of the East had reached high levels of civilization and organization, but through all the centuries of their intellectual and commercial development they had been under the sway of the foreigner. In the West there was even less national consciousness[1], for there Rome had faced not nations, but clans, never united except by accident and always ready to quarrel. When at last the peoples of Gaul and Spain began to feel conscious of their race, they voiced their feelings in Latin. Rome thus had not to extinguish nationalities, but rather she replaced here despotism and there anarchy with the solid advantages of a steady government, if severe, at least conscientious.

If Rome's yoke was heavy (and at times it weighed very heavily on some unlucky province), still hardly any attempt was made to throw it off. Rome had not as a rule to dread rebellion when once the charm of a hereditary dynasty was broken. Almost the sole exception is the Jewish people, a race made self-conscious by its own prophets, by its Babylonian captivity and by the tyranny of Antiochus Epiphanes and his like. Here the Roman met his match, and here was the one people to impose its will upon him. While everywhere the Roman government was sensitive to local peculiarities of administration and religion and careful to respect them where it was possible not to alter them, with the Jew special terms had to be made wherever he was. His Sabbath, his synagogue, his temple dues, the jurisdiction of his elders were all conceded to him; but even so Rome had to face rebellion after rebellion, and when that stage was past there still survived the Jewish riot in Alexandria. Here alone Rome failed, but with every other race once mistress she was mistress for ever, making all peoples equal and members one of another under her sway.

The Roman roads bound the Empire together. They were kept

---

[1] Cf. Seeck, *Gesch. des Untergangs der antiken Welt* i. (second edition), pp. 207—212, on "diese Schwäche des Staatsbewusstseins und des Nationalgefühls" among the early Germans.

in order and they were safe, and freedom of travel and trade prevailed as never before. In the West the schoolmaster was the sturdy ally of the government, and Latin culture bound Gaul and Spaniard to Rome till any other form of rule became inconceivable. Roman law found one of its most famous seats at the university of Berytus in Syria, while in the West it shaped the thoughts and conceptions of men to such an extent that it imposed itself at last upon the Church and its theology, from which it is not yet eradicated nor likely to be. East and West agreed in the belief that Rome's rule was eternal. Afrahat the Syrian and Tertullian the first great Latin father alike inculcate that the fall of the Roman Empire will not come till the Day of Judgment and the world's end. In a certain sense they are no doubt right, but their prophecy was of the formal government of Rome. The distress caused by the Gothic invasions is partly to be traced to the feeling that, if Rome fell, there was no possible power to take her place. Thus she stood for law, for peace and quiet, and for the general order of the universe. She was a necessary part of the universe, and her rule was a postulate for all rational thought on society.

Yet there was a bad side to all this. All power was centralized in the Emperor, more and more so as the generations passed, partly from the jealousy of the *Its weakness.* ruler and partly from the habits of obedience and reliance induced by long dependence. The faculty for self-government was paralysed by long disuse. Men were at first afraid and afterwards unable to think and move for themselves[1]. The consequences of such a decline are hard to compute, but the general helplessness of the Roman provinces in the face of invaders, numerically inferior but strong in the self-reliance of a free people without much government, is perhaps the most striking evidence of decay.

Another source of mischief was bad finance. From very early days the prejudice that trade is an unworthy occupation for a noble and high-spirited man had survived. No great industries were developed, and the world was poorer for want of the ingenuity they stimulate and the wealth they bring. The slave system was no doubt in part responsible for this, but not altogether. Industries depend

---

[1] Tacitus already remarks an *inscitia reipublicae ut alienae*—a striking phrase (*Hist.* i. 1). Seeck, *op. cit.* pp. 287—8, calls attention to the effect of the proscriptions in removing the brave and independent, and leaving only the weaker to be the fathers of a new generation—themselves and their children alike cowed by these examples of the results of independence. See p. 343.

on intelligence and observation, and these were depressed by the conditions of absolute government, and there was no foreign society to quicken them by competition and correspondence. As if this were not enough, taxation was arranged on fatal principles. The middle classes paid all the taxes, and, the towns being taxed as units, with every loss to the circle of tax-payers the burden was more and more intolerable for the rest. The lower classes, at least in Rome, were fed, amused and bathed for nothing. Free grain, free wine, free pork and free oil may trace their descent from the laws of Gaius Gracchus. The extravagant beast-shows and gladiatorial games were another legacy from senatorial Rome, and these were a tax on the rich all over the Empire. Symmachus spent £80,000, equivalent I suppose to four times the sum to-day, on one set of shows. Beast-catching was indeed a flourishing, if an unproductive, industry. Money was wasted in other ways, especially after Diocletian's remodelling of the imperial system and his establishment of two Emperors and two Caesars, each of the four with an extravagant court. Presents to the Emperor were another form of extortion.

Beside these elements of decay, and connected with them, was the terrible legacy left by the Republic in debased morals. The Roman character had its fine side, as we see in the qualities a Roman loved—*gravitas* and *modestia*, and in the ideals to which he aspired—*honores* and *auctoritas*, and while this is written for good all over the face of the Roman Empire and Roman institutions, there was another side. It may seem fanciful to go back to Hannibal for the beginning of Rome's decline, but he began the decay of Italian agriculture, and from his day Italian yeomanry died away. Following immediately on the Hannibalic war came the conquests of Greece and Western Asia, and the simultaneous flooding of Rome with Greek philosophy and Asiatic wealth. The one taught the Roman to despise the rustic gods of his fathers, and the other their thrifty, farm-bred ideals. Sudden wealth joined forces with a flippant scepticism to sap the Roman character, just as a successful rebellion and an enormous and rapid accumulation of wealth in the hands of persons without traditions have given a modern people a bad repute for lawlessness and want of taste. Neither in the one case nor in the other are redeeming features wanting, as we have seen, but the Roman aristocracy and the middle class were almost entirely corrupted. The last century of the Republic is marked by reckless and tasteless selfishness of the most violent type and by its fruits in chaos, massacre and paralysis. Over all this rose the Empire, heir to a weakened manhood and lowered ideals. It stopped in some measure the rapid progress of the disease, but the germs of Rome's decay it could not reach. It could not touch the essential scepticism of Roman society; it might try to revive a discredited religion and restore a forgotten ritual, but the profound unbelief underlying all the ideas of the upper classes was beyond its power to cure. Slavery was too deeply rooted in the social scheme to be meddled with, and indeed it seems to have occurred to no one to meddle with it. Marriage fell into disuse, as was natural when the sceptical and self-indulgent had the slave-system in their homes. And in spite of wars and proscriptions there was still the great wealth and still the tradition of replenishing it more or less honestly by the spoliation of the provinces. There was still the passion for the gladiatorial games and for the theatre—the schools of murder and of lust whose lessons were only too faithfully learned.

The wars of the year 69 A.D. mark a stage in Roman history. It is as though the world now definitely accepted the fact of the Empire. The restlessness that marks its first century is past. *Then* the sons of men, who, if not statesmen, had played great parts on the world's stage, were settling sullenly down to splendid and caged insignificance in Rome, eating, drinking, conspiring, raging and failing. *Now*, a quieter mood comes over the world. There is less rage and less extravagance, and the fruits of a quiet movement of thought begin to appear. Scepticism is yielding place to Stoicism, the philosophy of endurance. It was followed by a genuine revival of religion, genuine in that men believed in their convictions of its truth, but after all a sentimental revival. Scepticism and despair had yielded to philosophy, but the human heart wanted more[1]. Still sceptical it turned to religion, and of this mood of faith and unfaith, of this wish to believe and this doubt of the possibility of belief, came the revival. It was not of the best or the strongest, but it did good. It had an air of asceticism about it, and decency revived and society grew purer. But it could not check the decline.

---

[1] Cf. Strauss, *der Romantiker auf dem Throne* p. 20, "In such times of transition in the world's history, men in whom feeling and imagination outweigh clear thinking, souls of more warmth than clearness, will ever turn backward toward the old." This is written of Julian, but it applies to the whole revival in question.

At the end of the third century Diocletian orientalized the

The Empire in the 4th century. Empire—to borrow an expression of Synesius[1]. I give the story in the words of a hostile critic, Lactantius (if he wrote the *De Mortibus Perse-cutorum*). "This man ruined the world by his avarice and cowardice. For he set up three to share his kingdom [remark the word at last, *regnum*], and divided the world into four parts. This meant the multiplication of armies, since every one of them strove to have a far larger number of soldiers, than former princes had had, when they governed the state single-handed. So much greater did the number of those who received begin to be than of those who gave, that the strength of the farmers was exhausted by the enormity of taxation, the fields were deserted and cultivated lands returned to forest. And, that everything might be full of terror, the provinces also were cut into scraps, many rulers and more officials swooped down on the various regions and almost one might say on the several cities...[He enlarges on their number and greed.] ...He was also a man of insatiable avarice, and wished his reserves never to be lessened ; but he was always gathering in extraordinary sums of money and 'presents,' in order to keep what he was storing intact and inviolate......To this was added his boundless passion for building, no less a tax on the provinces in supplying workmen and artificers and waggons and every sort of thing neces-sary for building. Here basilicas, there a circus, here a mint, there an armoury, here a palace for his wife and there for his daughter...... Such was his constant madness, his passion to make Nicomedeia equal to the city of Rome" (*de Mort. Pers.* 7).

This is the bad side of the story. There was, however, another. The division of the imperial power, it is fair to assume, was to secure the world against being left without a head, as it had so often been in the third century, when the murder of an Emperor again and again plunged society into anarchy and civil war. The removal of the capital from Rome was a necessary and wise step[2].

---

[1] *de Regno* 10: τὴν περὶ τὸ βασιλικὸν σῶμα σκηνὴν καὶ θεραπείαν, ἣν ὥσπερ ἱερουργοῦντες ἡμῖν ἐν ἀπορρήτῳ ποιοῦνται καὶ τὸ βαρβαρικῶς ἐκτεθεῖσθαι τὰ καθ' ὑμᾶς. Lactantius, *M. P.* 21, had already said Galerius deliberately copied the Persian court. See Seeck, *Untergang der antiken Welt* (opening pages), for a brilliant portrait of Diocletian, an Emperor with a Radical M.P.'s love of reforming everything with one fresh plan after another. In his reign of twenty years the Empire was more fundamentally changed than in all the preceding three centuries.

[2] Rome personified says in a poem of Claudian's *His annis qui lustra mihi bis dena recensent | nostra ter Augustos intra pomoeria vidi* (vi. *Cons.*

The populace of Rome were no longer masters of the world, and their opinions not now being needed, there was no reason, but that of sentiment, for the seat of government remaining in a town remote from all important points. Nicomedeia was convenient, for it allowed the Emperor to be so much nearer both Danube and Euphrates. Thirty years later Constantine further developed the new system, making the Emperor the splendid head of a hierarchy of officials and transferring the capital across the sea to Europe. The foundation of Constantinople is no unimportant moment in the world's history[1].

Constantine was succeeded by his three sons, of whom Constantius became sole ruler. He was followed by Julian, who reigned some two years; and when, on Jovian's death (following speedily that of Julian), Valentinian became Emperor, he was bidden by his soldiers to name a colleague. He chose his brother Valens, and they divided the Empire. Valens became Emperor at Constantinople, and Valentinian in the West. Theodosius succeeded Valens, and in 395 left the world to his two sons, Arcadius, Emperor in the East, and Honorius in the West. From this point East and West begin to fall more conspicuously apart.

I have said nothing so far of the Goths. For some generations German barbarians had been menacing the Empire. Sometimes they were driven off or killed; sometimes they were given lands in the Empire and admitted to service in the army; but still they pressed on and on. The Goths' first really great victory was at Adrianople in 378, where they killed Valens. It seemed then as though they would at once finally overflow the Eastern half of the Empire, but they were beaten back, and it was not for thirty uneasy years that they had their will of the Roman world, and then it was not Constantinople but Rome they captured (410). They had little mind to destroy what they found; rather they wished to share and to control.

With bad finance, cruel taxation, civil wars, slavery and Gothic inroads the Roman Empire suffered terribly, but its most serious danger was the steady loss of population resulting from these causes, or at least speeded by them. The army was sterile; for

Hon. 392). These Emperors were Constantine, Constantius, Theodosius (twice). Diocletian may be added a little before (Lactantius, *M. P.* 17), but in any case this habitual absence of the Emperor is noteworthy.

[1] For one thing it gave the Bishop of Rome a much freer hand than he could otherwise have had, for now the only serious competing world-power was hundreds of miles away.

till the reign of Severus soldiers were forbidden to marry during service[1], and did not care to afterwards[2]. The Christian apologists never fail to bring home to the heathen their exposure of their new-born children. At the same time the tendency to asceticism and celibacy which went with the general revival of religion did not help the world, the finer natures leaving no children. The same unhappy result followed the persecutions of the Christians. The great plague, which lasted for twenty years in the latter half of the second century, also contributed to the depopulation, which had long ago begun to be marked, in Greece for example[3]. German immigration to some extent re-peopled the Empire, and greatly modified its character. The army and the peasant class became predominatingly German; and when the great inroads of the fifth century came, the Empire in the West was half German already. In the East the Persians and in Africa mere barbarians, neither easy to assimilate, wrought havoc with the Roman world, plundering, murdering and kidnapping.

This then is the Roman world, a society splendidly organized; training in laws and arms the Goths who were to overthrow it; giving its character and strength to the Catholic Church which was to check, to tame and to civilize these conquerors; and all the while gradually decaying, yet never quite losing all power of staying for a little its decline, as the wonderful history of Constantinople shews. We can see in some measure why the Empire fell, but how it was able to endure so long in the East is a harder question, which is not to be solved here. There its story is somewhat different, but there too it shaped a church and made nations, and held barbarism at bay for a thousand years after Rome had been taken by the Goths. Even the victorious Turks but adopted the traditions of government which they found.

Virgil had seen aright the genius of his countrymen, when he apostrophized the Roman;

> Thou, do thou control
> The nations far and wide:
> Be this thy genius—to impose
> The rule of peace on vanquished foes,
> Show pity to the humbled soul
> And crush the sons of pride.

---

[1] Dio lx. 24, 3.

[2] *Neque conjugiis suscipiendis neque alendis liberis sueti orbas sine posteris domos relinquebant*, Tac. *Ann.* xiv. 27. See also Boissier *Roman Africa* (tr.) p. 120 f.

[3] See Seeck's excellent chapter on "die Entvölkerung des Reiches" in his *Untergang der antiken Welt.* In the next essay (die Barbaren im Reich), p. 398,

Under the Empire there was a general decline in nearly all
the activities of the human mind, art, literature *II. Art,*
and philosophy alike falling away. Not all the *Education, and*
blame for this is to be laid upon Rome or her *Literature.*
government, for the impulse in all these things came from Greece
and was already well-nigh exhausted with the general exhaustion
of the Greek world. Faction, with its retaliatory massacres,
had in Greece steadily eliminated eminence and capacity. In
Rome much the same thing had befallen in the last century
of the Republic and in the years of usurping and suspicious
Emperors. The level therefore of Greek and Roman genius steadily
fell[1].

By the fourth century, says Gregorovius, "the creative art,
like the poetry and learning of the ancients, was taking its leave
of mankind; the date of its disappearance being manifested in the
Triumphal Arch of Constantine, the border of two epochs. This
arch the Roman Senate adorned with sculptures robbed from
another arch dedicated to Trajan. As these were not sufficient,
the artists of the time, to whom some of the reliefs were entrusted,
were obliged to confess that the ideals of their forefathers had
vanished and that the day of the barbarians had dawned. The
Triumphal Arch of Constantine may thus be described as the
gravestone of the arts of Greece and Rome[2]." The Christians
borrowed the form of the court of justice, the Basilica, for their
churches. St Peter's, the foundation of Constantine, like many
later churches, was built in some measure of relics and fragments
of paganism. The so-called chair of Peter, set in the church by
Pope Damasus, is typical of much. It is an ancient sedan-chair
decorated with minute carvings in ivory—heathen pictures of beasts
and centaurs and the labours of Hercules, some fastened on upside
down. Statues were still made and so were pictures, but the great
arts of the day, as we learn from Claudian and Prudentius, were
embroidery and mosaic, and where all else failed a lavish profusion
of gold and jewels did instead of art.

he alludes to the plague, which he estimates cost the Empire half its population, and goes on to shew the influence of German settlers on the Empire from
the days of Marcus Aurelius.
    [1] See Seeck, *Gesch. des Untergangs der antiken Welt*, pp. 280 ff. Seeck
holds that in the fourth century thought and literature throve only where there
was some Semitic element in the people—Syria, Egypt, Africa. Certainly one
Semitic stock has not even yet declined if we may trust a Disraeli and a
Heine. Seeck's chapter *Die Ausrottung der Besten* is well worth study.
    [2] *Rome in the Middle Ages*, vol. i. p. 85 and following pages.

In literature we find the same sterility. Latin literature had
from the first been imitative, but imitation is one thing in strong
hands and another in weak, and the surest road to decline is to
copy the copy. Virgil and Horace had drawn their inspiration from
Greek poets; Lucan and Statius from them; and these last almost
as much as the former were the models of later poetry. It was no
better in the Greek world. East and west, education and literature were infected with rhetoric, and the chief task of culture was
to echo and distort in echoing the ideas of the past. Here and
there a poet has something of his own to say, and then the old
language has something of the old power. Claudian's poetry is
quickened by the thought of Rome, Prudentius' by the victory of
the Church and the unity of mankind in her, and both poets rise
conspicuous above their age. In Greek the best is Quintus, the
quiet amiable imitator and completer of Homer, the longest is
Nonnus, whose poetry is like nothing so much as the playing of a
prismatic fountain, the waters of which on analysis in a cold light
prove to be dirty and full of infection.

Serious prose, apart from the church and technical writers, was
almost unknown. History was a dying art, but for Eusebius and
Ammianus—a very large reservation it is true. Letter-writing on
the other hand was never so flourishing or so sterile; as a few
pages of Symmachus will shew. Yet Neo-Platonism, if it could not
re-create, could revive literature, and the fourth century has much
more to shew than the third—more books and books worthy of
study for the light they throw on a great change taking place
under the cover of old forms. It was an age of schools and universities, but all of a conservative type. Education flourished, but
it was rhetorical. Chassang remarks that there was no chair of
history in any of the foundations, but a certain amount would be
involved in the study of literature, which was a branch of grammar[1].
Philosophy still lived, but it was not satisfactory. It was concerned
more with the tradition of *dogmata* than with the independent
investigation of reality, and magic followed it like a shadow.
There was some astronomy and a little other natural science, but
these too were traditional. But all these studies were overshadowed

---

[1] Chassang, *le Roman dans l'antiquité*, p. 98. Among the *Professores*
commemorated by Ausonius is a rhetorician, Staphylius (20), who besides
being a consummate grammarian is described as *historiam callens Livii et
Herodoti*. Chassang is however right in his main contention that the subject
was held of minor importance. There had always been a tendency in Rome to
regard history from the point of view of style almost exclusively.

by the baleful rhetoric, infecting everything with pretentious un-
reality, as every system of education will that teaches style first and
forgets nature.

One of the most striking facts about the education of the day
is the undeniable charm it exercised over men, partly no doubt
because in sterile ages men most prize correctness, but partly
because it introduced them to masterpieces which they must have
felt beyond them, however much they called one another Ciceros
and Virgils. The Christians are as much captivated as the pagans,
as we see in Augustine's enthusiasm for the *Aeneid* and Jerome's
studies of Cicero and Plautus, and above all in the intense passion
roused by Julian's decree excluding Christians from the teaching
profession. This enthusiasm was not always healthful, as it limited
the range of interests with the most cramping effects. Macrobius
for example devotes himself to Virgil (whom he does not really
understand) and only touches his own day in Neo-Platonism. He
knows something of Christianity, but his culture forbids his mentioning it. When all is weighed, perhaps Ammianus, with all his
naïve "readings of Antiquity" and "sayings of Tully" and his
wonderful style, is as honest and wholesome a man as any who
wrote in the century. And he had seen life and death as they are,
before he began his studies. It is this contact with reality that
lifts Augustine and, in his own way, Sulpicius into a spirit that
speaks to the heart.

Literature was one of the great strongholds of paganism and
the other was philosophy. It was not the philosophy
of the great days of Greece, and indeed it could not
be expected to be. The fall of Greek civic independence, the breaking down of barriers of tribal, communal and

*III. Philo-
sophy.*

religious tradition, and the levelling of mankind under the weight
of the immense empires that followed Alexander's conquest of
Asia, affected philosophy profoundly. It is hardly saying too much
to assert that the philosophers "despaired of the republic" and
turned to the individual instead. There were no doubt still
Utopias, but kings and armies made them look even more foolish
than demagogues and assemblies had done, and the main concern of
thought was the sad adaptation of oneself to the new world without
landmarks. The schools of Epicurus and the Porch, both appealing
directly to the individual man, carried all before them. The Stoics
had no disreputable following to give them a bad name and they
appealed more to the serious and manly with their doctrine of

living according to nature. Thus while Epicurus made disciples of honest Romans like Lucretius and Horace, Stoicism had more influence on Rome, particularly affecting the development of Roman law. This is not very surprising when we consider what the Roman character was.

As in the Greek world, so in the Roman, philosophy became a more important factor in life with the fall of the Republic and the rise of the Empire. There had been many Romans before this interested in philosophy, but now there was no alternative for serious people, except perhaps literature, and that also shews the influence of philosophic teaching. Stoicism had its popular preacher in Seneca, a more genuine exponent in Epictetus, and in Marcus Aurelius its last great example, and he indeed gives us a hint of the change that was coming.

Mr Pater in his *Marius* seizes this singularly interesting moment of the world's history, and exhibits to us this great Stoic Emperor with his assiduous sacrifices standing as it were between the two extremes represented by Lucian, the most distressing advocate of the blankest unbelief, and Apuleius the philosopher, the disciple of Plato and the magician, while in the background, as yet without prominence, is the new school gently bringing home to man that his soul is "naturally Christian." The great African who coined this phrase was a younger contemporary of the other three. With Tertullian and with Apuleius lay the future. Lucian might shew his age the rottenness of all its beliefs and mock it for their vanity, and Sextus Empiricus might give a philosophic account of Pyrrho's doctrine of scepticism, but the world swung violently away from them and beyond the cautious and melancholy Marcus. It would believe and it must believe, and a new spirit filled the third century.

The New Pythagoreanism found its literary exponent in a sophist—Philostratus, and its patroness in an Empress of Syrian extraction. It led the way to the New Platonism, a form of thought that had more and longer influence. Plotinus is its great thinker, Porphyry and Iamblichus brought it into common life; nearly all the pagan writers of the fourth century are touched by it, and still later Proclus taught it in Athens and Boethius found it his consolation in prison.

Neo-Platonism.

It owed its popularity to the fact that while retaining for the simple-minded all the gods of all the creeds as legitimate objects of worship, supporting their service and defending them against attack, it allowed more cultured minds to transcend them[1] and soar unfettered by literalism into an ecstatic communion with the divine beyond all gods. It justified every heathen religion, for all things were emanations from the one divine, and the gods were intermediaries between it and man and deserved man's worship by their larger measure of divinity or real being, and by their benevolent care for men, their weaker brethren or children. Every heathen god had thus his place in a splendid fabric, that reached from Absolute Being down to "the lowest dregs of the universe." Man was not left alone in a godless world to face riddles he could not guess. The world swarmed with gods as it did with demons, divine and beneficent powers contending against the demons of matter. The riddles were now beautiful mysteries man might see into, if he could overcome the divine reticence by a holy abstinence, an even more potent ritual and, more awful still, the strange powers of magic. By all of these man might learn how he could rise from one plane of being to another, ever growing more clear of matter, which was *not-being*, and ascending gradually into heights of purer and purer existence. It will be readily remarked what freedom this gave the wandering fancy—a pantheon wide as the world ; a creed broad enough to include everybody, except Epicureans, for, if Christians would but permit it, Christ might be an emanation as well as Dionysus ; a theory of the universe, superior to reason, far above proof, and remote from the grimy touch of experience. Everybody might believe anything and everything, and practise all rituals at once, and thus storm by a holy violence the secrets of all the gods. Naturally then we find very different types of Neo-Platonists, as they incline to this or that side of the general teaching of their school.

Loose and fanciful thinkers like Julian, pagan antiquarians like Macrobius, conjurers like Maximus, pious and beautiful natures like Praetextatus and Hermes Trismegistus (whoever he was), were all captured and held by this wonderful mixture of philosophy and religion. Stronger men too than they were attracted by it, and it left permanent traces of itself on Augustine's theology. It was the greatest of all heathen systems, recognizing and satisfying

---

[1] St Augustine (*de Vera Religione* v. 8) makes the point that in the Church philosophy and religion are entirely at one, while pagan philosophy is really at issue with popular religion. It was at least the aim of the Neo-Platonists to avoid this.

every impulse and energy of the human mind, except inquiry. It felt the unity of nature, the divinity of man as God's kinsman, the beauty of a morality modelled after God, the appetite of the human heart for God, and something of man's hunger for redemption. It had an explanation for everything, but it was not concerned to verify its explanations. Happy in imagination, it had no interest in observation. It was in one way essentially claustral. The common people it left to worship their gods unintelligently. For them it had no communion with the divine, no salvation from sin, no consolation for sorrow. Celsus had long ago sneered at Christianity as a faith for fullers and bakers. Porphyry calmly warns off athletes, soldiers and business men—he is not writing for them. The Neo-Platonist thus has the Greek temper still, preferring the life with advantages, and inculcating the old Greek ideal of self-rule, and progress toward a goal to be reached by contemplation. All things are divine in so far as they really exist, so the Neo-Platonist is not properly ascetic. But they are not always quite consistent, and some of them have an Oriental tinge about their views. Evil, they say, is not-being, but here a negative term covers a force felt to be positive, and they have not clearly explained their attitude toward matter. They say that it is failure-to-be, that it is nothing ; but their " flight " from it and their general conduct with regard to it seem to imply that they feel sometimes it is something more. They make guesses at it, but they do not inquire.

The general effect of Neo-Platonism was, I think, for good. Any belief is better than none, and a great faith, however confused, is apt to raise the moral tone. The literature of the fourth century has not the swing and surge of that of the first, but it is gentler and graver and purer. The general mind of man is not so robust, but it feels elements in the problem, which escaped it in its younger and more impetuous days. It cannot solve them, it can hardly state them, but in a confused way it recognizes them as affecting the general solution, and, where once it was dogmatic even to arrogance on the one side, now it instinctively takes the other, feeling it is nearer the truth but not realizing why. So though human nature was the same and people loved pleasures, they sought them after all with more restraint. In no previous century could a historian, without meaning to sneer, have coined the phrase *imperialis verecundia*. Most of these Emperors were Christian, but Julian morally the peer of the best was a Neo-

Platonist, and Jovian, the one licentious Emperor, said he was a Christian[1].

Neo-Platonism with its acceptance of *dogmata* was essentially a religion of disciples. It will be remarked how it fits in with the literary tendencies of the century—philosophy and literature explaining each other, both content with transmission, and happy in imitation, neither fertile in fresh discoveries or new ideas. They were alike exhausted.

So far we have discussed the heathen world, picking up the main threads separately for clearness' sake, and one has been omitted, which now calls for attention.

IV. The Church.

The old Jewish prayer, "I thank thee, O God, who hast made me a Jew and not a Gentile, a man and not a woman, a free man and not a slave," was repudiated by St Paul in an utterance which expresses a fundamental doctrine of Christianity—a doctrine to which the Roman Empire with its gradual levelling must have helped thoughtful men. Yet it should be noted that Paul proclaimed all human beings equal in the kingdom of God a century and a half before Caracalla made them equal in the world, and Paul included the slave whom Caracalla did not. The Stoic had already reached the dogma of the equality of all men, and Roman law was slowly working towards it. Thus the tendency of Greek philosophy and Roman imperialism co-operated with the new religion[2].

Again, the revival of paganism, of which I have spoken as a reaction against scepticism and despair, may or may not have been affected by the spreading of the Gospel. If not at first it was so at a later time. But here too there was common ground. Both the new paganism and the new gospel were helped by that pressure of circumstances, which drove men to seek in their own hearts for a stronger comfort to meet a more searching need than their fathers had known. This relation between the state of the Empire and

[1] Seeck, it should be said, believes the improved tone of morals to be due largely to the intermixture of German blood and German ideals. Like Gregorovius, he has a high opinion of the German invaders, and they can both present a good case, though when one learns elsewhere that Virgil must be semi-Celtic and Tertullian semi-Semitic, one accepts racial panegyrics with reserve. The English seem to be the only race "whom there are none to praise, And very few to love."

[2] When Tertullian (*Apol.* 38) said *unam omnium rempublicam agnoscimus mundum*, it was at once an expression of the unity of mankind and in some degree of revolt from the narrower conception involved in the Roman Empire.

the Church should not be forgotten, for it will also help to explain the rapid spread of monachism.

The Church was thus in contact with the whole life of the Empire, and though it was some time before she could much affect it, it helped to mould her. Her earliest organization was on secular models. She first held property under the law of burial associations. Her bishops were developed out of the presidents of these, and her architecture was in some degree influenced for ever by memories of her catacombs. But more significant were other contacts. She soon caught the ear of the philosophical world, some members of which merely sneered, some borrowed from her and some joined her. She had to reckon with all three, and first by the necessity of apologetic against heathen and heretic, and thence by that of a clear presentation to herself of her vital doctrines, she became philosophic. Then by the interaction of thought and organization the office of the bishop gained a new importance, when he became the repository of true doctrine, the test by which doubtful views were to be tried. But the world was wide and there were many churches ; the world was one, and the churches needed some common base and found it in a united episcopate which held truth *in solidum,* as the converted lawyer said—as a corporation. *Episcopatus unus est cujus a singulis in solidum pars tenetur*[1]. These examples may serve for many that might be brought to shew how not only Greek philosophy, but Roman law, influenced the Church, shaping her theories of government and moulding her theology[2].

The State came first into collision with the Church by accident, and merely added a new form of crime to be suppressed to those it knew already. The Christian, according to the statesman, divided families and spoiled trades, and from both causes public disorder resulted. In the next place the Christian by asserting the supremacy of a higher power than the Emperor's introduced a disturbing element into society, and an *imperium in imperio* was not to be tolerated. So efforts were made to extinguish the Church —*non licet esse vos.* Persecution failed because the persecutors were less in earnest about it than the persecuted and had other interests. The last persecution inaugurated by Diocletian and his circle shewed by its failure the solidity of the Church, and it was the real instinct of a statesman that led Constantine to make peace with it.

---

[1] Cyprian, *de Eccl. Cath. Unitate,* c. 5.
[2] See Sir Henry Maine, *Ancient Law,* ch. ix.

"By doing so," says Seeley[1], "he may be said to have purchased an indefeasible title by a charter. He gave certain liberties and he received in turn passive obedience. He gained a sanction for the Oriental theory of government; in return he accepted the law of the Church. He became irresponsible to his subjects on condition of becoming responsible to Christ."

The Nicene Council in 325 was a revolution. The bishops were here recognized by the State as constituting the Church, and as the Church they met to decide what was its faith. Constantine awaited their decision and then made his pronouncement. This was the Christian faith and no other; consequently all bishops must accept it. A number of new principles were involved here, and many consequences followed. First there was a series of fresh councils to re-try the question, which continued through the century. And it had to be settled by move and counter-move how far the Emperor was bound to accept the ruling of the Church which he had recognized.

The battle of the councils was about a diphthong according to one account; it was a fight between Christianity and paganism according to another. If the Son was ὁμοούσιος, he was God while still man—that is, the antithesis of God and man is superficial, the ideal man being at the same time God's best expression of himself; but if the Son was ὁμοιούσιος, he was not God but a creature, a demigod perhaps or a Neo-Platonist emanation, and neither on the other hand was he man. It is no wonder that the conflict raged.

There were other results of the peace between the State and the Church. It was no longer dangerous to be a Christian, but it was even profitable, and the stalwart Christians Diocletian had killed were replaced by time-servers and half-converted pagans. I do not say there was less Christian life at once, but at least the average Christian was of a lower type. This soon meant the general lowering of ideals, and was followed by the inevitable reaction, just as in former days the succession of easy times to difficult had meant first a lower tone in the Catholic Church, and then a Montanist and a Novatian revolt. Now the revolt took another form. Novatianism was conceived by an essentially Roman mind which worked from a new point of view to a new organization. The new revolt was more Oriental in character.

[1] *Lectures and Essays*, iii.

We have seen how Neo-Platonism had, like most serious forms of faith, a leaning to self-discipline which might fall into asceticism. Every eastern worship which the Roman world knew, except Judaism and Christianity, laid stress on asceticism. Celibacy had early invaded the Church, and Montanism had brought in asceticism. But monachism was a combination of both which was new to the Church in the fourth century, and its entrance coincides with the conversion of the monasteries of Serapis. It must not be lightly supposed that this was the source of the monastic movement in the Church, but rather it gave a new idea which fitted well with tendencies long since at work. The *Life of Antony* is a Greek novel telling about a Coptic monk, a simple tale but on fire for those prepared for it. It offered in the desert a holy life, dependent on grace alone, victorious over all devils, Neo-Platonist or otherwise, free from all the cares and sorrows of a sinful world and unvexed by the worldliness of a sinful church. For though Antony is habitually respectful to clergy and bishops, other monks, *e.g.* Sulpicius Severus, thought and spoke less well of them. The feelings that moved the unknown author of *Antony* and Sulpicius were shared by thousands. In a world of distress and despotism, in a church engaged in perennial debates about a question the simple-minded could not fathom, the ascetic ideal, preached by Neo-Platonist and Christian, triumphed and carried monachism with it. Neither was a part of primitive Christianity any more than the passion for relics and pilgrimages and the building of martyries, which invaded the Church from much the same quarters at the same time.

In the essays that follow I shall try to shew how the threads here separated interlace in the lives and thoughts of men and women. In this man one influence overweighs the rest; in that, another, but none wholly escape them all, while in some men all the influences of their time seem to meet and require expression. In Augustine, for example, we have the rhetorician, the man of letters, the Neo-Platonist, the admirer of *Antony*, the Christian believer in grace, the Christian bishop, the Christian statesman and the thoroughly Roman constitutionalist of the Church.

It is hard to form a completely unprejudiced judgment, but the conclusion is forced upon me when I survey the fourth century, its interests and its energies, that the Church had absorbed all that was then vital in the civilized world. It had not assimilated all of the beauty and wisdom of the great Classical period, for much of them was lost to that age and was not to be recovered for centuries. The Church of that day had her weaknesses, she made grave mistakes and she was not without sins that bore bitter fruit, but she rose superior to all the world around her, and to whatever sphere of work and thought we turn, literature, philosophy, administration, we find her marked off from all her environment by one characteristic it had not and she had—life and the promise of life.

CHAPTER II

AMMIANUS MARCELLINUS

I have at last begun my historical labours....The materials for an amusing narrative are immense. I shall not be satisfied unless I produce something which shall for a few days supersede the last fashionable novel on the tables of young ladies.

MACAULAY Letter to Macvey Napier

A MAN must have fine qualities so to write the history of his own times that his judgments on his contemporaries shall be sustained on appeal to the court of History, and posterity, after fifteen centuries, accept them still. He must be cool and dispassionate in his survey, and yet sympathetic. He should be alive to every aspect of the problems that beset his fellows, and take into account every advantage or disadvantage arising from age and environment. Commonly to attain the true perspective one must stand a century or at least a generation away. But in the fourth century, in the midst of the quarrels of Arian and Nicene, through all the turmoils of civil strife and barbarian war, lived and wrote a man, whose verdict on most of the men of his time is with some reservations substantially our own.

Ammianus Marcellinus[1] was born of Greek parents at Antioch[2],

---

[1] The Abbé Gimazane, not finding "fifteen consecutive pages" on Ammianus, has written 400 in his *A. M. sa vie et son œuvre* (Toulouse 1889), a work of some interest with some rather improbable theories. Max Büdinger's *A. M. u. die Eigenart seines Geschichtswerkes* is careful but too severe. The various historians of the period, and writers on Julian, generally refer to him more gratefully and, I think, more truly.

[2] We are curiously reminded of his birthplace when he speaks of Julian's invective against the Antiochenes (the *Misopogon*), which he wrote "in a rage...adding a good deal to the truth." Socrates, the fairest of Church historians as became a lawyer of Constantinople, lets the book pass with the

somewhere about the date of the Nicene Council, 325 A.D. It is not possible, nor is it necessary, to name the exact year. More we cannot say than that he was of noble birth. Sooner or later he was as well read a man as any of his day, but we cannot say what his early education was. We first find him in the army among the Protectores Domestici, for admission to whose ranks personal beauty and noble birth were necessary[1]. He tells us himself incidentally that at one critical moment he found it not pure gain to be *ingenuus*[2].

We first find him in 353 at Nisibis, in Mesopotamia, on the staff of Ursicinus[3], to which position the Emperor Constantius had appointed him. Ursicinus had been in the East for ten years[4], we learn, without disaster, in spite of the rawness and inefficiency of his troops. Four years after we first see him, Ammianus includes himself among the *adulescentes*[5] who were sent back to the East with Ursicinus, while the older men were promoted. Men vary so much in their ideas of what is young and what is old, that it would be hard to guess his exact age in 357.

He saw a good deal of travel and warfare first and last. How long he was with Ursicinus during his first period of Eastern service we cannot say. However, in 353 whisperers round the Court suggested to the greedy ears of Constantius that it might be dangerous to leave Ursicinus in the East after the recall of Gallus Caesar, and he was summoned with all speed to Milan to "discuss urgent business." All conveniences for rapid travel were supplied[6], and with long stages they made all haste to Milan to find they had come for nothing. Perhaps they were not greatly surprised. It was Constantius' method. Gallus had been hurried home in the same way to have his head cut off.

The next thing was the trial of Ursicinus for treason. Constantius was jealous[7], and the creatures of the Court whispered. His friends at once deserted him for men in the ascendant, "just as when the magistrates in due course succeed one another, the

remark that "it left indelible stigmata on Antioch." Sozomen says it was "excellent and very witty." Zosimus, a heathen, says it was "most witty, and blended such bitterness with its irony as to make the Antiochenes infamous everywhere." After twice reading the *Misopogon*, I must say my estimate is nearest that of Ammianus.

[1] Procopius, *Hist. Arcana*, 24.   [2] xix. 8, 11.
[3] xiv. 9, 1.   [4] xviii. 6, 2.
[5] xvi. 10, 21.   [6] xiv. 11, 5.
[7] Cf. Julian's comment on him; *Or.* vii. 233 c ἡ πρὸς τοὺς φίλους ἀπιστία ruined him.

lictors pass to the new from the old[1]." Ammianus could hardly express his contempt more significantly. A plot was actually made to kidnap and kill Ursicinus untried. It seems the Emperor was cognizant of it; a defect in our text may be used to defend him, but he was quite capable of the treachery. Delay prevented its execution.

In 355 they left Milan[2] under circumstances which seem strange perhaps, but are characteristic of the age. There was an officer in Gaul, Silvanus by name, loyal enough to the Emperor, but he had enemies, and they went to work in the usual way. They babbled to Constantius of treason till the wretched Silvanus found his only hope of life lay in treason—a desperate card to play, but his only one—and he boldly proclaimed himself Emperor. This was a thunderbolt indeed. But Constantius was not at a loss. He despatched Ursicinus (with Ammianus in his train) to quell the rebel, prepared to be glad to hear of the death of either of his generals. A mere handful of men went with Ursicinus, for craft or treachery was to be the tool employed. Ammianus felt, and they all felt, that they were in the position of gladiators condemned to fight beasts in the arena. They had to make haste to keep the rebellion from spreading to Italy, and so successful were they that Silvanus' reign was one of only four weeks[3]. They went, with a keen sense of their risk, to Silvanus as friends; they heard his complaints of unworthy men being promoted over his head and theirs; and after much discussion in private, and many nervous changes of plan, they managed to tamper with the troops. In a day or two at daybreak a body of armed men burst out, slew Silvanus' guards, and cut down himself as he fled to a church for safety. Thus fell at Cologne "an officer of no mean merits, done to death by slanderous tongues, so immeshed in his absence that he could protect himself only by going to the extremest measures." Such is Ammianus' comment on a wretched affair which gave him nothing but disgust. Constantius, however, was so delighted as to feel himself "sky high and superior to all human risks now[4]."

Ursicinus and Ammianus remained in Gaul for a year perhaps[5]. In 356 they saw at Rheims the Caesar Julian, who had been sent to Gaul, as they had been themselves, to crush Constantius' enemies,

[1] xv. 2, 3.   [2] xv. 5.
[3] Julian, *Or.* ii. 98 c γελοῖος ἀληθῶς τύραννος καὶ τραγικός. Julian says Constantius spared Silvanus' son afterwards.
[4] xv. 5, 37.   [5] xvi. 2, 8.

and if possible meet his death in doing it. Towards the end of the year came a welcome despatch summoning them to Sirmium[1], whence the Emperor sent Ursicinus once more to the East and Ammianus with him.

They were two years in the East, and meanwhile plots thickened. "The Court, hammering as they say the same anvil day and night at the bidding of the eunuchs, held Ursicinus before the gaze of the suspicious and timid Emperor as it were a Gorgon's head[2]," assuring him that his general "aspired higher." Chief among the enemies was the rascal chamberlain, Eusebius, "with whom," says Ammianus bitterly, "Constantius had considerable influence"; and the "piping voice of the eunuch" and the "too open ears of the prince" meant ruin for the brave soldier. But a good deal was to come first.

War with the Persians was imminent. A Roman subject of rank and some knowledge, harassed as Silvanus had been, though by smaller enemies, found life impossible within Roman frontiers, and fled to the Persians, and there he and his knowledge were welcome. A Persian invasion followed. Meanwhile the order had reached Ursicinus at Samosata to yield his command to one Sabinianus and come West[3]. The Syrians heard with consternation, and all but laid violent hands on him to keep him[4]. But Ursicinus and his staff had to go, and they crossed the Taurus, and after a short delay had travelled through Asia Minor, and were already in Europe when fresh orders turned them back whence they came. Sabinianus was recognized by the Emperor to stand in need of a soldier at his side. Back they went to Nisibis, and there they found their "little fellow gaping" (*oscitante homunculo*)[5]. Throughout the campaign this seems to have been Sabinianus' attitude. He visited Edessa and spent time among the "tombs," "as if, once he had made his peace with the dead, nothing were to be feared[6]." I suppose Ammianus means shrines and martyries[7]. Abgar, king of Edessa, so a very old story goes, wrote to our Lord and had a letter from Him, both letters being preserved for us by Eusebius. In the *Doctrine of Addai* we have the whole story of our Lord's sending Addai to Edessa, the healing of Abgar

---

[1] xvi. 10, 21.   [2] xviii. 4, 2.
[3] xviii. 4, 7.   [4] xviii. 6, 2.
[5] xviii. 6, 8.   [6] xviii. 7, 7.
[7] It was believed by some that Julian, on his Anabasis, avoided the place for the very fact of its early Christian associations. (Sozomen, vi. 1.) It also happened to be out of his way.

and the conversion of the whole place with such success and speed
that they read the *Diatessaron* in the churches nearly a century
before it was made. As our Lord's reputed letter or a copy of it
was shewn to St Silvia twenty years later than this, it is just
possible this relic occupied Sabinianus' attention.

Leaving Sabinianus to his devotions, Ursicinus had to take
what steps he might without hindrance. And now we are in the
thick of the campaign. It was reported at Nisibis that the enemy
had crossed the Tigris and that plundering bands were scouring the
country[1]. "So," says Ammianus (and I translate his account of an
incident commonplace enough perhaps, but illustrative of the times
and the region), "to secure the roads we set out at a trot, and at
the second milestone from the city we saw a child of gentle appearance, wearing a necklace, and about eight years old we supposed,
sitting crying on the middle of a bank. He was the son of a free
man, he said, and his mother, as she fled in hot haste for fear of
the enemy who was hard upon them, had found herself burdened
with him in her panic and left him there alone. The general was
moved to pity, and at his bidding I took him up in front of me on
my horse and returned to the city, and meanwhile swarms of
marauders were surrounding the walls far and wide. Alarmed at
the idea of an ambush, I set the boy within a half-closed postern,
and rode hard to rejoin our troop in some terror; and I was all
but caught; for a hostile squad of horse in pursuit of a certain
Abdigidus, a tribune, and his groom, caught the slave while the
master escaped, and, as I galloped by, they had just heard in reply
to their question, "Who was the officer who had ridden out?" that
Ursicinus had a little before reached the city, and was now making
for Mount Izala. They slew their informant, gathered together in
some numbers, and, without taking rein, made after us.

"Thanks to the speed of my animal, I outrode them and at
Amudis, a weak fort, I found my comrades carelessly lying about
with their horses grazing. I flung out my arm, and waving the
ends of my cloak on high (the usual signal) I let them know the
enemy was at hand. Joining them I rode off with them, my horse
already in distress. What terrified us was the full moon and the
dead level of the country, which offered no hiding place in case of
pressing need, as no trees or bushes or anything but short grass was
to be seen. We therefore devised this plan. A lighted torch was

---

[1] xviii. 6, 10—16.

set on a single horse and tied so as not to fall. The animal without a rider was sent off toward the left, while we made for the foot of the mountains on the right, so that the Persians, in the belief that it was the torch to light the general as he quietly rode along, might go in that direction. But for this device we should have been surrounded and captured and come into the enemy's hands.

"Escaped from this peril we came to a wooded spot planted with vines and apple trees, Meiacarire by name, so called from its cold springs. Its inhabitants had fled and we found but one man hid away in a corner—a soldier. He was brought to the general, and in his terror gave confused answers which made us suspect him. In fear of our threats, he sets forth the real state of affairs, and tells us he was born at Paris in Gaul and had served in the cavalry, but to escape punishment for some offence he had deserted to the Persians. On his character being established he had married and had a family, and had often been sent as a spy among us and brought back true information. He had now been sent by Tamsapor and Nohodar, the nobles at the head of the marauding forces, and was on his way back to tell what he had learnt. On hearing this and what he knew of what was going on elsewhere, we slew him."

I pass over a reconnoitring expedition made by Ammianus, and the disgraceful loss of an important bridge through the carelessness of a force of cavalry fresh from Illyricum, and the rout which followed, in which Ursicinus' party got separated, Ammianus escaping to Amid[1]. The path up to the gate was narrow, and he spent a curious night jammed in a crowd of living and dead, with a soldier in front of him held erect by the press though his head was halved to the neck. Then followed the siege of Amid, the story of which told in his nineteenth book may rank for vividness and interest with the sieges of Quebec or Louisbourg. Remember that the story is told by a soldier, an eye-witness and the man of all men then living most fitted to tell such a tale.

The Persian army moved on to Amid[2], "and when next dawn

[1] xviii. 8, 11—14.

[2] Amid (now Diarbekr) on the Tigris was one of the most important places strategically and commercially in the country, though less so than Nisibis, which was the key of the situation. This should be borne in mind when we come to Jovian's surrender. That Diarbekr is still the seat of the patriarch of the Jacobites shews its ancient importance (Stanley, *Eastern Church*, i.). It is now a town of 70,000 to 80,000 people, Turks, Kurds and Armenians, but not many Greeks, a great centre for trade, and capital of the vilayet of the same name (*Diar*, land; *Bekr*, *Abu Bekr*, the early caliph). It is surrounded by ancient walls which stand some seventy feet high, and make it the most remarkable place of the kind in Turkey.

gleamed, all that could be seen glittered with starry arms, and iron cavalry filled plains and hills." The phrase is curious, as many of his phrases are. The sunlight caught a thousand bright surfaces and the reflexions suggested the starry heavens. The iron cavalry are the cataphracts or men in armour mounted on horses in armour. We hear a good deal of them in Ammianus and Julian, who compares them to equestrian statues. "Riding his horse, and towering over all, the King himself (magnificently if tersely described as *ipse* without another word) rode down his lines, wearing as a diadem a golden ram's head set with gems, exalted with every kind of dignity and the attendance of divers races." He was intent on a siege, and, though the renegade advised against it, the "divinity of heaven" (*caeleste numen*) ruled that all his force should be concentrated on this corner of the Roman world and the rest should escape.

Sapor the king in a lordly way advanced to the walls, called for a surrender, and nearly lost his life for his pains, and retired raging as if sacrilege had been committed. Next day a subject king, Grumbates, came near losing his life on the same errand, his son falling at his side. Over the prince's body there was a fight, which recalled the death of Patroclus. The Persians at last bore him off and for seven days he lay in state while they held his funeral, feasting and dancing and singing sad dirges in lamentation for the royal youth, much as women wail for Adonis. At last they burnt the corpse and gathered his bones to send home to his own people, and after a rest of two days war began again with a great display of Sapor's troops, cataphracts, elephants and all[1]. Next day Grumbates, in the character of a *fetialis*, hurled a blood-stained spear at the city, and fighting began. Catapults, "scorpions" (for hurling great stones) and engines of all kinds[2] came into play, and many were the deaths on both sides. The night fell and both armies kept watch under arms, while the hills rang as "our men extolled the prowess of Constantius Caesar as lord of the world and the universe, and the Persians hailed Sapor as *saansaan* (king of kings) and *pirosen* (conqueror in war)[3]."

[1] This proceeding, strange as it may seem, occurs again at Daras, 530 A.D. On the second day fighting began and Belisarius won a great victory.

[2] Elsewhere (xxiii. 4) Ammianus gives a description of these various machines.

[3] Mr E. G. Browne informs me that this is a *locus classicus* with Orientalists, which some have tried very needlessly to emend. The passage is historical proof that the official language of the Sasanian kings was not pronounced as it is written, but for Aramaic words in the script their Persian equivalents were read. *Saansaan* is Shahin-Shah, *pirosen* Firuz.

Before dawn fighting began again. "So many evils stood around us, that it was not to win deliverance but with a passionate desire to die bravely we burned." At last night put an end to the slaughter, but brought little help for the wounded. There were seven legions in the city and a great crowd of country people beside the citizens, and there was no room or leisure for the burial of the dead.

Meanwhile Ursicinus was chafing to go to the rescue, but Sabinianus "sticking to the tombs" would neither let him go nor go himself. It was believed Constantius was to blame for this in his anxiety "that, even though it ruined the provinces, this man of war should not be reported as the author of any memorable deed nor the partner in one either."

Now came pestilence from the bodies of the slain, and for ten days it raged till rain fell and stopped it. All the time the siege was pushed on, and the defenders' difficulties were increased by the presence of two Celtic legions fresh from Gaul and itching to be "up and at them." It took a good deal to hold them inside the walls at all. A deserter betrayed a secret passage leading to a tower, and, while engaged with foes without, the defenders suddenly found some seventy archers shooting at them from a post of vantage within the walls, and with difficulty dislodged them. A half day's rest, and then "with the dawn we see a countless throng, taken on the capture of the fort Ziata, being led away to the enemy's land, thousands of men going into captivity, many among them frail with age, and aged women; and if weary with their long march they failed, all love of life now gone, they were left hamstrung." The sight was too much for the Celtic legions who raged like beasts of prey in their cages, and drew their swords on the gates which had been barred to keep them in[1]. They were afraid "lest the city should fall and they should be blotted out without a single brilliant exploit, or if it escaped it should be said that the Gauls did nothing worth while to shew their spirit. We were quite at a loss how to face them in their rage but at last decided (and got a reluctant consent to it from them)" that they should make a sortie on a dark night. The dark night came and

---

[1] Cf. Silius, *Punica* viii. 17, on Hannibal's Gauls:

> *vaniloquum Celtae genus ac mutabile mentis*
> *respectare domos: maerebant caede sine ulla—*
> *insolitum sibi—bella geri, siccasque cruore*
> *inter tela siti Mavortis hebescere dextras.*

with a prayer for heavenly protection the Gauls sallied out to the Persian camp, and but for some accident of a step heard or a dying man's groan caught they would have killed Sapor; but Sapor had twenty years of mischief before him yet.

Towers and elephants in turn were brought against the city, but the "scorpions" were too much for both; and the siege dragged on so that Sapor created a precedent and rushed into the fray in person. At last banks were raised, and the counter work put up by the besieged came crashing down as if there had been an earthquake; and the end had come. After a siege of seventy-three days the Persians had their way open, and now it was every man for himself, and all day long the streets were shambles.

"So at eventide, lurking with two others in an out-of-the-way part of the city under the cover of night's darkness, I escaped by a postern; and, thanks to an acquaintance with the country, now all dark, and the speed of my companions, I at last reached the tenth mile-stone. Here we halted and rested a little; and just as we were starting again, and I was giving out under the fatigue of walking, *for as a noble I was unused to it,* I saw a dreadful sight, but to me in my weary state it was to be a relief exceedingly timely." It was a runaway horse trailing its groom behind it, and as the dead body checked its speed, it was quickly caught, and Ammianus mounted. After a journey through the desert they reached the Euphrates to see Roman cavalry in flight with Persians in hot pursuit. "All hope of escape lay in speed, and through thickets and woods we made for the higher hills, and so we came to Melitina, a town of lesser Armenia, and there we found the general and his staff setting out for Antioch."

After these adventures Ammianus probably went West again with Ursicinus, who, as *magister peditum,* was kept near Constantius till slander prevailed and drove him into private life, and we hear no more of him, though his faithful follower tells us that a son of his was slain at Adrianople in 378[1].

Ammianus had by no means seen his last of war in the East. In some capacity he went with his hero, the Emperor Julian, on the fatal expedition against Sapor in 363. From point to point we can follow their Anabasis in the twenty-third and twenty-fourth books, and ever and again we find the verb in the first person, *vidimus, venimus.* It is, however, needless to trace their march, as

[1] xxxi. 13, 18.

Ammianus records practically nothing done by himself, though we may well believe he was not the least interested of the men who gazed on the wall paintings of battle and the chase at Coche[1]. Wherever he went we seem to see him with eyes open, quietly taking note of men and things.

When Julian was brought wounded to his tent, is it hazarding too much to suppose that Ammianus was at his side, and heard the manly farewell he made to his officers? Ammianus, unlike other Latin historians we have read, does not *make* speeches for his characters to deliver. With very few exceptions, if any, the speeches he reports are formal, set harangues delivered by emperors at coronations—the sort of utterance which is read from paper and preserved after delivery; and though he may very properly have condensed Julian's words, he is not the man to have invented them[2]. At all events he says nothing about *Vicisti Galilaee*, which is almost enough of itself to stamp that story a legend[3].

Whether he had a share in the deliberations which led to Jovian's election as emperor he does not say[4]. If he had he was certainly not proud of it, for he tacitly apologises for the choice made "when things were at the last gasp[5]." He shared the privations and the shame of the retreat, and a burning indignation betrays itself in the calm historian. Jovian accepted Sapor's terms and surrendered five provinces, including the all-important city of Nisibis, "when ten times over the thing to do was to fight[6]." The surrender was made "without any hesitation," and we may picture the feelings of the old soldier, whose own two leaders had been men indeed, when he penned the words *sine cunctatione tradidit*[7]. It was indeed a *pudenda pax*[8]. He witnessed the rage and grief of the betrayed Nisibis, when Jovian to save his soul respected his oath so far as to forbid the inhabitants to stand up for themselves,

---

[1] xxiv. 6, 3. Coche was practically a suburb of Ctesiphon the Persian capital, lying across the Tigris.

[2] Gibbon believes the speech to be authentic, but wickedly suggests that Julian must have prepared it in case of an emergency. Vollert, *K. Julian's relig. u. phil. Ueberz.* p. 94, says Réville and Ranke do not accept this speech.

[3] Theodoret (c. 430) tells the story. Socrates and Sozomen, historians of a higher type and about the same date, do not hint at it. Vollert (p. 95) accepts it as very like Julian.

[4] It has been conjectured that he was himself the *honoratior aliquis miles* who urged postponement. Gibbon (c. 24) and Hodgkin (i. 119).

[5] xxv. 5, 7.

[6] xxv. 7, 10. *Cum pugnari decies expediret.* Joshua the Stylite, c. 7, says Nisibis was surrendered for 120 years, but at the end of this period the Persians would not restore it—a local tradition perhaps.

[7] xxv. 7, 11.   [8] xxvii. 12, 1.

as they were quite capable of doing, independently of Roman support[1], and looked on, Roman Emperor as he was, while a Persian noble "hung out from the citadel the standard of his people."

He tells us of his return to Antioch, and then we are left to conjecture where he went and what he did. He was writing history, and personal details would have been biography; and he more than once protests that history cannot mention everybody's name, nor record what everybody did. *Minutiae ignobiles* are outside its sphere. Where he has mentioned himself it has always been because he was an eye-witness[2]. At some time or other he visited Egypt, to which visit he twice alludes, once with a quiet *vidimus*[3], once *visa pleraque narrantes*[4]. He also saw Sparta, and took note of the effects of an earthquake which had stranded a ship two miles inland[5].

Though he does not say so himself, we know at once from a letter Libanius[6] wrote him in 390 or 391, and from the vivid and satirical pictures he draws, that he lived in Rome, and wrote and read his history there. Seemingly he did not like Rome, and it has been suggested that Libanius' letter was meant to encourage him. At any rate the great orator says that the honour Rome does the historian, and the delight she takes in his work, do credit to Antioch and his fellow-citizens.

In 371 he had the ill luck to be back in Antioch[7] at the time when the affair of Theodorus was at its height. The story may be told quickly—he tells it us in full himself. Some men, speculating as to who was to be Emperor after Valens, tried a sort of planchette to find out, and learning that his name began with the four letters ΘΕΟΔ, they leapt to the conclusion that it was their friend Theodorus, a man of high rank[8]. Theodorus heard it, and perhaps was half inclined to accept a manifest destiny—*quo fata trahunt retrahuntque sequamur*—but the day planchette was tried was an evil day for him and for all concerned, and many more beside who were innocent. Attempts had been made on Valens' life before, and this time at least he left nothing undone to discourage them

---

[1] They were quite equal to this as Sapor could testify, for they beat him off in 340, though he had got so far as to make a breach in their wall.
[2] Gimazane (p. 54) is quite right in saying, "C'est un des rares écrivains qui savent parler du *moi* sans le rendre haïssable."
[3] xvii. 4, 6.   [4] xxii. 15, 1.
[5] xxvi. 10, 19. A ship suffered this at Galveston, Texas, in Sept. 1900.
[6] *Ep.* 983.   [7] xxix. 1.
[8] The man of fate was Theodosius, not Theodorus; so after all the prophecy came true. He was co-opted as Emperor by Gratian in 378.

for the future. A reign of terror followed. "We all at that time crept about as it were in Cimmerian darkness, as frightened as the guests of Dionysius who saw the swords hanging each by a horse hair over their heads[1]." There was probably no man with so little taste for rebellion in the empire. Writing of treason trials under Constantius he says[2]: "No sensible person condemns a vigorous inquiry into these matters; for we do not deny that the safety of a legitimate Emperor, the champion and defender of good citizens, to which others are indebted for their safety, ought to be protected by the associated enthusiasm of all men. To uphold this the more strongly the Cornelian laws allow in treason cases no exemption of rank from torture even if it cost blood." This is loyal enough, "but unbridled exultation in suffering is not befitting." He knew, and few better, what it meant to the empire to have no Emperor. That lesson was learnt in the desert and at Nisibis; and when after some months of tarnished glory Jovian died, the Roman soldiers were right when they forced Valentinian on his election at once to name a colleague.

While Ammianus lived in Rome he wrote his great history[3]. It consisted of thirty-one books, of which the first thirteen are lost. His work began with the reign of Nerva, 96 A.D., where Tacitus stopped; but in book xiv. we are in the year 353, and book xxxi. ends with the death of Valens at Adrianople in 378. It has been suggested[4] that there was not room in thirteen books on this scale for 250 years, and that perhaps, like Tacitus, he wrote *two* historical works, and that the history, eighteen books of which we still have, was that of his own times, while another is lost. This is a large supposition, and, I think, not very necessary[5]. At the beginning of book xv. he announces that what follows will be done *limatius*, which may refer as much to the matter as to the style, and would then imply greater detail. As I believe there is no external evidence of any kind, every one may freely form his

---

[1] xxix. 2, 4.
[2] xix. 12, 17.
[3] An English version was brought out by Philemon Holland, *of the Citie of Coventrie*, in 1609, in a flowing, if free, style. Pope sets Holland's translations (many and mainly historical) in "the library of Dulness," but Abp Trench thinks very highly of them, and his is probably the more serious judgment.
[4] By Hugo Michael. Büdinger, p. 4, rejects the theory.
[5] Zosimus, in his history of Rome's decline and fall, devotes one book, his first, to the first three hundred years of the empire, and gradually gives more space to events as he approaches his subject proper.

own opinion from that passage, and the little epilogue at the end of book xxxi.[1]

We do not know anything of his death. If his reference in book xxix to a young officer, Theodosius, *princeps postea perspectissimus*, implies that Theodosius' reign and life are done (as it may), then Ammianus died in 395 or later. The latest date to which an event he mentions can be assigned is Aurelius Victor's Praefecture of the City in 391. In speaking of the Serapeum he says nothing of its destruction in 391 by a mob, but he deals with the Serapeum in book xxii., and we have nine books on later history, so this gives us no further help. However it is quite unimportant when he died. He lived long enough to leave mankind a legacy, for which we cannot be too grateful.

As all we know of him is gathered from his history, we may consider his work and himself together. Let us begin with his epilogue, as good an account of him as there is:—" All this from the principate of Nerva Caesar to the death of Valens, I, a soldier in my day and a Greek, have set forth according to the measure of my powers. Truth being the boast of my work, never, I think, when I knew it, have I dared to corrupt it by silence or falsehood. What follows, let better men write, in the flower of life and learning ; and when, if they so choose, they undertake it, I bid them sharpen their tongues for a higher style." Elsewhere too he promises truth to his readers—*siqui erunt unquam*, as he modestly says.

He was a man of very wide reading, as his constant references to literature shew. They are so many in fact that it has been surmised he did his learning late in life. He is evidently proud of it, and the value he put upon it may be read in his apology for Valens, who had " a countrified intelligence, unpolished by any readings of antiquity[2]." Valens again shewed " a very unbridled exultation in various tortures (of supposed criminals), *being unaware of that saying of Tully's*, which teaches that they are unhappy men who think everything permitted them[3]." It is quite surprising how many Imperial and other crimes are sins of ignorance. Sometimes it is that the Emperor forgot or had not read his Aristotle, but we hear most of Tully. He is rarely at a loss for a historical parallel in the annals of Rome or Greece.

When he sums up the character of a good Emperor, he first of

---

[1] It is also believed by some that one book is missing before book xxxi.
[2] xxx. 4, 2 *Subagreste ingenium nullis vetustatis lectionibus expolitum.*
[3] xxvi. 10, 12 *Sententiae illius Tullianae ignarus.*

all tells us his faults—and quite freely too—and then sets forth his good points that they may leave the stronger impression, while with a bad Emperor he reverses the process. Let us follow his example and pay him the compliment implied by first giving an account of his foibles.

Critics almost without exception abuse his style, some even finding fault with him for trying to write in Latin at all[1], and certainly his style is curious and peculiar to him. It reminds one somehow of Apuleius, though it is less successful[2]. His vocabulary is good in itself, but his composition and grouping have a very odd effect. Partly it may be, as is suggested, the disturbing influence of Greek. Partly it is because he aims a little too much at rhetoric. The manner is more suited to the novel than to the history. In fact his style is rather more modern[3] than classical, so modern as to be nearly journalistic at times. It abounds in metaphor— "The trumpets of internal disaster were sounding[4]"; "the horrifying gang of furies lighted on the necks of all Asia[5]"; "he left the provinces waltzing[6]"; "the destiny of the East blared on the dread shawms of peril, mingling her plans with the shades of Tartarus[7]." He does not, in describing the situation of a town, care to say North, South, East and West simply, but "facing the arctoan stars," "whence the dawning sunbeam rises[8]." (Of course these phrases are more unnatural when translated.) Once or twice he

---

[1] It is remarkable in view of the fact that the Greeks had always been studiously ignorant of Latin (*e.g.* Plutarch), and that a century later than this we find but few in the East who knew it at all, that the two great men of letters of this age, Ammianus and Claudian, a Greek-speaking Egyptian, should write in Latin. The Emperor Julian seems guiltless of the most rudimentary acquaintance with Latin literature. Latin was still, however, the official language. Libanius (Sievers, p. 13) needed an interpreter to read a Latin letter, and was indignant at young Antiochenes going to Italy to learn Latin (*ib.* p. 162). Trench (*Plutarch*, p. 10) cites *one* quotation of Horace in Plutarch against Gibbon's assertion that there is no allusion to Virgil or Horace in Greek literature from Dionysius of Halicarnassus to Libanius. Is the statement or the exception more striking?

[2] E. W. Watson, *Studia Biblica*, iii. 241, compares Ammianus' style with Cyprian's, finding them "closely akin in their literary aspect."

[3] *E.g.* in the purely picturesque use of the adjective. xiv. 3, 4 *Aboraeque amnis herbidas ripas*, balancing *solitudines*.

[4] xxix. 1, 14 *internarum cladium litui sonabant.*

[5] xxix. 2, 21 *coetus furiarum horrificus...cervicibus Asiae totius insedit.* This rather curious phraseology is not unlike Apuleius, *e.g. Metam.* v. 12 *sed jam pestes illae taeterrimae furiae anhelantes vipereum virus et festinantes impia celeritate navigabant*—the description of Psyche's two sisters.

[6] xxviii. 3, 9 *tripudiantes relinquens provincias.* Others use this verb in the same way.

[7] xviii. 4, 1 *Orientis fortuna periculorum terribiles tubas inflabat...consilia tartareis manibus miscens.*

[8] xxvii. 4, 6 *arctois obnoxiam stellis.* 7 *unde eoum jubar exsurgit.*

breaks out in a declamatory apostrophe, which comes oddly enough in a history.   In fact we may borrow a phrase of his own, used of Phrynichus, to illustrate and describe his own style—*cum cothurnatius stilus procederet*[1].   *Cothurnus* is strictly the buskin worn by the tragic actor to give dignity to his stature, and is commonly enough used in Latin as equivalent to Tragedy itself, just as *soccus* represents Comedy.   *Cothurnatus* is "wearing the buskin" and may be employed of a man in a "tragic" humour.   To turn this into an adverb, and use it to describe the march of a style, is a somewhat unusual manner of writing, but characteristic of Ammianus.   It also hits him off admirably, for there is very often "a hint of the buskin in the strut of his style."   At the same time a good deal too much may be made of this, and has been made, for, as I hope the extract above translated will shew, he can write straightforwardly and simply when he pleases[2].   When his diction and his rather obtrusive learning are forgiven, I think we have exhausted the list of his sins, which must be admitted not to be very great.

When we come to his virtues, we find that his severe truthfulness and his dispassionate impartiality might set him in the very front rank of historians.   But a man may be fair and truthful without having the other necessary qualities of a historian, and these Ammianus has in a strongly marked degree.   He realizes the perspective of the picture he sees, and he selects and groups his matter with the eye of a master.   A modern author has this advantage over an ancient, that he can by grace of the printing press pack his digressions into footnotes and appendices, while so long as manuscripts held the field, everything had to go into the text. But for this the light reader would have a higher opinion of Ammianus.   Setting apart his geographical excursuses which really recall Herodotus[3], and those on scientific subjects such as earth-

[1] xxviii. 1, 4. So Mr Bury describes the style of Cassiodorus, "each epistle posing as it were in tragic cothurni and trailing a sweeping train."   *Later Roman Empire*, ii. p. 187.

[2] One must be careful of speaking of oneself after the Abbé's dictum, but I may be allowed to say I once read Ammianus steadily and almost exclusively for a fortnight and found him fascinating.   *Quot homines*, of course.

[3] Sievers, *Libanius*, p. 17, n. 2, says Geography was a Lieblingswissenschaft of the day.   Claudian stops the course of an epic to tell about Sicily and its volcanoes in 36 lines (*R. P.* i. 142—178).   While Peter (*die gesch. Litteratur über die R. Kaiserzeit bis Theod. I. u. ihre Quellen*) characterizes these excursions of Ammianus as Dilettantismus, Gimazane on the other hand (p. 207) says that after the French conquest of Algeria a French officer, Nau de Champlouis, took Ammianus' story of Theodosius' campaign in Africa, went over the ground and found the historian exact.   I have referred to de Broglie, whom the Abbé cites, but he is not quite so explicit.

quakes, the rainbow, comets, and so forth, which are generally borrowed, and naturally fall short of modern accuracy[1]—all of which would to-day be relegated from the main body of the work— we may say that he knows the use of light and shade, and shifts his scene so skilfully that the various parts of his work set off and relieve one another. No part of the Roman world is left out, and he gives us a vivid panorama of that world, borrowing no doubt at times from earlier writers. Huns, Goths, Egyptians and Persians are all surveyed, and though we may be surprised at an omission or a slip here and there, such as his neglect to notice the change from the Arsacid to the Sassanid dynasty in Persia[2], which from other sources we find meant much to Rome and her Eastern provinces, we really learn a great deal.

Then he has a keen eye for colour, and in a touch, a hint, an incidental phrase, lets us have glimpses that make the life of his time real and living to us to-day[3]. We are seeing his world for ourselves, almost with our own eyes. For instance, we learn thus that the Germans dyed their hair. Jovinus[4] "hidden in a valley dark through the thickness of the trees" surprises them, "some washing, some of them staining their hair red after their custom, and drinking some of them." In the same way we mingle with the Roman soldiers (too many of them barbarians), and see the way they do things. They are anxious to fight, and they let their commander know it by banging their spears on their shields[5]. To wish him good luck they make a din with the shields on their knees[6]. Here is a man who cuts off his thumb

---

[1] Gibbon, who had a high opinion of him, magnificently rebukes him on one occasion. "Ammianus, in a long, because unseasonable, digression, rashly supposes that he understands an astronomical question, of which his readers are ignorant." Nemesis overtakes him at once, for Dr Smith has remarked an error of a preposition in Gibbon's account of Ammianus' mistake.

[2] The Arsacids yielded place to Artaxerxes in 226 A.D., and the new dynasty which was supposed to derive from the Achaemenids (the family of Cyrus and Darius) lasted till 651 A.D. They restored the religion of Zoroaster and the authority of the Magi, persecuting Christians and Manichaeans alike. The long wearisome wars between them and the Romans (to be read of in the vivid if very unadorned history of Joshua the Stylite) left both an easy prey to Islam. We hear now and then of the Saracens already in Ammianus.

[3] Büdinger (*per quem non licet esse negligentem*), pp. 27—30, is very severe on some of Ammianus' picturesque touches—especially the scene where the Persians are crossing the bridge (xviii. 7, 1), asking, could he see so far and did Sapor really sacrifice at all? A little lower (p. 31) he laments that Ammianus did not know "Eusebios Pamphilos' *Sohn*." Ramsay, *Impressions of Turkey*, p. 193, mentions one or two odd little slips of Mr Hogarth into inaccuracy about small matters—a bolt on a door and a woman's petticoat—and asks what would be said of such blunders in St Luke.

[4] xxvii. 2, 2.   [5] xvi. 12, 13.   [6] xv. 8, 15.

to shirk service[1]. Julian makes a speech, and in delight the troops stand waving their shields in the air[2], or in anger they brandish their spears at him[3]. In the troops of Constantius[4] are soldiers who lie on feather-beds and have a pretty taste in gems. Alas! for Julian's heathen revival! his soldiers had too many sacrificial feasts, too much to eat and too much to drink, and rode home through the streets of Antioch to their quarters, mounted on the necks of passers-by[5]. Now they all but mutiny because Julian has only a donative for them of a hundred pieces of silver a man[6]. Again we find them marching into battle, while they raise the *barritus*[7], "so called in their native tongue, a martial note that began low and swelled louder." Mr Keary[8] very reasonably finds the origin of this in the German forests, where the wind sweeping over and through leagues of trees roared like the sea, and hence through barbarian recruits, of whom we hear a good deal, it came into the Roman army.

All these are small points, perhaps, but they add variety to the work; and though a history may be great without them, or dull with them, they are in their right place in Ammianus, and brighten his canvas without lessening the effect of the great outlines of his picture.

Ammianus was a soldier, but he saw that the army was not the State, and ever and again we find him intent on the provinces and the troubles of the tax-payer. He recognizes the merit of Constantius, whom he did not like, in keeping the army in its proper place[9], "never exalting the horns of the military"; and he tells us with a proud satisfaction in his hero that Julian reduced the land tax in Gaul from twenty-five to seven *aurei per caput*[10], and in his financial arrangements would not countenance one particular practice because it was merely a relief to the rich without helping the poor at all. It is not the picture of Julian we are generally shewn, and we must bear in mind that the man, whom the ecclesiastics abuse for "pillaging" them, was careful for finance and had the interests of the empire at heart. A burning question of the time was the shirking of "curial" duties by men who tried to

---

[1] xv. 12, 3.
[2] xxiii. 5, 24.
[3] xxi. 13, 16.
[4] xxii. 4, 6.
[5] xxii. 12, 6.
[6] xxiv. 3, 3.
[7] xxxi. 7, 11. Cf. Tac. *Germ.* 3.
[8] *Vikings and Western Christendom*, p. 43.
[9] xxi. 16, 1.
[10] xvi. 5, 14. Cf. Marquardt, *Röm. Staatsverwaltung*[1], ii. p. 222.

evade paying their share of the heavy taxes exacted from the *curia* of each town as a body. It is clear that every evasion made the burden heavier for the rest of the body, but Julian is severely criticized by Ammianus for being too sharp with men whom the *curiae* accused of such dereliction[1]. The system was vicious, and in fact was one of the main elements in the decay of the empire[2].

Another such element was officialdom. He tells us how when Julian was quartered at last in the palace of Constantinople, and sent for a barber, there entered a gorgeous official, who proved to be the court barber, and, as such, had a splendid income[3]. This roused Julian, who at once made a sweeping clearance of barbers and cooks and eunuchs, and till Valens became Emperor their *régime* was at an end. Other official nuisances were less easy to get rid of, and again and again we find Ammianus telling of tumult and war and disaster brought on by the cruelty and insolence of civil and military authorities. Valentinian, he complains, did nothing to check the irregularities of his officers, while he was very severe on the private soldiers. Finally, the terrible Gothic war, which culminated in the defeat and death of Valens at Adrianople, was occasioned, if not caused, by the rapacity and cruelty of a magistrate charged with the transport of the Goths over the Danube.

Here it may be remarked that while Ammianus has no political or economical views to set forth, and accepts the fact of the empire as part of the world's fabric, as everybody else then did, without criticism, he does permit himself to criticize and complain of the administration. Though he laments that his contemporaries have not the recuperative power which "sober antiquity, unstained by the effeminacy of an ungirt life," possessed in its unanimity and

---

[1] Rode, p. 58, refers this criticism to Julian's edict (*Ep.* 14) putting back Christian clergy into the curiae from which they had been released on ordination. Amm. Marc. xxv. 4, 21; and xxi. 12, 23.

[2] Priscus in his account of his interesting journey among the Huns in 448 A.D. (p. 59 B in the Bonn Corpus of Byzantine History, a translation of which is to be found in Mr Bury's *Later Roman Empire*, i. 213—223) tells us of a renegade Greek he met who had turned Hun and pled that he was better off; "for the condition of the subjects [of the empire] in time of peace is far more grievous than the evils of war, for the exaction of the taxes is very severe, and unprincipled men inflict injuries on others because the laws are practically not valid against all classes," and so forth. Priscus upheld the empire, and "my interlocutor shed tears and confessed that the laws and constitution of the Romans were fair, but deplored that the governors, not possessing the spirit of former generations, were ruining the State." It might be difficult to identify those "former generations," but the whole story is very significant.

[3] xxii. 4, 9.

patriotism[1], he has no regrets for the republic, no sorrow for the Senate of Rome in its glorious effacement, none of the narrow Roman feeling of the city-state days. Three hundred years had brought a good many changes, and all the world was Roman now together, apart from Germans, Goths, and Persians beyond the pale. The Greek of Antioch is as much a Roman as any one. The result is a striking difference of tone in the historian—a change for the better. We are rid of the jingoism of Livy, and the gloom of Tacitus[2]. Ammianus himself is tenderer and has larger sympathies than the historians of old. He can value human life even if it is not a Roman life, and pity the child though a Syrian who begins his experience by being taken captive. The Roman in Ammianus poses no more. He is far more frankly human. As a result we feel more with him. In fighting German[3] and Persian he is battling for light and civilization, and Christianity itself; and if in the last great fight in book xxxi. we incline to the Gothic side in some degree, it is the fault of a criminal official, and not because our historian alienates our sympathy by a narrow and offensive little patriotism. Things are more fairly and squarely judged on their merits now when the cramping caste distinction of *civitas* is gone. Even the line between Roman and barbarian was growing faint, when the Frank Nevitta was made consul by Julian, bitter as he was against Constantine for his barbarian consuls.

But I have said nothing so far of one great change that had come over the world in the triumph of the Church. We hear of it of course from Ammianus, but less than we might have expected. This is easily accounted for. One of our chief interests in the fourth century is the Arian controversy, and Ammianus was a heathen. A heathen of the latter-day type, that is, a rather confused, because so very open-minded a heathen. We hear little about the gods and a great deal about the vaguely-named *caeleste numen*, which shews its interest in mankind again and again.

In particular he digresses on the occasion of the downfall of Gallus, which he considered a well-deserved catastrophe, to give us his view of Nemesis or divine justice. The passage is characteristic in several ways. " Such things and many more like them are

---

[1] xxxi. 5. 14.

[2] Mr Bury (*L. R. E.*, ii. 179) characterizes Tacitus very justly as "out of touch with his own age."

[3] Büdinger (p. 21) discovers an "unusual bitterness against Germans" in Ammianus though he notices it less in the later books. If this is true it can hardly be surprising (compare Synesius), but it had not occurred to me.

often wrought (and would they were always!) by the avenger of evil acts and the rewarder of good, Adrastia, whom we also call by a second name Nemesis, a certain sublime Justice with divine power, set, if human minds may judge, above the orbit of the moon, or, as others hold, a guardian being, with universal sway over our several destinies, whom the theologians of old in their myth call the daughter of Justice, saying that from an unknown eternity she looks down on all earthly things. She, as queen of causes, arbiter and disposer of events, holds the urn of fate, varying the lot that befals us; and by bringing what our free wills begin at times to a very different end from that intended, she utterly changes and involves the manifold actions of men. With the indissoluble clamp of necessity she fetters the empty pride of mortality, and disposing as she will of the hours of growth and decline, now she brings down the neck of pride and cuts its sinews, now she lifts the good from the depths into prosperity. Antiquity, in its love of myth, gave her wings, that men might realize with what flying speed she is everywhere present; it gave her to hold the helm and set the wheel beneath her, that men might know she courses through all the elements and rules the universe" (xiv. 11, 25—26).

Here, while aiming at expressing his view in the style he loves, he gives us the conclusion of a man of affairs. Men propose this and that; powers above them "shape their ends," and the world presents a great appearance of confusion. Yet his experience and observation lead him to believe that in general it is possible to recognize some higher power (to-day we might say law or principle) which is acting towards justice. We do not always see justice entirely triumphant, but we often do, so often as to be justified in believing that above the play of "changeful and inconstant fortune" is a divine justice, however we may define it. He is not a philosopher, but he leans on the whole to Neo-Platonic theology, from which he derived "the orbit of the moon," the lowest of the seven heavenly planes.

Auguries and auspices are still to the fore, not that the mere birds can tell the future, but a kindly *numen*[1] guides their flight to allow us by it to see what is coming. Omens are very real

---

[1] xxi. 1, 9. *Amat enim benignitas numinis, seu quod merentur homines, seu quod tangitur eorum adfectione, his quoque artibus prodere quae inpendunt.* Surely there is something pathetic in this, if only in the *quoque*. This too is Neo-Platonic; see footnote 2 on p. 187.

things—an idea mankind still cherishes in a confused and half ashamed way. Prodigies still occur, but "nobody heeds them now." Ammianus has great respect for the philosophers and the *theologi* of old, though he draws a curious picture of Julian's camp with its Etruscan soothsayers and Greek philosophers[1]. Some sort of portent occurred on Julian's march into Persia, and the soothsayers declared that it meant disaster if the advance were continued. But they were slighted by the philosophers, "who had much respect just then, though they do make mistakes sometimes, and are stubborn enough in things they know nothing about." This time the event justified the soothsayers, we know.

But a historian of the fourth century, whatever his creed, has to deal with Christians. Ammianus is quite free from bias; Christian or heathen is much the same to him—*Tros Tyriusque mihi nullo discrimine agetur*. He has no *animus* whatever, and is so far unique among his contemporaries. He finds grave fault with Julian for forbidding Christian professors to teach ancient literature, stigmatizing the decree as one *obruendum perenni silentio*[2], "to be overwhelmed in eternal silence"—strong words to use of a man he loved and honoured, and speaking volumes for the fairness of the writer. As an outsider, however, who will have other outsiders among his readers, he will often half apologize for a technical term —"a deacon as it is called," "synods as they call them." A bishop is *Christianae legis antistes*, though he slips into *episcopus* now and then. A church is *Christiani ritus sacrarium*, or *Christiani ritus conventiculum*, or frankly *ecclesia*. These roundabout phrases are largely due to his environment; for the traditions of literature and good society ignored the new religion[3].

[1] xxiii. 5, 8—11. He was disgusted with the quacks and pretenders who swarmed round Julian. Augury and so forth were degraded when practised in irregular ways and by the inexpert. Cf. xxii. 12, 7, and Socrates, iii. 1, 55.

[2] xxii. 10, 7.

[3] This might of itself, I think, dispose of Gutschmid's ingenious attempt to correct a defective passage in xxii. 16, 22. Ammianus is enumerating the great men whose teaching has been influenced by Egypt (Pythagoras, Anaxagoras and Solon) and his last name is lost. *Ex his fontibus per sublimia gradiens sermonum amplitudine Jovis aemulus non visa Aegypto militavit sapientia gloriosa.* Gutschmid wants to read, after *his, ihs, i.e. Jesus*; Valesius would prefer correcting *non* into *Platon*. When one remembers that even Christians of the type of Augustine and Jerome found the style of the Bible bad and unreadable at first; that heathen writers habitually ignore the Church, its doctrines and usages as far as possible; that the use of the name *Jesus* alone is unusual, coming on one with a surprise in Jerome, while Tacitus says *Christus* and Suetonius *Chrestus* and dismiss the matter; that Ammianus, who was an admirer of Julian and generally in literary matters wishful to be correct, would have been a revolutionary among educated pagans if he had

But Ammianus was no pedant, and can speak in terms of admiration of the men[1] "who, to hold their faith inviolate, faced a glorious death and are now called martyrs." In another passage, speaking of the sufferings inflicted on the followers of the pretender Procopius—which were very much those undergone by the martyrs of Palestine according to Eusebius—he says[2] he had rather die in battle ten times over than face them.

Side by side with this stand his startling words on the warring of the sects. Julian, on the principle of *Divide ut imperes,* recalled the Nicene exiles with a view to fresh theological quarrels[3]; "for he knew that there are no wild beasts so hostile to mankind as most of the Christians are to one another." It was only two centuries since Tertullian heard the heathen remarking *ut sese invicem diligunt.* He records the terrible fight in a church at Rome[4] between the followers of Damasus and Ursinus, the rival candidates for the See, when one hundred and thirty-seven dead bodies were found on the victory of Damasus. Here is his comment— "I do not deny, when I consider the ostentation of Roman society, that those who are ambitious for this thing (the See) ought to spare no effort in the fray to secure what they want, for, if they get it, they will be sure of being enriched by the offerings of matrons, of riding about in carriages, dressed in clothes the cynosure of every eye, and of giving banquets so profuse, that their entertainments shall surpass the tables of kings[5]. They might be happy indeed, if they could despise the magnificence of Rome, which they count a set-off to the crimes involved, and live in imitation of certain bishops of the provinces, whom their sparing diet, the cheapness of their clothes, and their eyes fixed upon the ground, commend as pure and holy men, to the eternal deity and his true worshippers."

Once he seems to express a preference, when he complains of Constantius "confounding the pure and simple Christian religion with old-wife superstition[6]." Probably *anilis superstitio* is his

---

found "sublime eloquence" or "glorious wisdom" in Christianity; and finally that he nowhere shews any acquaintance with any Christian literature whatever, and fails to realize what Arian and Nicene were disputing about around him; the brilliance of Gutschmid becomes more and more impossible.

[1] xxii. 11, 10.   [2] xxvi. 10, 13.
[3] xxii. 5, 4.   [4] xxvii. 3, 12.
[5] Cf. Augustine's early judgment on Ambrose, *Conf.* vi. 3, 3.
[6] xxi. 16, 18. *Christianam religionem absolutam et simplicem anili superstitione confundens in qua scrutanda perplexius quam componenda gravius excitavit discidia plurima, quae progressa fusius aluit concertatione verborum,*

summary criticism of all theological speculation. Constantine took the same view and wrote to Arius and Alexander remonstrating about their quarrel which he called "childish folly"—they were "too precise" (ἀκριβολογεῖσθε, exactly Ammianus' *in qua scrutanda perplexius*) about these "entirely trifling questions." Constantine complained that these clergy caused disorder and discord; and Ammianus says the same of Constantius (*quam componenda gravius*)[1]. In any case, in view of his treatment of Athanasius and the curt dismissal of the Athanasian question[2], it is hardly clear that he censures Arianism, which in fact was less likely to seem *anilis superstitio* to a heathen than Nicene Christianity. At all events Constantius was too "curious about the Christian religion," and ruined the State's arrangements for the quick travelling of genuine officials by giving free passes to swarms of bishops who did little but go from one synod to another.

I think we may surmise Ammianus' own feelings from his remark about Valentinian[3]. Valentinian was rather a savage ruler on Ammianus' own shewing, but "this reign was glorious for the moderation with which he stood among the different religions and troubled no one, nor gave orders that this should be worshipped or that; nor did he try by threatening rescripts to bend the neck of his subjects to what he worshipped himself, but he left the parties untouched as he found them." Surveying all his references to Christianity, I am afraid we must admit that he did not realize what it meant, nor understand how vital was the issue between Arian and Nicene. How should he, when there were hundreds in the church who did neither? We must also always remember that, beside being a man who kept himself in the background, he was writing for a society which avowedly had no interest at all in Christian affairs[4].

Ammianus did not lack for dry humour; witness the soldiers who would have won a certain battle "if only they had displayed the vigour in standing which they shewed in running away"; and "Epigonus, a philosopher so far as clothes went"; or Mercurius "who was like a savage dog that wags his tail the more sub-

---

ut catervis antistitum jumentis publicis ultroque citroque discurrentibus per synodos quas appellant dum ritum omnem ad suum trahere conantur arbitrium, rei vehiculariae succideret nervos.

[1] See Constantine's letter *apud* Euseb. *V. C.* ii. 69—71 and Socr. i. 7.
[2] xv. 7, 6—10.   [3] xxx. 9, 5.
[4] The Abbé Gimazane is very anxious to make Ammianus a Christian, at least so far as to have been baptized, though he admits that his supposed faith is lukewarm. I see neither the gain nor the grounds.

missively for being a brute inside"; or the would-be Emperor Procopius, "about whom the wonder was that his life through he shed no man's blood"; or that governor of Africa "who was in a hurry to outstrip the enemy in plundering his province"; or finally, those lawyers of Antioch who, if you mentioned in their presence the name of some worthy of old, took it to be some foreign term for a fish or other eatable[1]. But what would have been in Tacitus one of the bitterest of epigrams, is in Ammianus no epigram at all. *Imperialis verecundia*, the chastity of an emperor, was the great phenomenon of the fourth and fifth centuries, whose emperors, whatever else they may have been, were in this matter above scandal.

There is a beautiful picture of the triumphal entry of Constantius into Rome[2]. He was a little man, long in the body and short and rather bandy in the legs, but

> He nothing common did nor mean
> Upon that memorable scene.

He rode in a golden chariot, and for all the noise and applause never flinched, but stood immovable; but "on passing through lofty gateways he would bow his little person; and as if his neck were fortified, he kept his gaze straight in front of him, and looked neither right nor left, as if he had been a dummy; the shaking of the wheels did not make him nod, and he was not seen to spit, or wipe his mouth or his nose, or move his hand throughout."

A grim humour hangs about the coronation of Procopius[3], who, after months in hiding, blossomed out as an Emperor. He appeared before the soldiers without a cloak, and so emaciated as to look as if he had risen from the dead, and all the purple he could muster was his boots and a rag he waved in his left hand :—"you would have thought him some figure on the stage, or some ridiculous burlesque that had popped through the curtain." His procession was hardly a success; for the soldiers were afraid of being assailed with tiles from the roofs, and marched along holding their shields over their heads.

Of Ammianus' residence in Rome we have many reminders, some of very great interest, some very amusing. His description of the city on the occasion of Constantius' visit shews the hold Rome still

[1] The same doubt has arisen in our own day as to whether Botticelli is a cheese or a wine, if we may trust Mr Punch.
[2] xvi. 10.   [3] xxvi. 6, 15.

had on the world's imagination. "Whatever he saw first he thought supreme above all." There was the temple of Tarpeian Jove, the baths as big as provinces, the solid mass of the amphitheatre built of Tiburtine stone, to whose top the human eye could hardly reach, and so forth. "But when he came to Trajan's forum —a structure, I suppose, unique under heaven, which even the gods would agree with us in admiring—he stood in amazement[1]." Rome was the one thing in the world about which exaggeration was impossible. The Emperor was so much impressed that he determined to add his item to the ornaments of the Eternal City, and sent an obelisk from Egypt. Of this and the inscription it bore, and its journey and arrival, Ammianus gives us a most interesting account[2].

But more entertaining are his digressions on Roman manners, which abound in sketches as good as Juvenal's[3]. The snobbery and extravagance of the great men of Rome may not have been more excessive than such things are elsewhere; but the grandee who with the greatest dignity (though no one has asked) extols to the skies his patrimony and the income it yields, how fertile it is, how far it reaches; the noble gentleman who welcomes you, though an utter stranger, as if he had been yearning for you, asks you endless questions till you have to lie, and makes you regret that you did not settle in Rome ten years earlier, but next day has no idea who or what or whence you are; the fashionable people, who loathed sensible and well-educated men like the plague, and learning like poison—all these impressed Ammianus so much that he has left them gibbeted for ever in his pages. The troops of slaves and eunuchs (his particular abhorrence), the luxury of the banquets, the Roman preference for the musician rather than the philosopher, the organs and lyres as big as waggons, the libraries closed like the tomb, the absurd fear of infection that has the slave washed after he has been to inquire about a sick friend before he is allowed into the house again, the gambling and horse racing, the effeminacy and the slang[4] of Rome, waken disgust in this old soldier, as well they might. The rabble that will fight for Damasus or Ursinus, and

---

[1] xvi. 10, 15. Cf. Symmachus, *Rel.* 3, 7, on Constantius' toleration of the temples.

[2] xviii. 4.

[3] xiv. 6; xxviii. 4. Boissier, *F. P.* ii. 187, says: "Dans ces passages qui ne ressemblent pas tout à fait au reste il est plus satirique et rhéteur qu'historien."

[4] *E.g. Per te ille discat.* Cf. Jerome, *Ep.* 55, 5, When they see a Christian, *statim illud de trivio ὁ γραικός, ὁ ἐπιθέτης.*

riot if the corn ships are late or wine is not forthcoming, are no better than the nobles. The most absurd figure of all, perhaps, is Lampadius, who was at one time prefect—"a man who would be indignant if he should so much as spit without being complimented on being adept at it above the rest of mankind." But even in Rome there were good men and true, such as Symmachus "who is to be named among the most illustrious examples of learning and decorum."

If this is comedy there is tragedy enough in book xiv. Gallus Caesar is in the midst of a career of tyranny and bloodshed in the East[1], when he is summoned to Italy. To disarm his suspicion he is bidden to bring his wife Constantina[2]—a helpmeet indeed for him, "a death-dealing Megaera, the constant inflamer of his rage, as greedy of human blood as her spouse"—a lady who listens from behind a curtain to keep him from weakening. She did not feel easy about the invitation, yet thought she would risk it, but she died of fever in Bithynia on her journey, and Gallus felt more nervous than ever, for he knew Constantius and "his particular tendency to destroy his kin." He knew his own staff hated him, and were afraid of Constantius, for wherever civil strife was involved the "luck" of Constantius was proverbial. A tribune was sent to lure him to his ruin; "and as the senses of men are dulled and blunted when Destiny lays a hand on them, with quickened hopes he left Antioch, under the guidance of an unpropitious power, to jump as they say from the frying pan into the fire." On his journey he gave horse races at Constantinople, and the Emperor's rage was more than human. A guard of honour (and espionage) accompanied him. From Adrianople he was hurried on with fewer attendants, and now he saw how he stood and "cursed his rashness with tears." The ghosts of his victims haunted his dreams. At Petobio he was made a prisoner, and at Histria he was beheaded, and all of him that reached Constantius was his boots, which a creature of the Court hauled off to post away to the Emperor with this glorious spoil.

What is the general impression left on the mind by the history of Ammianus? One cannot read him through without a growing conviction of his absolute truthfulness and a growing admiration of

---

[1] Even his brother Julian admits "fierce and savage" elements in his character. *Ep. ad Athen.* 271 D.

[2] Honoured since the 13th century as S. Constanza. Gregorovius, *Rome*, i. 106.

his power, and the two together present the Roman Empire to the mind exactly as it was. He makes no predictions, he expresses no regrets, and apart from observations on the characters he draws, he leaves the reader to form his own opinions on the Empire. Nobody foresaw that in twenty years after his death Rome would have fallen to the Goth, that the Empire as an effective power in the West was nearing its end, but yet, wise after the event, we can see in his pages that it is all coming. There were, we learn, strong men and honest men to stave it off and delay it, who, if they could not save Rome, did save Europe in virtue of those ideals of law and order which the younger peoples of the North found in the majestic fabric of Roman administration. Ammianus lets us see the exhaustion of the Roman world, the ruin of the middle classes under an oppressive system, and often still more oppressive agents, of taxation, the weakness all along the frontier, Rhine, Danube, Euphrates, and African desert, caused by bad principles of government within as much as by attacks from without, and the crying need of men which led to the army being filled with barbarians, who did not quite lose all their barbarism and brutality at once, and were often as terrible to those they protected as to the enemy they were supposed to keep off; and at the same time we read in him the grandeur and the glory of Rome, who had welded the world into one and made the nations members one of another, had humanized and civilized them with law and culture in her train wherever she went, and was even now training in her armies the men who should overthrow her, and then, as it were in horror at their own work, should set her on high once more, and keep her in her place as the world's Queen for a thousand years.

CHAPTER III

JULIAN

Perfidus ille Deo, quamvis non perfidus orbi.

PRUDENTIUS *Apoth.* 454

ONE of the amiable traits in man's nature is to love what is old for its own sake. Our affection for progress is not always utterly disinterested, but the love of the past is the purest of passions. And we are so made, or many of us are, that we love the old the more because it is the lost cause. It may be a weakness, but it is a gentle weakness. Yet it is apt to mislead us, and we sometimes allow age and defeat to obscure in our lost cause or our fallen hero features that would repel us in a triumph. Thus in some measure has it come about that there is a kindly feeling for Julian beyond what his worth really merits, and it is reinforced by the malignity and hatred with which ecclesiastical writers have, or are supposed to have, pursued his memory. The tradition grew that he was a champion of reason and enlightenment against the crudity and darkness of Christianity, and indeed these words are practically Julian's own. But the reason and enlightenment of which he thought and wrote would have seemed to many, who have admired him for their sake, as crude and foolish as the dogmas of the Church against which he protested. After all he owes something to the spiteful nickname he bears.

The Julian of sentimental atheism is really as far from the truth as the Julian drawn by over-zealous ecclesiastics. The real Julian is more interesting than either, because a more complicated character. He found fault with Old and New Testaments very much in the style of Voltaire, but he was not a sceptic. He was hated as a persecutor, though again and again he declares his

wish and his intention to maintain religious freedom. Many rulers
have upheld religion, very few have felt so deeply conscious of
divine guidance or so utterly dependent upon it as he. For most
men the religion of Christ seems to supply the closest, the most
vital and the most absorptive communion with the divine; to some
it has seemed to draw too much upon faith. But Julian decided it
was a cold sectarianism that cut a man away from heaven and left
him godless in a godless world. For some it has been a divine
alchemy transmuting everything it touched to gold. For Julian
it did the reverse, and for the gold of Homer and Plato offered the
lead of Matthew and Luke. It was a blight upon the Greek spirit
which had given life to the world for a thousand years. We can
now see that this Greek spirit had died long since a natural death,
but the Greeks of Julian's day fondly hoped it was living in them
still, and Julian voices the horror with which they began to feel
the chill of death and the natural, if rather irrational, hatred they
felt for what they supposed to be its cause[1].

"Draw me as you have seen me," wrote Julian to a painter. In
one way this is easy to do, for few men have ever let mankind see
into their inmost feelings as he did; but it is difficult, too, for the
atmosphere in which he lived was not ours, and many things look
strange to-day which were not felt to be unnatural then. Zeus and
Athena are not now, and we can only with difficulty conceive them
ever to have been for thinking men, even with all the generous
allowances philosophers might make, a possible alternative to Christ.
Yet are they stranger than Krishnu and Kali? Is it not possible
to-day for a man to halt between two opinions in India, and find
in the philosophy or theosophy of thirty centuries of Hinduism an
attraction which may outweigh Christianity? When we think of
the age of Julian we must not forget that the Brahmo-Somaj
exists to-day. Even Christians of his day believed his gods to be
real beings, of course demons.

[1] Perhaps the best thing is to quote a Latin view to supplement this.
Rutilius (i. 383—396) attacks the Jews and involves Christians with them.

> atque utinam nunquam Judaea subacta fuisset
> Pompeii bellis imperiisque Titi;
> latius excisae pestis contagia serpunt
> victoresque suos natio victa premit.

Further on he assails the monks, and concludes

> non, rogo, deterior Circaeis secta venenis?
> tunc mutabantur corpora, nunc animi.

The fourth century saw the last great persecution of the Church end in failure, and the new religion recognized and honoured by Constantine With him a new spirit came into the Roman Empire. Hitherto so long as a man did a loyal citizen's duty, the State did not intervene to regulate his belief. But now Constantine, weary of the civil disorder the Arian quarrel made at Alexandria and then communicated to other places as the infection spread, called a council of the Church and invited the bishops to decide what the Christian faith was, and he would then see to it himself that there should be no more quarrelling about it. He was, however, disappointed, for the quarrels went on, and when he died in 337 they were still unsettled. Whatever might have been Constantine's own religious position, his son's was clear. Constantius carried to the inevitable haiting-place the theory that a man's belief is the State's concern. He did not aim at reconciling the factions for the sake of concord, but at converting them all to his belief. His aim was that of Justinian or Henry VIII.—to dictate to his realm what it was to believe. This affected Christians at once, and signs were not lacking that the heathen ere long must in their turn be Arian, Semi-Arian or Nicene, as the ruler might require.

Constantine left behind three sons and a number of nephews and other relatives, but, whether the deed was the army's, done to secure "the seed of Constantine"—a phrase a man might conjure with at this time—or whether it was the work of Constantius, this great family was thinned down, and the sons of Constantine were left to rule the world alone[1]. Two of their cousins survived, the sons of their father's half-brother, Gallus and Julian. Gallus was thought to be so ill as to render murder unnecessary, and Julian was so small—six years old—as to be overlooked. It was a dark beginning for a life, like "the unspeakable tale from some tragedy" rather than the record of a Christian house, and Julian lays the guilt on Constantius, "the kindest of men." (*Ep. Ath.* 270 c.) In later days Constantius, who, too, had a conscience, looked upon his childlessness as Heaven's criticism of his deed. Had he lived a month or two longer, to see his daughter, he might have had to

---

[1] Licinius had thirty years before set the precedent by clearing away as far as he could all persons who by marriage or descent were connected with any pfevious Emperor. This was to exclude the possibility of a pretender. Such as it is, this is the justification of Constantius—"the sixth commandment," says Seeck, writing of Constantine killing the younger Licinius, "must yield to the safety of the empire."

50   *Life and Letters in the Fourth Century*

revise this opinion. The heathen world, if Libanius[1] voices a general feeling, saw in the extinction of the whole of Constantine's family the vengeance of the injured gods.

Julian was left to the care of his kinsman, the great Semi-Arian Bishop of Constantinople, Eusebius of Nicomedeia[2], and of a faithful eunuch Mardonius, who had been his mother's tutor. Some have tried to lay the blame of Julian's apostasy on the theology of Eusebius and his party. It would be nearer the truth to lay it on their unscoured morals as exhibited in the court of Constantius. Eusebius himself we may acquit of direct influence on Julian. Great ecclesiastical statesmen have rarely, perhaps, the leisure to teach little boys, and whatever leisure and inclination Eusebius may have had to teach Julian, he died when his charge was still a child. Mardonius had been reared by Julian's grandfather and was a faithful servant who watched well over the boy. He had a passion for Homer and Greek literature[3], and when the lad would ask leave to go to races or anything of the kind, the old man would refer him to the 23rd of the *Iliad* and bid him find his races there. Two things resulted from this training. Julian's moral character was thoroughly sound throughout life. He never entered the theatre till his beard was grown, and as a man he hated the races (*Misop.* 351, and 340 A). On the other hand Mardonius does not seem to have spent much time with his pupil on the Christian scriptures, and Julian's earliest and happiest associations were with Homer, whose poetry he always loved.

---

[1] See Sievers, *Das Leben des Libanius*, p. 192.

[2] Amm. Marc. xxii. 9, 4. A pedigree of the maternal connexions of Julian may be found in Seeck's great edition of Symmachus, p. clxxv. It is not quite complete, as the bishop is omitted.

[3] For Mardonius see *Misopogon*, 352 A. He was a Hellenized Scythian, and perhaps it was in some measure due to him that Julian was so entirely out of touch with Latin literature, but the Greek sophists with whom he consorted were of one mind in neglecting Latin. *E.g.* Libanius (Sievers, *op. cit.* p. 13) needed an interpreter for a Latin letter. See Rohde, *der griechische Roman*, p. 298, on this preference felt by the later Greeks for themselves—a preference which Julian shared but which did not gain him support in the Latin world. If *Epistle* 55 be written from Gaul or the West, as I think, we have Julian's views on the tongue half his Empire used—playful no doubt :— τὰ δὲ ἐμά, εἰ καὶ φθεγγοίμην Ἑλληνιστί, θαυμάζειν ἄξιον· οὕτως ἐσμὲν ἐκβεβαρβαρωμένοι διὰ τὰ χωρία. Elsewhere (*Or.* ii. 72 A) he speaks of what *they* (the Latins) do with the letter V. Eutropius (x. 16, 3) remarks his one-sided education—*liberalibus disciplinis adprime eruditus, Graecis doctior atque adeo ut Latina eruditio nequaquam cum Graeca scientia conveniret.* Constantine, on the other hand, addressed the Nicene Council (mainly Eastern and Greek-speaking Bishops) in Latin, but when presiding over the debates he intervened in Greek. (Euseb. *Vita Constantini*, iii. 13.)

A sudden edict from Constantius removed his two cousins to a rather remote place in Cappadocia. Macellum has been described as a castle or a palace. Very probably it was both. Julian, when he is attacking Constantius' memory, asserts that there he and his brother were shut off from schools, companions and training suitable to their age and rank (*Ep. Ath.* 271), but from another source we learn it was a place with a magnificent palace, baths, gardens and perpetual springs, where he enjoyed the attention and dignity his rank deserved, and had the literary and gymnastic training usual for youths of his age. (Sozomen v. 2, 9.) His teachers, it is suggested, were Christian clergy, who probably had the less influence for seeming to be the creatures of Constantius[1]. Consequently their instructions had not the charm of Mardonius', and it may be to them that he owes his repugnance for the Bible. It was not admired as a rule by the educated of the day—a terrible reflexion on the system that left them incapable of appreciating it. Longinus (ix. 9), it is true, quotes the passage "Let there be light : and there was light" as an instance of the sublime, and Porphyry occasionally cites the Old Testament in a friendly spirit, but they are exceptions. Wherever he may first have read the Scriptures, Julian never understood them. He had a good superficial knowledge of them, but no idea of their spirit and significance. The anthropomorphisms of the old Hebrew stories he found less wise and more crude than those of Greek legend ; while, for the New Testament, little is to be expected of a critic who can pronounce that Paul "outdid all the quacks and cheats that ever existed anywhere[2]."

Of course he would have no noble companions save his brother, but this was inevitable. Constantius seems to have meant to keep them in reserve, out of his way and safe from plotters who might make tools of them, but still available and properly trained in case of his needing them himself. Later on it was easy to represent these years at Macellum as bleak exile.

As to Gallus, Julian says that "if there were anything savage and rough that afterwards appeared in his character" (and it seems generally agreed that there was a good deal) "it developed from this long residence in the mountains." Whether Gallus would have done better in Constantinople is very doubtful. Nero, Domitian and Commodus do not seem to have derived much benefit

[1] So Rode, p. 27, and Vollert, p. 15.
[2] See Neumann's reconstruction of his book against the Christians, p. 176.

from the atmosphere of Rome. For himself, "the gods kept him pure by means of philosophy." Some of this "philosophy" was no doubt previously learnt, but some, it is possible, was acquired from the books "many philosophical and many rhetorical" which George (afterwards bishop of Alexandria) "gave him to copy when in Cappadocia[1]." There is nothing very original about any of his philosophical ideas.

From Macellum Gallus was summoned to be made Caesar by Constantius, to govern Syria in true tyrant fashion, to rouse the Emperor's ill-will, to be recalled and put to death. Julian later on tried to make political capital out of his being put to death untried, but from the pages of Ammianus Marcellinus we learn that whether tried or not (and those were not days when political offenders were over-nicely tried), Gallus richly deserved his fate.

The suspicions of Constantius extended to Julian, and for some time he was kept at court under his cousin's eye or within reach. But the Empress Eusebia was his friend, reconciled her husband to him, and obtained leave for him to live in Athens. For this Julian was always grateful to her memory[2].

Julian had spent six years at Macellum, and since then had attended at Constantinople and Nicomedeia the lectures of some of the great teachers of the day. He was made to promise he would not hear Libanius, and he kept his promise but obtained written reports of the lectures[3]. He was still nominally a Christian and a "reader," though really at heart a heathen already, when he went to Athens in 355, to meet there men whose acquaintance he counted among the best gifts of his life[4].

We have a picture of him drawn by his fellow-student, Gregory

----

[1] *Ep. Ath.* 272 A and *Ep.* 9 (on the rescue of George's books). I owe this suggestion to Vollert, p. 15, and Rode, p. 26.

[2] *Oration* iii. p. 118 D.

[3] Sievers, *op. cit.* p. 54 and Rode, p. 29.

[4] An interesting study of students and professors in the Athens of Julian's day will be found in Mr Capes' *University Life in Ancient Athens* (Longmans). He brings out the connexion between the city government and the "University," which explains Julian's addressing his manifesto in 360 "to the Council and People of the Athenians." It was a little pedantic in any case to send it to Athens at all, but the act is characteristic of Julian.

See also Sievers, *op. cit.* ch. iii. on universities, rhetoricians and scholars, and ch. iv. on Athens; and Wachsmuth, *Die Stadt Athen im Alterthum*, pp. 709—711, who emphasizes that Athens was purely a university town now and quotes Eunapius (*v. Prohaeresii*, p. 492) for Constantius' endowment of the university with some islands οὐκ ὀλίγας οὐδὲ μικράς. The two letters of Synesius, 54 and 136, quoted on p. 337, are of great interest in this connexion though of a later date.

of Nazianzus[1], which has been described as "a coarse caricature,"
but which, nevertheless, seems to me not unlikely to be fairly true
if a man's nature does reveal itself in look and gesture. Julian's
own writings give us the impression of a fidgety, nervous temperament, and his admirer, Ammianus, tells us a number of stories
which betray a want of repose. Gregory in Athens remarked (or
says he remarked) a certain changeableness and excitability in
him, beside a rather loose-hung neck, twitching shoulders, a rolling
eye, a laugh uncontrollable and spasmodic, a spluttering speech,
and an inability to stand or sit without fidgeting with his feet[2].
All these signs seem to point one way, and if we realize that his
temperament was restless, and that his training had not been of a
kind to correct his natural tendency to be nervous and emotional,
we may find less difficulty in explaining the variety of his religious
opinions.

He enjoyed the student's life, but he was to be called away
from it. The exigencies of the Empire had compelled Constantius
to associate Gallus with himself as Caesar, and the fact that Gallus
had been a failure did not alter the situation. Julian was the
only available person to fill his place, and Constantius, with some
constitutional hesitation and reluctance, made him Caesar and sent
him to Gaul to free the country from German invaders. It was an
honour Julian could have done without, and as he drove back to
the palace in his purple robe he kept muttering to himself the
line of Homer (*Il.* v. 83):

ἔλλαβε πορφύρεος θάνατος καὶ μοῖρα κραταιή.
Him purple death laid hold on and stern fate.

The story is told by Ammianus (xv. 8), and it sums up the situation.
The scholar is dragged from his study to be invested with the purple,
which had been his brother's ruin and may be his own as easily, if a
eunuch whisper it at the right moment to the suspicious Constantius;
and he cannot draw back, for stern fate wills it so, and all that the
purple means is that he will die with less leisure for the development
of his inner life[3].

So "torn from the shades of academic calm," Julian was plunged
"into the dust of Mars[4]" in Gaul, at first with but little direct

[1] Cited by Socrates, *E. H.* iii. 23, 18.
[2] Sir William Fraser tells us Disraeli's one mark of nervousness as he sat
in Parliament was a restless crossing, uncrossing and re-crossing of his legs.
[3] Amm. Marc. xv. 8, 20: *nihil se plus adsecutum quam ut occupatior interiret.*
[4] Amm. Marc. xvi. 1, 5.

responsibility. For this he was very angry with Constantius, though
at the time he could say nothing, and he believed (or it was said so)
that it was a matter of indifference to the Emperor whether he slew
the Germans or the Germans slew him, for in either case the Empire
would be freed from menace[1]. But, as Sozomen points out, if
Constantius had merely wanted to kill Julian, he could have done it
without marrying his own sister[2] to him and putting him in so
conspicuous a position. Constantius indeed loved to keep things
in such a way as to be able to have both of two mutually exclusive
alternatives, but it was surely not strange or outrageous of him to
entrust only a little power to begin with to an untried man. As
Julian proved himself worthy of more power, and his colleagues
shewed themselves unfit for it, Constantius gave him more, till
he had supreme command in Gaul. After his wont, however, he
surrounded Julian with creatures of his own and withdrew from him
almost his only friend in the provinces, the trusty Sallust.

It was not to be expected that Julian would be successful as
a soldier, but he was. Indeed a modern critic has said that it was
only as a soldier that he was great[3]. He was popular with the
soldiers, for he would share their privations and he led them to
victory. He won the regard of the Gauls by ridding them of the
Germans, and by reducing the land tax about 70 per cent., and he
had the respect of the Germans[4], for he could beat them in battle
and keep his word with them when his victory was secure. His
ambition was to be like the Emperor Marcus Aurelius[5], and though
a different man, and a weaker, he may be said to have resembled
him at least in honourable devotion to duty and the cultivation of
the higher life.

[1] Zosimus (iii. 1) puts this very amiable suggestion into Eusebia's mouth!
[2] It is curious that Julian only twice refers to her in his extant remains—
Or. ii. 123 D, *Ep. Ath.* 284 B.
[3] Boissier, *La Fin du Paganisme*, i. 138. I do not know enough of military
matters to be able to criticize this statement or to give any account of his
campaigns that could have an independent value. The reader may be referred
to J. F. A. Mücke (*Flavius Claudius Julianus*, part I. *Julian's Kriegsthaten*,
Gotha 1867) who is however criticized as generally too friendly to Julian, and
to W. Koch (*Kaiser Julian*, Leipzig 1899). Mücke, *op. cit.* p. 50, calls the
German wars "ein grosses Werk, werth der Unsterblichkeit."
[4] He seems to have respected the Germans, remarking their characteristics—τὸ φιλελεύθερόν τε καὶ ἀνυπότακτον Γερμανῶν (Neumann, p. 184).
He did not so much admire their beer, disliking its smell, if we may judge
from his epigram on it.
[5] Amm. Marc. xxii. 5, 4. Amm. Marc. xvi. 1, 4 *rectae perfectaeque rationis
indagine congruens Marco ad cujus aemulationem actus suos effingebat et mores.*
Eutropius x. 16 M. *Antonino non absimilis erat quem etiam aemulari studebat.*
This ambition was avowed likewise by Diocletian (*Hist. Aug. M. Antonin.* 19).

He was too successful in Gaul to retain the good-will of Constantius, and the wits of the court amused themselves with jokes about the "goat" (in allusion to his beard), the "purpled monkey," and the " Greek professor¹," and with darker insinuations that must ultimately mean death for him. Constantius grew nervous, and, as war with Persia was imminent, he sent to Julian to demand a considerable number of Gallic troops. Whether they were really wanted for the war, or the order was sent merely to weaken Julian, it was a blunder. He could reply that Gaul could not safely be left without them in view of the Germans, and the troops could say, and did say, that the terms of their enlistment exempted them from service so far from home². Julian wrote and the troops mutinied, and exactly what Constantius was trying to prevent occurred. The soldiers hailed Julian Emperor. He was reluctant, but without avail. They raised him aloft on a shield, and crown him they must and would³. It is interesting to note that, a crown not unnaturally not being forthcoming, Julian rejected the first two substitutes proposed, a woman's gold chain and some part of a horse's trappings, but submitted to be crowned with a soldier's bracelet (360 A.D.)⁴.

The fatal step was taken, but it is characteristic of the Roman Empire, though neither of the men was strictly Roman, that though civil war was inevitable, each should go on with the work he had in hand for the State⁵. Sulla had not returned to deal with his enemies in Italy till he had crushed Mithradates. Negotiations, if such they can be called, went on for a while, till in 361 the two Emperors marched against each other. They never met. Happily for everybody, Constantius died on his march, and all Julian had to do was to have him buried.

Julian was now sole Emperor, and could at last freely avow the faith he had held in secret for some ten years and openly proceed

¹ Amm. Marc. xvii. 11, 1 *Capella non homo—loquax talpa—purpurata simia—litterio Graecus.* xx. 4, 1 *Constantium urebant Juliani virtutes.* Julian himself (*Ep.* 68) says his relations with Constantius might be summed up as λυκοφιλία.

² Amm. Marc. xx. 4, 4.

³ Cf. Sulpicius Severus *Dial.* ii. (=i.) 6, 2 *magnum imperium nec sine periculo renui nec sine armis potuit retineri.*

⁴ Amm. Marc. xx. 4, 17 *primis auspiciis non congruere aptari muliebri mundo.* The whole affair shews a German rather than a Roman tone prevalent in the army. We may compare Julian's sneer at the usurper Silvanus and his purple robe ἐκ τῆς γυναικωνίτιδος (*Oration* ii. 98 D—a work written some years earlier than this).

⁵ Mr Bury, *Later Roman Empire*, i. 127, n. 4, remarks that Julian, though Greek in sympathies, was in many ways more Roman than Greek.

with the religious reformation he intended to effect[1]. He could plead the precedents of Constantine and Constantius for his attempts to remould the belief of his subjects, and his first step was to recall the Nicene bishops his predecessor had banished and to proclaim toleration for all religions.

Before following out the steps of his reformation, it will be well to study his own mind and learn if possible how he came to change his faith, and what he found in Hellenism that Christianity could not offer[2].

The first thing we have to realize clearly is that Julian was essentially a weak man, by nature inclined to a sentimentalism and a conceit which an evil environment developed. He was not an original thinker at all, but a born disciple, readily amenable to the mysterious and to flattery.

When the Antiochenes made a watchword of the letters "Chi and Kappa"—the initials of Christ and Constantius[3], it was not a random shot, but a deliberate combination of two names, which were already connected in Julian's mind. Constantius was above all things a Christian Emperor, and a Christian who could not content himself with the popular view of his religion, but kept restlessly intruding into the discussion of theological subtleties, better left to bishops, till he excited the disgust of honest, practical men like Ammianus[4]. And this man, the nervous student of creeds, ever on the alert for a diphthong too many or too few, was also the murderer, who had executed the "tragic curse[5]" on his family, as ready to add Julian to his list of victims as to take part in a battle of bishops. A Christian and a murderer, he was for years the baleful figure in the background of Julian's thoughts. His friends and satellites were no better than he—men as unscrupulous in currying favour at court as in maintaining their faith at a council.

[1] He writes to Maximus in triumph (*Ep.* 38) φανερῶς βουθυτοῦμεν. There is a pervert's excess of devotion about him. Ammianus, a pagan born and bred, felt this, and called him *superstitiosus magis quam sacrorum legitimus observator* (xxv. 4, 17).

[2] On this Wilhelm Vollert's *Kaiser Julian's religiöse und philosophische Ueberzeugung* (Gütersloh 1899) will be found most useful and suggestive.

Socrates, *E. H.* iii. 1, has a long chapter devoted to Julian, and a large part of the book (iii.) concerns him. Similarly Sozomen's book v. comprises the story of Julian, and though not perhaps equal to Socrates, contains some important original matter. Theodoret (iii. 28) is a lighter weight.

In what follows I have generally of set purpose avoided the testimony of the more hostile authorities, not that it is necessarily unreliable.

[3] *Misopogon* 357 A.

[4] Amm. Marc. xxi. 16, 18. See p. 41.

[5] *Or.* vii. 228 B ἡ τραγικὴ κατάρα.

On the other side stood the gentle and loyal eunuch Mardonius, as sympathetic a companion for his old master's grandson as he was an interpreter of Homer. Homer was their common study and inspiration, their daily reading, and from him they passed to Plato and perhaps Aristotle. Thus all that was horrible in the life of this sensitive, lonely orphan boy was Christian; while all that was helpful and delightful was drawn from Greek literature. When this period ended and the boy was sent to Macellum, the Christian clergy and the Christian Scriptures must have been equally repugnant to him, but he was alone (for Gallus could hardly be very congenial) and he allowed himself to be led along Christian paths and to make professions which he did not feel. It was here that he became a " reader."

Released from Macellum, he began to frequent the company of philosophers and rhetoricians ; and though he was prevented from hearing Libanius[1], the prohibition did not save him from the influence of this man, the greatest pagan teacher of the day, and perhaps even inclined him to be so influenced. These men were dangerous companions for him, as vain as peacocks (to adapt Synesius' description of Dio) and, as far as men so entirely self-centred could be religious, utterly pagan.

They read the young prince quickly, they praised him and they encouraged him in his classical studies, they made themselves agreeable to him and they shewed him the beauty and the breadth of Neo-Platonism. Here was a faith, whose scriptures were the beautiful books from which he had learnt his earliest lessons with Mardonius ; a faith which had no persecuting bishops but was quietly upheld by suffering scholars, men of rare genius, the successors of Plato himself ; a faith with a range and sweep far beyond the Church's, embracing all the truth and charm of the ancient poetry and philosophy of Hellas and all the passion and revelation of the religions of the East. It was a wider faith than Christianity, including all that was true in Judaism, of which Christianity was after all only a perversion and a misunderstanding. They would not be slow to shew him the absurdities and contradictions of the Old Testament, the difference between the New Testament and Nicene Christianity, and the sublime morality of a Plato and a Plotinus as contrasted with Constantius and his bishops. Surely the truth could not be with the barbarous, dull and incon-

[1] Sievers, *Libanius*, p. 54. Rode, *Gesch. der Reaction Kaiser Julians*, p. 29.

sistent authors of the Christian books rather than with Homer and Plato.

We can see in his later writings the general trend of the arguments which influenced him against Christianity and the Scriptures and brought him nearer Neo-Platonism. But there was more. He was young and sentimental, and the sufferings of the old religion and its adherents, which, as we can read in Hermes Trismegistus, were keenly felt, would be emphasized and the hope held out that on some future day he might himself be the restorer of the faith, to which Constantine and Constantius had done such injury. He might indeed be himself the chosen messenger of heaven, for it was a Neo-Platonic doctrine that the gods stoop to give mankind a saviour and a regenerator whenever the divine impulse in the world is in danger of being exhausted[1]. It might be that his name would be thus added to those of Dionysus and Herakles. This thought, whoever may have inspired it, was never lost by Julian, and its fatal consequences may be seen in the ever-increasing arrogance and self-conceit which mark his career.

To crown all, Julian came under the influence of "a certain Maximus, who at that time wore the outward look of a philosopher but was a magician and boasted he could foretell the future[2]." In these words of a Christian historian we have a true description of the man who did most to ruin Julian's character. Neo-Platonism made communion with the Supreme one of its cardinal doctrines, but while Plotinus and his followers pronounced this communion to be dependent on contemplation and a matter of consecrated intelligence, another school took the easier and more imposing route of theurgy. By theurgy, which Augustine says is merely a more splendid name for magic, by charm and ritual, by fast and offering, heaven could be stormed. The gods could be "compelled" (ἀναγκάζειν) to speak, and more, to appear in bodily form before their worshipper. The theurgist held secrets which enabled him to command the attention and the presence of the gods at will, and of this school Maximus was at this time the most eminent. The mind of Julian was prepared for him. They met, and, though

---

[1] Synesius, *de Prov.* i. 10, 11.

[2] Theodoret iii. 28, 2. Hellenism did not produce many martyrs, and an attempt has been made to beatify Maximus to fill the gap, but the true charge on which he was put to death, on which Christians also were often enough put to death, was magic. Magic may seem to us a harmless thing if foolish, but to the Roman government it generally connoted political disaffection, as it does in modern China. The context of Amm. Marc. xxix. 1, 42 implies that this was a political case. Vollert pp. 18—23 is excellent on Maximus.

circumstances for a while parted them, Julian never shook off the influence of this quack, but to the end of his days had for him a deep affection and respect, almost awe[1].

But for some ten years, however much he might fancy himself a new Dionysus, and whatever delight he might draw from intercourse with the gods[2], he had to practise deceit, to hide his powers of commanding heaven, to cloak his own godhead. It was not a good training—a conscious godhead, the control of gods and constant hypocrisy. It weakened Julian and accentuated his natural deficiencies. The marvel is that he suffered so little, and the reason perhaps lay in the steadying fear of Constantius, for when that was removed Julian rapidly lost in sense and self-control.

It will hardly be necessary to attempt a systematic exposition of his theology, which is neither original nor clear, but it may be of interest to see what Neo-Platonism as a religion offered him for the daily affairs of life. He had gone to Athens already a heathen in heart, and thence he was summoned to Milan, to be made Caesar eventually, though this was not quite clear at first. "What floods of tears and what wailings I poured forth," he writes to the Athenians, "how I lifted up my hands to your Acropolis, when this summons came to me, and besought Athena[3] to save her suppliant and not forsake me, many of you saw and can testify ; and above all the goddess herself, how I asked that I might die there in Athens rather than face that journey. That the goddess did not betray nor forsake her suppliant, she shewed by what she did. For she led the way for me everywhere and set around me on every side angels (or messengers) from the Sun and Moon to guard me. And it befel thus. I went to Milan and lived in a suburb. Thither Eusebia used often to send to me in a kindly spirit and bid me boldly write for whatever I would. I wrote her a letter, or rather a supplication, with language of this nature, 'So may you

---

[1] His public attentions to Maximus annoyed Ammianus, who sums them up as *ostentatio intempestiva*. xxii. 7, 3. The historian was perhaps more genuinely Roman than his hero.

[2] *Or.* v. 180 B εὐδαιμονίαν ἧς τὸ κεφάλαιον ἡ τῶν θεῶν γνῶσίς ἐστι.

[3] The hymn of Proclus to Athena is an interesting parallel. He prays Athena of the Athenian Acropolis for mental light, forgiveness of sin, freedom from disease, a fair gale on the voyage of life, children, wife and wealth, oratory and eminence (προεδρείην δ᾽ ἐνὶ λαοῖς). Proclus, it may be added, was the philosopher of the fifth century A.D., who won the proud title of ὁ διάδοχος *the successor*, *i.e.* of Plato! The prayers of Synesius, both as a Neo-Platonist and as a Christian, were mainly for freedom from anxieties, from attacks of demons and from the influence of matter. He also prays that he may be enabled to act worthily of Sparta and Cyrene.

have heirs, so may God give you such and such, send me home as
soon as possible'; but then I thought it might not be safe to send
such a letter to the palace to the Emperor's wife. So I besought
the gods by night to shew me whether I ought to send the document
to the Empress. And they threatened me with a shameful death
if I sent it. And that this is true I call all the gods to witness.
So I refrained from sending the letter. From that night a reflexion
came to me which it is, perhaps, worth while you should hear.
Now, said I, I am thinking of resisting the gods, and I have thought
I could better plan for myself than they who know all things. Yet
human reason looking only at what is present is lucky if it can just
avoid error for a little......but the thought of the gods looks afar,
nay, surveys all, and gives the right bidding and does what is
better; for as they are authors of what is, so are they of what will
be. They must then have knowledge to deal with the present.
For the while, my change of mind seemed wiser on that score, but
when I looked at the justice of the matter I said, So you are angry,
are you? if one of your animals rob you of your use of itself,
or run away when called—a horse, perhaps, or a sheep or a cow—
and yet you yourself who would be a man, and not one of the
many or the baser sort either, rob the gods of yourself and do not
let them use you for what they would. Look to it that, in addition
to being very foolish, you are not also sinning against the gods.
And your courage, where is it? Absurd! You are ready to toady
and cringe for fear of death, though you might cast all aside and
trust the gods to do as they will and divide with them the care for
yourself, as Socrates bade, and do what concerns you as best you
can and leave the whole to them, hold nothing, catch at nothing,
but accept what they offer in peace. This I considered not merely
a safe but a fitting line of conduct for a wise man...and I obeyed
and was made Caesar[1]." (*Ep. Ath.* 275—7.)

Ever thereafter he walks by faith, trusting the gods to look after
him[2]. While in Gaul he wrote two panegyrics on Constantius,

---

[1] We may add his expression of acceptance of the Divine Will—*Or.* vii.
232 D χρῆσθέ μοι πρὸς ὅ τι βούλεσθε. Similar views will be found in other
Neo-Platonists, *e.g.* Hermes Trism. (Bipontine edition of Apuleius, vol. ii.
p. 313) *Justo homini in Dei religione et in summa pietate praesidium est.*
Deus enim tales ab omnibus tutatur malis; and Porphyry to Marcella, esp. c. 16
καὶ τιμήσεις μὲν ἄριστα τὸν θεὸν ὅταν τῷ θεῷ τὴν σαυτῆς διάνοιαν ὁμοιώσῃς...εἰ δὲ
χαίρει τῷ ἀρχομένῳ τὸ ἄρχον καὶ θεὸς σοφοῦ κήδεται καὶ προνοεῖ. καὶ διὰ τοῦτο
μακάριος ὁ σόφος ὅτι ἐπιτροπεύεται ὑπὸ θεοῦ.
[2] See his myth in *Or.* vii. 233 D ἡμεῖς .γάρ σοι (the gods say) πανταχοῦ
συνεσόμεθα.

which does not seem an entirely honest performance. But perhaps, as Vollert (p. 86) suggests, he is ironical, and he is certainly not exuberant, though a reader, who did not well know their relations, might feel more kindly to Constantius from what he says of him. But I refer to them because, beside doing his duty as a citizen by his ruler, he yields to his besetting temptation which clung to him through life, and preaches. In the second panegyric he says, "The man, and still more the ruler, all whose hopes of happiness depend on God and are not blown about by other men, he has made the best disposal of his life[1]." (*Or.* ii. 118 D.) In a very undisguised homily he wrote in Gaul on the Mother of the Gods, he gives thanks that, whereas he was once in Christian darkness, he is not now[2]. When Constantius recalled Sallust, Julian consoled himself with another homily : "Perhaps the god," he says, "will devise something good ; for it is not likely that a man, who has entrusted himself to the higher power, will be altogether neglected or left utterly alone." (*Or.* viii. 249.) (We do not always allow enough for the awful loneliness of a monarch or of one in Julian's position, yet it must be considered in estimating them.) "It is not right," he goes on, "to praise the great men of old without imitating them, nor to suppose that God eagerly (προθύμως) helped them but will disregard those who to-day lay hold on virtue, for whose sake God rejoiced in them[3]."

He feels that in a very special sense he is the chosen vessel of heaven. In his myth[4] in his seventh oration the conclusion of a very easily-read riddle is that he, the least and last of his house, is directly chosen by the gods to restore the old faith, and to this end is particularly entrusted by Zeus to the care of Helios—the Sun. In his letter to Themistius he accepts the rôle of a Herakles or a Dionysus, king and prophet at once ; he feels the burden more than man can bear, but neither desire to avoid toil, nor quest of pleasure, nor love of ease, shall turn him away from the life of duty. He fears he may fail in his great task, but he counts on aid from the philosophers and above all commits everything to the gods[5].

In the moment, perhaps the supreme moment of his life, when the soldiers sought him to hail him Emperor, he tells us he was in

---

[1] Cf. Dio Chrys. *de Regno, Or.* i. 15.
[2] *Or.* v. 174 B; so also *Or.* iv. 131 A.   [3] Compare also *Or.* vii. 212 B.
[4] "Dans toute cette allégorie Julien ne fait que se répéter à lui-même, *Tu Marcellus eris.*" Chassang, *Hist. du Roman*, p. 194.
[5] Notice in the concluding prayer to Cybele in *Or.* v. an entreaty that she will aid τῷ Ῥωμαίων δήμῳ μάλιστα μὲν ἀποτρίψασθαι τῆς ἀθεότητος κηλῖδα.

his chamber—"and thence I prayed to Zeus. And as the noise grew louder and louder, and all was in confusion in the palace, I besought the god to send a token, and forthwith he sent a token [he quotes a word or two from the *Odyssey*][1] and bade obey and not resist the will of the army. Yet, though these signs were given me, I did not readily yield, but held out as long as I could, and would accept neither the title nor the crown. But as one man I could not prevail over so many, and the gods, who willed this to be, urged them on and worked upon my will. So about the third hour, some soldier tendering his bracelet, I put it on with reluctance and went into the palace, groaning from my heart within as the gods know. And yet I ought, I suppose, to have been of good courage and trusted to the god who gave the token, but I was terribly ashamed and wanted to escape, in case I should seem not to have been faithful to Constantius[2]." (*Ep. Ath.* 284 c.)

Elsewhere, in the *Misopogon* (352 D), which is not, like the letter just quoted, a manifesto of the date of his revolt, he uses the same language. "This office the gods gave me, using great violence, believe me, both with the giver (Constantius presumably) and the receiver. For neither of us seemed to wish it, neither he who gave me the honour or favour, or whatever you like to call it—and he who received it, as all the gods know, refused it in all sincerity." Again, writing to his uncle Julian (*Ep.* 13) he says, "Why did I march (against Constantius)? Because the gods expressly bade me, promising me safety if I obeyed, but if I stayed—what I would have no god do......So I marched, trusting all to fortune and the gods, and content to abide by whatever pleased their goodness." Before he started he "referred all to the gods who see and hear all things, and then sacrificed, and the omens were favourable." (*Ep. Ath.* 286 D.) In this feeling of dependence on heaven and the constant reference of everything to the divine he is very like Constantine, his uncle.

The preceding Emperors had left him precedents for the imperial control of religion, and when Julian found himself at last sole

[1] But he does not say what the token was—the line of Homer (*Od.* iii. 173) merely illustrates his request and its gratification. It was believed at the time that the philosophers by the aid of magic and theurgic rites had not unfrequently such manifestations.

[2] The same kind of plea, however, was made twenty years later by the tyrant Maximus to St Martin. (Sulp. Sev., *vita Mart.*, 20.) *se non sponte sumpsisse imperium sed impositam sibi a militibus divino nutu regni necessitatem defendisse et non alienam ab eo Dei voluntatem videri, penes quem tam incredibili eventu victoria fuisset.*

Emperor, with power to carry out in act the restoration which he had long felt was laid upon him by Heaven, he had to consider practical measures for the maintenance and propagation of his religion. He saw at once its weakness. The old faith, which he re-christened Hellenism, fell short of the new both in creed and conduct. Three centuries of Christian experience and thought had built up a body of doctrine, point by point tried and proved, and the Christian could rest on the rock of the Church. The heathen had no dogma, no certainty. This philosopher said one thing, and that another, and every man could choose for himself and be uncertain, solitary, a lonely speculator, when he had chosen[1]. Hence the Church was stronger than her adversaries. To meet this difficulty Julian revived Maximin Daja's great idea of the Holy Catholic Church of Hellenism[2]. All the great philosophers conspired to witness to the truth; all said, if rightly understood, one thing[3]. By dint of a little confusion, a little judicious blindness, one might believe this. Thus the teachings of the Neo-Platonists were not mere "hypotheses" but genuine "dogmata," and rested on a solid basis (*Or.* iv. 148). As substitutes for the Father, the Son and the Holy Ghost he set the usual group of Neo-Platonic conceptions, to which he linked the gods, proceeding from the great original τὸ ὄν, ὅλος or ὅλη ἐξ ὅλου. The Sun played a great part in all these speculations, "for whom and by whom are all things[4]." The Jews were built into the wondrous fabric, for they, too, worshipped the great Supreme, though clannish narrowness made them exclude the other gods[5]. What were the relative places of these other gods, whether separate beings or merely different names for one being, it is a little difficult severally to

[1] Cf. Lucian's *Hermotimus*, a great part of which may be read in Mr Pater's English in *Marius the Epicurean*. A good criticism of this piece of Lucian's is given by Chassang, *Hist. du Roman*, pp. 191—2.

[2] Eusebius, *E. H.*, ix. 4, and Lactantius, *M. P.* 36.

[3] *Or.* vi. 185 A τοὺς πρωτεύσαντας δὲ ἐν ἑκάστῃ τῶν αἱρέσεων σκοπείτω καὶ πάντα εὑρήσει σύμφωνα.

[4] For the adoration of the Sun compare the hymn of Proclus (412—485 A.D.), *e.g.* 1. 34:

εἰκὼν παγγενέταο θεοῦ, ψυχῶν ἀναγωγεῦ,
κέκλυθι καί με κάθηρον ἁμαρτάδος αἰὲν ἀπάσης, κτέ.

[5] Julian seems always to have been very friendly toward the Jews, and endeavoured at one time to rebuild the Temple for them, but the design fell through, baffled by the accident or miracle of fire and earthquake. See *Ep.* 25, a striking letter, and *Ep.* 63.

Elsewhere (Neumann, *op. cit.*, p. 185) he says the Jewish god is in charge of the Jewish race just as there is καθ' ἕκαστον ἔθνος ἐθνάρχης τις θεός; (p. 178) προσήκει τὸν τῶν Ἑβραίων θεὸν οὐχὶ δὴ παντὸς κόσμου γενεσιουργὸν ὑπάρχειν οἴεσθαι καὶ κατεξουσιάζειν τῶν ὅλων.

determine, but his system of Divinity had but a very few years to grow in and must not be inspected too closely, as at best it was but patchwork. His homilies were generally "knocked off" in two or perhaps three nights, "as the Muses can testify[1]." They ramble and digress and leave us confused. But the great thing was that Hellenism had a system of Divinity and that all the philosophers bore witness to it. If it were a little abstract, it was not after all for the common people[2]. This was a fatal weakness, but it could hardly be helped.

In the second place there was no doubt in Julian's mind that his new Catholic Church suffered from disorder, and from the careless lives of its adherents. He tried to organize his priesthood and to improve their morals. He is most emphatic on their sacred character, which he means to make others respect, and which the priests would do well to respect themselves. He writes them charges like a bishop[3], lecturing them on their social deportment and on their sacred duties. They must not frequent theatres or wine-shops, nor read erotic novels[4] or infidel books like the works of Epicurus[5] ("most of which the gods, I am glad to say, have allowed to perish"); they must speak and think no unseemly thing. Their families must be orderly and go regularly to the temples[6]. Their sacred robes are for temple use, for the honour of the gods, not to flaunt in the streets. Decencies must be observed in temple service[7]. The magistrate or officer within temple walls is as any other man. He is annoyed when men applaud him in a temple[8]; there they must adore the gods and not the Emperor. Again, the Galilaeans (for so he calls the Christians) beside influencing people by their

---

[1] Cf. *Or.* vi. 203 c.

[2] *Or.* vi. 196 D, τοὺς μὲν οὖν πολλοὺς οὐδὲν κωλύει ταῖς κοιναῖς ἕπεσθαι δόξαις— a common feeling of Neo-Platonists.

[3] *E.g. Ep.* 49 from which I have taken some of what follows. Harnack (*History of Dogma*, tr. vol. i. p. 336) remarks that "the ethical temper which Neo-Platonism sought to beget and confirm was the highest and purest which the culture of the ancient world produced."

[4] Rohde, *der gr. Roman*, p. 349, calls attention to this prohibition as a striking proof of the wide and general popularity of such novels in Julian's day.

[5] Epicurus and his school were hated by all the adherents of the pagan revival from the days of Lucian. Cf. Macrobius, *Comm.* i. 2, 3. Lucian's sham prophet Alexander had coupled them with the Christians, *Alex.* 38.

[6] He was highly annoyed to find that the wives and families of some of his priests preferred the churches. Sozomen v. 16.

[7] In *Ep.* 56 he directs that attention be paid to sacred music in Alexandria, τῆς ἱερᾶς ἐπιμεληθῆναι μουσικῆς, and that choir boys of good birth (εὖ γεγονότες) be chosen for their voices—ἐκ φωνῆς καταλεγέσθωσαν, trained and maintained at the public charges.

[8] *Ep.* 64.

sober lives gain great influence by their hospitality to the poor and
the wayfarer, and to counteract this Julian ordains great guest-
houses and provision for their maintenance, that Hellenism, too,
may win men by its charities. Above all things he preaches holiness.
All service done in holiness to the gods is alike acceptable[1].

One thing was wanting. When this life is done, the Christian
Church offers a sure and certain hope of a joyful resurrection.
What had the Catholic Church of Hellenism to bid against this?
Neo-Platonism, as we can see in Macrobius, in Hermes and elsewhere, inclined to a belief in reward and punishment beyond the
grave. Even Plotinus holds that a man's position in the next life
is determined by what he has reached in this. Julian no doubt
went with his teachers here as elsewhere, but he does not speak so
clearly of the other life as we might have expected of him. In one
place (*Fragm. Epist.* 300) he writes hopefully: "Consider the
goodness of God, who says he rejoices as much in the mind of the
godly as in purest Olympus. Surely we may expect that he (πάντως
ἡμῖν οὗτος) will bring up from darkness and Tartarus the souls of us
who draw near to him in godliness? For he knows them also who
are shut up in Tartarus, for even that is not outside the realm of
the gods, but he promises to the godly Olympus instead of Tartarus."
In another place (*Or.* iv. 136 A, B) he says that the souls of those
who have lived well and righteously will go upward to Serapis—
not the dread Serapis of the myths, but the kind and gentle god
who sets the souls utterly free from becoming or birth (γενέσεως),
and does not, when once they are free, nail them down (προσηλοῖ)
to other bodies by way of punishment, but bears them upward and
brings them into the intelligible world—the region next to Absolute
Being, according to the Neo-Platonists.

There is however another passage, where one feels it odd that he
says nothing of all this. In *Letter* 37 he writes to a friend to say
he wept to hear of the death of the friend's wife, but here is
nepenthes for him as good as Helen's. Democritus of Abdera told
King Darius, who was sorrowing for his queen, that he could raise
her from the dead, if he would write on her grave the names of three
that never were in mourning. "But if you cannot, why weep as if
you alone know such a sorrow?" The same story, or one very like
it, is told of Buddha, but its comfort is a little cold.

[1] Some of his ideas are curious: *e.g.* funerals by day dishonour the Sun
(*Ep.* 77) εἰς ὅν πάντα καὶ ἐξ οὗ πάντα.

Julian's relations with the Christian Church remain to be discussed[1]. To an erring priest he wrote (*Ep.* 62) that he would not curse him, as he does not think it right, for he remarks that the gods never do it. It was only consistent with such a temper not to persecute, and he sedulously maintained that he did not and would not. But, says Ammianus[2], on the bench he sometimes asked litigants their religion, though it never affected his decisions. While all creeds were lawful, he felt it only right to give higher honour to the true faith and its adherents. Any other course would be dishonouring to the gods[3]. But, of course, this was not persecution. When he recalled the exiled bishops, when he made the Catholic restore Novatian churches, when he coquetted with Donatists, he was only carrying out a liberal measure of toleration. No doubt, but English Nonconformists have never felt specially indebted to James II. Heathen men said Julian recalled the exiles to kindle anew the flames of discord in the Churches[4]. But it was bad policy. Nicene and Arian were at least unanimous in opposing a heathen. Moreover when the two parties were thus left on an equal footing, and the Nicenes had their leaders again, the Nicene party gained ground steadily, and they after all were the more serious opponents[5]. When he forced bishops to rebuild heathen temples they had destroyed, they called out on persecution; they, too, had consciences and might destroy but could not build up heathenism. So far, perhaps, no one could say Julian was strictly unjust. But when the mob of Alexandria rose and slew George the bishop, all he did was to write a letter of gentle rebuke—they ought not to have broken the law; they should have trusted to him and justice; but for Serapis' sake and his uncle Julian's he would forgive them (*Ep.* 10). Indeed he seems to have been less anxious that no more bishops should be killed than that none of George's books should be lost (*Epp.* 9, 36). When bishop Titus of Bostra[6] wrote to inform him of his efforts and his clergy's to preserve the peace, he wrote to the people of Bostra and put an unpleasant

---

[1] In addition to the books dealing specifically with this (to which I have already referred) Sievers, *Leben des Libanius*, c. xi., may be consulted.

[2] Amm. Marc. xxii. 10, 2.

[3] *Ep.* 7 προτιμᾶσθαι μέντοι τοὺς θεοσεβεῖς καὶ πάνυ φημὶ δεῖν.

[4] Amm. Marc. xxii. 5, 4 is very explicit about this.

[5] See Gwatkin's *Studies in Arianism*, ch. vi. p. 201 (first edition). I am afraid I do not take so high a view of Julian as my former teacher does, though I once inclined to take a higher.

[6] Famous otherwise as the author of three books against Mani—extant partly in Greek and partly or wholly in Syriac.

construction on the bishop's letter, and invited them to rid themselves of him. (*Ep.* 52, August 362.) The Emesenes burnt the tombs of the Christians, and were held up in consequence as an example to easy-going Antioch (*Misopogon*, 357 c). But of all men Julian hated Athanasius most, the man who seemed, as Vollert says, to unite in himself all the force of Christendom. The bishop in virtue of the decree of recall had returned to his see of Alexandria. Julian wrote to the Alexandrians in March, 362, to say he had never meant to recall the bishops to their sees ; it was enough for them not to be in exile ; Athanasius, who has been banished by so many decrees of so many Emperors, might have had the decency to wait for one restoring him to his so-called episcopal throne before boldly claiming it to the annoyance of pious Alexandrians ; he must now depart (*Ep.* 26). When, instead of going into exile, Athanasius dared to baptize some Greek ladies, Julian wrote in October of the same year peremptorily ordering his removal (*Ep.* 6). A month or so later he had to write again, for he had miscalculated Athanasius' influence in Alexandria. He is surprised and shocked at the Alexandrians, but they may trust him, for he knows all about Christianity after twenty years of it, and now he has been following the gods twelve years. Still, if they will not be converted, there are other possible bishops beside Athanasius, whom he banishes from the whole of Egypt (*Ep.* 51)[1]. The great bishop was not concerned. "It is but a little cloud and will pass," he said[2], and went into hiding in Alexandria itself, and in less than a year the little cloud had passed away and he was free again.

Gregory of Nazianzus said Julian veiled his persecution under a show of reasonableness[3], and it may be held that nothing very terrible has been mentioned as yet. Perhaps it was not going too far when he cancelled all the immunities and exemptions granted to the clergy by Constantine and Constantius, though if he did (as alleged[4]) compel widows and virgins to refund grants made to them in past years, he would seem to have been a little too exacting. But a zealot, whose principle is the equality of all sects and the preference of one, stands in slippery places. The Syrian historian is highly indignant about this robbing of the Churches. Western indignation was greater on another score, as we shall see. The

[1] He concludes with a flout at Athanasius' person—μηδὲ ἀνήρ, ἀλλ' ἀνθρωπίσκος εὐτελής—which, if a little unnecessary, still reveals one side of his own character.
[2] Sozomen, v. 15, 3.
[3] x. p. 166 : ap. Sievers, *op. cit.*, p. 118.   [4] Sozomen, v. 5.

great old centre of Christianity in Syria was Edessa, and the Arian Church there, by its attack on the Valentinians, gave Julian an opportunity which he gladly seized. He confiscated the Church property by an edict, assigning as one of his grounds "Blessed are ye poor, for yours is the kingdom of heaven[1]." This may have been rough and ready justice, but the next step to which I refer was oppression of a most irritating kind.

It is a strange thing, perhaps, in view of the general carelessness about education, that a government has only to incur suspicion of playing with it in the interests of one or another religion to arouse ill-will. Of all acts passed to worry the English Nonconformists, few angered and alarmed them so much as that of Queen Anne's reign, which checked their educational freedom. In the same way Julian roused the Church to fury through the western world by a rescript forbidding to Christians the teaching of ancient literature. It was in more ways than one an unhappy thing for his new Catholic Church that the real Catholic Church was devoted to the old literature. In the east Christians read Homer and Plato, and in the west they steeped themselves in Virgil and Cicero, and in both east and west they were a match for the heathen in all things pertaining to a liberal education, more than a match, for there is a marked difference in general between heathen and Christian writing of the day. This was unfortunate for Julian, for it disproved one of his theories—that the Galilaeans were illiterate and barbarous and divorced from that ancient world which meant so much to all educated people. If his theory had been right, his policy was absurd and unnecessary; but he bore witness against himself, that Christians were not without a share in the old culture. He realized in fact that they valued it so highly that they would not give it up. Accordingly he enacted[2] in June 362 that whereas a man cannot teach aright what he believes to be wrong, and whereas it is highly desirable that those who teach the young should be honest men, and it is incompatible with honesty for a Christian to expound the poets, orators and historians of old, who held themselves (Thucydides[3]

---

[1] *Ep.* 43 ἵν' εἰς τὴν βασιλείαν τῶν οὐρανῶν εὐοδώτερον πορευθῶσι.

[2] See *Ep.* 42. Without citing Christian testimony, it is enough to quote the opinion of an honourable heathen, Ammianus, who pronounces this decree *obruendum perenni silentio* (xxii. 10, 7). Comparetti, *Vergil in the Middle Ages* (tr.), p. 80, gives a good account of this decree, its meaning and results.

[3] On the other hand, Dean Stanley (*Eastern Church*, Lect. i. p. 123) says, "Along the porticos of Eastern Churches are to be seen portrayed on the

among them, it seems) sacred to the gods, while he himself believes
in no gods, henceforth it is forbidden to Christians to teach ancient
literature, unless they first prove in deed their honesty and piety by
sacrificing to the gods. This edict was to produce one or both of
two results, either young Christians must grow up without classical
education, which was not likely to be their choice, or they must go
to the schools of heathen, who would if they did their duty give
them a bias toward Hellenism. Probably Julian was thinking of
his own youthful studies, but heathen teachers were not all alike
and were not in general propagandists.

The immediate result of the decree was that some of the
most famous teachers of the day threw up their profession. Then
came a strange phenomenon[1]. A father and son, both called
Apollinaris, set to work and made a new Homer out of the
Pentateuch, and a Plato out of the Gospels. It has been suggested
that the Christian people admired these works, but from the
synchronism of their disappearance with the death of Julian it
seems that Socrates, the most admirable of Church historians,
is representing the common view when he applauds them rather
as products of enthusiasm than as literature. If the Apollinares
failed of fame as authors, the younger, the Gospel Platonist,
made his mark in Church History as an independent thinker,
though the Church did not finally accept his views. Another
result of this decree was that Valentinian and Valens two years
later began anti-pagan legislation with an edict forbidding the
performance by night of heathen rites and sacrifices. Julian had
made the declaration of war and Christian Emperors accepted it.
In yet another way the decree had a great effect, for it emphasized
the distinction between Christianity and pagan philosophy, and
while, as Prof. Gwatkin[2] says, this told heavily against Arianism
at once, it was not in the long run a good thing for the Church
to doubt the value of ancient wisdom and poetry. "In the
triumph of Christianity," writes a recent biographer of Julian[3],
"he foresaw the Dark Ages." This is a most extravagant state-

walls the figures of Homer, Solon, Thucydides, Pythagoras and Plato, as
pioneers preparing the way for Christianity." We may wonder which character
would have most surprised Thucydides.

[1] Socrates, iii. 16, 1.
[2] *Studies in Arianism*, p. 199.
[3] See *Julian the Philosopher* (p. 174), in the Heroes of the Nations Series, a
careful work but marred by the writer's admiration for Julian and a mis
understanding of his opponents. It would perhaps hardly be going too far to
call the book an apology for Julian.

ment, but, if Christianity and the "Dark Ages" are connected at all, it is in some measure the result of this prescient pagan's decree. Christianity is really no more responsible for the "Dark Ages" than is Neo-Platonism.

Such, then, was Julian's religious policy, but what was its success? Was society with him? It might be expected that the hour for a reaction had come, and there were certainly a good many heathen left. The philosophers, whose spirit he had caught, and the nobility of the city of Rome, with whom he had no relations, were ready to welcome a return to the old ways. But Julian was at heart a Greek, leaning eastwards, and had not much support in Italy, while the philosophers, after all, were out of touch with the world at large. It must be confessed that the reaction was not very spontaneous; it was an attempt to galvanize a revival by the *fiat* of a ruler, and though there was an appearance of life about it, it was not living. Julian has to admit (*Ep.* 49) that Hellenism does not yet thrive as he would wish, but the fault does not lie with the gods, but with their worshippers. The heathen were past revival. They might resent being forced into the background by the Christians, but they only wished to live in quiet as they pleased. They had no mind for martyrdom, and almost as little for Julian's violent revivalism. They would not be regular in attendance at temples, they did not care to sacrifice very much, and in short they would make no efforts for their religion. The women, as Julian himself complained, were against him (*Misop.* 363 A). The mob enjoyed breaking Christian heads[1], and creatures of the court affected conversion and a quickened life, but Julian was hardly pleased with either. He had practically no converts from among the Christians—none of any weight. Hecebolius, a rhetorician, came over, to return to the Church promptly on Julian's death. A bishop, Pegasius, who seems to have been a pagan at heart under his episcopal robes, now avowed his faith or unfaith[2].

Julian had a measure of support in the army, which had a large non-Roman element, which was not Christian[3], but such officers as Jovian and Valentinian were probably not alone in being loyal to the Christian faith. In fact, from whatever point of view,

---

[1] Theodoret (iii. 6) gives a lively picture of heathen processions—"Cory-banting" through the streets (λυττῶντες καὶ κορυβαντιῶντες) and abusing the saints. He adds the information that they got as good as they gave, without much advantage to public order.

[2] See *Ep.* 78, a very interesting letter, for this curious person.

[3] Sievers, *Libanius*, ch. xi. p. 109.

the revival was a failure from the beginning, and the final proof of this was given by its complete collapse on Julian's death.

Julian's reign was short (361–363), and the most interesting part of its history is the period he spent at Antioch[1]. He reached there in 362, and personally conducted his pagan campaign. There was a considerable number of pagans in the city, but, though he was well received and made bids for their good-will, the pleasure-loving populace was no more to be influenced by Julian's exhortations to a godly, righteous and sober life than by Chrysostom's twenty years later. His attempt to transform Daphne from a pleasure resort to a shrine again was a ludicrous miscarriage. A martyr, Babylas, had been buried there by none other than the Emperor's own brother, Gallus[2], and before a martyr Apollo was mute. Julian ordered the "dead body[3]" to be removed, and it was removed by a great procession singing, "Confounded be all they that serve graven images[4]." One of the singers was arrested and tortured, so angry was Julian, but only one; for his constancy shewed what might be expected from others, and Julian resolved to "grudge the honour of martyrdom[5]."

His failure as a revivalist was supplemented in Antioch by his blunders as an economist[6]. He was massing forces there and prices rose in consequence. The mob however did not understand how prices were so high, and greeted the Emperor with the cry, "Everything plentiful, everything dear." Anxious to win applause, for his admirer Ammianus says he ran too much after cheap glory[7], he summoned the leading citizens and gave them three months to find a remedy. When none was forthcoming, he lowered the price of grain by an edict, which had the surprising effect of driving it out

---

[1] See Amm. Marc. xxi. 9, 4. *Videre properans Antiochiam orientis apicem pulcrum* (here speaks the Antiochene)...*in speciem alicujus numinis votis excipitur publicis, miratus voces multitudinis magnae, salutare sidus illuxisse eois partibus adclamantis.* But was it a good omen that he should arrive just when the women were wailing for Adonis? Claudian on the Antiochenes, *In Rufin.* ii. 34, *adsuetumque choris et laeta plebe canorum...imbellem...Orontem.*

[2] Sozomen, v. 19.

[3] *Misopogon*, 361 B.

[4] Theodoret, iii. 10.

[5] Eutropius (a heathen) says Julian was *religionis Christianae nimius insectator perinde tamen ut cruore abstineret* (x. 16, 3). This is a considerable admission for a writer who never elsewhere mentions Christianity, not even in writing of Constantine. Whether by Julian's orders or not, blood seems to have been shed none the less.

[6] For this story see *Misopogon*, 368 c; Amm. Marc. xxii. 14, 1; Socr. iii. 17, 2; Soz. v. 19, 1.

[7] Amm. Marc. xxii. 14, 1 *popularitatis amore*; xxii. 7, 1 *nimius captator inanis gloriae.*

of the market. Then he fetched grain himself from the Imperial granaries and sold it at his own price, and the dealers reappeared as buyers. Altogether he effected nothing but the irritation of every class, and jokes about making ropes of his beard were bandied round the city[1]. He had made himself ridiculous at once with his corn laws, his sacrifices, his mob of court philosophers (instead of Constantius' court bishops), his homilies and his pietism. He was not always very tactful[2], he lacked ballast, and his virtues won him as much ill-will as his foibles. With the best intentions, the purest motives, and the highest character, he had made Antioch thoroughly hostile, and, the world over, his reformation was producing disorder and ill-will. He now wrote a "satire" on Antioch, which he called *The Beard-Hater* (*Misopogon*), perhaps as undignified a production as was ever penned by a monarch[3]. Under cover of shewing up his own faults, he lets out all his spleen at the Antiochenes, till one is really sorry to see the man giving way to such littleness. The final jest of Antioch was superb. Felix, an officer of high rank, and Julian, the Emperor's uncle, had recently died, and the populace went about shouting *Felix Julianus Augustus*[4]— a *double entendre*, which must have been doubly exasperating for being strictly loyal. Julian finally left the city, vowing he would never see them again—a vow which was grimly fulfilled—and taking a cruel revenge on his enemies by setting over them a governor well known to be oppressive[5].

Julian was now once more in the camp, where his earliest successes had been won, and where he was less likely to be brought into humiliating conflicts. He meant to end the long-standing Persian quarrel which Constantius had left unsettled. That the expedition had any close connexion with his pagan reformation,

[1] Amm. Marc. xxii. 14, 2, gives some other jokes—none very brilliant. Julian, it seems, was a "monkey-face," with a goat's beard and the walk of Otus and Ephialtes.

[2] He confesses to being λαλίστερος. *Ep.* 68.

[3] Socrates, iii. 58, complains not unjustly τὸ δὲ διασύρειν ἢ σκώπτειν οὐκέτι φιλοσόφου ἀλλὰ μὴν οὐδὲ βασιλέως. Ammianus, an Antiochene, is not at all pleased with this production of his hero. (xxii. 14, 2.) A keen, almost acrid, humour ran in the family, Constantine being noted for his εἰρωνεία, etc. (Socr. i. 9.) The best instance of Constantine's humour is his retort to the Novatian bishop that, if he was so exclusive, he had better take a ladder and go to heaven by himself.

[4] Amm. Marc. xxiii. 1, 4.

[5] Ammianus (xxiii. 2, 3) actually says Julian remarked *non illum meruisse sed Antiochensibus avaris et contumeliosis hujus modi judicem convenire.* On any other authority the story might seem doubtful. Libanius had a great deal to do to keep this man's energies for paganism within moderately decent bounds. See Sievers, *Libanius*, pp. 118—121.

as has been suggested[1], is, I think, not at all certain. His paganism
seems to have been a hindrance to him here, in shaking the loyalty
of the Christian Armenians[2].

Julian set out on a punitive expedition. One or two letters
written by the way survive—one telling of a little address on
Hellenism he gave at Beroea to the city council, convincing, he
regretfully adds, but very few, and they were converted already
(*Ep.* 27). If the expedition was not very richly blessed with
triumphs for Hellenism, it was in other ways more of a success[3].
The Persians were thoroughly cowed and their land laid waste, till
an unfortunate act of rashness altered the look of things. When he
had gone as far as he meant and was outside Ctesiphon, the capital,
Julian was induced to believe that the fleet of vessels which had
escorted him down the Euphrates was of no further use, and, to
avoid its falling into Persian hands, he gave the fatal order to burn
the ships, only to realize at once, but too late to save them, that it
was a blunder. Even so the retreat might have been free from
disaster but for an accident. The Persian cavalry harassed the
army on its march, and in one of the frequent skirmishes Julian
was fatally wounded. He was carried to his tent, and there he
died after some final words to the friends about him[4]. He surveyed
the principles that had guided him in life, care for his subjects'
good and trust in the wisdom of Providence. He had sought peace,
but when duty called to war he had gone to war, though he had
long well known he was "to die by iron." His life had been
innocent, his conscience was at rest, he had only thanks to the
eternal divinity for the manner of his departure. So he died, and
the Empire had immediate cause to regret his death in the shameful
surrender of Jovian to the Persians. For himself his early death
was probably a good thing, for had he returned victorious, he must
inevitably have been carried into a war without truce against
Christianity, and have stained his name with tyranny and persecution.

As I have already quoted passages at length from his writings, a
word or two will suffice for them in conclusion. They reflect his
personality in a striking way. His style is very fairly good. The

---

[1] Vollert, *op. cit.*, p. 90.
[2] See Gwatkin, *Studies in Arianism*, pp. 209, 210, on the Persian War—
an interesting account of it.
[3] Hodgkin, *Italy and her Invaders*, vol. ii. p. 538.
[4] Amm. Marc. xxv. 3, 15.

effect is marred, however, by a tendency to digression and after-thought, and an unnecessary concern for side issues[1]. It was not to be expected that he could help being didactic ; he had a mission, and in season, and sometimes out of season, he is pleading and exhorting. His three panegyrics, two on Constantius, the third on Eusebia, roam off into discussions on education, true kingliness, books and so forth. His other five so-called orations are really treatises. Two are theological, dealing with the Sun and the Mother of the Gods, but far from clear. Of the other three, which are concerned with morals, two deal with the Cynics and are a little wearisome in their fault-finding. The eighth is addressed to himself —a series of reflections to console him for the loss of Sallust.

His letters fall into two classes, those of the elaborate polite type consisting of a quotation, a compliment, and perhaps an invitation, many of them addressed to philosophers, and those of a practical character, some of them edicts, some letters on religious thought and life, some friendly and intimate. Three long letters stand apart, those to Themistius and the Athenians, and one which is fragmentary, and these shew him at his best and most serious. They give the clearest picture of his manliness, his purity and piety —of the intense earnestness and dutifulness of his nature.

His elaborate work against Christianity has been pieced together by Neumann so far as possible from the citations of Cyril, who wrote a book to refute it, as he found it did harm. Like the Manichaeans he emphasized the readily assailable parts of the Old Testament—in what language did the serpent speak with Eve ? If all the earth had been made into bricks, could the tower of Babel have been a success? Why did Jehovah, if the Universal God, choose the Jews and neglect the Greeks? What is good in Moses' law is common to all peoples. Jehovah's character as "a jealous God" and "an angry God" is really unworthy. The effect of the Christian books is not (like that of Greek literature) to make men better—it makes them no better than slaves. Old Testament monotheism cannot be reconciled with the Christian account of Christ. John first called Jesus God, when he found a mass of converts in Greek and Italian cities worshipping the tombs of Peter and Paul. Since then "many fresh corpses have been added to the old one," and so forth. The difficulties he raised were after

---

[1] Cyril (Neumann, p. 195) complains of his πλατὺ διηγημάτων πέλαγος— a very fair criticism.

all obvious, and were felt already. The Church however explained
many of them by the allegorical method, which it seems was legitimate enough for Porphyry. This was no doubt an unscientific
and unsatisfactory treatment of Scripture, but it had this merit
that it enabled the Church to reach a deeper truth and one more
vital than the literal meaning gave; to escape an obvious interpretation involving an outgrown position; and to gain for Scripture a
higher value in a spiritual significance, which, if it did not strictly
answer to the view of the original writers, at least corresponded
with Christian experience. Thus Julian's polemic was really beside
the mark. Though he says he knew Christianity, he really did not
know it, and the Christians were right in their allegation that he
did not understand.

Two other books remain, the *Misopogon* and *The Caesars*. Of
the former I have spoken. The latter is humorous with an
underlying seriousness. There is a banquet of the gods at which
the Caesars are in turn subjected to criticism, and a select few
are bidden set forth their ideals. While Julius and Constantine
might, perhaps, complain of their treatment (the latter particularly,
as self-indulgence does not seem to have been his aim[1]), Marcus
Aurelius carries the day, for his theory of life was "the imitation of
the gods." The piece concludes with a burlesque view of Christian
baptism. Constantine rejected by the gods turns to Luxury, who
welcomes him, clothes him with fine robes and takes him to
Profligacy, and "there he found Jesus proclaiming to all, 'Whoever
is a seducer, whoever is a murderer, whoever is accurst and filthy,
let him come boldly; for I will make him clean at once by washing
him in this water; and if he again fall into the same state, I will
grant to him that, by beating his breast and smiting his head, he
may be cleansed'." So to Jesus Constantine goes, but the avenging
demons overtake him, while Julian is made the special child and
charge of Mithras the Sun-God. I need not, I think, repeat that
Julian did not understand Christianity. As for the rest, let me
quote M. Chassang :—" The book of the Caesars is a work of great

---

[1] Julian is always unfair to Constantine, cf. *Or.* vii. 227 c. Though
Constantine's conduct was not above reproach, his conscience on the question
of chastity was keener than might fairly have been expected, and he at least
contributed to the growth of that tradition of *verecundia imperialis* which
Ammianus records. See Gwatkin, *Studies in Arianism*, p. 106, for a wise and
sympathetic judgment on him; also Seeck, *Untergang der Ant. Welt*[2], i. pp.
65—67. In short, Constantine displays, though with fluctuations, a gradual
development of high character from his accession to empire onwards through
life; Julian on the other hand degenerated.

originality. Yet is there not more pride than sureness, more caprice than justice, in this general reprobation of his predecessors? And when we reflect that Marcus Aurelius alone is excepted, are we not led to suppose that Julian *a fortiori* excepts himself, and that, in making those who went before him thus stand their trial, he means to glorify himself at their expense[1]?"

The general effect of Julian's life was to prove how dead a thing heathenism was. His Hellenism was not the old religion, it was a blend of various philosophies with some admixture of Christianity and more of magic. It testified at once against Greek philosophy, Greek religion and Greek morals The philosophy led from nowhere to nowhere and was a confusion of everything, with nothing in the long run to rest a life on. The religion was worse, a vacuous and external thing of ritual, trance and superstition. The morals were, in spite of Neo-Platonism, essentially uninspired. To reinforce all, Julian borrowed from the faith he hated—borrowed partly consciously, as when he conceived of the Catholic Church of Hellenism, but largely unconsciously, and there, perhaps, he shews more conspicuously the strength of the Church. Of all attempts made by Roman Emperors to crush the Church, his was the best conceived—he alone realizing that to crush without offering an alternative was impossible, and the alternative he did offer was the best then conceivable. He saw, as others had not seen, that it would be easier and more satisfactory to convince than to force men, and though events seemed trending to the use of more force as time went on, the fact remains to his credit that he at all events began by repudiating it. His life was a failure, and for this his religion is to blame. He had not a strong nature, and his religion made him weaker in the same measure as it inflamed his conceit by teaching him to fancy himself a god. But even this is of minor importance. He took the wrong way, and turning back to a creed and a philosophy outworn he suffered the fate of all who, from whatever cause, prefer a lower to a higher truth.

[1] Chassang, *Hist. du Roman*, p. 197.

CHAPTER IV

QUINTUS OF SMYRNA

My songs are now of the sunset;
Their brows are touched with light,
But their feet are lost in the shadows
And wet with the dews of night.

HENLEY

NOT the least remarkable figure in the history of Greek literature is Quintus of Smyrna. Not that he is in any great sense of the word a poet; not that he has any special gifts of insight and interpretation, of narrative or style; but that such a work as his should be produced at such a time must ever remain a marvel. The *Iliad* and the *Odyssey* belong to the dawn of Greek letters; the poem of Quintus was written to complete the story of the *Iliad* and to connect it with the *Odyssey*, and it was written a thousand years or more after them. The age of Homer, if the name may be used with perhaps something of a collective sense, may be reconstructed from his poems. The age of Quintus was removed from it in every aspect of man's life that can be affected by progress. It would be difficult to say whether in politics or in economics, in social, intellectual or religious life, the gulf between the two poets is widest. There had intervened thirty generations of mankind, who had seen the rise and fall of the Empires of Athens, of Alexander, and of the Ptolemies, the growth and decline of the Roman Republic, the development of the Roman Empire from the veiled monarchy of Augustus to the open sultanism of Diocletian; and associated with these political changes were the names of poets and philosophers, who had summed and had interpreted in the literatures of Athens, of Alexandria and of Rome the life and thought of the ages. From the vivid anthropomorphism of Homer men had climbed to conceptions of loftier and purer deity, till the Zeus and Athena of the poet

were names outworn, and if they still survived they served but to
cloak philosophical abstractions beyond the reach and outside the
needs of the men who first enjoyed the Homeric poems.   Strange
and barbarous gods from Egypt and Persia had supplanted the gods
of Greece and Italy with those who were not philosophers.   And
slowly Zeus and Athena had joined forces with Isis and Mithras,
enlisting philosopher and devotee, to do battle with another faith,
which had taught men to look death in the face and had risen by
being cut down to rule the world.   The labarum[1] with its cross and
monogram had proclaimed for half a century to Roman, Persian and
German that the world was Christian, when Quintus wrote his poem
to link the *Iliad* to the *Odyssey*.   Constantinople had been for
almost as long the seat of the Roman government, when he gave
the world the rest of the story of Troy.   And here is the marvel of
his work.   There is scarcely a hint that the world has moved since
Homer sang.   One allusion is made, and one only, to history, and
apart from this, which is introduced as a prophecy, there are but
two or three slight anachronisms which betray a society later than
Homer's.   With the literature of the intervening ages, it has been
maintained with much show of reason that Quintus was unac-
quainted, but for his study of Hesiod and Apollonius Rhodius.
And it was Quintus' endeavour to let it appear that in thought
and faith he stood where Homer had stood, though here it was
harder to deceive posterity, and we shall find evidence against him
in the confusion of his ideas.   Yet the illusion is wonderfully
successful, and so far as form and fashion are concerned, the work
of Quintus might at times pass for that of Homer himself.   But,
however Homeric, Quintus is not Homer, and as we read we realize
the feeling of the Trojan hero, who sought his wife and found, not
herself, but

infelix simulacrum atque ipsius umbra Creusae.

Still there is an interest, though it may not be a keen one, in the
study of this pale Homer of the fourth century.

Cardinal Bessarion first discovered Quintus in the monastery
of St Nicholas near Otranto, and because this town, once called
Hydruntum, lay in the ancient Calabria, the poet long bore the
surname Calaber, a title as suitable, says his editor Tychsen, as
Sangallensis would be for Quintilian in view of the fact that he was

---

[1] Prud. *c. Symm.* i. 487 *Christus purpureum gemmanti textus in auro Signabat
labarum.*   The institution of this change is told by Lactantius, *M. P.* 44.

first found by Poggio at St Gall. The manuscript bore no name
but Quintus, and there has been much speculation to account for
it. One scholar maintained it was rather the name of the owner of
the manuscript than that of the author of the poem. Another would
have corrected Cointos to Corintos, in order to attribute the author-
ship to a grammarian Corinthos, who unfortunately proved to have
lived in the twelfth century A.D., when such work would have been
flatly impossible. Then who was Quintus? Was he Aemilius
Macer, who according to Ovid filled in what Homer left out? or
was he Alcibiades? or perhaps Quintus Ennius, the favourite of
Cicero[1]? Strange as it may seem, no one has suggested Quintus
Cicero, a most energetic and productive poet, nor the greatest
Quintus of them all, who certainly tells us he thought of writing
in Greek and would have written but for the miraculous intervention
of Quirinus—why not as well then as any, Quintus of Venusia?
Time has however settled the question, and a number of references
and quotations in later grammarians make it clear that his name
was Quintus and give no indication that he ever had another. And
as he takes pains to inform us himself, whether he means it or not,
that Smyrna was the home of his youth, he is by common agreement
styled Quintus of Smyrna.

It will readily be supposed that when his name is a matter of
discussion, many questions may be raised about the man himself,
the answers to which must be largely conjectural. As regards his
date all serious critics are very much at one, some putting it toward
the beginning of the fifth century, most however toward the end of
the fourth and roughly about the time of the Emperor Julian. The
evidence for this is almost entirely internal, and the conclusion rests
on the relations of his versification to that of Nonnus and his school,
on the confused character of his paganism and on one or two faint
references to the contemporary world. Arguments dealing with
style have necessarily a subjective element about them, and the
rather large mass of Epic poetry and other poetry in hexameters
produced under the late Roman Empire is little studied to-day.
Yet on the whole it seems agreed that Quintus is earlier than
Nonnus, and this is an aid towards fixing his date. He has one
clear reference to the Roman Empire, which might refer almost
equally well to any Imperial family from Julius to Julian.

The scene is that of the fall of Troy, and Aeneas, like a crafty

[1] A new sense for Persius vi. 10: *cor jubet hoc Enni postquam destertuit esse
Maeonides Quintus.*

steersman taking to the boat when the ship is doomed, is leaving Troy under his mother's guidance. He is remarked by the Greek seer Calchas, who bids the Greeks to spare him, "for it is decreed by the glorious counsel of the gods that from the Xanthus he shall come to the Tiber's broad waters and build an holy city, famous with posterity, and himself shall reign over mortals of many seeds, and his race after him shall be kings to the rising and to the setting of the tireless sun; yea, and it is granted to him to be with the immortals, because he is the son of Aphrodite of the glorious locks. ...So spake Calchas and the Greeks obeyed and looked upon Aeneas as a god, all of them; and he gat him quickly from his city, whither his feet bore him in his haste[1]." This is not Virgil's story, nor Homer's, and I am sure Quintus never learnt of Juppiter Indiges from Livy, but he clearly implies a well-established Empire.

A simile from the arena, not unlike one of Claudian's, has been used to give a nearer date. The two sons of Atreus find themselves surrounded, "and, hemmed in on every side, they turned this way and that, even as boars or lions in the enclosure, on a day when kings gather men together, and with cruel mind shut them in, devising an evil destruction for them by great beasts, and they within the ring tear in pieces the slaves, whosoever cometh near them; even so they in the midst did slaughter with a will[2]." The Greek word he uses (βασιλεύς) served for the Homeric King and was the usual term for the Roman Emperor. It has been pointed out that an end was put to the beast-fights about the beginning of the fifth century, and though games were still held they were not bloody after that day.

It may be complained that the evidence for his date is not very strong, but on the whole it must be admitted when everything is weighed that the margin of error is slight, and while recognizing that absolute certainty is out of the question we may accept the general verdict that puts Quintus in the age of Julian.

Sainte-Beuve, in his very interesting study of Quintus, to which I shall have to refer more than once, remarks that the only biography we can form of Quintus must deal with his ideas and

---

[1] xiii. 336—343, 350—52. Homer hints at a royal destiny for Aeneas (*Il.* xx. 302—308), but does not particularize. Quintus lacks Virgil's power, as he well may, but even Dionysius of Halicarnassus (i. 46—47) is more spirited in his tale of Aeneas holding first the citadel and then Ida, and making terms for an honourable departure—all this from Hellanicus he says. There was yet a fourth story, that Aeneas was a traitor; and Servius says Virgil knew of it; so Chassang, *Histoire du Roman*, p. 364. This last is followed by Gower, *Confessio Amantis*, bk i. Hypocrisy.   [2] vi. 531—7.

his character, and this part of the French critic's work is admirable. The *Posthomerica* contains one solitary reference to the poet's life, but for the rest his character and his mind reveal themselves clearly in the course of the poem. His poverty precludes the possibility of mistake.

He waits till, in his twelfth book, the Greek heroes are preparing to enter the Wooden Horse, and then he invokes the aid of the Muses in dealing with their names. A list rarely lends itself to poetic treatment and perhaps his invocation was timely, though the reader will regret that it was unavailing. At all events it gives us our one piece of knowledge about Quintus. He says :—" Tell me, O Muses, in response to my asking of them each and all, who went down into the capacious Horse. For ye filled my soul with all song, or ever the down was spread upon my cheeks, when I fed the splendid sheep in the plains of Smyrna, thrice so far from Hermos as a shout will carry, by the temple of Artemis, in the free garden, on a hill not very low nor yet very high[1]." Nothing could well be plainer, and yet Lorenz Rhodoman in the sixteenth century turned the shepherd into a professor and was sure the splendid sheep were pupils. If such a theory needs attention at all, it may be said Bernhardy pronounces that Quintus' grammar and constructions stamp him as anything but a grammarian or teacher. Sainte-Beuve reaches a higher plane of criticism, when he says of this passage that "all is drawn with the precision of reminiscence inspired by the heart; every circumstance is given with love." The curious details were to define the exact region, and one would need to know the topography of Smyrna to pronounce upon them. I have, I should say, no confidence at all in my rendering of Ἐλευθερίῳ ἐνὶ κήπῳ ; it is a point that requires local knowledge.

Why the poet introduced this personal touch, it is easy to see. He had before him Hesiod's account of his inspiration by the Muses, and it encouraged him to tell of his own. Hesiod says he will begin his *Theogony* with the Muses "who taught Hesiod a beautiful song, as he fed his lambs under divine Helicon," for they came to him and gave him a staff and bade him sing of the race of the blessed who live for ever, and of themselves first and last and always[2]. There is the source of Quintus' courage, and while there may be something, there is probably not very much, in the suggestion that he dwells on his own Smyrnaean origin because Smyrna was one of the seven or

[1] xii. 304—311.　　　[2] *Theogony* 22—34.

more birthplaces of Homer. No doubt the city's claim to have
given Homer to the world moved him as it would not have moved
him to remember Polycarp, but to hint that he claimed to be from
Smyrna because he was a second Homer is extravagance. Let us
take him at his word, especially as everything tends to confirm the
literal interpretation of it.

It is when he speaks of his own country, of Lycia, Caria, Lydia,
Phrygia, the Hellespont and so forth, that this second Homer nods
least. He knew the ground and he loved it and dwelt with pleasure
on one and another striking scene. For example, Dresaios is a
person of no consequence, killed on his first appearance in the
story, but he was born near "snowy Sipylus, where the gods turned
Niobe to stone, and her tears still freely flow from the great crag on
high, and with her wail the streams of loud-roaring Hermus and the
long heights of Sipylus, on which ever hangs the mist, the shepherd's
foe ; and she, she is a great marvel to them that pass by, so like is
she to a woman of many sorrows, who mourns a bitter woe and
sheds a thousand tears ; and this thou wouldst say she was of a
truth, when thou sawest her from afar ; but when thou comest near
thereto, it is seen to be the craggy rock, a spur of Sipylus. But
she, fulfilling the baleful wrath of the gods, wails among the rocks,
like unto one in sore grief[1]." His interest is clearly not in Dresaios
but in Niobe. Now compare the account given about 180 A.D. by
the traveller Pausanias, himself said to be a native of Lydia. "This
Niobe I myself saw when I went up Mount Sipylus. Close at hand
it is a rock, a precipice with no sort of resemblance to a woman,
weeping or otherwise ; but if you go further away, you will think
you see a woman downcast and in tears[2]."

Again another unimportant warrior, killed at once, had previously "dwelt in sheep-bearing Phrygia, under the divine cave of
the fair-tressed Nymphs, where once as Endymion slept among
his kine the fair Moon saw him from on high and descended from
heaven ; for keen longing for the youth seized her, immortal virgin
as she was, and to this day is the token of her couch under the
oaks ; for all about it in the glade is the milk of the kine ; and
men see it there still. Looking from afar thou wouldst say it was
white milk, and white water sent it forth, but when it cometh near
it is dried up in its channels and is but rocky ground[3]." It would

[1] i. 294—306.
[2] Pausanias i. 21, 3: Sophocles, *Antigone* 823—832; Nonnus ii. 160.
[3] x. 126—137. There is some doubt as to the integrity of the passage.

seem to have been some white marble or an incrustation of some sort, but I have found no other allusion to it, though Pausanias and Strabo speak of the shrine and tomb of Endymion being on Mount Latmos, by the Maeander and just above Heraclea.

There are other similar references to scenery, but let us take the voyage of Neoptolemus as a stepping-stone to something further. "And the divine dawn came to the sky ; and to them appeared the heights of the mountains of Ida, and Chrysa [an island to their left], and the shrine of Smintheus, and the headland of Sigeum and the tomb of the prudent son of Aeacus [Achilles], but the wise son of Laertes shewed it not to Neoptolemus, lest his spirit in his breast should be troubled. And they passed the Calydnaean islands, and Tenedos was left behind, and they saw the place of Eleûs[1], where is the tomb of Protesilaus overshadowed by tall elms, whose tops wither away so soon as they have seen Ilion, as they shoot upward from the plain. And the wind bore the boat as they rowed onward nearer Troy, and they came where by the beach were other ships of the Argives, who then were being sore bestead as they fought about the wall they had builded aforetime to be a safeguard for the ships[2]."

This is a good passage, but it is hardly Homeric. When Odysseus sails home from Scheria, he sleeps and is landed asleep. No points of interest are remarked. But when Aeneas voyages westward[3], he cannot do so without Virgil remembering Odysseus' description of his native islands to Alcinous (*Od.* ix. 21—24) :

> *Jam medio apparet fluctu nemorosa Zacynthos*
> *Dulichiumque Sameque, et Neritos ardua saxis.*
> *effugimus scopulos Ithacae.*

We have Homer's epithet (ὑλήεσσα Ζάκυνθος) ; and before very long another and a different reminiscence follows :

> *Actiaque Iliacis celebramus litora ludis[4].*

And then we remember Homer again :

> *Protinus aerias Phaeacum abscondimus arces.*

Koechly marks a lacuna in the middle. I have here followed Zimmermann, whose remedies for Koechly's lacunae are sometimes heroic, but often helpful. See Pausanias v. 1, 5; and Strabo c. 636.

[1] Eleûs, on the Chersonnese, cf. Pliny, *N. H.* 4, 11 (18), 49; Pausanias i. 34, 2; Arrian i. 11, 5, who all mention Protesilaus. Herodotus ix. 116 has a story about the stealing of Protesilaus' treasures by a Persian governor. For the elms, see Pliny, *N. H.* 16, 44 (88), 238, and Wordsworth's *Laodamia.*
[2] vii. 400—416.   [3] See the passage in *Aen.* iii. 270—293.
[4] Virgil, it seems, followed Varro in letting Aeneas visit Actium, but the memories the name awakened were of an event after Varro's day.

Virgil, in fact, and Quintus would seem to have sailed through scenes they had read of, and their books were in their minds, just as the modern traveller sails up the St Lawrence and picks out with Parkman's aid the positions held by Wolfe as they appear, the heights of Levis, the Point of Orleans, the East cliffs of the Montmorency, and then marks the citadel and the plains of Abraham, and, as the steamer leaves the quays, watches anxiously for Wolfe's cove, "the little bay with the tall chimney[1]."

Quintus tells us he was or had been a shepherd, and in agreement with this statement is the remarkable number of similes drawn by him from country-life and from the calling of the shepherd in particular. No doubt many of these are imitated from Homer ; at all events I know of no evidence for the existence of lions in Western Asia Minor in Quintus' day, and one in ten of his similes boasts a lion. It may also be noticed how large a proportion of the similes deal with mountain scenery, the sphere of a shepherd's life. Bush-fires, landslips, storms in the hillside forests, hunting episodes, rivers in flood, the melting of the snow in the mountains, the swarming of bees, the flight of locusts, the migration of cranes, and the frolicking of a calf in a garden, all supply him with similes. And these have a warmth and a truth about them and speak of observation rather than of other men's books An example or two may serve.

As when amid rain the mist hangs upon the mountains, when the brawling channels are filled with rushing water, and every torrent roars aloud, and all the shepherds tremble at the floods and at the mist, dear to the savage wolves and the other beasts, bred in the depths of the forest[2]....

As when starlings and jackdaws, on outspread wings, swarm upon the olive-berries, for desire of the sweet food, nor can the lads for all their shouting turn them to flight before they eat, for hunger stirs their soul to shamelessness[3]....

---

[1] Conington however, on *Aen.* iii. 76, and 275, seems to question the accuracy of some of Virgil's island geography and quotes Clark (*Peloponnesus*, pp. 20, 21) who doubts Virgil's "personal acquaintance" with the scenery Aeneas saw before reaching Italy. In any case Virgil wrote in an age of tours and memories more akin to Quintus' than Homer's. Lechevalier, whose *Voyage en Troade* (1829) is referred to by Sainte-Beuve, confirms the truth of Quintus' topography, praises him with enthusiasm, and wishes his work were really Homer's own. The first part of this criticism is probably of more value than the rest.

[2] ii. 471.

[3] viii. 387. A simile which recalls the most beautiful scene in the *Daphnis and Chloe* of Longus (iii. 5, 6), quoted on p. 374.

As when, upon the shore of the deep-voiced sea, men take the long ropes from the well-wrought pegs and scatter the long baulks and timber of a towering raft, and all the broad beach is filled with them and the black water splashes amidst them[1]....

It may be said that there is not here perhaps the most perfect finish in the language, yet there is at least the note of observation and experience, which tells of country life. One point I have noticed which is not, I think, to be observed in Homer. Quintus has a curious habit of watching the horses in his battles. The plunging of the horse in death, tangled with the chariot and another horse on top of him, affects him as it does the soldier in Kipling's ballad *Snarleyow*. One of the few really living touches in his account of Troy's capture is his description of how "when the houses fell, horses and dogs stampeded through the city in terror at the cruel flames, and with their feet they trod down the dead, and kept galloping about, a danger to the living." It is the same story that Zola tells of the horses after the battle of Sedan, and it is startling to find so vivid and unexpected an episode in Quintus.

On the other hand there is scarcely a trace in Quintus of the magic that brings the unconscious environment into a real sympathy with the mind of man. Musaeus, a somewhat later and greater poet, in his epic-idyll of Hero and Leander, gives the last touch to the description of the loneliness of Hero's tower with the words :

αἰεὶ δ' ἀνὰ νύκτα καὶ ἠῶ
ἐξ ἁλὸς ἠνεμόεντος ἐπιβρέμει οὔασιν ἠχή.

But this is perhaps modern after all. Tennyson, for example, in his *Death of Oenone*, a tale avowedly taken from Quintus, puts a different atmosphere into his scene by telling how the branches of the vines that covered the mouth of Oenone's cavern

were wither'd long ago,
And thro' the sunless winter morning-mist
In silence wept upon the flowerless earth.

Such treatment is quite beyond Quintus.

Whether Quintus went to the school of rhetoric at Smyrna, it is impossible, and indeed needless, to say. His education was

---

[1] xi. 309. Allusions to "rafting" in classical literature are rare; but from what I have seen of it on Lake Ontario his picture seems true. To-day for ropes, saplings twisted by machinery are used ; and "towering" (ἠλίβατος) would be rather a large word for the rafts I have been on, which rise not more than a few feet above the water. See Torr, *Ancient Ships*, p. 122, though the authors he quotes refer mainly to rafts as used in war.

Homer and little else, and though he has some few of the foibles of the rhetorical school his taste was really moulded by Homer and almost by Homer alone.   After a careful study of his metre, which is wonderfully Homeric and varies from Homer's in but a few insignificant features, Koechly pronounces that Quintus wrote by ear rather than by written rule, and this means a freedom, an ease, and a naturalness quite foreign to the school and its artifices.   The difference may be perhaps most readily felt by reading a page of Quintus and a page of Colluthus, who is a weaker member of the family of Nonnus.

Homer dominated him, and it was not very strange that it should be so.   Witness is borne to Homer's power at this very time by the writings of Julian, who was steeped in him, and by the marvellous *tour de force* of Apollinaris of Laodicea, who, when Julian forbade Homer to Christian teachers, made a new Homer out of the Pentateuch.   This work does not survive, and if it did the student of the *Posthomerica* would hardly wish to read it.

The great work of Quintus was to bridge the gulf between the *Iliad* and the *Odyssey*.   This had perhaps been done long before by the Cyclic poets, and the question has been raised as to how far Quintus used them.   Schow believed that his work was a mere cento made from them, in which case one would be surprised to remark that he never stole a line from Homer—not a καί ποτέ τις εἰπῆσι; not an αὐτὰρ ἐπεὶ πόσιος; perhaps not even a τὸν δ' ἀπαμει-βόμενος.   As a matter of fact however, the right view of the case has been put by Tychsen, who on reading and re-reading the book found the same quality throughout—which is fatal to the theory that half of it was Arctinus and half Lesches.   Koechly also shews that in a large number of cases Quintus did not follow the versions given by the Cyclici of famous episodes, that he owed far more to the handbooks of mythology, and finally that in all likelihood he never so much as saw the Cyclici.   To this one may add that, while the manner of writing is the same, there is a great change at book xii., where the fighting stops, and the Wooden Horse is built.   Here and in the story of the capture of Troy and the departure of the Greeks, there was no Homer for him to follow, and one realizes then how very dependent on the *Iliad* he has been throughout.   A fight between Eurypylus and Neoptolemus can be modelled quite well on one in Homer, but when Homer will no longer serve and the poet is left to his own devices, he flounders terribly and has to fall back on a storm at sea to finish his book.   His task in the actual taking of Troy was a hard one. Virgil's was easier, for he had to tell the story of one man's part in it. Napoleon found even Virgil's account deficient from a military point of view, but it has a unity and a completeness as the tale of Aeneas' experience. Quintus gives us nothing but a string of second-hand horrors, without movement or connexion, neither Greek nor Trojan having any plan of action.

Of course he has a few anachronisms, but he falls far short of Virgil in this. His heroes ride on horseback; they torture Sinon to get the truth out of him[1]; and Odysseus suggests and tries the formation known as the *testudo*. More noticeable are series of portents which he intermittently gives. Omen and portent are rare if they occur at all in the *Iliad*, and though they are found in the *Odyssey* they are not so awful as in Quintus, who piles them up after the manner of Lucan, some of them curiously like those familiar to the reader of Livy. We may also remark a difference from Homer in the gentler character of the warriors when not engaged in actual fighting, who " have respect unto the slain," "for there is no wrath against the dead, for they are to be pitied and are foemen no longer when once their life is gone[2]." The most remarkable example of this new feeling is the sudden love of Achilles for the maiden-warrior Penthesilea, whom he has just slain. The episode is hardly Homeric, but it has justly won the warm praise of Sainte-Beuve.

This last feature appears in the story of Ajax and the arms of Achilles, to which we may give some further consideration There is an allusion to the quarrel of Ajax and Odysseus in the *Odyssey*, but no hint that Ajax thought of murdering the Greek captains. The arms were awarded on the decision of the Trojan captives and Athena[3]. Pindar lets the Greek chiefs decide "by secret votes." Sophocles, in taking the theme for a tragedy, was bound to adopt a less simple version of the story, which would allow more variety of character and motive, but was in consequence less epic in its movement. Quintus however was writing an epic, and realized that Sophocles' rendering was not for him, and his work has a simplicity, and his characters a nobility, in striking contrast with the play.

---

[1] Even the gentle Synesius countenanced this method of examination. *Ep.* 44, 1373 A.

[2] ix. 38; i. 809. Compare Virgil, *Aen.* xi. 304. We must not however forget *Od.* xxii. 412 οὐχ ὁσίη κταμένοισιν ἐπ' ἀνδράσιν εὐχετάασθαι.

[3] *Od.* xi. 547. Aristarchus however rejects the line, but W. Christ and others maintain that it is the oldest form of the story. Probably Quintus had no doubts.

When the arms were first set out by Thetis and claimed by the two heroes, Nestor, with some pertinent remarks on the wisdom of age, suggested that the decision should rest with some Trojan captives, and Agamemnon accepted the proposal. Then the two heroes rose and pled. Here Quintus was going outside Homer, but, as their pleadings had long been themes for declamation in the schools, he had little to do but to go along the lines laid down. There are in fact close resemblances between the speeches in Quintus and in Ovid's *Metamorphoses*, but Ovid is three times as long as Quintus. More than that, Ovid, as might have been expected, puts into the mouths of the Homeric warriors speeches too full of quirks and conceits for the Roman bar. There is no difference between Ajax and Odysseus; both make neat little points and both are practised rhetoricians, versed in every artifice and prettiness. The warriors in Quintus are true to Homer—Quintus never has the strength of Homer, but he has at least the manner, and the speeches are not the terrible anachronisms of Ovid. Each says his say and emphasizes his own good points, and each makes a short rejoinder in conclusion, and the arms are given to Odysseus.

But here Quintus broke down and described how the madness came on Ajax, giving a list of symptoms[1], which betrays that he too had studied rhetoric, and had forgotten the wisdom of Hesiod that the half is more than the whole. In this state Ajax was led away. Then, fearing he would do mischief, Athena allowed the madness to fall heavily upon him, and with a series of similes Quintus lets us see him kill the sheep. Raging like a storm at sea, or a wild beast robbed of her whelps, or a bush-fire, or Orion, or a lion falling upon sheep, Ajax, his heart seething like a cauldron, threw himself upon the sheep and scattered them as the North wind scatters the leaves. Then he regained his senses, made a short soliloquy, debating on the courses open to him and cursing the Greek chiefs, and plunged Hector's sword into his neck. His speech shews, I think, points of contact with the two speeches of Sophocles, but this is implicitly denied by good critics.

The most marked divergence from the tragedy follows. The play dealt, according to Professor Jebb, with the death *and burial* of Ajax, the latter being as important as the former. But there is

---

[1] A similar deluge of pathology overtakes us, when Quintus tells of Laocoon, who was not, though his sons were, devoured by the snakes, but suffered blindness. Many and grievous were his symptoms, καὶ ἔδρακε διπλόα πάντα (xii. 411).

no such question in Quintus. Tecmessa mourns her widowhood and looks forward to slavery, but Agamemnon reassures her, promising that, on the contrary, the Greeks will honour her as if she were a goddess, as if Ajax yet lived ; while Odysseus, if a little prosy, expresses his regret at what has occurred and wishes he could have foreseen it, for then he would himself have given the arms to Ajax (For this Quintus seems indebted to the *Odyssey*, where Odysseus makes the remark to Alcinous.) Ajax is then buried with all pomp, "for they honoured him as much as Achilles," and the burning of his body was as the burning of Herakles.

It cannot be said that Quintus generally reaches the measure of success he attained in the episode of Ajax He had before him a large mass of traditions, many inconsistent with one another. It was difficult to deal with them without modifications, but though Quintus might select, he did not dare to modify. The story of Ajax permitted a reasonable treatment, but that of Philoctetes was harder. No valid explanation is given of the desertion of the suffering hero. He was healed too easily—"swifter than thought" —by Podalirius on his arrival at the camp, and, though it is explained that Athena aided in this marvellous recovery, it seems odd still that some attempt had not been made at first. Nor is it very clear why he should have consented to come to Troy. The explanation of his abandonment, given on the island by Odysseus, is that no one was responsible for it but Fate, and so says Agamemnon later on. Men are driven by Fate as leaves by the winds, so a wise man must endure what comes his way. To this Philoctetes merely says briefly that he understands all this and suggests going to bed if they mean to fight next day. I do not think Quintus intended any humour here, but it would help the situation. Assuming then that for some inscrutable reason Philoctetes allows that no one is responsible for the wrong done him, and that he is willing to come to Troy, it cannot be seen in Quintus that he effects anything of the slightest consequence. The slaying of Paris cannot be considered a heavy loss to the Trojans, though he is a respectable warrior in the *Posthomerica*. Yet we were told how, before his coming, battle raged, "till, bidden by Calchas, the Greeks withdrew to their ships, and forgot their toils, for it was not fated that Ilion should be conquered before the mighty Philoctetes, skilled in tearful war, came to the throng of the Greeks[1]." The idea of some

[1] ix. 325—329.

kind of moral satisfaction being the cause is precluded by the Greeks' conviction that they were guiltless of any sin against him.

Again, there is a strange passage in book x. Hera is greatly cheered by the death of Paris, and the four Seasons tell her of the future course of the war, outlining with some precision events, which may have occurred but which are entirely omitted by Quintus in the remainder of his narrative. The capture of the Palladium is to be the turning point of the war, and no allusion is made to it. It has been suggested that the poem wanted the poet's final revision[1], but the last three books, as I have said, are beyond revision. To be mended they must have been re-written. In view of this it is going too far to suggest that Quintus wanted time. What he needed was something very different.

Yet Quintus was not without some of the gifts of the poet. He had the instinct to keep to the Homeric simplicity and to avoid the rhetoricians *et dona ferentes*[2]. Though, as we have seen, he owes them a little here and there, he is not a rhetorical poet. His verse is singularly Homeric in tone, though in no servile way. He abjures Homeric "tags," as he does the dainty but monotonous rhythm of Nonnus, which is more suited to the idyll than to the epic. There is a good deal of variety and freedom in his rhythm, and its excellence is remarked by all the critics. Here perhaps he is at his strongest.

He suffers from length, from *copia* rather than *inopia* to quote Tychsen. Pauw goes even further and declares that a third of him might have been removed with advantage, and perhaps he is right, but we must take the poet's work as he left it, redundant and iterative as it is. He has to express a Homeric idea, and Homer has done it in the directest way, so Quintus has to try another with the result that he is longer and less effective. For example, when Patroclus' body is burnt, Achilles says "let us gather up the bones of Patroclus, Menoetius' son, singling them well, and easy are they to discern, for he lay in the middle of the pyre, while the rest apart at the edge burnt confusedly, horses and men[3]." When Quintus describes the same being done for Achilles,

---

[1] Tychsen, p. li; Rohde (*der gr. Roman*, p. 110, n. 5) believes this little batch of prophecies to have been carelessly copied from the Hellenistic poet whom he supposes Quintus followed in the story of Oenone.

[2] What the rhetoricians had made of the actual story of Troy may be read in Chassang, *Histoire du Roman*, part iii. c. 5, on Philostratus' *Heroicus*, Dares and Dictys.

[3] *Il.* xxiii. 239—242.

he says, " And his bones were clear to behold, for they were not
like unto the others, but as it were the bones of a mighty giant, nor
indeed were others mixed with them, since the kine and the horses
and the sons of the Trojans, confusedly with other slain also, lay a
little apart round about the corse, and he in the midst, overcome by
the breath of Hephaestus, lay alone[1]." He has tried to say a little
more than Homer but has achieved less.

He is chiefly praised for his similes, to which I have alluded,
but here again he suffers from excess. When Homer adds simile
to simile, each illustrates some new point, but it cannot be said that
Quintus' comparisons always effect their purpose. Too often they
block the narrative. We have seen how they tumble over one another
when he describes the madness of Ajax. Yet it is in his similes
that he is after all most successful, which implies unhappily that his
general work is not successful. It is one of the marks of the
rhetorical school, that it endeavours to storm the reader's admiration by a rapid series of brilliant attacks, blow upon blow, and
sometimes it succeeds as in the case of Lucan, and perhaps of
Claudian, though his case is rather different. Quintus, either from
judgment or want of strength, avoids the manners of the school,
antithesis, mythology, obscurity and other Alexandrine arts, but he
is not strong enough or wise enough to resist the temptation to
carry the reader by a brilliant use of simile. It is a half measure, a
compromise between the rhetorician and the poet, and it fails. Still
we must admit that if his similes, as too often his epithets, are not
always wholly appropriate, they are at least very often happy in the
sympathy they shew with wild nature and country life. Some of
them, to quote Sainte-Beuve, are "refreshing, exact and uncommon."

But more than rhythm and taste and the power to describe external scenes is required of a poet, and it may be asked if Quintus has
the higher gifts. It may seem from what I have already said that I
have already given judgment. But first let us take the judgments
of scholars and critics. Tychsen found passages in the *Posthomerica* "worthy of a great poet," while the faults were in some
measure due to a "great and fertile nature." Koechly brushes aside
such estimates as "the fond imaginations of lovers and not the
judgments of critics," pronouncing Quintus to be without any really
poetic faculty, his characters devoid of flesh and blood and his

---

[1] iii. 723—9.

poem of unity. Bernhardy is still more savage and declares that Quintus "registers his material without the slightest psychological consideration." On the whole the scholars are against Quintus.

Turning to another school, we find Sainte-Beuve has a remarkably high opinion of Quintus, whom he finds simple and easy in style, possessed of affection and sensibility, able to describe striking scenes with exactness and truth, and, in short, well worthy of study. Of the story of the death of Paris he writes, "Ceci est de la grande et vraie passion, de la pure et sincère nature; je donne entier tout ce morceau, admirable selon moi et le plus beau du livre de Quintus....Il me semble qu'il ne se peut rencontrer dans un récit épique, de scène plus profondément naturelle et plus moralement émouvante....Il avait certes un grand talent, celui qui à une époque de décadence savait ainsi choisir, élaguer les circonstances frivoles et vaines, et rendre ou conserver à ses récits un cachet de réalité qui les fait paraître intéressants encore aujourd'hui et si émouvants par endroits."

And yet Sainte-Beuve had read Koechly's introduction to the poet[1]. Whether Tennyson referred to any of these editors and critics or formed his views on independent study alone, his judgment is as clear and, I think, as true here as in the cases of Virgil and Catullus. In his dedication of *The Death of Oenone* he bids the Master of Balliol lay down his Plato for one minute,

> And read a Grecian tale re-told,
> Which, cast in later Grecian mould,
> Quintus Calaber
> Somewhat lazily handled of old.

Has Quintus indeed that realization of life, that feeling for humanity, which Virgil sums up in such lines as

> *Sunt lacrimae rerum, et mentem mortalia tangunt?*

Do his men and women suffer real anguish, feel a real smart, or know "infinite passion and the pain of finite hearts that yearn" as Virgil's do? Sainte-Beuve admits he is not a Virgil. Few episodes in the *Aeneid* are so terribly true as the story of Mezentius and Lausus. Quintus has a somewhat similar opportunity in the story of Nestor and Antilochus. But he does little more than remark that "no more cruel sorrow comes on mortal men than when sons

---

[1] Mr Andrew Lang (*Contemporary Review*, Aug. 1882) says "The *Argonautica* of Apollonius Rhodius seems to me a much less moving poem, much less Homeric in spirit, than the *Posthomerica*."

are slain before a parent's eyes." (Virgil omitted to say this.) He continues; Nestor was grieved in his heart and called to his other son, "Rise Thrasymedes, glorious of renown, that we may drive the slayer of thy brother and my son away from the poor corse, or ourselves upon him complete the tearful sorrow. But if there is fear in thy breast, thou art not my son nor of the stock of Periclymenos, who dared to stand even against Herakles. But come let us toil, for necessity ofttimes gives great strength to men doing battle, though they be of little worth." Memnon warns him to go away and he goes, remarking that he had once been a better man, but now retired like an old lion before a sheep-dog. At the beginning of the next book the Greeks wail for Antilochus, "but Nestor was not greatly overcome in mind, for it is the part of a wise man to bear a grief bravely, and not abjectly to give way to grief." So, very soon (a day or two later) we find him chanting a hymn in honour of Thetis and Achilles, when the sea-nymph was giving the funeral games for her son. Of course we may remember Virgil's *at pius Aeneas* after the last scene with Dido, but there is a difference.

Quintus delivers himself of two reflexions in this story and they may serve to shew his manner. Where Homer and Virgil draw a man and let us see him suffering, doing battle, working, and leave us to feel with him, Quintus explains his feelings. It may be an affectation, an attempt to reproduce the epic simplicity, but it is a false simplicity—*simplesse*. Homer could hardly have shewn us Andromache a widow and explained that "great grief springs up for honourable women when a husband dies[1]." Priam asks the young Neoptolemus to kill him that he may die and forget his sorrows, and he replies, "Old man, ready and willing am I whom thou biddest. For I will not leave thee, being a foeman, among the living; for there is nothing dearer to men than life[2]." When the Trojans fall into a drunken slumber after their feast of triumph, we are informed that darkness covered their sight, "for the eyes and mind of young men are darkened by strong drink, when it cometh into their heart in plenty[3]."

Perhaps his best episode is that of Deidamia. It is quiet and, it may be, a little obvious, a theme, therefore, well suited to the gentle mind of the poet. A mother's emotions, when her son goes to battle, are intense but not complicated. Hence Quintus can treat them with truth and feeling. In one or two points his treatment

---

[1] i. 116. [2] xiii. 238—40. [3] xiii. 11.

recalls Claudian's picture of the sorrow of Ceres for the lost Proserpine. Once before Quintus makes a touching reference to such a theme, when he tells how Thetis "bethought her of her own son, as she looked on Ajax ; and sorrow fell upon her soul[1]."

Odysseus and Diomedes went to Scyros to fetch Neoptolemus, and that night "sweet sleep came not to Deidamia as she remembered the name of the wily Odysseus and of the godlike Diomedes, the twain who widowed her of war-loving Achilles, prevailing upon his brave soul that he should come to the war; and the Fate that turneth not away met him and cut off his return and brought infinite sorrow to his father Peleus and to her, Deidamia. Therefore fear unspeakable held her heart lest, if her son went to the war, sorrow should be added to bitter sorrow." She asks her son, "Why is thy stout heart set on going with the strangers to tearful Ilion (Ἴλιον ἐς πολύδακρυ), where many fall in the cruel fight, though they know war and battle? And now thou art young and knowest not yet the works of war, that ward off from men the evil day. But hearken thou unto me and abide in thy home, lest an ill report come to me from Troy that thou art fallen in the battle."

Neoptolemus however was a fatalist and would go. " And he with a bright smile was eager to hasten to the ship. But his mother's tearful whispers (δακρυόεις ὀαρισμός) stayed him yet in the hall...and she, grieved to her heart, was yet proud of her son." When he had gone, she lamented like a bird over an empty nest, "and now she threw herself on her son's bed and wept aloud, and now by the posts of the door ; and she put in her bosom any toy that there was in the house, wherewith when a tiny child he had delighted his tender heart. And for his sake, if perchance she saw some javelin left behind, oft and again she kissed it, and aught of her son's that she saw through her tears. But he heard no more the ceaseless weeping of his mother, but went unto the swift ship[2]."

The story of Oenone's death is well known. Paris was at last wounded by a poisoned arrow of Philoctetes, and knew none could cure him but Oenone. She would not and he died. Too late she repented and threw herself on his funeral pyre. Erwin Rohde[3], who speaks of the narrative as one of real feeling which stands out " in the wilderness of Quintus," believes the tale to be of Alexandrine origin. Quintus' treatment displays once more an epic simplicity.

[1] iv. 498.
[2] vii. 240—345.
[3] *Der griechische Roman*, p. 110, n. 5, and generally pp. 109—112.

He omits the additional feature used by William Morris in *The Earthly Paradise,* and does not tell how Oenone brought Paris back to life and how, when with returning consciousness his first word was "Helen," she let him die.

Paris, says Quintus, went to Oenone "against his will, but dire necessity led him to his wife's face" while birds of ill omen hung and screamed around him. "And thus he spake with his faint strength: O lady wife, hate me not in mine anguish, that of old I left thee a widow in thy house, not of mine own will, but the Fates that none may escape led me to Helen, and would that before I had known her bed I had died in thy embrace! But come! by the gods who dwell in heaven, and by thy bed and our wedlock, have a gentle heart, and stay my cruel pain, putting upon the deadly wound drugs that shall avail, that are fated to drive grief from the heart, if thou wilt. For it rests with thee to save me from grim death or not; but take pity quickly and stay the strength of the swift-slaying arrows, while still my force and my limbs abide; nor remembering baleful jealousy leave me to die unpitied at thy feet. It were a deed displeasing to the Litai (Prayers) who are the daughters of thundering Zeus and in anger at such as are overweening stir up against them the dread Fury and wrath; but do thou, lady, ward off the Fates and quickly, even if I have sinned at all in folly."

There are wasted words in this, otiose epithets and draggling clauses, but that is not all. There is a suggestion of the sensualist, selfish and peevish, who has hardly a word of regret, hardly a thought of his baseness, and is in more hurry to be healed than to offer any amends for his treachery. If this were, as may be said, Paris' true character, why allude so terribly directly to Helen? Tennyson has borrowed a good deal from Quintus here, but the speech as a whole is very different.

> 'Oenone, *my* Oenone, while we dwelt
> Together in this valley—happy then—
> Too happy had I died within thine arms,
> Before the feud of Gods had marr'd our peace,
> And sunder'd each from each. I am dying now
> Pierced by a poison'd dart. Save me. Thou knowest,
> Taught by some God, whatever herb or balm
> May clear the blood from poison, and thy fame
> Is blown thro' all the Troad, and to thee
> The shepherd brings his adder-bitten lamb,
> The wounded warrior climbs from Troy to thee.

My life and death are in thy hand. The Gods
Avenge on stony hearts a fruitless prayer
For pity. Let me owe my life to thee.
I wrought thee bitter wrong, but thou forgive,
Forget it. Man is but the slave of Fate.
Oenone, by thy love which once was mine,
Help, heal me. I am poison'd to the heart.'
'And I to mine' she said 'Adulterer,
Go back to thine adulteress and die!'

So writes Tennyson, and every line is a criticism. Of course it was not to be expected that Quintus should look at the story in the same way. Some of his plain-spokenness is an endeavour after epic simplicity and directness, yet it may be doubted if Homer would have told the same tale as his imitator.

Oenone's reply is long (20 lines) and sarcastic, but on a sudden another strain appears. " Would that I had at my heart the great strength of a wild beast, to rend thy flesh and then to lap thy blood, for the woes thou hast given me in thy wickedness." She bids him go "a curse, a grievous curse to gods and men ; for because of thee, wretch, mourning has befallen the immortals too, some for sons and some for grandsons slain. But go from my house and betake thee to Helen, by whose bed it befits thee to whimper night and day in dudgeon, pierced with bitter grief, till she heal thee of thy sore pains." Hecuba breaks out in a similarly savage strain in the *Iliad*, and Zeus taunts Hera with a readiness to eat Priam raw and Priam's sons, but after all Paris was a suppliant and in distress, and the coarse vein in Oenone, though not alien from the Greek character, gives an unpleasant impression. The reference to the gods, who lost some their sons and some their grandsons, may be primitive in its exactness, but hardly seems probable.

As in the case of Philoctetes' abandonment, no guilt seems to attach to those who have done the cruel deed. They are merely automata in the hands of Fate, a point to be remembered in view of what follows.

For if there is one thing Quintus takes pains to assert, it is the supremacy of Fate. Of course he has the Homeric gods, but they are dull and bloodless, ornaments more than agents. The conception of Fate however appears in three forms ; there are the Keres, there is Aisa, and there is Moira. The first chiefly appear with death—θάνατον καὶ κῆρα μέλαιναν. Yet the functions of them all overlap and nice distinctions are hardly to be drawn ; but Aisa and Moira have perhaps a wider range of activity.

The Keres hang about the doomed man, pitiless, robbing him of his senses, deceiving him and exulting in his doom. The gods cannot check them, and though Quintus follows Homer in the occasional use of a phrase ὑπὲρ κῆρας where people narrowly make lucky escapes, yet the Keres are normally and properly inevitable (ἄφυκτοι).

Aisa and Moira similarly dog the doomed, deceive him and cannot be escaped, but Quintus has a little more to say of them. Of Aisa, Calliope says to Thetis "Dost thou not know that about all men upon earth, about them all, the baleful Aisa, the invincible, hangs, recking not even of the gods, such strength has she alone? And she shall sack Priam's rich city, slaying of Trojans and of Greeks whomsoever she will, and there is no god that shall stay her[1]." When in battle a Trojan prayer rose for deliverance, "the gods heeded not at all, for other was the mind of Aisa, giver of mourning; and she regarded not mighty Zeus, nor any of the other immortals; for her dire mind is not to be changed, whatsoever be the lot she spin with inevitable thread for men at their birth, for men and for cities; but under her, this will fall and that rise[2]." Again, "not even Zeus himself can easily put aside Aisa beyond what is fated, Zeus who excels all the immortals in power, and of Zeus are all things[3]." Aisa made Ajax to sin and before her men are like leaves before the wind[4].

Moira sometimes appears in the plural. The Moirai are daughters of holy Chaos (ἱερὸν Χάος iii. 756) and Zeus yields to them. They control the varying destinies of men. The most curious passage is where Nestor is comforting Podalirius for the death of his brother. First he tries one line—the fatalist's.

" On high, good things and bad lie on the knees of the gods, a myriad all mingled; and of the immortals none seeth them, for they may not be foreseen and are covered in thick darkness. And on them Moira alone layeth her hands, and without looking she flingeth them from Olympus to earth; and they fly hither and thither as on the breath of the wind. And often great sorrow overwhelms a good man, and to a bad cometh wealth unmerited. Man's life is blind, therefore he walketh not in safety but stumbleth oft with his feet, and his changing steps turn now to sorrow and

---

[1] iii. 649—654. The gods themselves might not care to stay her, if we may trust Thetis (xii. 206)—"It befits not, when Zeus is angry, that for men, mere men (μινυνθαδίων), the eternal ones should fight."
[2] xi. 271—7.   [3] xiv. 98—100.   [4] v. 594 and ix. 502.

now to good; and none among mortals was ever wholly happy."
The moral is endurance, but a world governed by pure chance has
small consolation for the bereaved, and as Podalirius will not so be
comforted, Nestor drops fatalism and tries another approach before
he ceases to speak. So in one speech we have two distinct theories
of the universe—not to say three.

"Hope ever for the better; for there is a saying (φάτις) among
men that the good go to heaven that fadeth not, but the bad man
to hateful darkness. And thy brother was both kind to mortals
and the son of a god, and I think that he will ascend to the race
of the gods by the bidding of his sire[1]."

"Il ne faut pas trop presser la théologie du vieillard de Pylos,"
says Sainte-Beuve, who justly describes the general philosophy of
Quintus as "the paganism of the second or third period." It
blends certain elements of fatalism, a hint of a Neo-Platonic
heaven, and a preference for the salvation of the well-born which
is neither one thing nor the other, but is perhaps a good deal
nearer Homer than either.

The other world offers great uncertainties to Quintus, for which
he may be forgiven[2]. We have seen Nestor's views, and there are
other cases, which add to the confusion. Memnon after his death
is, we learn, "in the house of Hades, or else with the blessed on the
Elysian plain[3]." Paris is uncertain about Hector's lot, but proposes
a course of action to please him "if indeed there be for men in
Hades either mind or law[4]." When Achilles dies, Poseidon
tells his mother of his future shrine at Leuce and his glory as
Pontarches, Lord of the Euxine, a position he actually held till
displaced by St Phocas of Sinope after Quintus' day[5]. Agamemnon
speaks of him as with the immortals, and when he appears to his
son in a vision he says the same. Homer had him a ghost with
other ghosts below, and ignorant alike of the story of his own
burial and of his son's prowess. The bitter cry of Achilles to
Odysseus in the *Nekyia* is famous—"Rather would I live on ground

---

[1] vii. 70—92. This happy destination of the "good" is the theme of
Macrobius' long Commentary on Scipio's Dream. So Hermes Trismegistus
(Ed. Bipont. Apuleius ii. p. 312), but he, like Claudian, says nothing of rank
counting, and anticipates a strict examination of merits by the *summus daemon.*

[2] It may be pled that Virgil handles the next world with some uncertainty,
but after all his fluctuations are distinctly within narrower limits, and his
greatness, lying in another direction, is unaffected.

[3] ii. 650.

[4] iii. 197.

[5] On the worship of Achilles at Borysthenis, a Greek town on the Dnieper,
see Dio Chrysostom, *Borystheniticus,* 9, 14, 25.

as the hireling of another, with a landless man who had no great livelihood, than bear sway among all the dead that be departed." A similar divergence may be remarked between Homer and his imitator, when the one speaks of the dead at Troy and the other of Herakles. The wrath of Achilles "sent to Hades many strong souls of heroes and gave themselves (αὐτούς *i.e.* their bodies) to be a prey to dogs and all winged fowls." But when Herakles was burnt on Oeta "his soul left the goodly man and mingled with the air, and himself (αὐτός) was enrolled among the gods, when earth had received his long-suffering body[1]." Here a man's *self* has travelled from meaning his body to be his soul.

Now there falls to be added to the confusion another element. We have seen the pleas advanced to Philoctetes and Oenone, that the wrong-doer is the victim of fate, which implies that there is no such thing as guilt or sin. Even so we saw that prayers rejected become avengers, which implies that there is guilt. Is there such a thing or not? No blame is to be attached to Helen, says Agamemnon, for the fault was all Paris', and therefore has he been requited. Quintus accepts this view, and though Helen feels some shame, as Aphrodite might in the lay of Demodocus, the Greeks look on her as a goddess, as of course they had to in view of the *Odyssey*. This distinction between guilt and freedom from guilt is frail and will not stand rough usage. Quintus however manages to put it immediately side by side with some reflexions on the fall of Troy. "Justice, chief among the gods, brought much evil on the Trojans, for they first wrought evil deeds in Helen's case, and first did despite to oaths, hard men, when in the wickedness of their heart they trampled under foot the dark blood and the sacrifices of the gods; wherefore the Erinnyes wrought woe for them thereafter and so they perished, some before the wall and some in the city as they feasted with their fair-tressed wives[2]."

---

[1] v. 647—9. It may be objected that in the *Odyssey* (xi. 601—604) Herakles' image is with the dead—εἴδωλον· αὐτὸς δὲ μετ' ἀθανάτοισι θεοῖσι τέρπεται—but the distinction is probably post-Homeric and an addition while the antithesis is not the same as in Quintus. Herakles at all events met the common fate of man, without achieving divinity, in the *Iliad* (xviii. 117—9). Quintus may be illustrated by the words of Hermes Trismegistus (the Latin translation printed with Apuleius' works but not his, Ed. Bipont. Apul. vol. ii. p. 321) on Asclepius, *in quo ejus jacet mundanus homo, id est, corpus, reliquus enim vel potius totus, si est homo totus in sensu vitae melior, remeavit in caelum.* See Geddes, *Problem of Homeric Poems*, p. 149.

[2] xiii. 377—384. There immediately follow the recovery of Helen and Agamemnon's plea, helped out by the special intervention of Aphrodite who gives her fresh beauty.

That nothing may be wanting, the ghost of Achilles appears to his son in the character of Polonius and all but quotes Hesiod to him[1]. He explains that he is now with the gods, "forbear then to be troubled for me, but put might into thy heart. Ever stand first among the Greeks, yielding place to none in courage; but in debate hearken unto older men, and all will call thee wise. Honour such as are blameless and have wisdom abiding with them, for the good is a friend to the good, and the grievous man to the froward. But if thou think what is good, good shall befall thee. But that man never reached the goal of Virtue, who had not a righteous mind; for the stem of her is hard to climb and her shoots reach unto the sky, but such as strength and toil attend, win from their labour pleasant fruit, when they have ascended the goodly tree of Virtue of the fair garland. But come, be valiant, nor in thy wisdom vex thy mind overmuch for sorrow, nor delight greatly in good fortune, but let thy heart be gentle to thy friends and thy sons and to women. Men are like the flowers of the grass, withering and blooming. Therefore be tender, and tell the Greeks, and most of all Agamemnon, Atreus' son, if they remember all my travail about the city of Priam, and the prey I took ere we came to Troy, to grant me according to my desire, from among the booty of Priam, the well-clad Polyxena[2], that they sacrifice her with speed, for I am yet angry and more than aforetime for Briseis," and, as ruler of Pontus no doubt, he will raise a storm against them if they do not. So Polyxena is sacrificed, and if Achilles does not raise a storm, Athena does, in alarm lest, if Ajax the son of Oileus go unpunished, men will not heed the gods and justice and shame perish utterly. And with the elaborate drowning of Ajax, Quintus ends his poem.

Our study has been long and tiresome, and what is the conclusion? "The gods give not all things at once unto men, but by some destiny evil standeth hard by good. So for Nireus, the king, along with fair loveliness was ordained impotence[3]." Quintus tells us of the weariness and exhaustion of his age which could admire but not create, which could echo the words of the thinker but not realize his thought, and which clung to the past because it did not believe in the

---

[1] xiv. 180—222.

[2] Chassang, *op. cit.* 368, remarks how utterly Quintus ignores the romance that had, since classical times but long before his day, been woven round Achilles and Polyxena (see Philostratus, *Heroicus* 323). This romance was one of the most popular in the middle ages.

[3] vii. 11.

future. It may be said they felt, as the Church did not yet feel, the value of beauty, but the beauty they loved wanted life, and the life within the Church was in time to give birth to richer and fuller beauty than they knew, to beauty embodying more of truth and containing more elements of permanence.

Quintus with many another stood midway between the fervent Julian and the bitter Palladas. He loved the Homer Julian loved, but had he been able to understand his own mind, he would have realized that his thought was as godless and as hopeless as that of Palladas. But he did not understand, and the sense of life's hollowness only came on his gentle soul now and then, and was lost again in the dreamy pleasantness of living in the country and completing Homer.

CHAPTER V

AUSONIUS

Possem absolute dicere,
sed dulcius circumloquar
diuque fando perfruar.

Ep. xii. (xvi.) 7—9

THE amiable Gibbon[1] remarks that the "poetical fame of
Ausonius condemns the taste of his age." So cultured a man
as Symmachus, the Pliny of his time and the mouthpiece of Roman
paganism, declares on his honour that he ranks Ausonius' poem
on the Moselle with the works of Virgil[2]. If corroboration be
needed for the statement of a heathen, St Paulinus of Nola supplies
it. He gently deprecates being called a yokefellow of Ausonius;
"scarce Tully and Maro with thee could bear the yoke[3]." The
Emperor Theodosius writes a most friendly letter begging the poet
to favour him with copies of his poems, as the greatest authors of
olden days, "whose peer your merits make you," did by Augustus[4].
He and the Emperor Valentinian gave the poet commissions for
epigrams and so forth on the sources of the Danube, their favourite
horses and Easter, in which he was neither remarkably above nor
below the average of Poets Laureate. Finally it was to Ausonius
that Valentinian entrusted the education of his son Gratian, who
himself, when Emperor, raised his teacher to the very highest
dignities. It is clear then that by Ausonius we may in measure
judge his age.

---

[1] Gibbon vol. iii. p. 356 (Milman and Smith).
[2] Symm. *Ep.* i. 14, 5 *ita dii me probabilem praestent ut ego hoc tuum carmen
libris Maronis adjungo.*
[3] *Ep.* 11, 38.
[4] *Praef.* 3. Note *illius privatae inter nos caritatis.*

In the works of Ausonius, whatever else may be wanting, there is no lack of interesting detail about himself, his family and his friends, and on the whole it is here that the chief interest lies. He had no theories about poetry, no thought-out criticism of life, to give mankind; but sometimes trivial, always kindly, and incorrigibly and invariably leisurely, he strings together verses to please himself, to amuse his friends or to do honour to those he loved. I shall follow in the main the order of chronology in dealing with himself and his writings, and if any one blame me for occasional digressions of some length, I am sure the amiable poet himself would have to defend me.

There is probably no poet of antiquity, and few of modern days, of whose birth and connexions we know so much. The father of Symmachus amused his old age by writing a series of memorial verses for his old friends, and Ausonius did the same for his family and the professors he had known from his youth at Bordeaux. His verses, I need hardly say, are much better than those for which Avianius won such praise from his dutiful son[1]. Ausonius tells us all about his father, and not only him, but his grandparents, his sons, sons-in-law and grandsons, and, in a word and literally, "his sisters and his cousins and his aunts," regretfully owning that he does not know much about his wife's sister and knows still less of her husband, but he cannot leave them out in the cold[2]. It will hardly be necessary to enumerate them all here.

The poet's maternal grandfather, Arborius[3], came of old Aeduan stock and lived to ninety, leaving among his papers a forecast of his grandson's greatness which came true. He was an astrologer, though he preferred to conceal the fact. The maternal grandmother is described in language curiously near the account the Barrack Room Balladist gives of Gunga Din—

> For all 'is dirty 'ide
> 'E was white, clear white, inside.

The poor lady was of dark complexion and was nicknamed Maura (the Moor), "but she was not black in her soul, which was brighter than a swan and whiter than untrodden snow." She was an austere old lady, and kept her family "on the straight" (*ad perpendiculum seque suosque habuit*[4]).

---

[1] Symmachus, *Epp.* i. 2 and 3.   [2] *Parentalia* 21.
[3] *Parentalia* 4.   [4] *ib.* 5.

Ausonius' father[1] was the leading physician of Burdigala (Bordeaux) and apparently a fine man. With all his foibles Ausonius was a good son, and time and again he tells us of his father's qualities. He preferred "rather to live than to talk by the rule of the wise"; he was moderate in his ambitions, kindly, modest, a good neighbour; and he hated gossip and scandal.

> *Famam quae posset vitam lacerare bonorum*
> *non finxi et veram si scierim tacui.*

In his son's wake he too rose to glory and was Prefect of Illyricum and lived to ninety, a hale and hearty old man. The poet's mother, like a Roman lady of the good old days, had a reputation for modesty, wool-making, conjugal fidelity and good discipline.

Ausonius was born at Bordeaux about 310 A.D. He was still living in 390 according to Seeck, and as late as the end of 393 according to Peiper. Seeck however fixes no limit for his life, as he came of stock so remarkable on both sides for longevity[2].

His life, roughly, began with the reign of Constantine and ended with that of Theodosius, and covered the period of the victory of the Church over the Empire, of its struggle with Arianism and its victory there, of the reaction of Julian and the final establishment of well-defined orthodoxy. Nor are these eighty years without interest in what is called secular history. Yet his life, as mirrored in his poetry, is unruffled and serene, and this, though he lived to see his imperial pupil murdered, a tyrant established in his country, and religious persecution in learned circles. He was undisturbed by the Arian controversy. He displays indeed a certain carefulness to establish a good character as became one of rank so high, but it gives the impression that the poet was not interested in the dispute and contented himself by adopting at second-hand the resultant and victorious creed. To his religion, which though null in itself is important as a sign of the times, we shall have to recur.

He was educated at Toulouse and Bordeaux. He had, to begin with, eight years of training at Toulouse under his uncle Arborius (c. 320–328), who was called about 328 to Constantinople to bring up a son of Constantine (perhaps Constantius

---

[1] *Parentalia* 1, and *Epicedion*. Notice especially the preface to this latter piece—*post Deum semper patrem colui...alia omnia mea displicent mihi; hoc relegisse amo,* not an unworthy feeling.

[2] Seeck's *Symmachus,* Intr. p. lxxxi. Peiper's edition of Ausonius is one of the most helpful of the Teubner series.

himself). Then he returned to Bordeaux to finish his education, and after some six years he became himself a professor of " Grammar " and married Attusia Lucana Sabina.

As the life-work of Ausonius was education, and as his poems are full of reminders of it, a discussion of the subject may not be out of place[1]. Education had by his day been reduced to something like system, but in Rome's greater days it was not so. Then every man brought up his son after his own method, and the result, if not precisely culture, was generally manhood. In 92 B.C. an innovation crept in and was promptly stopped for the time[2]. A Latin school of rhetoric was opened in Rome, but forthwith closed by order of the Censors as contrary to Roman tradition (*mores majorum*). The Greeks had been and continued to be in private families the educators of Rome. They had introduced the usual subjects of study in Greece, but had not been uniformly successful with them. Philosophy the Roman reckoned to be verbiage. Geometry was useless. About Rhetoric he was doubtful. Grammar was obviously above suspicion. Grammar started by meaning "the art of speaking correctly," and then fell to illustrating itself from the poets, whom it bodily annexed, finally extending its borders beyond prose to scansion, music and even astronomy, philosophy and geometry. In fact, Grammar meant a liberal education. One regrets therefore to see the old name Grammar school dying out. Rhetoric was the art of setting forth what one knew and concealing what one did not, and was therefore more important than Grammar. It was generally agreed that the two together made an education, though men complained that the rhetorician poached on the grammarian's preserve and gradually drove him out.

At first, as I have said, the teachers were private adventurers, and some succeeded and some failed. Remmius Palaemon, we are told, made £3200 a year[3], and Orbilius, the famous teacher who flogged Horace, lived to see a long old age of penury[4].

---

[1] I am indebted to M. Boissier's *La Fin du Paganisme* for a good deal of what follows—a charming book from which I have derived much advantage in many matters.

[2] Cf. Cic. *de Or.* iii. 24, 93.

[3] Suetonius, *de illustribus Grammaticis* 23. This man was a freedman of vicious habits but of ability. He used to maintain that Virgil's use of his name in the Third Eclogue was a prophecy. He was one of Persius' teachers (*Vita Persii*).

[4] Suet. *de ill. Gramm.* 9.

Hence there was a tendency to accept positions under a scheme which, if it meant no more Palaemons, at least excluded the grosser forms of starvation. Julius Caesar recognized teachers of the liberal arts and gave them exemptions from public service. Quintilian was a professor in Rome for twenty years and rescued Roman taste by preaching Cicero[1]. Vespasian fixed the salaries in Rome at £800 a year (a very respectable minimum for a professor)[2]. Marcus Aurelius founded chairs in Athens at £380 a year in Plato, Aristotle, Epicurus and Zeno (a catholic selection of subjects), and wisely left the choice of professors to a scholarly friend—Herodes Atticus. Theodosius II. in 425 established a university at Constantinople, with thirteen professors in Latin (three Rhetoric, ten Grammar), fifteen in Greek (five Rhetoric, ten Grammar), and two in Law. One in Philosophy seemed enough in a Christian university[3]. They were forbidden private teaching, but could retire after twenty years' service.

Turning to less advanced education, we find two grades of school—the village school and what we may call perhaps the Grammar school, verging now and then into a college. These schools were widely spread. We have an interesting letter of Pliny (iv. 13) to Tacitus telling him about an arrangement for a schoolmaster at Como. Hitherto the boys had gone to school at Milan, which Pliny thought a pity, so he offered the Como people part of the salary of a teacher. This, he shrewdly remarks, was to make them take an interest in the investment of their own money in the other part of the salary. The village schoolmasters may have been prodigies of learning compared with the villagers, but they were not so regarded in the higher walks of letters. *Litterator* has not a very honourable connotation[4]. The poor man had to teach unwilling children their lessons, and St Augustine speaks feelingly of the *odiosa cantio—unum et unum duo; duo et duo quattuor*[5].

---

[1] x. 1, 112; *Ille se profecisse sciat cui Cicero valde placebit.*

[2] Suet. *Vesp.* 18, *primus e fisco Latinis Graecisque rhetoribus annua centena constituit.*

[3] Chassang remarks the absence of History (*Hist. du Roman*, p. 98), but it might be included under Grammar or Rhetoric. Staphylius, a rhetorician at Bordeaux (Auson. *Prof.* 20), knew Livy and Herodotus at any rate. The rhetorical conception of history was held by very respectable people.

[4] Suet. *de ill. Gramm.* 4; Gellius, *N. A.* xvi. 6, an amusing story. Macrobius is particularly contemptuous, *Sat.* v. 19, 31. The word is applied to sciolists in general.

[5] *Conf.* i. 13, 22. In 13, 20, he says even Latin, as taught by these *primi magistri*, was tiresome.

Ausonius writes an interesting poem to his grandson who is going to school, and writes with a good deal of sense[1]. He begins by hinting at holidays—

> The due vicissitudes of rest and toil
> Make labour easy and renew the soil.
> (*Sed requie studiique vices rata tempora servant*
> *Et satis est puero memori legisse libenter*
> *Et cessare licet.*)

But the gist is that little Ausonius (*qui nomen avi geris*) must not be afraid. It is pretty clear that the discipline in some of the schools did not fall far short of being ferocious. The grandfather urges that a master should never be a sight of terror, even if he is stern with age and rough of tongue, and his wrinkled brow bodes trouble. Let the little boy think of Achilles and Chiron who was half horse—truly a terrible schoolmaster. "So fear not you, though the school resound with much thwacking and the old man your master wear a truculent frown. 'Fear proves a soul degenerate' [a half line of Virgil from his lesson book to encourage the boy]. Be yourself and be bold, and let not the noise and the sounding rods, nor terror in the morning, make you afraid. The ferule, the birch and the tawse, and the nervous fidgeting of the benches of boys, are the pomp and show of the place. All this in their day your father and mother went through. You too will be a man some day, and I hope a great man." From this he passes on to tell him what they (grandfather and grandson) will read together at some future time. After this he speaks of his own methods of teaching, which seem much milder. "Your grandfather knows about it all, after making trial of a thousand natures in his teaching. Many in their years of infancy have I nurtured myself...With soft bidding and gentle terror I woo'd them to seek the pleasant profit at cost of trouble, to pluck the sweet fruit of a bitter root." No one can read the affectionate words Paulinus addressed to his old teacher without feeling there must have been a charm about his teaching. He calls him "a father, to whom God has willed I should owe all sacred rights and all dear names[2]."

The "grammar schools" managed by municipalities were apt to be badly and unpunctually paid. Constantine legislated in the

---

[1] *Ep.* 22. The boy was the son of Ausonius' daughter and his father was dead.

[2] Paulinus, *Ep.* xi. 91 (=xxx. in Peiper's edition of Ausonius).

teacher's interests in this matter, and Gratian, Ausonius' pupil, fixed a scale of salaries to be paid by the cities according to their size and importance. It would seem to have been the' aim of the Emperors to control the schools—a very significant fact. Some of the positions were directly filled by the Emperor, some by the Decurions (the long-suffering upper class). As these men probably had to pay the teacher, this seems just; but they needed looking after. Sometimes they would ask advice from a man of eminence, and in this way, on the recommendation of Symmachus, Augustine (not yet a saint) was sent to Milan to the great advantage of Christendom. Julian, who had particular reasons for wishing to direct education, enacted that the choice of the Decurions should be submitted to the Emperor. His more famous "schools" decree forbade Christians to teach heathen literature.

This brings us (for I have said grammar schools and colleges ran into one another) to the subjects of education in Ausonius' day. That "idolatry which is midwife to us all[1]" still ruled the schools despite Tertullian, and was still to rule them despite Jerome. It was an incalculable boon to the Church that she could not control the education of the young. They were still taught Virgil and Cicero, Horace and Terence, and gained a wider outlook on life, a larger range, and (not the least) a purer and more nervous style in consequence. Virgil haunted the minds of such men as Tertullian, Jerome and Augustine to their dying day. So we find a Christian world full of schools and colleges where Christian men trained the youth in heathen things. Literature was still heathen. The exquisites still affected to sneer at Tertullian and Cyprian, the strongest and the suavest of Latin prose writers since Tacitus and Pliny[2]. Nay more, it was unbecoming to know anything about Christianity. Dio Cassius never mentioned the word—"Jewish superstitions" served instead. So it went on. Panegyrics were addressed to Christian Emperors without a hint that the world's worship had undergone a change. Where allusions must be made to higher powers, it is *numen divinum*—"Divinity"—a colourless word[3]. Roman writers of learning and intelligence like

---

[1] Tertullian, *de Anima* 39.

[2] Lactantius, *Instit.* v. 1 of Cyprian, *denique a doctis hujus seculi quibus forte scripta ejus innotuerunt derideri solet.* He had himself heard Cyprian called Coprian.

[3] So St Cyprian, whose training was rhetorical too, uses *divina protectio, majestas, pietas, benignitas,* etc. He at all events was not "hedging," and his use of the abstract shews it was a point of style as well as a most convenient ambiguity.

Macrobius and Eutropius manage to ignore the new faith entirely, the latter mentioning it only once, the former never alluding to it even indirectly. Claudian is even more triumphantly pagan and flaunts the old gods and the altar of Victory in poems written to celebrate that family of Christian Emperors who did most to stamp out paganism, but he never alludes to Christianity except in one flippant epigram. Rutilius does not mention the name though he attacks the thing, bitterly mocking the folly of monachism and sighing over that conquest of Judaea, which had spread the Jews and their infectious superstition over the world[1].

While dealing with the relations of the schools and of literature to Christianity, we may return to Ausonius and inquire where he stood. His position is interesting, not because it is thought out, but because it is typical of a class which must have been very numerous.

Ausonius, as we have seen, was a Christian, but he does not proclaim it on the housetops. He has a group of little poems which he calls the *Ephemeris*—the day's work. He begins in bed with elaborate Sapphics to waken his slave, but when "the rhythm of Lesbian calm" fails, he gets him up at last with iambic dimeters and concludes with an intimation that he will say his prayers. This he does in dactylic hexameters, which have been pronounced to be "nervously orthodox." The Father lacks beginning and end and is older than time past or to be. The Son sits at the Father's right hand, the Maker of all things, the word of God, God the word, begotten in the time when time was not, God born of Father unborn. This is to give the lie direct to the Arian ἦν ποτε ὅτε οὐκ ἦν—there was when the Son was not—though he shews he is not a professional theologian by inserting the word "time" in the first half of the phrase, which the Arians were exceedingly careful to avoid. Point after point in his prayer may be illustrated from the creeds of the Nicenes. He prays for the longed-for ray of eternal light, "if he does not swear by gods of stone, and does recognize Thee, the Father of the Only Begotten Lord and God, and One with both the Spirit that brooded on the watery waves." Elsewhere he is as careful. Dr Hodgkin sees more in his prayer, and certainly he offers up some petitions for a manly moral life to which Horace might have said Amen, but which I think St Paul

[1] *Atque utinam nunquam Judaea subacta fuisset
  Pompeii bellis imperiisque Titi!
latius excisae pestis contagia serpunt
  victoresque suos natio victa premit.* i. 389.

would have considered not very far-going, if quite unexceptionable
so far as they go. To my mind the significant thing is the outburst
following the Amen :—*satis precum datum Deo.* "Enough of
prayers, though of course guilty mortals can never pray enough.
Give me my outdoor things, boy, I have to call on some friends."
This may be very natural, but it is hardly suggestive of a specially
deep piety. Contrast it with Prudentius' *Daily Round*, where
every part of life is touched by religion—

> *Christus et influat in pateras;*
> *seria ludicra verba jocos*
> *denique quod sumus aut agimus*
> *trina superne regat pietas.*

Thus much for the system and the subjects of study, but we
can go further. Ausonius has been admirably summed up by
M. Boissier as "an incorrigible versifier[1]," but we may readily
pardon him, for the little obituary tributes, in which, as I have
mentioned above, he commemorated his Professors, let us see a
little of the life of a professor in those days, with hints of student
life too which we can supplement from elsewhere.

He begins with a man called Minervius, a teacher of rhetoric,
who gave a thousand pupils to the bar and two thousand to the
Senate (probably round numbers). Minervius was a second Quintilian, with a torrent of language, which rolled gold and never mud.
His memory would have made him a good whist player, for after a
game at backgammon (or some game of the kind) he could repeat
the throws in order from beginning to end. He was very witty, lived
to sixty, and would have been an ideal man for a combination room,
and "if there is a future life, he is still living on his reminiscences :
and if there is not, he lived for himself and enjoyed life here[2]."

It is hardly necessary to detail them all. Two call for notice,
a father and a son, of Druid descent, Attius Patera and Attius
Delphidius by name. It is interesting to remark that where Roman
arms went, Roman culture followed, and often effected as much in
securing Roman domination[3]. At an early stage we learn that
eloquent Gaul has taught the Britons oratory, and Thule at the
world's end is thinking of engaging a rhetorician[4]. This mission of

---

[1] *F. P.* i. 175.
[2] He may very well, it is suggested, have been the *senex Garumnae alumnus*
who taught Symmachus, *Ep.* ix. 88.
[3] Cf. Tacitus, *Agricola* 21.
[4] So Juvenal vii. 148. We might add that Spain, in Quintilian of Calagurris,
taught Rome herself.

education, for which Rome does not always receive credit, is one of her noblest works. In Ausonius' day the best of Roman literature came from Gaul, Spain and Africa. The elder Attius was a cultured kindly rhetorician, who had the old age of an eagle or a horse. The younger soared higher and fared worse—

> *Felix quietis si maneres litteris*
> *opus Camenarum colens—*

but even he had alleviations in his lot, for he did not live beyond middle age and so did not see his wife and daughter turn Priscillianists and meet a sad end at the hands of a persecuting usurper. This murder, prompted by bishops and executed by Maximus to gain the support of the Church, shocked the conscience of the world, Christian or otherwise[1].

Ausonius writes a Sapphic ode to his Greek professors, confessing that he got very little from them, but generously owning it was his own fault, "because I suppose a certain dulness of perception stood in my way, and some baleful mistake of boyhood kept me from applying myself to my studies." Too true, for, though he amused himself in translating Greek epigrams, I have caught him in a false quantity here and there This perhaps served him right for writing a barbarous jargon of Greek and Latin words mixed. He only did it once, but that was once too often. Such plays of humour as κοναιστωδέα *lucrov* and οὐίνοιο βόνοιο have little to recommend their being written, nothing their publication. I am afraid Ausonius was in good company, when he did badly at the Greek. St Augustine asks, "Why did I hate Greek literature? I greatly loved Latin—not indeed what I learnt from the man who taught me the elements, but what the Grammarians teach." (He is no doubt thinking of Virgil.) Even Homer was bitter to him as a boy. The Professors of Bordeaux and Toulouse seem to have been on the whole a genial and agreeable set of men, not very great perhaps nor always very good. One had to flee to Spain owing to a damaged name (*saucia fama*), but there he took a new one and a rich wife, and let bygones be bygones. They moved from chair to chair—from Bordeaux to Constantinople, and back again—looking out for heiresses and not unfrequently finding them, for they were cultivated men and above all good company.

---

[1] See chapter xii. pp. 292—293. Cf. Pacatus, *Panegyric to Theodosius* 29...*ut unco ad poenam clari vatis matrona raperetur. Obiciebatur enim atque etiam probabatur mulieri viduae nimia religio et diligentius culta divinitas.*

Of one we are told that he did not know much, but quite enough for the poor chair he held. In general, they were all that could be expected. Paulinus complains that all they could do was to "train the tongue and fill men's hearts with falsehood and vanity"—by which he means heathen literature. They lacked, and Ausonius lacked, the root of the matter, and those who knew them best and loved them best had to admit it. Style, polish, grace, neatness were there, but not life, and its absence vitiates all the excellence they attain.

The students were much like other students, but treated their professors much worse or much better. Sometimes they would pay no fees, or would desert a teacher just before they fell due, or would leave him for one less strict. Here and there the teachers had absolutely to form a sort of "union" (συνθήκη) to safeguard themselves[1].

At Rome Theodosius had to make regulations for the students, including the production of certificates of origin, registration, police control and finally departure at the age of twenty. The students from Africa in particular were so disorderly in Rome that Valentinian ordered that if they went too much to the theatre and festivals at night, or did not generally conduct themselves according to the dignity of liberal studies, they were to be deported home[2]. At home, in their own Carthage, they made the streets terrible with their *eversiones*, interrupted classes, and in their "foul and reckless licence" did things which were punishable by law—*nisi consuetudo patrona sit*, says Augustine[3]. Freshmen seem to have divided with professors the attentions of the energetic. But on the other hand students would now and then as a mark of respect escort their professor home, or do battle hand to hand with the students of another professor to maintain the reputation of their teacher, or to kidnap a freshman for their own class. Thus Libanius went to Athens to study under a certain Aristodemus apparently, but one evening he fell into the hands of the students of Diophantus, who arrested him and kept him in durance till he would swear allegiance, when they let him go, now one of themselves[4].

Ausonius then became a professor in the university of Bordeaux

[1] See Sievers, *Libanius*, p. 30.
[2] Boissier, *L'Afrique Romaine*, c. vi. 1, p. 224.
[3] *Conf.* v. 8, 14 on students at Carthage; v. 12, 22 Rome.
[4] Sievers, *Libanius*, p. 46.

about the age of twenty-four (334), and there he married Attusia
Sabina, and very proud of her he was. Among his epigrams, which
are many, some neat, some nasty, the best are addressed to her.
One is an apology, for which there is some need. Catullus apolo-
gised on the ground that, while the poet ought to be pure, his
verses need not be, in fact were better not to be[1]. Ausonius pleads
variety as his excuse, but as his dirtiness is purely conventional
and imitative it is the harder to pardon. However to his wife
he pleads thus—

> Lais and Thais, neither name
> Of very specially good fame,
>   My wife reads in my song :
> "'Tis nothing but his way to jest,
> He makes pretence," she doth protest,
>   "He could not do me wrong."   (*Epigr.* 39.)

Probably this was the case. Another epigram bears witness to
their happy relations.

> Be life what it has been, and let us hold,
> Dear wife, the names we each gave each of old ;
> And let not time work change upon us two,
> I still your boy, and still my sweetheart you.
> What though I outlive Nestor ? and what though
> You in your turn a Sibyl's years should know ?
> Ne'er let us know old age or late or soon ;
> Count not the years, but take of each its boon.
>
>   (*Epigr.* 40.)

This tender hope was not fulfilled. She died after some nine
years of married life at the age of twenty-seven, leaving two children, a boy and a girl, their first little son having died when about
a year and a half old and learning to speak (*Parent.* 9).

At seventy, when he wrote his lines to his relatives (*Parentalia*),
Ausonius addressed her again. Her loss is still after thirty-six
years *nec contrectabile vulnus*, a wound he cannot bear touched.
"Old age permits him not to soothe his grief : it is ever sore and
ever new. Other sufferers find consolation in time's flight. Time
but the impression deeper makes…It makes his wound more cruel

---

[1] Catullus 16, 5 f. Tennyson alludes to this, saying "I don't agree with
him ; his verses fly much further than he does. There is hardly any crime
greater than for a man with genius to propagate vice by his written words"
(*Life*, vol. ii. 400). See also Boissier on Martial's apology: *Revue des deux
Mondes*, 15 July, 1900.

that he has none to whom to confide his sorrows or his joys"
(*Parent.* 9). His elevation and distinction, much as he enjoyed
them, had still this *amari aliquid.*

To his father he wrote a pleasing letter in elegiacs on the birth
of his son. "I thought that nothing could be added to my
affection, that you my honoured father should be loved the more
......What I owe as a son, a parent's care for your grandson tells
me. We must give my father the extra honour of a grandfather."
This must be the elder son, who died, and to whom he gave his
own and his father's name, Ausonius. To the younger, who lived,
he gave the name Hesperius, in which Seeck finds a variant for
Ausonius, the words being synonyms in Virgil. In the same way
the old grandmother's name Maura reappears in Melania, and
Arborius in Dryadia. Thus he called both his sons after himself.
The idea seems pretty, but, as Seeck points out, the ingenuity and
the easy invention of a new name betray that the family was not
of really high station, for then old names of the paternal and
maternal houses would have almost inevitably prevailed[1].

Years passed while Ausonius still taught at Bordeaux, missing
his wife and attaching himself instead to his children and pupils;
and in 359, when he was already forty-nine, a child was born who
was to raise him to glory. Valentinian, an officer in the army
under Constantius, had a son whom he called after his grandfather
Gratian. Nothing specially remarkable seemed to be destined for
him, and yet this child was to be an Emperor and meet a cruel
death at the hand of the usurper Maximus at twenty-four (383 A.D.).
Constantius had no son, and, beside the heir presumptive Julian,
there were none of Constantine's family living. But in four years
Julian was dead in Mesopotamia, and the wretched Jovian had
succeeded him to the shame of the Roman world. Luckily this
person soon died (Feb. 17, 364), and a month later Valentinian
was made Emperor by the soldiers.

But before we touch further on Valentinian, an interesting point
may be raised about the reign of Julian. Julian forbade the
teaching of Classics by Christians in his famous schools decree of
362. Did this affect Ausonius? His correspondence with Paulinus
seems to shew that literature came before religion in his affections,
nor does he otherwise seem to have been the stuff of which martyrs
or even confessors are made. What did he do? Victorinus, one

[1] See Seeck, *Symmachus,* Intr. p. clxxiv., n. 885.

of the most famous Latin professors of the day, at once resigned
his position. I can hardly imagine Ausonius doing the same, and
yet I cannot well account for his subsequent history if he apostatized.
Rode, in his book on Julian, opens a way out of the difficulty by
pointing out that in the West little effect was given to the pagan
reaction. Probably then Ausonius was not questioned at all about
his religion—a happy thing for him.

Valentinian, established as Emperor in the West, now called
Ausonius to undertake the education of Gratian—an action bearing
witness to the repute of the poet, or rather the professor, after his
thirty years of teaching. In his capacity as tutor he was attached to
the court, accompanying the Emperor on his expeditions against the
Alamanni, there making the acquaintance of Symmachus (369), and
writing poems at the Imperial bidding, amongst others the famous
cento from Virgil. In it by ingeniously connecting a series of lines
and half-lines and phrases from Virgil he constructed a series of
hexameters on the subject allotted him—I will not say a poem.
The method was at best trivial, and the production a disgrace to
its author as a scholar and a man.

Before we speak of his *Moselle*, it may be well to survey his
other attempts at literature. To his letters I shall return. He
was essentially a man of learning, of more learning than taste, and
like many Latin poets he liked to air it. He loved list-making
and trick-versifying, weaving into rhyme everything that went
by thrées[1] or by fours or by thirties, collecting all the monosyllabic
nouns in the language, and making 130 lines of verse each ending
in a monosyllable. " He has been at a great feast of languages
and stolen the scraps," and cooks them up into odd little messes
of his own, very ingenious but hopelessly trifling. The rhythm
of our Latin grammars

> *a abs absque coram de*
> *palam clam cum ex et e*

might have been his model. It is quite as poetical and every whit
as valuable. " Thirty days hath September," or a Latin variety of
it, is one of its gems. A line a-piece to each of the Roman
Emperors makes an historical poem. A catalogue of the cities of

---

[1] In this "poem" (*Griphus* xvi.) there is a sort of accidental confession of
faith. After Cerberus' heads, the three Punic wars, the threefold nature of
Scylla (dog, woman and fish) he magnificently concludes *ter bibe : tris numerus
super omnia, tris Deus unus.* "With three sips the Arian frustrate" represents
surely a higher piety than this.

the Empire, a series of epitaphs for the heroes of the Trojan war, and a jingle about the Zodiac, five lines here on the Greek games, a summary there of the twelve labours of Hercules, are things he loves. Very many of his single lines are forceful or epigrammatic as may be. Claudius *non faciendo nocens sed patiendo fuit:* Titus was *felix imperio felix brevitate regendi:* admirable as historic summary, even as neat verse, but hardly poetry. So in his *Moselle* he cannot resist a list of the fishes found in the river, and we have the names of fifteen varieties. In the same spirit we have a hexameter letter cataloguing all the oysters he can remember, but a humorous letter and a poem are different.

The *Moselle* was written in 370 or 371, when he was about sixty years of age. It is his best work—one might almost say his only good work, were it not for the kindliness and feeling of some parts of his *Parentalia.* It is a leisurely poem descriptive of the river and its waters, its transparent shallows, its pebble beds and swarms of fish, its banks with their vine-clad slopes and farm-crowned heights, the rustic rivalry of the peasants, the merry nonsense of boatman and wayfarer, the reflexion of everything in the water till the river seems in leaf, the boys in their boats playing at sea-fights· or fishing, and so forth. The remarkable thing is his escape from the conventional view of nature common in his day. He does not exclusively contemplate the river as an adjunct to man's environment, but takes a pleasure in it for itself. Take this picture and contrast it with similar scenes in the Greek novelists—

> cum vada lene meant, liquidarum et lapsus aquarum
> prodit caerulea dispersas luce figuras:
> quod sulcata levi crispatur harena meatu,
> inclinata tremunt viridi quod gramina fundo;
> usque sub ingenuis agitatae fontibus herbae
> vibrantes patiuntur aquas lucetque latetque
> calculus et viridem distinguit glarea muscum.   (61—7.)

Or again—

> quis color ille vadis, seras cum propulit umbras
> Hesperus et viridi perfundit monte Mosellam!
> tota natant crispis juga motibus, et tremit absens
> pampinus et vitreis vindemia turget in undis.   (192—5.)

These last two lines were particularly admired by Edward FitzGerald. The two passages shew the poet at his best. He is looking at nature at last, and, as he realizes her in his thought, his language rises with his conception. His stream is a real stream, the water flows and the weeds are waving, we can see the ribbed sand and the gleam of the pebble ; and, as so often in Virgil, the verse and the picture explain each other.

Again, the lines are happy in which he describes "the village Hampdens" the stream has known—

> *quin etiam mores et laetum fronte serena*
> *ingenium natura tuis concessit alumnis.*
> *nec sola antiquos ostentat Roma Catones*
> *aut unus tantum justi spectator et aequi*
> *pollet Aristides veteresque illustrat Athenas.* (384—8.)

Such passages by their music, their dignity, and their graciousness might warrant Symmachus in his daring comparison of their author with Virgil. But Ausonius pleased his friends, or at least himself, almost as much with that itch of his for petty scribbling (*nostra illa poetica scabies*) and the lists of triplets—if one may judge from the amount of such matter, though in justice to Symmachus it must be added that he gently quizzes his old friend about his fish.

In 375 Valentinian died and was succeeded by Gratian, and Ausonius rose to glory and his house with him[1]. Between this date and 380 all the highest offices in the West were held among the family, and the laws of the time betray the genius of Ausonius. Laws were passed in favour of the literary and medical professions and in defence of monuments of ancient art. Symmachus calls the poet *consilii regii particeps, precum arbiter, legum conditor* (*Ep.* i. 23), and indeed Ausonius' very style has been recognized in the wording of some of the laws. His son and son-in-law were given high office, and his father too became in extreme old age honorary prefect of Illyricum. Later on Ausonius was himself made prefect of the Gauls, and with this prefecture Italy was for a while united. Towards the end of 379 he gave up his prefectures, but he had climbed still higher if possible, for he had given his name as consul to the year 379. As he managed in the years remaining to him to make a good many allusions to these distinctions, and obviously felt them to be the crown of his life, we may look into them.

It was Diocletian who introduced the system of prefectures to secure the better administration of the Empire and maintain

[1] In what follows I have used Seeck's Introduction to his *Symmachus* (pp. lxxix., lxxx.)—a wonderfully thorough piece of work (*Monumenta Germaniae Historica*).

peace. The Roman world was divided into four prefectures—the East, Illyricum, Gaul, and Italy. The last two more closely concern us. Italy comprised the dioceses of Italy (in modern nomenclature Italy, the Tyrol, the Grisons, and South Bavaria), Illyricum proper (Austria between the Danube and the Adriatic, and Bosnia) and Africa (Algeria, Tunis, and Tripoli). Gaul included Spain (Spain and Morocco), the "Seven Provinces" (France up to the Rhine) and Britain (south of the Forth)[1]. It is thus seen that either prefecture was more than a modern Empire. Each was ruled by a praetorian prefect. This official in early days was a military officer in command of the praetorian guard, but with time he had developed into a civilian from whose sphere the army was jealously kept. He stood in the highest grade of senatorial rank, and was an *Illustris.* It was not generally a cheap thing to hold this rank; for though it gave immunity from local taxation, which was heavy enough, it involved other burdens, but from these retired civil servants, court physicians, and professors and a few others were relieved. This covered Ausonius. It may seem odd that professors should attain rank so high, but there was a reason, and to it we shall return.

The praetorian prefect within his prefecture was a little Emperor, responsible only to the Emperor himself, and the Emperor, by a law of Constantine, would hear no appeal against his decisions. Justice, finance, the coinage, the highways, the posts and the public granaries were under the prefect's direct control. He could appoint or dismiss at will the governors of the provinces in his prefecture. These were not the old provinces of the Republic by any means. We have seen that each of the western prefectures had three dioceses (a word the Church has borrowed from the State amongst much else), and these again were subdivided into provinces. In the prefecture of Italy there were thirty provinces, and twenty-nine in that of Gaul. Well might Lactantius growl that the provinces were "snipped to scraps[2]." Ausonius would thus have the appointment of fifty-nine provincial governors. While all other offices were annual it is easy to see why the Emperors should have preferred the prefect's tenure to be very irregular, when the prefect

---

[1] Claudian curiously gives us a metrical account of both Ausonius' prefectures in his poem on the Consulship of Manlius Theodorus; Gaul in lines 50—57, and Italy in lines 198—205. Neither is very poetical. See Gibbon, vol. iii. p. 315; Hodgkin, *Italy and her Invaders,* i. 600 ff. ; Bury, *Later Roman Empire,* i. 37.

[2] See p. 6.

was, as Dr Hodgkin sums it up, "a Prime Minister plus a Supreme Court of Appeal." Eusebius puts it, that as he is to the Emperor, so is the Eternal Son to the Eternal Father[1]. (One hesitates to say which way the Bishop's illustration is the more tremendous.)

Apart from all this real power the trappings of office were magnificent. The prefect wore a purple cloak reaching to his knee (the Emperor's went to his feet). He rode in a lofty chariot with four horses caparisoned in silver. He took precedence of everybody, and even the officers of the army bowed the knee to him.

No doubt in an administration like that of the Empire which imprinted itself upon Europe, in many matters a prefect would only have to follow a routine, to approve what was done by the officials under him. It must also be remembered that the prefect's work was not complicated by the necessity for any foreign policy, and that Rome's idea was to allow the magistrate room to work, but not opportunity for excessive individuality. Yet it has been elicited by careful study of the Theodosian Code that a special arrangement was made to relieve Ausonius. His son Hesperius was in 377 prefect of Italy. In 378 Ausonius received the prefecture of the Gauls. Very soon both prefectures were united in the hands of Ausonius— nominally, while really the burden of both fell on Hesperius, willing enough, doubtless, to bear it for his father's sake. When in the autumn of 379 Ausonius resigned the double duty, the prefectures were separated, Hesperius retaining his own[2].

The consulship however was Ausonius' special joy. To have one's name added to a list nearly nine hundred years old, and to know that through eternity the year will be officially dated *Ausonio Olybrio coss.*, must have quickened the dullest imagination. Of course it could be foreseen by no one how soon a new reckoning was to replace the old, and every Roman citizen believed in the eternity of Rome, even if Juvencus did say that like the rest of the world "golden Rome" would know an end some day. The consulship was by now a name and no more, involving social preeminence without practical power, but it was an object of ambition none the less. Who would refuse a dukedom without a pang? Julian tells us there is no one who would not consider it a prize (ζηλωτόν) to be named consul, for the honour of it *per se* reft of all else was

[1] Quoted by Bury, *L. R. E.* i. 43.
[2] See Seeck, Int. to *Symmachus*, p. lxxx. From Symm. *Ep.* i. 42, 2 it would seem Ausonius had felt his greatness a burden or had said so.

as much as any power. It was a high title for an Emperor (ἄγαλμα καὶ κόσμος), so for a subject what must it have been[1]? At his inauguration the consul gave great games and festivals, after which he retired, as Gibbon says, "to enjoy during the rest of the year the undisturbed contemplation of his own dignity."

Ausonius was so much overwhelmed by his own glory that he thought of little else for long. He wrote a sort of panegyric, a *Gratiarum Actio*, to Gratian. He had panegyrised the Emperors before, but that speech is, I believe, lost. This one is senile and very grovelling. His consulship, thanks to Gratian, involved no canvass with awkward episodes of names forgotten; no voting, no election, no bribery. The Roman people, the Campus Martius, the knights, the rostrum, the booths, the Senate, the Senate-house—all were summed up in Gratian. Nay, more, the Emperor had written a letter—honour above honours!—and had actually said he was paying a debt in making Ausonius consul—" O gilded saying of a golden mind!" (*O mentis aureae dictum bratteatum*). He contrasts himself with other Imperial tutors, is very unfair to Seneca, and remarks that Fronto was consul merely for two months in somebody else's year; and in any case he "prefers a Gratian to an Antonine." He rapturously analyses the Emperor's letter—its style and its kindness, and when he comes to Gratian's instructions that he is to wear Constantine's robes, his joy knows no bounds. He was an old man, and had bred the Emperor from a child of five; so we must try to forgive him.

It is a little hard to-day to understand why the Emperors attached so much importance to so obviously inflated and extravagant panegyrics, and consequently to the rhetoricians and professors who made them. The explanation lies in the fact that, as Julian and others who discoursed on monarchy put it, the goodwill of his subjects is the strongest buttress for a monarch. In the absence of a press subsidized by government, the panegyric conciliated public opinion, toned down awkward facts, emphasized the advantages the Emperor daily conferred on his people, extolled his character, his kindliness, his prowess, his glory, and, above all, brought out the fact that there never had been an Emperor like him[2]. (Also we may be sure there were Emperors who were able to accept the most tasteless flattery, the supply creating a demand.)

---

[1] *Cod. Theod.* ix. 40, 17 (xvi. Kal. Febr. Theodoro Cons.), the edict on Eutropius, speaks of *divinum praemium consulatus*.

[2] So Schiller, *Gesch. der r. Kaiserzeit*, ii. 447.

Such a panegyric would circulate as a pamphlet, and as the public taste was for rhetoric, and here it was at its most rhetorical, we can see how valuable the rhetorician was to an Emperor. This explains in part[1] the deference paid by Julian and others to Libanius, and the high regard the class had in general. In 392 a professor, Eugenius, was actually made Emperor by Arbogast the Frank, who modestly thought the world was not ripe for a Frankish Emperor. Even to-day we see millionaires testifying to the influence of professors by removing them if they hold by free trade or free silver or any other uncongenial heresy, but as a rule the money goes to-day to buying the press[2]. How much exactly mankind has gained by having the press instead of the professor to mould its views, we may leave optimists to compute.

The rest of the life of Ausonius need not detain us long. Gratian passed under the influence of a much stronger man—Ambrose of Milan—and met his tragic death in 383 at Lyons. Maximus[3], his murderer, held his court awhile at Trèves, where Ausonius was. The poet may have witnessed the sufferings of Priscillian and his followers, among them the widow and daughter of a former professor of Bordeaux. One wonders whether he met St Martin, and if they did meet what the rather lukewarm professor and the very militant saint thought of each other. But Ausonius may have got safely back to Bordeaux before Maximus had to deal with either Priscillian or Martin. At all events at Bordeaux he spent his declining years, versifying as ever. Theodosius demanded verse of him, and he wrote it—not that he had anything to say, but Caesar's bidding was inspiration enough. (Theodosius was not a man to be trifled

---

[1] Symm. i. 20 (to Ausonius), *iter ad capessendos magistratus saepe litteris promovetur.* At the same time there seems to have been some genuine respect for learning, in spite of Ammianus' gloomy views.

[2] The position of a professor does not seem to be as secure in the United States as in England. The millionaire founder is too fond at times of having his own views taught.

[3] See Sulpicius, *Dial.* ii. 6; iii. 11 on Maximus, p. 291 f. Ausonius only alludes to him in congratulating Aquileia on having seen his end:

> *solveret exacto cui sera piacula lustro*
> *Maximus, armigeri quondam sub nomine lixa.*
> *felix quae tanti speculatrix laeta triumphi*
> *punisti Ausonio Rutupinum Marte latronem.*

> *Ordo Urbium* 9.

Rutupiae, Maximus' native place, is Richborough, near Sandwich, in Kent. If he had succeeded, Ausonius might have accepted him as Symmachus unhappily had already.

with—*blando vis latet imperio.*) His profession is at least in-
genuous

> *non habeo ingenium: Caesar sed jussit, habebo.*

He was still busy with extracts, *tours de force,* " April, June, and
dull November," but we shall find it more interesting to turn to
his correspondence.

I am afraid the letters of Ausonius can hardly be called very
interesting. Some are better than others, but as a rule he has
little to say and spends all his energies on his phraseology. Pliny's
was the first great series of letters written for publication, which
has reached us. After his day letter-writing became a regular
branch of rhetoric, and letters are no longer so much letters as a
form of literary parade. The nine hundred letters of Symmachus
are characterized according to Gibbon by a " luxuriancy, consisting
in barren leaves without fruits and even without flowers." Such
a criticism would no doubt have shocked their amiable author, but
it is just and applies to most of the surviving collections of the
day, apart from the theologians' epistles which are often in reality
treatises.

The correspondence of Ausonius (if I may borrow an epigram
of the combination room) is "like Hollandaise sauce—a lot of
butter and no flavour." Ausonius compliments Symmachus, and
is very modest : and Symmachus is very modest and compliments
Ausonius, till the reader feels that Symmachus for once has, in one
of his apologies, hit the nail on the head—*Videbor mutuum scabere.*
" Come and see me and bring a cart load of Pierian furniture (list
herewith) " is the burden of a number of these letters—the
characters figuring as " Cadmus' brunettes " (*Cadmi nigellae filiae,
Cadmi filiolis atricoloribus*). We must except from this condem-
nation the letters above-mentioned to his father on his son's birth
and to his grandson. To these may be added the letter to Paulinus
about the steward who, after failing in his proper duties, has gone
off trading, "enriching himself and impoverishing me" (*se ditat
et me pauperat*), and has got into trouble at Hebromagum. Here
at all events Ausonius had something to say at last.

But most interesting after all is the group which ends the
volume—the correspondence with Paulinus. Paulinus was a
favourite pupil of Ausonius, on which M. Boissier cruelly remarks
" On n'est guère disposé aujourd'hui à l'en féliciter," but he himself

thought it had been his making[1]. Certainly he owed his consulship to Ausonius' influence. He was a distinguished literary man as things went; his only fault was, according to Boissier, to be "eternal"; and in every way all promised well for his future. Whether it were his Spanish wife Therasia, or the influence of St Martin that was to blame, he suddenly forsook the world. He withdrew first to Spain and then to Italy, where he settled by the tomb of St Felix at Nola and wrote a birthday ode to the saint every year. Ausonius was puzzled to imagine what could have induced a man who had drawn so much from him thus to abandon all that during nearly eighty years had been to himself the interest and the worth of life[2]. He had left the Muses—for what? Ausonius wrote him letter after letter in a rambling, senile, affectionate way to win him back : picturing agreeably enough his own joy when his prodigal returns, and rather querulously asking why he was treated so. Well he might, for no answer came for some years, as his letters had gone astray (a curious illustration of the rather haphazard postal service of the day for private people)[3].

At last we hear from Paulinus, who explains the mishap to Ausonius' letters, and then sets forth why he has forsaken the world—*mens nova mi, fateor, mens non mea.* He writes kindly but clearly—and at enormous length. He has found something Ausonius' Muses could not give. He has learnt that life means more than an opportunity to versify Suetonius, as he had been doing in a desultory way. He owes Ausonius more than he can say—let Ausonius then be glad he has trained a servant for Christ. Rhetoric and rhyming have their place, but they cannot save the soul : that lies beyond a professor's power, and still it is life's end. So long as he lives, he must live for Christ, and prepare for the great day of the coming of the Lord. For " He who sits on the eternal Father's throne at His right hand, is set as a King over all, and, when the years have passed, He shall come to judge all nations with equal justice." This thought, he says, haunts him, as we know it did Sulpicius, his friend and correspondent, who

---

[1] It was a friendship of the second generation, as their fathers had been friends before them. *Ep.* 27, 106.

[2] The Christian leaders of the day understood Paulinus better and heralded him as a great example; see Ambrose, *Ep.* 58, etc.

[3] Synesius' correspondence may also illustrate this, *Ep.* 123 : Syn. was for two years away from home and the letters of Troilus were not forwarded to him but awaited his return. *Ep.* 129, Syn.'s letters to Pylaemenes (in Constantinople) went to Alexandria (probably the proper way) and after being held there or sent astray for a year came back to their writer in Cyrene.

fell into millenarism, and the poet Prudentius, who again and again tells of the Last Judgment.   He fears lest his soul,

si forte recluso
increpitet tuba vasta polo, non possit in auras
regis ad occursum levibus se tollere pinnis
inter honora volans sanctorum milia caelo.

If his course pleases Ausonius, let him congratulate his pupil; if not, *Christo tantum me linque probari.*

What Ausonius may have thought of this response, we are not told.   I doubt if he could have really understood the mind of his friend at all.   Paulinus was not a great man by any means—a dull, wordy, worthy creature.   Yet the weight in the correspondence lies with him, and one feels at once the contrast between the amiable inanity of the old poet and the glowing devotion of the younger man.   Ausonius stood for the past, so far as he understood himself.   But a new spirit was at work in the world, and a new age was beginning.   Prudentius represents this new age best among his contemporaries; and whether one weigh them as makers of music, as poets, as thinkers, or as men, Prudentius is greater than Ausonius every way.   Hippocrene was exhausted, and the poets, if they are to serve mankind, must go to Jordan[1].

Yet, with all his amiable doggerel and list-making, Ausonius has been set down as the first of French poets, as Sulpicius is of French prose-writers, for after all he wrote the *Moselle.*

---

[1] I may be allowed to adapt Fuller's happy epigram on Sternhold and Hopkins, who had "drunk more deep of Jordan than of Helicon." Juvencus had already prayed that his mind might be sprinkled with the pure waters of *dulcis Jordanis*, but, as all his readers know, he had drunk almost as deep of Mincius.

CHAPTER VI

WOMEN PILGRIMS

Non Hierosolymis fuisse sed Hierosolymis bene vixisse laudandum est.
JEROME, *Ep.* lviii. 1

THE pilgrim movement of the fourth century was not un-heralded. From the days of the earliest Greek mariners, who explored the new world of Italy and Sicily and voyaged to the old world of the Nile, a never-ceasing series of travellers had given their tales to mankind. The conquests of Alexander had thrown open fresh regions for adventure, and when the Romans with the widening of their empire came more and more under the influence of Greek literature, travel was at once safe and suggestive. The scenes of the Trojan war, and of the great wars of historical Greece, the spots hallowed by memories of Socrates, of Euripides and the famous names of the past, the monuments of ancient art and not least the holy places, where for generations men had by the mysteries found access to the unseen, all drew to themselves the more thoughtful and cultured among the Romans. Nor were the motives that took men abroad only those of the sight-seer, the scholar and the pious antiquary. New cults, which had not the associations of ancient Greece, now and again prescribed the penitential pilgrimage. Germanicus and Hadrian wandered in the course of their official progresses to one and another famous place, and from time to time were initiated into the ancient mysteries of Eleusis or Samothrace. Against this nothing could be justly said, but it was another thing when the priests of Isis bade Roman ladies go to the far bounds of Egypt and fetch waters from burning Meroe to sprinkle in the goddess' shrine in Rome[1].

[1] Juvenal vi. 527.

The novels of the early centuries of our era, if they do not aim at presenting the life of their time, at least betray some of its interests. Their scenes and dates are vague, but their adventures and travels are vivid. Pirates and Ethiopians and hair-breadth 'scapes crowd one another in quick succession. It is a poor heroine who is never kidnapped. So we range from Tyre to Alexandria and far beyond, and meet strange men with black hearts and black faces, and the heroine comes home unscathed. And every here and there the divine is introduced with a lavish hand, and thunders and lightnings and inspired dreams avert many an awful crisis. Stories like that of Apuleius are less common, good novels perhaps being a small minority in every age. The popular taste demands a certain style of fiction, and so it leaves behind it evidence on which posterity will condemn it. The novels are poor but they prove the interest felt in travel.

How easy, as compared with former days, travel was under the early Empire, is shewn by the rapid spread of Christianity[1]. There was universal peace, the great roads were kept in repair and free from brigands, one rule and two languages were universal instead of the many formerly prevailing, and Christians passed quietly in their obscurity from shore to shore. Their story was new and for the present, for the end of the world was at hand ; and though, as time went on, it included more of the future, it had hardly as yet a past to waken historic sentiment. And quite apart from this, the Christian world had scant leisure for retrospect. Men and women had ever to be ready for sudden travel, but it was to escape persecution, and wherever it scattered them they were more prompted to preach than to dream. Still as early as 212 a man, Alexander by name, is recorded to have made a journey from Cappadocia to Jerusalem to pray and to study the geography of "the places[2]." A little later (about 216) Origen, commenting on St John i. 28, remarks that "he is convinced the right reading is not Bethany but Bethabara, for he has visited the places to follow out the footsteps of Jesus and His disciples and the prophets[3]." In his reply to Celsus, he appeals to the evidence of the cave and manger of Bethlehem, which would seem to imply that he had seen them[4].

[1] See Ramsay, *St Paul the Traveller and the Roman Citizen*, p. 352, for an interesting account of Roman Imperial policy in promoting ease of communication within the Empire.
[2] Eusebius, *Eccles. Hist.* vi. 11.
[3] Origen, *Comm. Joh.* tom. vi. 24 (40).
[4] Origen, *in Celsum*, i. 51.

With the victory of Constantine a new age began, an age of more freedom and also in general of less spirituality. Foreign ideas had filtered already into the Church, now they streamed in, and the Christian was almost directed (in spite of such men as Augustine) to the external.

Christianity had given women a new honour in the world and a new outlook on life. From the first it was asserted that in Christ was neither male nor female, and though the Church in deference to old prejudice frowned on her performing some of the more exalted Christian duties, forbidding her the priestly office and trying to discredit the story of Thecla's baptisms[1], woman took her place with man in the maintenance and the extension of the faith by martyrdom and Christian living. The Church delighted to contrast the swarms of Christian virgins with the reluctant though well-paid Vestals[2], and it was in virginity that woman's great opportunity seemed to lie. It had taken asceticism some three centuries to capture the Church, a clear proof in a world, which could conceive of no other type of holiness, that it was not the original conception of the Church's Founder and His immediate followers.

While more than one of the great Fathers found it desirable to write treatises on the dress, the veils and the general deportment of Christian women devoted to the celibate life[3], it was not till the fourth century that there appeared so ardent a pleader for the convent and the extreme rigour of asceticism as St Jerome. The saint was a great scholar but a greater rhetorician. Rhetoric indeed formed a large part of the training of all the fathers of this century, but Jerome's rhetoric has neither the idle wordiness of Paulinus nor the spiritual intensity of Augustine. He has no lack of ideas, but they are generally apt to be superficial. He was rhetorician rather than scholar, and scholar rather than thinker.

Jerome is never so copious or so coloured as when he dilates on the glory of celibacy and the poverty, the pettiness and the ignominy of married life. There can be little doubt that the life of Pagan society in Rome was a dull round of splendour. It had culture, it had wealth, it had splendid lineages, but it lacked inspiration, life and perhaps intelligence[4]. But it is of Christian society that

[1] Cf. Tertullian, *de Bapt.* 17.
[2] *E.g.* Prudentius, *adv. Symm.* ii. 1063 and following.
[3] See Benson, *Cyprian* I. xii. p. 51 f.
[4] In Ammianus Marcellinus we read an indictment of Roman society, as scathing as anything of St Jerome's and more amusing (xiv. 6; xxviii. 4). The letters of Symmachus shew us Rome from within, a weary spectacle.

Jerome speaks so harshly. "I would not have you consort with matrons," he writes to Eustochium, aged seventeen[1], "I would not have you approach the houses of nobles; I would not have you often see what in contempt you renounced to remain a virgin...Will you, the spouse of God, hasten to the wife of a man? Learn here a holy pride; know you are better than they. Nor do I desire you to avoid those alone, who are puffed up by their husbands' glories, whom flocks of eunuchs surround, and in whose clothes mines of gold beaten to thread are woven; but avoid those too, whom necessity, and not their choice, has made widows—not that they should have wished their husbands to die, but that they did not gladly catch at the chance of a life of purity. Though they have changed their garb, their pride is unchanged. Before their litters march the ranks of eunuchs; their rouged cheeks and their plumpness suggest, not that they have lost, but that they are looking for husbands. Their houses are full of flatterers, full of banquets..." and he goes on to say the flatterers are clergy kept by a retaining fee. He sums up his position toward marriage, a little below;— "I praise marriage, I praise wedlock, but because they bear me virgins; I gather from the thorn the rose, from the earth the gold, from the shell the pearl[2]." A married woman may thus rise to be "mother-in-law of God" (*socrus Dei*).

The woman then who would live the perfect life must be a virgin, and more, a nun secluded from the world and knowing only the cloister and the church. In one of his letters (cvii.) Jerome sketches the education he would wish given to a little girl dedicated by her parents to the nunnery from her birth. The little Paula must not learn worldly songs (probably nursery jingles) but the Psalms. Her only play is to be with wooden or ivory letters of the alphabet. She is to be gently taught to read and love books, but she must not use baby-words (*dimidiata verba*)[3] or wear gold or purple. A grave nurse must teach her to chant Alleluia to her grandfather[4]. Her ears are not to be pierced for ear-rings, her face must know no white lead or rouge or any other cosmetic, her neck no gold or pearls, her head no gem, her hair no red dye—all

---

[1] Jerome, *Ep.* xxii. 16.
[2] *Id. ib.* 20.
[3] A celibate view, with which contrast Minucius Felix 2. 1 *et quod est in liberis amabilius adhuc annis innocentibus et adhuc* dimidiata verba *temptantibus, loquellam ipso offensantis linguae fragmine dulciorem.*
[4] He was a pagan, a friend of Symmachus, Publilius Caeionius Caecina Albinus by name, and he appears in Macrobius' *Saturnalia.* See Seeck, *Symmachus*, pp. clxxv.—clxxx.

which things savour of hell. Her only walk is to be to church.
She is not to eat before strangers, and she should drink no wine.
Musical instruments she must not touch. Latin and Greek, reading
and praying, psalm-learning and wool-work (not silk or embroidery)
should afford her day variety. Perhaps she had better not have
baths at all, for it is not pleasant for her to see herself unrobed[1].
How can all this be managed? It would be hard in Rome, so the
little maid had better be despatched to her grandmother and aunt in
Bethlehem, Paula and Eustochium.

The life here pictured might in time be tedious for a scholar.
The monks of the middle ages found it so. What must it have
been for a child, for a young girl? There is pleasure in the healthy
exercise of a natural function, and beings created to be active must
have chafed under such a vegetable life. One woman, of whom
St Jerome tells us[2], could not face it. Her name was Fabiola and
she was twice married. On the death of the second husband she
sold all and "was the first of women to found a hospital (νοσοκομεῖον),
in which to gather the sick from the streets and cherish poor folks'
bodies wasted by sickness and hunger." She nursed them herself
awhile and then suddenly astonished people by going off to Jerusalem. Another, Paulina, daughter of the more famous Paula, built
a ξενοδόχιον or guest-house in Portus[3].

But a more frequent resource to escape the dulness of secular
or religious life in Rome was the pilgrimage. Movement, change of
scene, novel situations and fresh society must have been salvation
to many a weary soul—from stagnation at least and perhaps from
loss of reason or character. It may be permissible to say that the
pilgrimage involved a certain amount of masculine society, if it were
only that of Egyptian monks. At times it would mean adventure
and real danger and a military guard. Beyond such motives,
however, there were higher ones, a genuine interest in following
intelligently the life of our Lord in the land where He had lived,
and in marking every spot associated with any episode of His
history; a desire to meditate and to pray with the impress on one's
mind of the holy places, where so many great ones of the past had
prayed and had been heard; a feeling that "it was part of the faith
to worship where the feet of the Lord had stood, and to see as if in
all their freshness the traces of the nativity, the Cross and the

---

[1] A monkish fancy shared by Antony and Amun according to the novelist
(*V. Ant.* 47. 60).
[2] *Ep.* lxxvii. 6.　　　　　[3] *Ep.* lxvi. 11.

passion[1]." Thus were combined the student's hope to understand and the mystic's to enter more fully into the life of the Lord. Over and above all this, we must remember that honour was being directed more and more to saints and martyrs everywhere, that prayer was paid at their shrines and martyries, and that their aid was reckoned a factor in the spiritual life[2]. And further a suspicious importance began to attach to relics of the saints, and the pilgrim to the East was often able to collect them. For example, Cyril of Jerusalem[3] and Paulinus of Nola both testify to the practice of pilgrims taking away fragments of the Holy Cross, the latter assuring us that the wood miraculously replenishes itself. St Silvia tells us incidentally of one covetous man who made a pretext of kissing the cross and surreptitiously bit out a mouthful as a relic[4].

Egeria

Of St Jerome's own residence in Palestine and of the visit paid to him at Bethlehem by Sulpicius' friend Postumian, I do not here speak. My subject is rather the pilgrimages of women, and I have to deal with Melania, with Paula and her daughter Eustochium, and especially with St Silvia of Aquitaine. All these were in Palestine between 381 and 388, and by comparing their stories we may get a clearer idea of the spirit of their times.

Egeria

Melania[5] was a Roman lady of noble origin, the daughter and granddaughter of Consuls. She early "suffered marriage" and was soon a mother. After a few years of married life, she lost her husband, and before he was cold or, at least, buried, two of three sons also died. "I am going," says St Jerome, "to tell a thing incredible, but, before Christ, true. Not a tear-drop fell; she stood immovable, and falling at Christ's feet, as she were laying hold on Him Himself, she smiled. 'More easily,' said she, 'can I serve thee now, O Lord, in that thou hast relieved me of so great a burden'." She came to Rome with one surviving infant boy, whom

---

[1] Jerome, *Ep.* xlvii. 2.

[2] Cf. Prudentius, περὶ στεφ. xii. 59, on pilgrims to St Peter and St Paul in Rome; and Sulpicius Severus, *Dial.* i. 3 *loca visitare sanctorum et praecipue ad sepulcrum Cypriani martyris adorare.*

[3] Cyril Jer. *Catech. Ill.* x. 19; xiii. 4; and Paulinus, *Ep.* xxxi. 6.

[4] Dio Cassius 51. 16 says that at Alexandria Augustus saw the body of Alexander the Great and broke off a piece of the nose. This story, most probably untrue, yet shews the early prevalence of the passion for keepsakes. Jerome, *In c.* 23 *Matth. l.* iv. says such things as fragments of the Cross or little gospels were worn as amulets by *superstitiosae mulierculae* after the manner of the ancient Pharisees. (Neander.)

[5] Her name is variōusly given as Melanius, Melania and Melanium. See Paulinus, *Ep.* xxix.; Jerome, *Epp.* xxxix. 4; xlv. 4; and *Chron.* ad an. Christi 377 for her story.

"she flung into the bosom of Christ," says Paulinus. Jerome more prosaically says she left him to the Praetor Urbanus, after transferring her property to him[1]. Then, though friends opposed and it was the middle of winter, she set sail for the East, taking Egypt on her way to Jerusalem, and there she stayed for some five and twenty years (374—399). Her virtues, of which humility was the chief, won her the name of a new Thecla. She lived through the Arian persecution of Valens, who fell at Adrianople in 378 ; she was arrested but dismissed from the court, and fed large numbers of monks through the troublous days[2]. When Jerome came to the East, she lived in close friendship with him and Paula, avoiding baths and unguents, and practising fasting and filthiness. At the end of the century she returned to Italy, and after landing at Naples went to Nola, where Paulinus says her arrival caused a great sensation, a great throng of people in purple and silk escorting her in her rags. She gave Paulinus a tunic of lamb's wool, and he read to her Sulpicius' life of St Martin, from which she might have learned that even at home life might be lived well. The tunic and part of a fragment of the true cross, given her by John bishop of Jerusalem, were passed on to Sulpicius. This "woman, if so manly a Christian may be called a woman[3]," lived some twenty years longer, probably in Palestine.

Melania's departure to Palestine attracted much attention in Rome, but perhaps even more was excited by Paula who left there in 382—3. Paula[4] was the daughter of Rogatus, who claimed a proud descent from Agamemnon, and of Blaesilla, as proudly descended from Scipios and Gracchi. She was married at sixteen to Julius Toxotius, a descendant of Aeneas and the Julii, who, as became one sprung from Venus, was true to paganism. She bore him five children, four girls and a boy, and then he died, leaving her for a while inconsolable, till she turned to the religious life. In

---

[1] Antony (*Vita Ant.* 36) represented μνήμη τῶν οἰκείων as actually a temptation of the devil. Sulpicius (*Dial.* i. 22) has a tale confirming this, how the devil tempted a monk to return and convert his wife and son.

[2] A footnote of Gibbon's may be transcribed (vol. iv. p. 316): "The monk Pambo made a sublime answer to Melania who wished to specify the value of her gift :—Do you offer it to me, or to God? If to God, HE who suspends the mountains in a balance need not be informed of the weight of your plate. (Pallad. h. Laus. 10.)"

[3] The phrase is borrowed from Paulinus. Cf. Porphyry, *ad Marcellam* c. 33, μηδὲ γυναῖκα ἴδῃς σαυτήν.

[4] Jerome, *Ep.* cviii. 3 and following. Also xlv. 4 *Nullae aliae Romanae urbi fabulam praebuerunt nisi Paula et Melanium, quae contemptis facultatibus, pignoribusque desertis, crucem Domini quasi quoddam pietatis levavere vexillum.*

382 a synod of bishops from East and West was held in Rome under Pope Damasus, and intercourse with some of these gave Paula new ideas, and "she yearned to go to the desert of the Pauls and the Antonies." Her eldest daughter was dead, the second married, and the third Eustochium practically dedicated to virginity, but the fourth was of marriageable age and had no mind for celibacy and joined with the son, the little Toxotius, in imploring their mother to stay, at least for a while. "Yet she raised dry eyes to heaven and overcame love of children with love of God. She knew not she was a mother, that she might prove herself Christ's handmaid."

Before following her on her journey, we may learn her feelings from a letter she wrote[1]. She was obeying, so she said, the teaching of Scripture, wherein God had said to Abraham, "Get thee out from thy country." Had Christ not loved Jerusalem, He had never wept over it. The Ark of the Covenant has indeed passed from it, but the Lord's sepulchre is there; "and as often as we enter it, we see the Saviour there, lying in the linen; and if we wait a while, we see the Angel sitting at His feet, and at His head the napkin rolled together." "In every place we venerate the tombs of the martyrs, and put the sacred ashes to our eyes, and if we may we touch them with our lips too." How many holy men have felt they had not received "the finishing touch in virtue, unless they had adored Christ in those places, whence first the Gospel had gleamed from the cross"? And what can be said of the place of the Nativity?

So to the Holy Land she went and left her son behind in Rome —to grow up a staunch heathen. If in later life he became a Christian (a point not certain), he did not owe his conversion to his mother. Paula sailed away, passed between Scylla and Charybdis, and threaded Virgil's Cyclades—

sparsasque per aequor
Cycladas, et crebris...freta consita terris[2].

At last she reached Antioch, and "the noble lady, who had once been borne on the hands of eunuchs, set out on a donkey."

---

[1] This is printed among St Jerome's letters, *Ep.* xlvi.

[2] Jerome quotes the *Aeneid* iii. 126. When the Angel with the scourge told him "*Ciceronianus es, non Christianus,*" nothing luckily was said about Virgil (*Ep.* xxii. 30). See Comparetti, *Vergil in the Middle Ages*, tr. pp. 82—3 for the saint's fluctuation in his feelings about the poet. In the short account of the travels which follows, I have made a mosaic of pieces from *Ep.* cviii. especially §§ 7, 8, 9, 14, 15.

Sarepta and Elijah's tower, the sands of Tyre where Paul had knelt, Megiddo, Caesarea and the house of Cornelius and the rooms where Philip's four daughters slept, Joppa whence Jonah sailed and where (though this is another story[1]) Andromeda was tied to the rock, Beth-horon, Aijalon, Gibeon,—all these and other places she saw, and came to Jerusalem, where "prostrating herself before the cross, she worshipped as though she saw the Lord hanging there." "She entered the tomb of resurrection, and kissed the stone the angel rolled away ; and the actual place where the Lord had lain, as one thirsty coming to waters long prayed for, she licked with a believer's mouth." She ranged over Palestine, passed through Egypt to the Nitrian desert and threw herself at the feet of the monks, to whom she gave gifts as to the Lord. Though she would have liked to stay with them, she returned to Bethlehem to build cells and lodgings for pilgrims by the road where Mary and Joseph found no shelter. This was her rest because it was the birthplace of her Lord. Here she continued till her death, reading the Bible in Hebrew and Greek, afflicting herself with various austerities, and doing despite to the face which, against God's precept, she had formerly decorated with all sorts of cosmetics. It was her prayer that she might die a beggar, and at last she attained what she wished and left her daughter deeply in debt, "as she still is, though she hopes, not by her own strength, but of Christ's mercy, to be able to pay."

When we pass from Paula to Silvia, there is a marked relaxation of tension. We are out of the region of extravagance and hysterics, and in the company of a lady who is quiet and has no rhetoric. It must be premised, however, that we are on less certain ground, for it may be that we are dealing not with a single person but with two. The case stands thus. There exists a considerable part of a narrative of three years' residence and travel in and about Palestine. It is avowedly written by a woman, seemingly from Gaul, for she comes "from the ends of the earth," she compares the Euphrates and the wash of its waters with the Rhone, the Red Sea with the Ocean, and its fish with those of the "Italic sea." She held some office in a monastery, to the sisters of which she wrote ; her journey ended in Constantinople where she was detained for some unspecified reason ;

---

[1] *Ut aliquid perstringam de fabulis poetarum* says Jerome. See Dr G. A. Smith, *Hist. Geography of the Holy Land*, pp. 162—4, on the linking of Andromeda's dragon to St George, and of St George to England, the whole story centring at Lydda a little way up the country.

and the courtesy and attention shewn her by military authorities in Egypt suggest that she was a person of some consideration. In view of all these facts Gamurrini, who discovered the manuscript in 1884, identified her with St Silvia of Aquitaine, who was in the East at the very same time as our pilgrim shews that she was, and whose brother was Rufinus, minister of the Emperors Theodosius and Arcadius at Constantinople from 384 to 396. When this man was murdered in 396, his widow and daughter were despatched to Jerusalem. Such a connexion would explain the ease of our pilgrim's travels and her lingering at the capital. The identification has been generally accepted, though Dr Bernard points out a curious little divergency. The pilgrim of the manuscript remarks that because it was impossible to ride up Mt Sinai, she had to go up on foot (MS p. 32), but the St Silvia of Palladius boasted she never was carried. Again, this Silvia, he says, never bathed, but our pilgrim does not betray personal asceticism. We may also remark that while the Silvia of Palladius was "a most learned lady," and read Origen and Basil and so forth, and while for her Rufinus of Aquileia[1] made a translation into Latin of the Clementine *Recognitions*, our pilgrim, though very well read in Scripture[2] and well informed in sacred geography and much interested in ritual, wrote a Latin so barbarous and so ungainly as to suggest that her literary attainments were slight indeed. Accordingly, if we agree that our pilgrim is St Silvia, we must bear in mind that her own narrative deals only with her travels in the East where we find her first at the foot of Sinai, and that all other knowledge of her connexions and subsequent history comes from outside sources.

Aquitaine was in the fourth century, and indeed later, one of the most cultured and most Roman of all lands of the Empire. The names of Ausonius and Sulpicius Severus stand for much in the history of the century's literature, and a brightness and a clear air hang over their country. From Elusa (Eauze), the poet Claudian tells us, came Rufinus and therefore presumably his sister. Of her early life we know nothing, but if we trust Palladius she was born somewhere about the date of the Nicene Council 325, for she says (according to him) that she was in her sixtieth year when travelling in Egypt. She herself tells us why she took her pilgrimage to

---

[1] Not her brother, but a man set over a convent of fifty virgins established by Melania in Jerusalem.

[2] It may be remarked that she shews no trace of Jerome's revision of the Latin Bible. So Dr Bernard on *St Silvia*, p. 34.

Palestine. She went to pray (*orationis gratia*, pp. 44, 47, 55) at
the bidding of God (*jubente deo*, p. 40), and also to learn for herself
(*tunc ergo ego, ut sum satis curiosa, requirere cepi*, p. 46). She
regarded it as a mark of divine grace that she was able to go so far
and see so much—"though I ought ever to give thanks to God in
all things, I will not say how much in the case of all that He has
bestowed on me in counting me worthy, unworthy and undeserving
as I am, to travel through all these places far beyond my merit"
(p. 36). On the way home, she says, "I crossed the sea to
Constantinople thanking Christ our God that to me unworthy and
undeserving He had deigned to give such grace, that is, not only
the will to go, but had deigned to give the power to traverse what
I would and to return again to Constantinople" (p. 55).

The record of her outward journey is lost, if it ever existed, but
our last reference may give us a hint. There were various possible
routes from Aquitaine to Palestine. Sulpicius Severus' friend,
Postumian, sailed from Narbonne to Africa, visiting Cyprian's grave
at Carthage, and from there to Alexandria. The first sail took him
four to five days, the second longer, for they had to land somewhere
on the coast under stress of weather, and from there they had a
voyage of seven days. Thence to Jerome at Bethlehem and back,
and then to the Nitria and Sinai. But Silvia's expressions[1] and her
account of her visits to all the churches and shrines of Constantinople on her return, shew that it had been her starting-point for
her eastern journey.

While of course she could have gone to Constantinople by sea,
it is interesting to note that another pilgrim from her country has
left us a record of his long overland route from Bordeaux to Jerusalem. Who he was is not known, but he dates his pilgrimage by
the consuls of 333, and gives the name of every stopping-place on
his way and occasional summaries of distances in miles—in leagues
from Bordeaux to Toulouse[2]. He passed through Silvia's town of
Elusa, and she may have followed his route—this of course is mere
conjecture. Picking out the points at which he adds up his miles,
we find he went by Arles, Milan, Aquileia, Sirmium (Mitrowitza),
Serdica (Sophia) and so to Constantinople, and he reckons that so
far he travelled 2221 miles, and made 112 halts.

The route from Constantinople was by Libyssa (where, confusing

[1] Cf. pp. 47, 55.
[2] An interesting survival. In parts of French Canada the *habitants* still
reckon by *lieues*.

Rome's greatest foe and the Emperor's brother, he notes "Here lies King Annibalianus who once was King of the Africans"), Nico-medeia, Nicaea (no word of the Council of eight years before), the farm of Pampatus ("whence come the horses for the magistrates"), Tyana ("hence was Appollonius (*sic*) the Magician"), Tarsus ("hence was the apostle Paul"), through Cilicia to Antioch, and so by Tyre and Caesarea to Jerusalem. He travelled, according to Professor Ramsay[1], mainly along the military road used by the Byzantine armies to reach Syria from Constantinople. Silvia tells us (p. 55) that she returned to Constantinople *faciens iter jam notum*—either a route already "described to you" or "familiar to me"—through the provinces of Cilicia, Cappadocia, Galatia and Bithynia, and the towns she mentions are Antioch, Tarsus, Mopsucrene (which with the Bordeaux pilgrim she calls Mansocrenae) and Chalcedon. All these names occur in reverse order in the Itinerary. It is therefore likely that she followed in the main the older pilgrim's course. On her way back she made a deviation to see St Thecla's martyry —a three days' journey from Tarsus by Pompeiopolis (Soli) and Corycus to Seleucia in Isauria, so that she may have made similar excursions on her way out. The Bordeaux pilgrim reckons 1159 miles and 58 stopping-places between Constantinople and Jerusalem. The journey there and back took him seven months in all. He left Chalcedon on May 30 and was back in Constantinople on December 26.

Her journal (if one may so call it) was written apparently for sister nuns in Aquitaine, whom she addressed in affectionate terms —"ladies of my soul," "ladies, my light," "your affection[2]," "venerable lady sisters." It would seem to have been put into its present form after her return to Constantinople, but from records previously made by her. Sir Charles Wilson, who describes her geography of Sinai as minute and correct, concludes—"I have been much struck by the accuracy of St Silvia's topographical descriptions; they are evidently those of a person who has seen the places described, and have apparently been compiled from notes written on the ground." If her geography is accurate, her grammar is not, and her style abounds in repetitions and awkward constructions, to

---

[1] See note to Bordeaux Itinerary, in the Palestine Pilgrims Society's texts.

[2] Cf. p. 56, *domnae lumen meum cum haec ad vestram affectionem darem.* This is partly convention. Symmachus addresses his son as *amabilitas vestra* (*Epp.* vii. 3, 6, etc.) and his daughter as *domna filia* (vi. 80); Ausonius, his old friend, the professor and prefect, as *eruditio tua* (i. 31).

say nothing of peculiar spellings, which shew a Latin wearing down towards French.

After so long a preface, it will be best to transcribe at length a passage, illustrative at once of the Saint's methods of grammar and travel and thought. It comes from the opening of what is left of her narrative and describes her visit to Sinai.

" We then entered the Mount late on the Sabbath (= Saturday), and coming to certain cells the monks who dwelt there received us there quite kindly, shewing us every kindness. For there is also a church there with a presbyter. There then we abode that night, and thence rather early on the Lord's day, with the presbyter himself and the monks, who dwelt there, we undertook the ascent of the several mountains, which mountains are climbed with infinite toil ; since you do not go up slowly and slowly in a circle, spirally as we say, but you go up straight as if up a wall, and it is necessary that the descent of the several mountains be made straight down, until you come to the real foot of the middle (mountain), which is Syna in particular. Accordingly therefore, at the bidding of Christ our God, and helped by the prayers of the holy men who accompanied me, and even so with great toil, because I had to go up on foot (because the ascent cannot be made at all on saddle)—yet the toil itself was not felt. The toil was not felt for the reason that I saw the desire, which at God's bidding I had, being fulfilled. At the fourth hour then we reached the summit of Syna, God's holy mount, where the law was given, in the place, that is, where the majesty of the Lord descended on the day when the mount smoked. In that place then there is now a church, not large, since the place itself, *i.e.* the summit of the mount, is not sufficiently large, a church however which of itself has great grace. When then at God's bidding we had got up to the very summit and had reached the door of the church itself, lo! there met us the presbyter coming [p. 33] from his cell, a man set apart to that very church, a sound old man and a monk from earliest life, and, as they say here, an ascetic, and in a word such a man as is worthy to be in such a place. There also met us other presbyters, and in fact all the monks who dwelt there by the mount, that is, all who were not prevented by weakness or age. But indeed on the very summit of that middle mountain no one lives. For there is nothing else there save only the church and the cave, where the holy Moses was. When the passage in the book of Moses had been read and the oblation had been duly made, ourselves too communicating, as we were now leaving the church, the presbyters gave us the blessings of the spot itself, that is of apples which grow on the mount itself. For although the holy mount Syna itself is all of rock so as to have no herbage, yet below at the foot of the mountains themselves, *i.e.* either round the foot of that which is in the middle, or round about that of those in the circle, there is a little soil. At once the holy monks of their diligence plant little trees and arrange little orchards or fields and hard by cells for themselves, just as if they were deriving fruit from the earth of the mount itself; which however they seem to have wrought with their own hands. And so after we had communicated and the holy men had given us blessings and we had gone outside the door of the church, then I began to ask them to shew us the several places. Then at once those holy men condescended to shew us the places. For they shewed us the cave where the holy Moses was, when for the second time he had ascended up into the mount of God in order to receive the tables anew, after he had broken the former in consequence of the people's sin ; and all the other spots we wished, or they themselves were better acquainted with, they condescended to shew us. I wish you to know, O venerable lady sisters, that from the spot where we stood, that is around the walls of the church, *i.e.* from the summit of the middle mountain, so far below us did those mountains, which we had climbed at first, seem beside that middle one, on which we stood, as if they were hillocks. Yet they were so unending, that I thought I had never seen higher, except that this middle one far excelled them. Egypt and Palestine and the Red Sea and that Parthenic Sea which leads to Alexandria, and moreover the endless frontiers of the Saracens we saw thence, so far below as to be hardly credible. All these several things those holy men pointed out to us.

"When then all our desire, for which we had hastened [p. 34] to ascend, was satisfied, we now began to descend from the actual summit of the mountain of God, unto which we had ascended, into another mountain which is joined to it ; which place is called Horeb ; for there is a church there. For this is the place Horeb where the holy prophet Elias was, when he fled from the face of Ahab, when God spoke to him saying "What doest thou here Elias?" as is written in the Book of the Kingdoms. For the cave too, where the holy Elias lay hid, is shewn there to this day before the door of the church which is there. There is also shewn there the altar of stone, which the holy Elias placed to offer to God, as those holy men too deigned to shew us the several things. We therefore made

the oblation and a very earnest prayer, and the passage itself from
the Book of the Kingdoms was read : for that had been my chief
desire for us always, that wherever we came, the very passage should
always be read from the book. When therefore our offering was
made there too, we came afresh to another spot, the presbyters and
monks shewing it to us not far away from there, that is to the spot
where the holy Aaron had stood with the seventy elders, when the
holy Moses received from the Lord the law for the children of Israel.
In that place then although there is not a house, there is yet a great
rock with level ground around it above, on which the holy men
themselves are said to have stood : for it has also there in the
middle as it were an altar made of stones. There too accordingly
the passage itself from the book of Moses was read and one psalm
said, suitable to the place ; and so after prayer we descended
thence.

"And behold now it began to be about the eighth hour, and still
there were three miles for us to quit the mountains themselves,
which we had entered at evening on the previous day : but we had
not to go out by the same part as we had entered by (as I said
above), because it was necessary for us both to walk round all the
holy places and to see whatever cells there were there, and so to
come out to the end of the valley that lies below the mountain of
God. It was necessary for us to go out to the end of the valley
itself, since there were there very many cells of holy men and a
church in that place where the bush is : which bush lives till this
day and sends forth twigs. Accordingly therefore when we had
descended the mount of God, we reached the bush at perhaps the
tenth hour. This is the bush, which I mentioned above, from which
the Lord spoke to Moses in fire, and it is in this place, where there
are many cells and a church at the end of the valley itself. In
front of the church itself there is a very pleasant garden [p. 35]
with an excellent and plenteous spring, in which garden the bush
itself is. The place too is shewn hard by there, where the holy
Moses stood, when God said to him "Loose the latchet of thy shoe"
and so forth. When then we had come to this place, it was already
the tenth hour, and because it was evening we could not make the
oblation. But prayer was made in the church, and in the garden
too at the bush. Moreover the passage itself from the book of
Moses was read according to custom, and so because it was evening
we supped there before the bush with the holy men themselves.
Accordingly therefore we abode there. And on the next day

waking rather early we asked the presbyters that the oblation might be made there too, as was also done."

No one after all this will be surprised to learn that Silvia saw a monolith with figures of Moses and Aaron, gratefully erected by the Israelites as they left Egypt. Yet not a word do we hear of the hardships and peril of the journey. It is only incidentally we learn that she had been outside the frontier of the Empire and needed a guard. Officers with soldiers escorted her from fort to fort till she reached a place called Arabia. "Here we sent back the soldiers, who had according to the Roman military system given us protection as long as we walked through suspected places." She lightly sketches the rest of the journey, and the stages by which she returned "to Aelia, that is, to Jerusalem[1]."

This was not her first visit there, as indeed we should have judged from her route. She made it for three years a centre for her archaeological expeditions, and though she gives us a very long and full account of the Christian year, as there celebrated, she does not (in the part of her story surviving) tell us much about the famous places and churches and relics of the city, except as they concern church practice. The special point that most pleased her in this was the appropriateness of the service and lessons of each day to the day. This was a novelty to a Christian from Gaul, and was only introduced into the Gallican churches in the fifth century by Musaeus, a presbyter of Marseilles[2].

Many wonderful relics she saw—the column at which our Lord was scourged and the horn used in anointing the Jewish kings—but many more she did not see, for the marvels were not all discovered at once. Two centuries later, pilgrims had the privilege of seeing the crown of thorns, the spear, the sponge and reed, the cup used at the last supper and the charger that received John the Baptist's head. But she saw what the Bordeaux pilgrim did not see—the Cross.

Now this is a wonderful story and a digression may be forgiven. Everybody knows Helena found the Cross. It was found, says Cyril of Jerusalem, in Constantine's reign[3], and Constantine died in 337.

---

[1] To find Jerusalem still called Aelia after three hundred years is very interesting. Ammianus Marcellinus about this time alludes to another town far in the West—"Augusta, formerly known as London."
[2] So Dr Bernard on *St Silvia*, p. 73, in the Palestine Pilgrims Society's text.
[3] Cyril Jer. *Ep.* 3. Cyril died in 386. This letter is said to be early, and a sermon (*Catech.* iv. 10) quoted in the same connexion is set down to 347. If this date is right, the silence of Eusebius is the more impressive.

Helena died in 328, so, if she found it, why did not the Bordeaux pilgrim know of it? He knows a great deal and saw a great deal, but is silent about the most remarkable thing of all And why is Eusebius silent? He only says that "the solemn and all-holy *martyrion* (token?) of the saving resurrection appeared, though beyond all expectation[1]." These two authorities are of great importance, and not at all outweighed by any unanimity of post-Cyrillian writers. But there is a curious cross-current to be considered. One of the most interesting of Syriac documents relative to the early church is *The Doctrine of Addai*. Its date or dates scholars fix differently, but Dr Wright puts it down in its present form to the second half of the fourth century[2]. Its main theme is Addai, the apostle Thaddaeus, sent by our Lord to heal King Abgar of Edessa. Incidentally Addai tells the story of the Invention of the Cross, not by Helena, but by "Protonice, the wife of the Emperor Claudius, whom Tiberius made second in his kingdom, when he went to make war with the Spaniards who had rebelled against him." Need it be said that each new fact makes the story more astounding? Protonice with two sons and a daughter stayed with Herod in Jerusalem, and at the request of the apostle James commanded the Jews to inform her where the cross was. It was in the grave with the crosses of the two thieves. Happily, her daughter fell down dead, and the brilliant thought of her elder son at once restored his sister to life and discovered the True Cross. We shall probably never know who the real discoverer was, and perhaps it is better that Helena should not be robbed of such renown as the story gives her[3]. At all events Silvia had no doubt she had seen the True Cross.

Another of her excursions was to Mt Nebo[4], and on her way she saw Moses' traditional tomb—his sepulchre having been discovered, though "no man knoweth his sepulture." More interesting still, she saw the place that bore the name of Lot's wife (where of course they read the passage in Scripture); "but believe me, venerable ladies, the pillar itself is not to be seen, but the place alone is shewn; but the pillar itself is said to have been covered by the

---

[1] Eusebius, *Vita Constantini* iii. 28. 'Token' is Dr Bright's rendering, and he refers it to the Holy Sepulchre. Eusebius lived in intimacy with Constantine and must have known it, if the Cross had really been found.

[2] *Syriac Literature*, p. 43.

[3] See Dr Abbott's *Philomythus*, c. vii. §§ 30, 31 for an interesting discussion of the Invention of the Cross and Cardinal Newman's handling of the evidence.

[4] *Peregrinatio Silviae*, pp. 40—44.

Dead Sea. Certainly though we saw the place, we saw no pillar, so I cannot deceive you about this. For the bishop of the place, that is, of Segor [Zoar], said to us that it was now some years since the pillar had been seen. For Segor is about six miles from the place where the pillar stood, which is now entirely covered by water." This was a distinct loss. However Theodosius (about 530 A.D.) says it is there and it waxes and wanes with the moon, and Antoninus (about 570) says it is not true that it is being wasted away by cattle licking it, but it stands as it was. A pillar about five feet high is still shewn.

After one more expedition to see Job's tomb, she tells us her mind turned toward home, but on her way she wished to see Edessa, where were the martyry of St Thomas and the authentic letter our Lord wrote to King Abgar. This story of Abgar is one of the most firmly asserted of early traditions. Abgar was the name of the princes of Edessa from the days of Pompey till the end of the second century, and the tale of our Lord's letter is given by Eusebius, who translates from the Syriac a part of the *Doctrine of Addai*, in a form however differing from the present Syriac text, which expressly says that our Lord sent a verbal message, and that Hannan, the keeper of the archives, afterwards wrote it down. Still our Lord's reputed autograph and His promise that Edessa should be inviolable had already, so Edessan historians declared, saved the city at least once from capture by the Persians[1]. As to St Thomas, it was he who had actually given Addai his orders to go to Edessa, and St Ephraem in one of his hymns tells us that St Thomas' bones had recently been brought from India to Mesopotamia by a merchant, "who was in truth a merchant[2]."

So to Mesopotamia Silvia went and saw the martyry and read there the *Acts of Thomas*, that most wonderful collection of the Apocrypha—or at least some of them, *aliquanta ipsius sancti Thomae*[3]. She was kindly received by the bishops of Mesopotamia,

[1] See Phillips, *Doctrine of Addai*, pp. ⁋ and 5; W. Wright, *Chronicle of Joshua the Stylite*, chapter 60, where Joshua (writing about 507 A.D.) speaks of our Lord's promise that Edessa should never be captured being once more fulfilled when Ḳawâd was driven off in 502—3 (814 of the Greeks); and Cureton, *Ancient Syriac Documents*, p. 152, and the authorities there quoted, Procopius, Evagrius, etc. Cureton alludes finally to the existence in England down to his own memory of a practice of keeping a copy of this letter of our Lord as a phylactery.

[2] *Carm. Nisibena*, 42.

[3] "The tale of Thomas the Apostle is a sea that cannot be exhausted," said Jacob of Serug. A better authority is Mr Burkitt's interesting book on *Early Christianity outside the Roman Empire*.

as her long journey "from the ends of the earth" deserved, and she was shewn perhaps the very letter of our Lord, or at least a true copy of it. (It depends on the pronoun *ipse,* which has hardly its classical meaning in Silvia.) She writes that on her return her correspondents shall see her copy of it. She says nothing about the picture of Christ, which Abgar was supposed to have had.

She went on to Carrhae (Haran), and as Nisibis was inaccessible, having been held since 363 by the Persians, she had the happy inspiration to go and see the place where Jacob kissed Rachel, or rather, to quote her correctly, where he watered Rachel's flocks. They read there the passage from Genesis and a suitable psalm (was it the forty-fifth?) and saw the well and the great stone and the inevitable church And so to Antioch and across Asia Minor to Constantinople, where her story ends with the anticipation of visiting Ephesus "on account of the martyry of the holy and blessed John and to pray."

We hear of her again a year or two after 400 from a letter of Paulinus to Sulpicius. He cannot himself spare "a grain of sacred ash" to Sulpicius' envoy Victor, who is in search of relics, "but Victor says he has abundant hopes of such a favour from the holy Silvia, who has promised him some relics of many martyrs of the East[1]." Elsewhere we learn she died at Brixia (Brescia) and left her sacred treasures to the bishop of the town, Gaudentius. Her memory is still celebrated there on Dec. 15.

So far we have followed the course of three women pilgrims, and it will easily be believed in what numbers both men and women flocked to Palestine. As Paula says, "The chief men in Gaul hasten hither; the Briton, remote from our world, if he advance in the faith, forsakes the setting sun and seeks the spot he knows by fame and from the Scriptures. What shall we say of Armenians, of Persians, of the tribes of India and Ethiopia, of Egypt herself hard by, so rich in monks, of Pontus and Cappadocia, of Coele-Syria and Mesopotamia and all the swarms (*examina*) of the East? They all hasten to these places and shew divers types of virtues[2]." Chrysostom more than once speaks of the world coming together to the manger, and tells of many taking a long journey over the sea from the ends of the earth to Arabia to see Job's dunghill[3]. It seems however

---

[1] Paulinus, *Ep.* 31. 1.
[2] Among Jerome's letters, *Ep.* xlvi. 10.
[3] *Homily* 5 *De Statuis,* p. 69 Migne, διὰ τοῦτο πολλοὶ νῦν μακράν τινα καὶ διαπόντιον ἀποδημίαν στέλλονται ἀπὸ τῶν περάτων τῆς γῆς εἰς τὴν Ἀραβίαν τρέχοντες ἵνα τὴν κοπρίαν ἐκείνην ἴδωσι, and they derive from the sight πᾶσαν ὠφέλειαν καὶ φιλοσοφίαν πολλήν.

that this concourse of strange races in Jerusalem and Bethlehem was not free from those attendant evils which mark similar mixtures in other places. Gregory of Nyssa visited Jerusalem about 380, that is just about the same time as our pilgrims, and his conclusion was that the effect of the pilgrimages was evil and not good. He was disturbed by the dangers to the fame and character of women, pilgrims though they might be, in the profligate cities of the East. Of Jerusalem itself he writes:—"There is no species of impurity that is not dared therein—flagitious actions and adulteries and thefts, idolatries and witchcrafts and envyings and murders; and this last evil, above others, is so common in that place, that nowhere else is there such a readiness to commit murder as in those places[1]." Even Jerome, the great advocate of pilgrimage, has to confess (about 394) that "if the sites of the Cross and Resurrection were not in a crowded city, where is a curia, a garrison, harlots, actors, jesters and everything there is in any other city; or if its only crowds were monks, then indeed it were a desirable abode for all monks[2]." Quite apart from the fact that many of the pilgrims attributed more value to the actual pilgrimage than to any spiritual impulse or impression connected with it, even for the more spiritually minded there was (and is always) a danger in religious excitement, as tending to supersede the moral standard. That contemporary criticism was not wanting is seen from Jerome's ferocious and filthy attack on Vigilantius, who had dared "to call us who stand for relics, ash-men and idolaters, worshippers of dead men's bones[3]." There were also bishops, who gently deprecated pilgrimages, but on the whole without much success.

But was there not, in spite of Jerome, an alternative type of Christian life for woman? Though ecclesiastics do not as a rule emphasize it, we find there was. Two instances may fitly close this essay.

There exists a curious little poem, dating from the middle of the fourth century, which generally bears the name of Faltonia Proba, and is therefore attributed to the granddaughter of the Roman lady who, it seems, actually wrote it. Proba, the real authoress, was the wife of Clodius Celsinus Adelphius, who was Prefect of Rome for

[1] Gregory of Nyssa, *Ep. ad Eustathium*, §§ 6—13.
[2] Jerome, *Ep.* lviii. 4. Letter cxlviii. deals with a scandal, which occurred at Bethlehem almost under his own eyes. Even the gatherings on a smaller scale at Nola were marked by drunkenness and disorder, see Paulinus, *Natal.* 9. 546 f. Also Augustine, *Conf.* vi. 2, 2.
[3] Jerome, *Ep.* cix. 1 *cinerarios et idololatras, qui mortuorum hominum ossa venerentur.*

half the year 351[1]. Her grandfather, her father, her brother, her son and many more of her male relatives held the office of consul, and her nephew Petronius Probus, who married her granddaughter Faltonia, was one of the greatest and richest men of his day. So Proba belonged to a family of the very highest repute and dignity. She had at least two sons, and was able to combine with her duties as wife and mother a close study of Virgil. Her surviving poem is a sort of epitome of Old Testament and Gospel history composed of lines and half lines from her poet, and very ingenious it is. Comparetti is no doubt right in pronouncing such work childish after all, though it was then regarded as glorifying the poet who was used as a quarry.

Proba's prologue tells of former attempts on a different theme, though she does not say whether they were in the same style. "Long since of chiefs who brake the gentle bonds of peace, moved, unhappy men! by dire lust to reign, of mutual slaughter and the cruel wars of kings, of armies of one race and fair shields stained with parents' blood, and trophies won but not from foemen, of blood-besprinkled triumphs that fame proclaims, and of cities so oft widowed of so many a citizen, I have written, I confess." But now "I will shew that Virgil sang the gentle gifts of Christ." And so forth for nearly seven hundred lines, one half dealing with Genesis and Exodus, and the second a harmony of the Gospels and of Virgil. She concludes with a gentle address to her husband, from which some have supposed he was not at first a Christian. "Of your grace, my friends, keep this way of worship: hold this thyself, my sweet spouse, and if our piety deserve, may all our grandsons hold the faith." At times she is hard put to it to match Virgil with Scripture[2], but the passages I have translated run smoothly enough, patchwork as they are.

Perhaps Proba was in his mind, when Jerome angrily wrote "The art of interpreting Scripture is the one all claim. *Scribimus indocti doctique poemata passim.* This the garrulous old woman, the drivelling dotard etc. lay claim to, mutilate, and teach before they learn...As if we have not read the centos from Homer and

---

[1] Boissier, *La Fin du Paganisme*, ii. 244; Gregorovius, *Rome in the Middle Ages*, tr. i. 97, and Comparetti, *Vergil in the Middle Ages*, tr. p. 54, give the poem to Faltonia, the two latter avowedly following Aschbach. But Seeck, *Symmachus*, Intr. p. xc., and Schenkl on Proba in the Vienna Corpus of Latin Ecclesiastical Writers, vol. xvi. p. 514, make it clear that this is wrong and that the grandmother is the authoress.

[2] Cf. the creation of Eve; *Quaeritur huic alius; nec quisquam ex agmine tanto | audet adire virum* (*Aen.* v. 378—the boxing match).

Virgil, and could not say Virgil was a Christian before Christ, when he wrote *Jam redit et virgo etc....*This is puerile[1]." Yet Proba found a place by her poem in at least one list of the Church's famous men, a solitary woman among them, because, as Isidore says, she sang the praise of Christ, "and if we do not admire her conception, we praise her ingenuity, and her work is still read among the apocryphal writings[2]." Thither Pope Gelasius relegated it by a decree between 492 and 496, and so it continued to be read through the Middle Ages.

But if to-day we do not read her poem, we have another and perhaps a tenderer memorial of her, which may well seem to outweigh the rhetorical laudation Jerome lavished on a Paula or a Eustochium. Among the Latin inscriptions is one, which at her death her husband had inscribed upon her tomb, which was also to be his.

CLODIVS ADELFIVS V C EX PRAEFECTIS VRBIS VXORI INCOMPARABILI ET SIBI.

(Clodius Adelphius Vir Clarissimus [his rank] Ex-Prefect of the City, to his incomparable wife and himself[3].)

Of Monnica, the mother of St Augustine, much has been written and but few words need be given to her here. From her son's writings we can piece her life together. A German critic has suggested that perhaps she was not throughout an ideal mother in every way, but at least she was always motherly. She, like her son, grew in grace and knowledge and rose with time to higher planes of thought and vision. She was early trained to sobriety and piety by an old Christian slave[4]. When it fell to her lot to be married, she was given to a husband, who if kindly was very quick-tempered, yet such was her tact that she never had a blow from him and they never quarrelled. Over her son she watched and prayed and wept to win him for Christ. At times she would have despaired, but now a vision told her she should "see him standing where she stood," and now a bishop with a splendid instinct told her "it was impossible that the son of those tears could be lost" and the words came to her as a voice from heaven. When the son deceived her by going away from her to Rome, "after accusing my treachery and cruelty she turned once more to pray for me." She followed him to Milan and underwent a storm on her voyage, but in

---

[1] *Ep.* liii. 7.   Tertullian, *Praescr. Haeret.* 39 on earlier centos.
[2] Isidore, *de Vir. ill.* 22 (18).
[3] *Corpus Inscr. Latin.* vi. 1712.
[4] *Conf.* ix. 8—9, 17—20, etc.

inversion of the natural order she comforted the sailors by telling of a vision, in which she had learnt they would arrive safely. It was, she told her son, her firm faith in Christ that she should not leave this life till she saw him a faithful Catholic. And when her dream was realized and he went with the small circle of friends to Cassisiacum to spend the few months before baptism in thought and discussion, she went with him, and her part in the dialogues held there is no mean one. From time to time she joins in aptly, with a happy anticipation of some philosophical conclusion, with a witty phrase that caps a process of reasoning, or a line from a hymn of Ambrose which is the conclusion of the whole matter[1]. The wonderful scene at Ostia, where mother and son held spiritual communion and in swift thought touched on that Eternal Wisdom, which abideth over all, and had reached for a moment the contemplation of God which is "the joy of the Lord," must be read in Augustine's own words[2].

Neither Monnica nor (so far as we know) Proba ever went on a pilgrimage. The common duties of domestic cheerfulness, peace-making and love sufficed them. We may contrast with Melania's relinquishment of her son to the Praetor and Paula's neglect which left Toxotius to grow up a pagan, the mother's feeling which glows through Proba's quaint mosaic and still more the very significant words of Augustine[3]. He is telling of the spiritual awakening he felt for the first time in his life when he read Cicero's *Hortensius*.

"And since at that time (Thou knowest, O light of my heart) the apostolic writings were not known to me, I was delighted with that exhortation so far only as to seek and pursue and hold and embrace—not this or that sect—but Wisdom herself, whatever she were; I was wakened and kindled and enflamed by the dialogue; and yet—this alone checked me in all my enthusiasm, that the name of Christ was not there; for this name, according to Thy mercy, O Lord, the name of my Saviour, Thy Son, even with my mother's milk my heart devoutly drank in and deeply treasured; and whatever lacked this name, however learned, exquisite or true it might be, it took not entire hold of me."

---

[1] See dialogue *de Beata Vita*. Note his high opinion of woman: *Conf.* xiii. 32, 47 *feminam quae haberet quidem in mente rationalis intelligentiae parem naturam.*

[2] *Conf.* ix. 10—11, 23—28.

[3] *Confessions* iii. 4, 8; cf. also i. 11, 17 on the contest between maternal and paternal influence. Also *de B. V.* 6 *nostra mater cujus meriti credo esse omne quod vivo.*

CHAPTER VII

SYMMACHUS

...Et in vetustatem perducens superbos et nesciunt...

AUGUSTINE, Conf. i. 4, 4

TWICE in the course of his history Ammianus pauses to describe the Roman society of his day, and his pictures are lacking neither in colour nor liveliness. But whether these portions of his history were as popular as other sections which he read in public at Rome, we are not told. St Jerome's account of the luxury of Rome, like Cicero's story of his own consulship, may be said to have "exhausted the cabinet of Isocrates, all the paint-boxes of his disciples and a good deal of the pigments of Aristotle[1]." On the other side Claudian is lavish of admiration, so lavish as to praise much that Jerome attacked. More moderate is Macrobius in his picture of the amiable and learned circle of Praetextatus, which shews us that society at its best.

But Fortune has preserved for us other means of judging the Roman nobility, for one of its number added to his great repute as an orator the fame of a great letter-writer. We have some nine hundred letters of Symmachus written to a large number of the best people in the Rome of his day. It might be expected that from these we could test the validity of the impeachment of Ammianus and Jerome and the defence of Claudian and Macrobius. To a certain extent we can. But the reader who hopes to obtain from the letters of Symmachus anything like the bright and varied impression of life he may gain from the accumulations of Sir Edmund Verney and his family, will be disappointed. The reason is not far to seek. The Verney papers remained untouched

---

[1] *ad Att.* ii. 1.

for some two centuries and they offered Parthenope Lady Verney a boundless variety of documents bearing on the daily life and private interests of a large and active family with a wide circle of relatives and acquaintances. The correspondence of Symmachus was edited by his son not long after his death, and Fabius Symmachus was, I am afraid, a dull man, thoroughly in subjection to the notions of propriety held by his class, which was not a very intelligent class. He carefully removed anything unsafe, anything beneath the dignity of a great man, anything relating to common life or business or passing events. Perhaps he should not have all the blame, for he was apparently a good son and only did what his father would after all have wished. Symmachus himself more than once speaks of subjoining in an *index* or *indiculus* or *breviarium* some account of what is occurring, and it is impossible for us to say whether his son cut these away, when he edited the collection, or whether he did it himself, when he filed his letters for preservation. For it has to be confessed that Symmachus kept copies of his letters from a genuine admiration of them, which of course he would have denied or put otherwise. Sometimes he used them again intact, and sometimes he culled a phrase from an old letter to weave into a new. Once, perhaps by mistake, he took a sonorous cluster of words from a letter of Ausonius he had by him[1]. At all events he wrote his letters to his noble friends with a keen sense of their value and dignity, and a strong impression of the likelihood of their being published. Here is at once a difference between such letters and those of Cicero. All is studied, all is for the public. *Ubique vitam agimus consularem* he wrote of himself a few years after his consulship (*Ep.* viii. 23), and the same spirit filled him throughout. He never forgot, as even Cicero so frequently did in writing to his friends, that he might be, or was, or had been a consul. Neither did he ever forget that he had a reputation to maintain as a stylist. Indeed it may be said he is most natural and most human when he is thinking about his health or that of his family.

This edition of his letters was not the only task Fabius undertook for his father. A monument erected by him was found on the Caelian hill in 1617. The inscription is straightforward and not without dignity. "To Q Aurelius Symmachus, Vir Clarissimus, Quaestor, Praetor, Pontifex Major, Corrector (Governor) of Lucania and the Bruttii, Count of the third order, Proconsul of Africa,

---

[1] *Ep.* iii. 6, quoting Ausonius ap. *Ep.* i. 32 (*delenifica et suada facundia*).

Prefect of the City, Consul of his year, a most eloquent orator—
Q. Fabius Memmius Symmachus, Vir Clarissimus, to the best of
fathers[1]." Symmachus' career was thus very typical of his class
in his day, splendid but not very important.

We may then take this man as a representative of the Roman
nobility. In nothing else is he of real importance to the historian.
He contributed no ideas to mankind and he left no mark on society.
He was a good son, a good father, a good friend, a gentleman in
a good sense of the word, but in no sense was he great. His
reputation for his speeches and his letters is not sustained by
posterity. It has become one of the strongest proofs of the de-
cadence of Roman taste. In fact, strange as it may seem, the
most important act of his life in its bearing on history was his
recommendation of St Augustine as a professor of rhetoric to the
people of Milan.

Symmachus came of a distinguished family, and he believed
that "good blood tells and never fails to recognize itself" (*im-
pulsu boni sanguinis, qui se semper agnoscit; Or.* viii. 3). His
grandfather, Aurelius Julianus Symmachus, had been consul in
the year 330, about ten years before his birth which is generally
placed about 340. His father, Lucius Aurelius Avianius Symmachus, to whom we shall return, was Prefect of the City in 364
and won the praise of Ammianus (who is chary of praise) as "one
of the most conspicuous examples of learning and modesty[2]."
Quintus Aurelius Symmachus, our subject, was consul in 391. His
son Fabius was never more than praetor, but his grandson was
consul in 446, his great-grandson, the father-in-law of Boethius,
in 485, and that man's grandsons, the sons of Boethius, in 522.

The education Symmachus received was that of his day—the
traditional education of a Roman gentleman for centuries—rhetoric
and literature. How much Greek he learnt, it would be hard to
say. It made very little impression on him, but this is not surprising in view of the decline of Greek studies[3]. Let an extract
from a letter to Ausonius tell of his philosophy[4]. " I pay no

---

[1] *Corp. Inscr. Lat.* vi. 1699. *Consul ordinarius* is the consul who gave his
name to the year as opposed to the *suffectus* who took his place during the year.
[2] Amm. Marc. xxvii. 3, 3.
[3] Boissier, *F. P.* i. 175—6, remarks this decline.
[4] Perhaps it is not for nothing that in the *Saturnalia* (vii. 1, 2) Macrobius
makes Symmachus deprecate the introduction of Philosophy at the banquet;
rather, he says, *tanquam censoria quaedam et plus nimio verecunda materfamilias
penetralibus suis contineatur*. The passage (including the simile) is modelled
from Plutarch's *Convivial Questions* i. 1, a work much used as a quarry by
Macrobius.

attention to others, the ignoble mob, who feign philosophy by air and garb. A few our age has produced, and among these in particular my friend Barachus, whose native wisdom approaches antiquity. 'But do *you*,' I hear you say, 'presume to judge of philosophers?'" (*Ep.* i. 29). Possibly it was enough for a gentleman to know the names of the philosophers and an anecdote or two about them. Aristotle was the tutor of Alexander; for the rest, "Plato taught us there are gods, and Aristotle reduced the nature of rhetoric to an art" (*Ep.* i. 4).

When Avianius Symmachus met Libanius the great Greek rhetorician of Antioch, "he saw," writes Libanius to Symmachus, "that I was not at all a contemptible person, and telling me much about your natural endowment, he asked the gods to grant something that might allow you to partake my studies." The prayer was not granted, and Symmachus was trained by "an old man, the child of the Garonne," who "dropped the precepts of rhetoric into his breast" (*Ep.* ix. 88). Gaul was famous for her rhetoricians, and this man has been identified with Tiberius Victor Minervius, in earlier days the teacher of Ausonius and commemorated by him in an interesting little poem[1]. A friend of St Jerome's was sent to Rome "that Roman *gravitas* might season the richness and resplendency of his Gallic oratory[2]," and it may not be fanciful to attribute to his teacher from the Garonne the permanently "rich and florid" character of Symmachus' rhetoric, for so Macrobius describes it[3].

He entered on the usual career of office for a young Roman noble, as is set forth on his monument, and began to acquire some repute as an orator. In fact his oratory won him his selection by the Senate to bear its offering of gold and voice its sentiments in a panegyric at the Quinquennalia of Valentinian, the festival to celebrate his five years of empire in 369. This panegyric, another to Valentinian and one delivered at the same time to Gratian, survive, though they are not complete. They are like other panegyrics, but have some additional interest in dealing with the German campaigns of the Emperor, to whose court the young orator was attached at the time. *Interfui*, he says, *ipse*

[1] *Professores* 1. See p. 110.   [2] Jerome, *Ep.* 125, 6.
[3] It may be well to give Macrobius in full, *Sat.* v. 1, 7 *pingue et floridum in quo Plinius Secundus quondam et nunc nullo veterum minor noster Symmachus luxuriatur*. This verb, picking up a previous *lascivit*, is very well chosen to represent Symmachus' style. Whether following Macrobius or not, Gibbon uses the same word—"the luxuriancy of Symmachus."

deprehendi. · He is able to emphasize real merit in Valentinian's
activity and his preference for active service at the front, but the
glory of the ten-year-old Gratian rings false. Of course the Roman
Empire is made much of ; the Rhine flows " from our Alps to our
Ocean " and mirrors Roman forts on either bank ; "from the
couch of the rising Aurora to the goal of the setting sun thou
seest nought that is not thine own," and the Neckar, before unheard of, is now for the first time made known to the world by
the Emperor's victories[1]. This last flourish was, however, a triumph
of loyalty over geography. It should be noted to what sources he
ascribes the Emperor's prosperity—"I said, O venerable Augustus,
that the gods were thy helpers. It is easy to prove this with the
Rhine for a witness, etc." The plural *dei* was the regular form
in panegyrics and its importance may be exaggerated. Still it is
significant. It was while he was with Valentinian that he made
the acquaintance of the poet Ausonius, then tutor of Gratian and
destined to rise higher.

In 373 Symmachus became proconsul of Africa, and cooperated
with Theodosius, the father of the future Emperor, in crushing
Firmus, whose revolt exhibited in the political world those ambitions of the Moors, which found their religious expression in
Donatism. He seems to have won the praise of Theodosius (*Or.* i.).

Either just before or just after his two and a half years in
Africa, he married Rusticiana the daughter of Orfitus. He received
with her a fine dowry, though in later years he was involved
in legal troubles by this connexion with Orfitus' estate. Orfitus,
according to Ammianus (xiv. 6, 1), was a man who conducted
himself with insolence as Prefect of the City, his elevation turning
his head, but otherwise he was sensible and a good business man,
though alas ! not so well equipped in liberal studies as a nobleman
should be. He was exiled on a charge of peculation but afterwards
recalled. Symmachus had by this marriage two children, a son
and a daughter, who seem to have been born about 384—5.

Meanwhile Avianius had had an interesting experience of the
Roman populace, for, says Ammianus (xxvii. 3, 4), "they burnt
his house, the most beautiful across the Tiber, for they had been
excited by some vile plebeian saying that Avianius had said
(though no one had heard him) that he would rather slake lime

---

[1] Ausonius says the same of the sources of the Danube, referring to this
campaign, *Mosella* 424, *Et fontem Latiis ignotum annalibus Histri,* | *haec
profligati venit modo laurea belli.*

with his wine than sell it at the prices expected. Ammianus
abounds in stories of rioting in Rome, when free corn and wine etc.
were not forthcoming for the populace. There are hints of this
in Symmachus' letters, and the reader will understand his pleasure
in watching from his seaside house the corn-ships on their way
to Ostia[1].

Avianius withdrew to the country and stayed there till the
Senate sent a deputation to ask him to return. An oration of
Symmachus' on this joyous occasion, and one on behalf of Trygetius
delivered about the same time (376), survive in fragments. The
latter has some significant flattery addressed to Gratian, in which
one may trace some side-references to Valentinian, of a nature
to diminish the faith one might place in the previous panegyrics.

All this is characteristic of the day. One might read the letters
of Symmachus without forming any clear idea of the dangers, internal and external, of the Empire, just as it is almost impossible
to gather from Miss Austen's pages that England was at war with
Napoleon. Yet here are stirring incidents in his family circle,
perils that might have broken his fortunes for ever, and he himself
was to face and escape even greater dangers. How much more
interesting his correspondence would be, if it had not been so
carefully edited!

Symmachus was now at the height of his glory. He was famous
as an orator; he had represented the Senate before the Emperor;
the Emperors "entrusted to his human voice their divine despatch,
and the Senate learned their victories from his mouth" (i. 95).
His correspondence now begins to be more extensive.

In 382 the Emperor Gratian, who had passed from the hands
of Ausonius into those of Ambrose, a much more aggressive Christian, began a campaign against paganism. He withdrew public
authority and money from the ancestral *sacra* of the *gentes*;
cancelled the grants and immunities of the Vestals and limited
their right to receive property by will; and removed the statue
of Victory and her altar from the Senate. A remonstrance was
addressed to him by the pagan members of the Senate, but (to
quote St Ambrose, *Ep.* xvii. 10), "the holy Damasus, bishop
of the Roman church, chosen by God, sent to me a statement

---

[1] Seneca, *Ep.* 77 (beg.), gives a pleasant picture of the excitement at Puteoli
on the approach of corn-ships, which are recognised from their rigging to be
Alexandrian. (See Torr, *Ancient Ships*, p. 90.) The sight must have meant
more to Symmachus with his experience of the Roman mob.

which Christian Senators beyond counting had given him, to the effect that they had directed no such thing to be done, did not agree with such petitions made by the heathen, and withheld their consent; and they stated publicly and privately that they would not come to the Senate if any concession were made." This statement (*libellus*) was given to Gratian by Ambrose, and the pagans, says Symmachus, "were refused an audience, thanks to unprincipled men (*improbi*), because justice could not have failed them" (*Rel.* iii. 1).

A year later Gratian was murdered, and Valentinian II. succeeded him. The pagan party regained some strength and Symmachus became Prefect of the City. In this capacity he had constant communication with the Emperor on all sorts of business, legal points, civil service disputes, compliments and so forth. Who was responsible for such and such a bridge? Puteoli and Tarracina quarrel over an imperial grant of grain, and it goes to the Emperor. Certain city guilds wish exemption from a new tax. The people are anxious about some games promised by the Emperor. Honorary senatorial rank is asked for a philosopher, brought according to precedent from Athens to instruct the young nobility. His name is Celsus, and men of letters generally agree in pronouncing him nearly equal (*subpar*) to Aristotle. Some novelties have been introduced into the processions of Roman magistrates, and Symmachus asks for their abolition. "Remove the chariot, which boasts greater magnificence; we prefer that which can claim greater antiquity."

Two most interesting *relationes* refer to the duel between Christians and pagans. The pagans made a move to recover from Valentinian II. the altar of Victory, which Gratian would not restore, and the Christians hatched a plot to ruin Symmachus. Both parties failed in the offensive.

As a good deal of literature rose round the *relatio* (*Rel.* 3) about Victory, an abstract of it may be given. Symmachus begins by a reference to the former deputation, which was not received through the machinations of evil men. However he now appears in a twofold capacity, as Prefect of the City and envoy of the Senate. There is no conflict of interests. All are concerned in the glory of the age and the maintenance of ancestral usage. So it is asked that the state of things which long blessed the republic may be restored. Earlier princes maintained and later ones allowed the old ceremonies, and what is so familiar as the altar of Victory?

Let the name (*nomen*), if not the goddess (*numen*), have its dignity.
The Emperors owe much to Victory. It has long been an orna-
ment of the curia, and the pledge of the honour of the Senate
who swore truth on it. Constantius may have interfered with
this, but he respected the Vestals. He came, he saw, he tolerated
and preserved Roman usages. Different nations have different
faiths. That is best which is most helpful to the State, so experience may decide where reason wavers. Rome personified asks
leave to live in her own way. The great secret can hardly be
reached by one only path, and it is only fair to suppose that whatever men worship is one after all. However, to turn from discussion to entreaty. What does the Treasury gain by robbing the
Vestals? Rather let it grow rich on the spoils of the foe than the
pillage of the priests. It is especially invidious to take money
without the plea of need. The Treasury will not allow the
Vestals to inherit land, though freedmen may. Thus it is better
to be the slave of man than the servant of the gods. Is not this
also to interfere with liberty of testation? It never was to the
State's advantage to be ungrateful. In fact disaster and famine
have even now followed in the steps of sacrilege. Let it not be
said this is to be given to a strange religion. It is not a gift, it
is a debt made so by long usage. It is not the Emperor who *gives*
this, as he may be told [as Ambrose did tell him], for it was given
long ago. The deputation only ask the continuance of the state
of things which gave the Emperor's father empire and heirs [a
tacit contrast with Gratian, perhaps]. That deified sire from the
starry zenith now looks down on the tears of the priests, and finds
himself condemned when the use he maintained is violated.

Ambrose was again too strong for the pagans. Now for the
Christian plot. Symmachus had been charged to recover temple
property, and the tale was invented that he had in doing so been
guilty of torturing Christian priests. It brought down on him
an imperial censure, but he triumphantly cleared himself by producing evidence to shew he had so far taken no steps at all, and
procuring a letter in his favour from Pope Damasus (*Rel.* 21).

Symmachus however had a real loss in this year in the death
of his friend Praetextatus, and he was subjected to a good deal
of annoyance in the matter of the property of Orfitus. So in
autumn 385 he gave up office   He was still a person of consequence and was regarded as the leading man of the Senate. It
was in this year he was asked, while still Prefect, to recommend

a teacher of rhetoric for Milan, who should travel at the public cost to take up his duties. Augustine tells us how he set his Manichaean friends to canvass for him, and how after giving an exhibition of his powers to Symmachus he was appointed, and on reaching Milan was kindly received by Ambrose, who was, notwithstanding controversy, a friend and correspondent of Symmachus[1].

In his despatches to Valentinian II. Symmachus had used some striking expressions of loyalty. "Believe me, you (the Emperors) possess the secrets of all hearts" (*Rel.* 9). He commits the gratitude which he feels, but cannot fulfil, to the powers of heaven (*Rel.* 7). "O city accepted of heaven and the stars, on which you have so freely lavished the good things of every land" (*Rel.* 9). The year 387 shewed (if it was necessary) the value of such phrases. The usurper Maximus, who had killed Gratian, now drove Valentinian from the West, and Rome made her submission. Symmachus delivered a panegyric in his honour and in the following year did so again. In 388 Maximus fell before Theodosius at the battle of Aquileia, and everyone had to make haste to change sides. Symmachus' adventures are not recorded by himself, but the tale survives in Socrates the Church historian (v. 14).

"This Symmachus was an eminent man in the Roman Senate, and was admired for his mastery of Roman eloquence, and there are in fact many speeches written by him in the Roman tongue. While Maximus then still lived, he wrote and recited a panegyric to him, and so became liable to the charge of treason. Accordingly in fear of death he fled to the church. Now the Emperor was so careful of the Christian religion that he not only exceedingly honoured the priests of his own faith, but he also gladly received Novatians who held the *Homoousion* (the Nicene symbol). At the request of Leontius, bishop of the church of the Novatians in Rome, he yielded and pardoned Symmachus. On obtaining forgiveness Symmachus wrote a speech of apology to the Emperor Theodosius."

It must have been an interesting speech, but it is lost. Theodosius became friendly with him and made him consul for the year 391. Once more the altar of Victory came up, and Ambrose again intervened and refused for some days to see the Emperor, whom he supposed to be wavering (*Ep.* lvii. 4). Symmachus intro-

---

[1] *Conf.* v. 13, 23. I believe Augustine was studying rhetoric and reading Cicero's *Hortensius* at Carthage while Symmachus was proconsul (*Conf.* iii. 4), but there is no suggestion of their meeting.

duced the matter into a complimentary oration he was making to the Emperor at Milan. Theodosius blazed into passion and had the orator seized, put on a carriage without cushions and driven posthaste to the hundredth milestone[1]. Even so the matter was again brought before the Emperor next year in Gaul, far away from Ambrose, as the saint points out, and he was still obdurate.

In 392 Eugenius was Emperor, the puppet of Arbogast the Frank. Symmachus, wise by experience, was careful, but still Fabius Symmachus was made quaestor. This was a mistake, and Fabius took pains to eliminate from his father's letters as far as possible all references to the usurper, though one or two escaped him. Flavian, Symmachus' friend, lost his life for Eugenius in the defeat on the river Frigidus, and the younger Flavian, Symmachus' son-in-law, had apparently to turn Christian to conciliate the victorious Theodosius—a fact worth remembering in view of Claudian's panegyric. Augustine (*C. D.* v. 26) curiously quotes Claudian's poem and refers to this laudable clemency in the same chapter. The young man was forgiven and became a little later Prefect of the City, but he had great trouble relative to the money matters of the department his father had filled under the usurper.

Once more in 397 Symmachus had to face danger. Gildo, the brother of Firmus, rebelled in Africa, and had the corn supplies for Rome at his mercy. To declare war on him meant to stop the corn-ships at once, and this meant riot at Rome. To make sure that the odium of this should fall not on the Emperors but on the Senate, and to save the former from any trouble with the latter in consequence of popular disturbance, Stilicho consulted the Senate and made it vote for war[2]. It was many years since the Senate had had such a compliment, but it was costly. The corn failed, there were riots, and Symmachus was for a little time the object of popular ill-will and had to withdraw, but all was soon tranquil.

His last years were devoted to his son, his son's marriage, the games Fabius was to give as praetor, and his health. It is not certain when he died. Seeck says the year is 402, but it seems clear he was living when Prudentius wrote his reply to the great *Relatio*, and that was just after the so-called victory of

---

[1] Prosper, *de promiss. Dei*, iii. 38, 2.

[2] Claudian (*Cons. Stil.* i. 325 f.) soars on this occasion; *Romuleas leges rediisse fatemur | cum procerum jussis famulantia cernimus arma*—a good phrase representing no doubt what Stilicho wished the Senate to think for the moment.

Pollentia in 403, so soon after it, apparently, that the doubts which Claudian found it so hard to lay, had not yet been raised about the result of the battle.

We may now turn to Symmachus in his relations with his family and his friends. The first thing that will strike the English reader is the extraordinary formality with which he addresses his correspondents. A very large number of the letters—a strangely large number—contain elaborate excuses for not writing, and as elaborate requests for letters, with studied admiration of the correspondent's style and profound humility on Symmachus' part on account of his poverty in composition[1]. "I am poor in speech," he writes (iv. 27), "and economical of paper." "I have always, like rivers in drought, shrunk from wide banks, that an affectation of brevity may conceal my poverty...I could wish that like the Aborigines we might exchange our greetings on a bit of stick or cork ; and let Egypt have devised her rolls of papyrus for the libraries and the forum" (iv. 28). Still he has to keep writing every day, though he has little to say. "How long shall we babble (*blaterabimus*) the words of mutual salutation, without other matter for the pen ? In days of old our fathers would fill their friendly pages with business of state—but of this there is little or nothing to-day. Of this resource the peace of our times has deprived us, so we have to hunt for untried seeds of correspondence (*semina scribendi*) to wipe away the weariness of commonplace letters" (*Ep.* ii. 35). It was after all the artificial style which appealed to his correspondents, as we may see in Fabius' method of editing. He sorted out the letters into groups, putting by themselves all addressed to the same person, and published them without any further effort at arrangement, and with no consideration for chronology. Indeed in one case at least he confused a father and son and left their letters mixed. After some time spent on this arduous work, he let it drop altogether and made his secretaries copy off his father's letters as they stood in his portfolios without attempting any order at all—books viii. and ix. are the result. The *relationes*, like Pliny's letters to Trajan, stand by themselves. Seeck has been at enormous pains to date as far as possible all the letters.

---

[1] All these are the constant characteristics of the epistolary style taught by the rhetoricians. There are letters enough of Julian and Synesius, both men of higher type, which shew the same features. See Volkmann, *Synesius v. Cyrene*, p. 116, and especially Rohde, *der griechische Roman*, pp. 341 ff., on letter-writing as a regular branch of sophistic composition.

If then the collection offers little aid toward an ordered life of Symmachus, we may still find in it abundant evidence of his character. His letters to his father speak the admiration and affection of a dutiful son. He submits verses to his father's criticism with much nervousness, though he knows his father cannot resist paying the most lavish compliments. "What could be neater than your letter, just received? what more delightful than its intermixture of verses?" writes Avianius, and he proceeds to tell his son he is writing poetical tributes to some eighty great men of his time, and he sends five samples. They consist of six tolerable hexameters each and are all very pretty and polite and nothing more. Their chief value is to shew how much better and more lively are Ausonius' similar productions

Rusticiana, Symmachus' wife, is hardly mentioned in the letters. Once or twice reference is made to her estates, once to her birthday, and once to her not being very well. Nearly all Symmachus' relatives cause him anxiety on this score.

There is a large number of letters addressed to his son-in-law and his daughter. One gathers the impression that the orator was a little in dread of the lady's temper sometimes. She must not be annoyed, he says on one occasion, at his delaying the horses she needs for some journey (vi. 12). He is very anxious about her health—is she taking care of it? Here is a letter (vi. 4)[1].

"The suffering I have to bear from the pain in my right hand your bad news has doubled. The keener anxiety racks me, that I know my daughter cannot be persuaded to be moderate in eating and drinking. Worried therefore by distress of mind and disease of body, I could not wait till I could write myself; but by a hurried dictation I have satisfied my alarm, if I have broken my rule. And first, I implore you to relieve my fears by a reply : and then, lady daughter (*domina filia*), I pray you in particular to avoid what does not suit your well-being and to mend your health, so often broken, by the aid of temperance. Because it not only promotes healthfulness, but is a testimony of our good sense, to abstain from what is dangerous. Farewell."

Then she needs rest and quiet (vi. 15). Is she really better or not? (vi. 20). By and by, she has overdone the abstinence and her health suffers again, and he is very anxious, beside being gouty (vi.

[1] There is a lively little note written by Synesius to a physician on ὀλιγοσιτία, to whom he quotes Hippocrates as his authority for its being the "mother of health," *Ep.* 115.

29). He is happy to hear a purge has given her relief and has also reduced the inflammation of her eyes—was it necessary to bleed her as well? he anxiously asks (vi. 64). His daughter's bad health requires the solace of her husband's presence, and the weakness of his stomach forbids him to go to her, so with other difficulties coinciding Symmachus hardly knows what to advise (vi. 59). Another source of anxiety is his little granddaughter Galla, who is ill at the same time as her mother, but by the gods' blessing (*opitulatio divina*) he hopes for good news. He will take it as a mark of true affection if his daughter will take care of herself and let him have better reports of their progress (vi. 22).

We have one or two letters acknowledging her birthday gifts. He is delighted with her *lanificium* ; it shews her love as daughter and her diligence as a matron ; it is quite like the famous women of old, but that they lived in a dull age which was congenial to the distaff, while she lived at Baiae (vi. 67). Another year, he says it was a tradition of many years for him to receive the gifts, and he is the more grateful for being brief in his thanks, but urges it on her as a filial duty to take care of her health (vi. 48).

To his son he was even more devoted. He personally took charge of his health, his education, and his future renown. *Pignus meum* and *unicus meus*, "my only son," come over and over in the letters. He writes to a friend ; "While my son is being initiated into Greek, I have once more taken part in his studies as if a schoolfellow. A father's feelings (*pietas*) bid one become a boy again, that the sharing of the toil may make the lessons pleasant to one's children. For you however things are not in the budding stage, but at harvest time ; for I find your son is most eloquent and pressing hard on the heels of his father's proficiency. O happy man, my friend, if you are surpassed! My care is still to encourage the blossom, and I cannot exact hard work from my only boy. Still between my fears and my persistence my dear one's progress is sure if slow " (iv. 20).

Fabius was made quaestor by Eugenius the usurper, an episode the family tried to forget, and later on the praetorship was given him by Honorius for 400, the date being changed however to 401. The only duty attached to these offices was to give on each occasion a great show in Rome. Symmachus felt this to be most important. He strongly disapproved of the neglect with which some Roman nobles treated this part of their duty, and emphasized with how little expense after all it might be done (ix. 126). Yet he got a law to limit extravagance in displays of the kind, and broke it for Fabius' glory.

Some half dozen letters refer to the quaestorship—contemporary letters. He writes to Paternus, who was a Christian, about hunters for the arena (v. 59), to some one else about ornaments and especially robes which he describes in a very modern way as partly silk (*subsericas*, v. 20). Flavian sent him seven Scottish dogs which were greatly admired (ii. 77), and Symmachus writes to him to ask his kindly offices with one Domitius, who has promised bears which are desperately needed and not to hand. Some few cubs have indeed arrived, but worn out by starvation and travel, and he can hear nothing of his lions (ii. 76). But there was a more cruel blow yet, and he had need to remind himself of Socrates' way of supposing all to be for the best, however disappointing, when he found that some twenty-nine Saxons (desperate race!) had laid impious hands on themselves and strangled themselves or one another to escape the arena and death before the populace (ii. 46). For Symmachus stood for gladiatorial shows and had as Prefect congratulated the Emperor after a victory over the Sarmatians on "reserving some of the prisoners for the pleasure of the people of Mars" (*Rel.* 47). They had been marched through the streets and "we saw the shackled column of the conquered race in procession, and those faces once so warlike altered to a wretched pallor."

On Fabius' praetorian games he is said to have spent £80,000, and we have a large number of letters appealing to his friends to aid him in purchasing Spanish horses[1] and to hasten their delivery. Bears, leopards, antelopes, charioteers, stage-carpenters, trappings fill his letters. This time the robes are to be all silk (*holosericae*, iv. 8). He had some crocodiles, which he exhibited, and he wanted to save them for his daughter and her husband to see, but for fifty days they would not eat and they had to be killed at the second show (vi. 42). In this connexion a couple of letters on the customhouse are interesting. An attempt was made to charge a friend of Symmachus a duty of 2 per cent. on some bears imported by him for the arena. Traders in beasts had to pay this, but candidates who gave shows for the people's amusement were usually and not

---

[1] So many letters relating to Spanish horses have been preserved, that one feels tempted to suppose Ammianus was not far wrong when he grumbled at the passion for horse-flesh among "grave men, and maintainers of the virtues, as they think" (xxviii. 4, 11). An interesting account of an African magnate's stud and the magical devices of the jockeys is given by Boissier, *L'Afrique Romaine*, ch. IV. § 3. (Engl. tr. p. 173.)

improperly freed from the impost (v. 62). Very soon Symmachus has to intercede for another friend, on whom an attempt has been made to levy 2½ per cent., also on bears. One burden is enough, he says (v. 65).

The business of capturing and transporting wild beasts had been for centuries an enormous one, and one of the most wasteful methods of exhausting the Empire. Claudian twice sets the minor powers of heaven to collect beasts for the circus, and his descriptions are contemporary with the letters of Symmachus. They are elaborate and have some interest as history, but as poetry they fail[1].

In 401 Symmachus married his son to the granddaughter of Flavian, and we have a number of polite little letters sending little gifts to friends in celebration of the occasion. The same had been done when Fabius was quaestor and praetor.

Symmachus had a wide circle of friends, and though it may be said that his views on friendship are by no means original, yet it is clear that friendships were a large part of his life. " My feeling is that my friends' prosperity is part of my own good fortune. And, in truth, how many happy days can a man have who only reckons his own advantages? He has a wider joy who can enjoy another's happiness" (iii. 24). "Is there any one so hard-hearted as to see the sorrow of many without feeling pain?" (v. 12). "Favours seem to me to confer more on him who gives them" (vii. 46). "The mind finds its own sorrow lightened, when it directs itself to kindly offices" (ii. 32). "True friendship feels such security, that it finds in its own loyalty an assurance of mutual affection" (iv. 30).

Full accounts of his friends, their fames and families, are given by Seeck in his great Introduction. To one or two of them I have already alluded. One however calls for special notice. Vettius Agorius Praetextatus (b. 330 or earlier, d. 384) was the most eminent of the heathen in Rome. He was a scholar, an antiquarian, something of a philosopher and a mystic. In his house Macrobius laid the opening scene of his *Saturnalia*, and he is a leading character in the discussions. He held a number of priesthoods and made a point of being initiated into all possible mysteries—a privilege he extended to his wife. He won high praise from Ammianus for his integrity and sense in his government of Rome

---

[1] See *Paneg. Manl. Theod.* 280—332 and *Cons. Stil.* iii. 237—369. Cf. too Amm. Marc. xxviii. 4, 28—31 on the races.

when he was Prefect[1]. He had the distinction of settling the quarrel of Ursinus and Damasus for the Roman See, by expelling the former from the city[2]. In this connexion a story of St Jerome's is interesting—"The wretched Praetextatus," he says, "who died when consul designate, a sacrilegious person and a worshipper of idols, used laughingly to say to the blessed Pope Damasus, 'Make me bishop of the Roman Church, and I will be a Christian at once'" Damasus might forgive this jest to the man who rid him of Ursinus. Some eight inscriptions to his memory have been found in Rome and one in Crete. To one of these I must refer.

His sepulchral monument[3] bears after his name a list of his priesthoods, Roman and non-Roman, and the last two titles call for attention—*tauroboliatus, pater patrum*. The *pater* was the seventh grade in the priesthood of Mithras, and the *taurobolium* was the baptism of that religion[4]. The participant stood in a pit, the throat of a bull was cut over him, and he was drenched with the blood. The bull was the sacred animal of Mithras and its blood meant new life and regeneration for eternity—*taurobolio in aeternum renatus*, says one man in an inscription (*C. I. L.* vi. 510). Women had usually no place in Mithraism, but the name of Praetextatus' wife, with her priesthoods and *tauroboliata*, follows his own.

On the same monument are two inscriptions addressed by Praetextatus to his wife, and one by her to him, which I translate, as it seems to me to exhibit the better side of Roman society in a tender and beautiful way. They were married for forty years, and she says:—

"The splendour of my parents gave me nought better than that I seemed worthy of my husband; but all my light and glory is my lord's name, thine, Agorius, who, sprung of proud lineage, dost illume thy country, the senate and thy wife, by thine honesty of heart, thy character and thy studies, whereby thou hast attained the highest pinnacle of virtue. For, whatever is set forth in either tongue by the thought of the wise to whom heaven's gate stands open, and all the songs the learned have written and all things set

[1] Amm. Marc. xxvii. 9, 8—10.

[2] The famous fight for the bishopric and the historian's comment, xxvii. 3, 12—15, which may have been suggested by Jerome's story, *contr. Johann. Hierosol.* 8.

[3] *C. I. L.* vi. 1779. I have taken it from Seeck, who quotes it in full.

[4] See an excellent article by A. Gasquet in *Revue des Deux Mondes*, April 1st, 1899, on *Le culte et les mystères de Mithra*. Also Prudentius, στεφ. x. 1010—1050—a most vivid and realistic account of the *taurobolium*.

forth in prose, thou givest forth, but better than thou didst find them in the books. But this is of light account; thou, holy and initiate, dost lay up in the secret of thy heart what thou hast learnt in holy rites, and well-skilled dost adore the manifold divinity of the gods, of thy goodness admitting thy wife to the sacred things of men and gods, a faithful partner. Why now should I tell of office or of power, the joys men seek in prayer? for thou, ever reckoning these to be but light and for a season, dost boast to be the priest of the gods and wear the fillet. Thou, purifying and cleansing me by the blessing of thy teaching, dost save me from the lot of death, lead me to the temples and dedicate me to the service of the gods; in thy presence I am initiated into all the mysteries. Priestess of Cybele and Attis, thou my holy spouse dost honour me with the rites of the bull. The handmaid of Hecate, thou teachest me the three secrets; thou makest me worthy the mysteries of the Greek Ceres. It is because of thee that all call me blessed and holy, for thou dost spread my fame through the world. Though unknown, I am known to all. For how should I fail to please, when thou art my husband? The matrons of Rome take an example from me, and count their offspring fair if it be like thine. Men and women alike covet and approve the glories thou hast given me by thy teaching. Now that all this is taken away, I am a sad wife and in sorrow, who had been happy had the gods let my husband survive me, yet happy still in this that thine I am and have been and thine shall ere long be after death."

Such a man was Symmachus' friend Praetextatus, and there were others like him, but he also counted among his friends men who were neither so pious nor so learned as Praetextatus. Stilicho and Bauto (father-in-law of the Emperor Arcadius) were soldiers and barbarians, a Vandal and a Frank. Petronius Probus was neither saint nor soldier. Ausonius was a poet and said he was a Christian. Ambrose was a Christian and a bishop, and not the only one of Symmachus' acquaintance, for beside Damasus who defended him against Christian calumny, we find two bishops receiving letters of recommendation from him. To his brother he wrote; "You may wonder at my recommending a bishop to you, but it is his cause and not his sect that has induced me." It was a bishop Clemens, whose Mauretanian diocese had been plundered, apparently by Firmus. Moneys belonging to the treasury had been taken, and now the treasury was trying to collect its taxes a second time to replace what was lost, and the bishop appealed to Symmachus and he sent him to his brother (i. 64). Another bishop he introduces as "my brother Severus, a bishop whom all the sects [*i.e.* including pagans] agree in calling praiseworthy" (vii. 51).

People in all sorts of need appealed to him. Here and there are letters recommending sons-in-law (ix. 7, 49). A betrothal has been cancelled and Symmachus writes on behalf of the incensed suitor. He thinks the lady's father had been unhandsome (*devenustare*), and that it will be a little rude of him to reject the intercession of Symmachus, when the young man's character and standing are, as he knows, excellent (ix. 43). A professor is in distress, and Symmachus writes to Flavian:—

"His dress and his hair proclaim Serapammon a man of letters, for if he had felt he had no share in such things, he would never have adopted the philosopher's garb. But about this I leave you to judge, who profess to understand such things. I felt I could not properly refuse an introduction at his request. It will be consistent with your character, if you aid the fortunes of the stranger with your resources and your kindness" (ii. 61).

Again, he intercedes for a professor, whose salary is in some danger (i. 79), and he lays down the principle that it is the mark of a flourishing State that good salaries be paid to professors. It is one of the pleasant features of Roman society, or at least of that part of it which Symmachus represents, that literature or learning is as good a passport into it as wealth or military glory. Ausonius and even Eugenius himself had begun as teachers of rhetoric.

Far too many letters of mere compliment are included in the collection—letters in which pretty nothings are "over-curiously trimmed," till the modern reader is apt to suppose both writer and recipient entirely frivolous. The language is certainly extravagant and the tone of mutual admiration unhealthy, but we must remember that the contemporaries of Drake and Shakespeare used the most extraordinary phraseology of their Queen. We have to go deeper than the form, and Symmachus apart from literature seems to have been a very sensible and kindly man.

I quote as an example of his happier style a letter to the young Olybrius and Probinus, the sons of Petronius Probus, who were consuls in 396, and for whom Claudian wrote his first great Latin poem—not nearly so sensible a production.

"Your hunting bears witness to your fulness of strength and vigour. So this is my first reason for pleasure about you, that you are benefiting your health by rustic pleasures. The second stage of my happiness is that I should have deserved what you took in the chase. For as we are permitted to dedicate the horns of stags to the honour of the gods and to fix the tusks of the boar at our thresholds, so the fruits of the woods are devoted to friendship. Meantime I repudiate the idea that hunting is a business for slaves. Granted that a writer [Sallust, *Cat.* iv. 1] laid this down, who is only to be praised for his style—for the damage his character sustained disqualifies him as a guide for life—I prefer you to enjoy country life with Atilius and follow the sport of strength than to be led aside by fair phrases into habits of idleness. At all events this exercise suits your years. Youths should be tested not by gaming-board or ball or Attic hoop and Greek palaestra, but by the ready endurance of fatigue and delight in innocent hardihood. It is to this I shall encourage my Symmachus, when he grows old enough, though he will have no brother to go with him (*quamvis unicum*). A day will come when, burdened with years, you will have to renounce this employment. Then hunting will rightly be called a servile business. For it is a sort of slavery, if, when our strength fails, we refuse to use the respite from toil which old age grants us" (v. 68).

That the reader may be able to judge from a specimen, I quote one of the too many letters of compliment with which Symmachus found himself bound to honour his friends. Some of the terms are a little hard to translate into rational English.

"Decency [the word is *religio*] demanded that I should write, especially when an opportunity coming from your own household encouraged me. For your man offered himself as letter-carrier, and I saw clearly that not to give him a letter would be monstrous guilt. So I hope you are well, I inform you that I am, and I hope in return that you will reward me with news of your good health" (v. 61).

The French scholar M. Morin, who published an interesting monograph on Symmachus in 1847, remarks on the value of the letters of Symmachus to the historian, while he gently complains that Gibbon made little use of him. Gibbon has however a footnote on him, which is very characteristic:—"The luxuriancy of Symmachus consists in barren leaves without fruit and even without flowers. Few facts and few sentiments can be extracted from his verbose correspondence[1]." It is certainly true that if

---

[1] Gibbon iii. 410, n. 16.

Symmachus were our only authority for his period, its history
would be all but a blank. It is only as a tributary to another
source of information that he is of the least value. One might
learn from him the names of the Emperors, but hardly another fact
but that Valentinian was a soldier. Maximus and Eugenius are of
course obscured. Apart from the affair of the altar of Victory and
the accidental allusions to a bishop or two, one hears nothing of
Christianity[1]. To the barbarians he makes no allusion in his
letters[2]. Now and then he speaks of the country districts being in
distress. "It has come to be the practice in our days," he says,
"that the country which used to feed us has to be fed" (i. 5). We
hear of brigandage (ii. 22), and there is an end of it.

He hardly refers to the Empire, except in the panegyrics already
quoted. The Emperor is always spoken of in the language of
worship. His words are oracles, his person sacred, himself actually
royal—"all men love him as the god who feeds mankind" (iii. 82).
(This phrase was meant for the sacred ears, though in a private
letter.) Once however he says to an Emperor that "the Empire
has grown because you rule over free men" (*Or.* iv. 13)—a sentiment
much elaborated by Claudian.

Of official tyranny and mismanagement, of the severity and
cruelty to which subjects were submitted with little consideration of
guilt or innocence, we hear a good deal. Take an example (v. 63).
The treasury officials of Italy have started a new trick (*stropha*).
They forge claims against persons as debtors to the treasury and
exact them. The weak give way because they are bullied; the
strong, because to resist may be made into treason. In this at all
events Symmachus confirms the impression we get from Ammianus.

The Senate is of course the centre of Symmachus' immediate
political life, and his friends are mainly of the nobility. Many of
them still had enormous wealth. Possibly Petronius Probus was
the richest, though Ammianus (xxvii. 11, 1) amiably says it is not
for his poor judgment to decide whether he came by all his estates
justly or unjustly. Symmachus himself had a surprising number
of country villas, residences and lodges at various places near and

---

[1] Eutropius, the historian, a friend of Symmachus, managed in the same
way to write of Constantine without a reference to his conversion, and concludes
atque inter Divos meruit referri (x. 2, 8).
[2] In his panegyric on Gratian, it was impossible not to allude to them when
the orator had followed a campaign against them on the Rhine and Neckar, but
he has found a prophecy "Thus far and no farther"—*Hactenus nomen stetisse
barbaricum* (*Or.* iii. 12).

about Rome and in Campania, and estates in Samnium, Apulia, Sicily and Mauretania. Seeck has collected a great list from the letters[1].

Yet the manners of these great men were not always nice. Symmachus hints at one brawl in the Senate, and "is ashamed to tell what charges and bad language the best men threw at one another" (vi. 22). He had however been absent. The times were, no doubt, improving in some ways, as we can see in Macrobius, but slavery still tainted society with cruelty. Apart from the gladiatorial shows, to which I have referred, we find once or twice in the letters allusions to slavery; *e.g.* the punishment of a slave, who went off without waiting for an answer to a letter, and "it lies in your hands whether you allow this to go unavenged [*inultum*, rather more than unpunished, but not quite so much as unavenged]" (vi. 8)[2]; and again a request to a magistrate, which may be quoted at length.

"My first reason for writing is to pay you the compliment of a greeting, my second to present a petition to the magistrate whose love of law I know so well (*probatam mihi modestiam*). For a good many slaves of my establishment have run away and lie hid in the region under your care. I should like you to hear my agent's allegations and restore these persons ; for it is only consistent with your character to consider our friendship and deny a refuge to the iniquity of slaves (*servili nequitiae*). Farewell" (ix. 140).

The letter leaves an uneasy feeling. It is too suggestive of Fugitive Slaves Bills. No doubt many masters shared the feelings Macrobius puts into Praetextatus' mouth in the *Saturnalia*, that slaves were men—"slaves no doubt, but still men; they are slaves; rather, say fellow-slaves, if you reflect that Fortune has equal power over both....He may be slave of stern necessity, but perhaps he is a slave whose mind is free (like Epictetus)" (*Saturn.* i. 11, 7). Yet Praetextatus in the same speech says, "We masters put on the minds of tyrants, and we wish to be limited in our treatment of our slaves not by what is fitting but by what is lawful" (*ib.* i. 11, 14). However gentle slavery may be, it still is slavery[3].

---

[1] Symmachus "had three villas in the immediate neighbourhood of Rome, seven in other parts of Latium, five on the bay of Naples and probably several others of which we do not know." Seeck, *Gesch. des Untergangs der Antiken Welt*, p. 379. See also his Introduction to the *Letters*.

[2] Ammianus (xxviii. 4, 16) speaks of 300 lashes being ordered by a Roman master for a slave, who was slow in bringing warm water—an ominous parallel, I am afraid.

[3] Both passages are from Seneca, *Ep.* 47, but as Macrobius considered the

It may be fairly urged that Symmachus was not writing history and that broad views were not required of him. Yet the narrow range of his interests is significant. He lived in a very narrow world. It was no longer the Rome of Cicero or Augustus. The seats of government were Constantinople and Milan; and Rome was a provincial town with a history. On that history Symmachus and his friends lived. They were subjects now and not rulers[1], and had little chance of making history except by accident or by attaching themselves to the court and leaving Rome. Symmachus had great difficulty in prevailing on Flavianus to go East to become secretary to the Emperor—"to utter in oracles the mind of the august prince" (ii. 8). Except in the case of men of learning and physicians, they had no concern with their fellow-subjects abroad[2]. Even for the "fellows without grandfathers" (*terrae filios*) and "plebeian society" Symmachus betrays his contempt (i. 3). In literature it was the same. They read the recognized Latin classics[3] and imitated them as carefully as they could. Pliny the younger was Symmachus' especial model. The writers of the day who can boast any life, are not Italian. Ammianus and Macrobius were Greek, Augustine a Latin of Africa, Prudentius a Spaniard, Sulpicius a Gaul, Claudian some kind of Egyptian, whether Greek or Latin. It is from such men and not from Symmachus that one obtains the truest picture of the Roman world.

Symmachus missed the meaning of Rome through his narrow conservatism. So in religion he held fast by paganism more from a sense of its traditional propriety than from faith. No doubt he constantly refers to the gods in such phrases as "by the divine blessing," "by the peace of the gods" and so forth[4], and he was in his dignified way a pious person, but without much religious enthusiasm or reflexion. He stood for the altar of Victory stoutly,

---

letter worth quoting in this way and re-inforcing with examples from Gellius, we may still consider it not without value as evidence for his own day.

[1] Lact. *de M. P.* 26, Galerius, devouring the world with taxation, *ad hanc usque prosiluit insaniam ut ab hac captivitate ne populum quidem Romanum fieri vellet immunem.*

[2] Ammianus (xiv. 6, 12—13) says even these distinguished strangers were only welcome once.

[3] Ammianus (xxviii. 4, 14) says the Roman gentry confined themselves to Juvenal and Marius Maximus, who are not in Seeck's list of Symmachus' authors. Lucretius seems not to have been read. His verse repelled the taste of the age, his philosophy its faith. Augustine refers to him once, *de Util. Cred.* 4, 10.

[4] That he should use such phrases at all marks the change of Roman feeling since the days of Cicero, whose mind is revealed by such passages as this to his wife (*ad Fam.* xiv. 4, 1): *neque di, quos tu castissime coluisti, neque homines, quibus ego semper servivi, nobis gratiam retulerunt.*

and he stood for the traditional rather than the modern chariot in the procession. He was careful about the expiation of a portent at Spoletium (i. 49). He was opposed to the erection by the Vestals of a monument to his friend Praetextatus—it was an innovation. But if he had been forced to state his ultimate belief about the divine, it must have been a general impression that it—or they— had a benevolent nature, or, if this be too strong, a preference for hoping it were true. Many ways might lead to the great secret, but it was a Roman's part to be content with the way his fathers took, and if necessary console himself with the thought that, if these things were obscure, antiquity was more likely to be right. His passion was for antiquity and for religion as part of its inheritance.

Is it any marvel that Julian was disappointed with a pagan community, of which Symmachus was a truer type than himself, which was content with lazy generalities and ready to turn Christian to oblige Theodosius or to soothe him, which in a word had no convictions?

Still, we must be just to Symmachus. The traditions of his family and of his city, his education and his environment made it difficult for a man of no great mental power to take a wide outlook, and if he preferred to spend his days "patching up his health, avoiding disturbance and always loving literature" (iv. 44), if his ideals were not strenuous, he passed through life with the respect of Christian as well as pagan, the type of an honourable and cultured Roman gentleman.

CHAPTER VIII

MACROBIUS

Vetustas quidem nobis semper, si sapimus, adoranda est.

Sat. iii. 14, 2

THE work of a commentator may be of interest in either or both of two ways. He may win attention for what he contributes to the explanation and interpretation of the author with whom he deals, or he may be interesting for what he reveals of himself or his age. In the case of a great commentator it is sometimes hard to say for which reason he is read. Do the majority of his readers study Calvin for the sake of St Paul or for Calvin's own sake? But there are men of far less note, men who cannot claim genius, originality or even insight, whose commentaries are of value for the light they throw upon the feelings and the tastes of their day. Among these we may place Macrobius. He preserves, no doubt, a great deal of matter, of which the student of Virgil would be sorry to be deprived, though it certainly could not be called indispensable, but it is mainly as an exponent of the mind of Roman society at the end of the fourth century that he merits attention. Claudian was a man of genius; Symmachus and Macrobius were not, but their remains help to complete his picture of the times. It is mainly to this part of Macrobius' work that I shall devote the following pages.

One point however demands notice first of all. One aspect of Roman life is carefully ignored by Macrobius as by Claudian, and is but accidentally mentioned by Symmachus. No reference is made to Christianity, or to any thing or any person connected with it. Yet it touched at many points the lives of the men Macrobius presents to us. Praetextatus, Symmachus and Flavian are chiefly conspicuous because they were its last great opponents, Flavian even falling in battle against it. Of the others Caecina Albinus, pontifex as he was, had a Christian wife; his daughter Laeta was a correspondent of St Jerome's ; and his little granddaughter Paula, who was dedicated to the nunnery from her birth, is pictured by the Saint (*Ep.* 107, 1) singing her childish Alleluia to her pagan grandfather, as she sat on his knee. The other Albinus is variously called Furius and Rufius in the manuscripts, and if Rufius was his name, as Seeck believes, he was a Christian himself. Macrobius then was not silent about Christianity because he knew nothing of it. His silence is, on the contrary, as significant as anything he could say. A contemporary of Augustine, Ambrose, Jerome, Chrysostom and Theodosius, he chooses to know nothing of their faith. It was victorious, and his revenge is silence.

Apart from his books little can be said of the man. The books are dedicated to his son Eustachius, and he hopes his son will find his language correct and a good model, though he was "born under another sky" (*nos sub alio ortos caelo, Sat. Praef.* 11). We might, from his knowledge of Greek literature, suppose this other sky to have been that of Greece, or, if not of the Greece of geography, of that wider Greece which embraced the Eastern World. But it is suggested he may have been born in Africa[1]. We have really no evidence. *A priori* probabilities are quite valueless here. Augustine was an African and knew Greek literature chiefly in translations ; Apuleius read Greek before he read Latin. Nor can we say with van Jan, his great editor, that, if a Greek, Macrobius would hardly have written in Latin. Ammianus and Hierius, and perhaps Claudian, were Greeks. Attempts have been made to identify Macrobius with one or other of several contemporary officials, who bore the name, and in one case we should have to suppose he became in later life a Christian, but there is no probability, or at least no certainty, in any of these identifications. We are thus left to what he says of himself. If we cannot learn his history, we can at least form some idea of his mind.

Three works remain which bear his name. One, to which I shall not further refer, is grammatical and deals with the differences of the Greek and the Latin verb. The *Saturnalia* and the

---

[1] Van Jan inclines this way. Petit (*de Macrobio Ciceronis interprete*, Paris, 1866) holds to the Greek origin. Macrobius in the mss has also the name Ambrosius, on the strength of which Petit identifies him with Ambrosius, a correspondent of Libanius. The evidence he cites from the letters is quite inconclusive: Ambrosius is an official; he is interested in reading; and a rhetorician, by name Eusebius, is introduced to him. Sixty persons named Eusebius are enumerated by Fabricius (v. Jan, i. p. xxx).

Commentary on *Scipio's Dream*, in spite of an elaborate fulness which betrays the professional teacher, are really interesting books and not unworthy of study. I shall not attempt a close analysis of them, but content myself with remarking the salient points which make themselves felt on a general survey of the books, and first of the *Saturnalia*.

That the book owes something to the *Noctes Atticae* of Gellius is very evident. Apart from material freely borrowed (without acknowledgment) the name Macrobius gave his book and the language of his preface suggest Gellius. Gellius tells us there were many books like his, with all sorts of fanciful titles to indicate the variety of their contents, books of extracts and notes and criticisms set down in any order or no order—*Amalthea's Horn*, for instance, *Muses*, *Honeycombs*, *Lamps*, *Quilts*, *Manuals* and so forth. He himself, in memory of the place and time of his studies' beginning, calls his book *Attic Nights*[1]. Macrobius avows the same design. His book is to gather together the fruits of his reading, but (and we are to understand the advance made here) it will present them in an ordered and digested form, for the mind, like the stomach, will not bear undigested matter ; it may load the memory, but it will not help the intelligence (*ingenium*). He chooses the form of a dialogue.

He would hardly do so to-day perhaps[2], but to say nothing of Plato and Cicero, whose dialogues have really something of discussion about them, there is abundant precedent for the use of this style of composition for matter frankly more suitable for the dictionary or the encyclopedia. The *Deipnosophists* of Athenaeus is the most terrible monument of energy turned in this direction. Again, the *Convivial Questions* or *Symposiacs* of Plutarch, a work from which Macrobius borrowed most of his seventh book, may also have suggested this method. The *Questions*, however, Archbishop Trench says[3], are no fancy pieces, but brief records of conversations which actually sprang up at entertainments in which Plutarch took part, and at the request of a friend they were cast into their present shape from notes taken at the time. Gellius too has chapters professing to be from life, and there was also the precedent of Varro.

[1] For Gellius, see Prof. Nettleship's essay in his *Essays in Latin Literature*, i. Comparetti, *Vergil in the Middle Ages*, pt. I. c. 4, and Boissier, *La Fin du Paganisme*, vol. i. pp. 178—180, will also be found interesting.
[2] Yet a Hebrew Grammar, widely used, consisted in its first edition of "Letters to a Duchess," and a much reprinted work on the Mystics was cast in the form of a series of conversations "over wine and walnuts."
[3] *Lectures on Plutarch*, 2nd ed. p. 20, an interesting work.

Nor indeed was the deliberate dialogue yet dead, as readers of St Augustine will remember. More than one of the discussions at Cassisiacum were reported there and then by *notarii*, though doubtless Augustine remembered Cicero, when he drew up the *De Beata Vita* and the rest for publication. Even points of grammar and etymology were sometimes discussed at the dinner-table. It was a favourite diversion of the Emperor Tiberius. No doubt, before Philology became scientific, it was a game at which all could play, who had a little fancy and a slight knowledge of Greek, a language from which Latin was largely derived [1].

With all these precedents, whatever may have been his special reason, Macrobius chose to make a dialogue of his material, and like Plato and Athenaeus put the whole thing into the mouth of a man with a memory, who had been present at the supposed gathering. We are apt to forget at times that we are reading the story of a conversation, though now and again Macrobius remembers to remind us of the fact. Servius, for example, in a discourse obviously transcribed from a note-book, speaks of "his memory serving him at the moment." Here and there we have some by-play, which we generally owe to the outspokenness of Evangelus, the "villain" of the piece. After some forty consecutive Teubner pages of theology, the author apologizes, we may perhaps say, by letting the guests express their admiration of Praetextatus by a wide-eyed stare in silence, broken at last by rapturous praise of his knowledge and his memory (i. 24. 1) [2].

Macrobius frankly avows that the conversation never took place, and he even says he is not sure that all his characters could very well have met for such a purpose. For they are all, so far as we know, real people, most of them undoubtedly so. And in this, in spite of passages where we forget it is dialogue, lies some of the value of the book. The characters were deliberately chosen for their parts, and we may thus use Macrobius to supplement what we learn elsewhere. So the book, with all its faults, illustrates the age, its tastes and feelings, social, literary, philosophical and religious.

The supposed gathering may, M. Émile Thomas says [3], be dated 380. To some of the characters I have already alluded. Two remain to be considered. One is the grammarian Servius, who is

---

[1] Nettleship, *Essays*, i. p. 213, on Verrius Flaccus.
[2] Yet we should remember that even grammarians like rhetoricians would sometimes improvise in the theatre addresses in comment on some passage supplied at the moment; see Rohde, *der Gr. Roman*, p. 309, n. 1.
[3] *Scoliastes de Virgile*, p. 135.

introduced as a young but very learned man. He is loth to speak among a company so eminent for learning and divine lore, and has to be pressed to conquer his blushes. It is curious to note that when the modest scholar does open his mouth, Macrobius puts some passages of Gellius into it. One of these may be taken as a fair illustration of Macrobius' method. Gellius says: "Some grammarians of former times, men of learning and of note, among them Cornutus Annaeus [the teacher of Persius], criticize the word *vexasse* in the following passage as carelessly used and without distinction" and so forth, to which he replies at some length. Macrobius lets Avienus make the criticism in the terms used by Gellius, and Servius the reply, sticking as closely to the *Noctes*. It is much as if one introduced a living scholar into a dialogue to-day and gave him some pages of Bentley or Ussher to recite without more ado. There are also coincidences between Macrobius and the Commentary of Servius, but opinions vary as to whether Macrobius quotes that work, or whether it at a later date was enriched or enlarged by an editor adding matter from the *Saturnalia*.

But perhaps the most interesting character in the book, though not in life, is Evangelus. His introduction like so much else is due to Gellius. In the *Noctes*, says Professor Nettleship[1], "as a foil to the instructed scholar or philosopher, there appears a conceited or affected or generally unseasonable individual, whose delusions are exposed by the light of superior wisdom." This person is generally young and often a schoolmaster. In Macrobius the part is played by Evangelus, in whose name some have found a reference to the Gospel—quite unnecessarily. Evangelus is fully as unconscious of Christianity as the rest, and indeed displays some recondite acquaintance with pagan ritual in his attempt to reply to Praetextatus' praise of Virgil. But he is not merely the holder of shocking and even impossible opinions about Virgil, for his manners are monstrous. About the others there is a prodigious politeness quite in the style of Symmachus' letters. He is frankly rude, even to the point of brutality. The repugnance, involuntarily displayed by the guests when he enters, warns the reader what to expect. And, most curious of all, he too seems to be a real person, to whom Symmachus in one of his letters attributes an *incautus animus*[2].

---

[1] *Essays*, i. p. 238.
[2] *Ep.* vi. 7. This quality is getting Evangelus into danger in his wild attempt, despite the roads, to attend Honorius' fourth installation as consul. Is he or another the *homo non amicus* there mentioned?

The scene of the dialogue is the feast of the Saturnalia, and the guests meet in succession during the three days at the houses of Praetextatus, Flavian and Symmachus. The conversations, or dissertations, range over literature (which is summed up in Virgil), science, manners, morals and religion. Without attempting to keep to the order of proceedings, we may deal with the book as a whole with reference to these points.

The work may be regarded as a sort of *Institutio* of the Roman gentleman—a presentment of what he should be and what he should know. Yet it is surprising how little is said or thought of Rome, of political life, or duty to State and Empire, or even of the significance of Rome. It is away from such things that attention is directed— they were not safe subjects perhaps for Roman society. Praetextatus is represented (i. 7, 5) as disturbed at the suggestion that they were discussing anything the world might not hear. The complete gentleman is to live rather in the past than the present, and he is not to take part in public life[1]. It may of course be said that after all literature and not statecraft was Macrobius' theme, but with all the ebb and flow of the conversation it never touches matters of public concern. Some slight reference is made in the commentary on Scipio's dream to a life of action in the public interest, but that is involved by the text and but lightly treated. In Symmachus' letters, in like manner, politics are avoided. In fact they were dangerous.

The complete gentleman's education is developed along two lines—antiquarianism and Neo-Platonism, generally with Virgil as a text-book. The whole is slavish and mechanical. "The fruit of reading is to emulate what you find good in others, and by dexterous borrowing to turn to your own use what you most admire in other people's utterances" (vi. 1, 2). What did this mean in literature? An extraordinary devotion to the superficial, phrase-hunting, grammatical and lexicographical pedantry of the most unfruitful type. One of the earliest discussions turns on the expressions *noctu futura* and *die crastini* (i. 4). When one of the party makes a stand for modern speech and old manners, his utterance is from Gellius, and where the unacknowledged quotation ends, in comes another archaism, which has likewise to be discussed (*mille verborum est*, i. 5, 3).

---

[1] Not so Synesius, though a Neo-Platonist too. See his spirited letter to his brother (*Ep.* 107) on his duty to fight the barbarian invaders at the risk of incurring the Government's displeasure.

From this it is but a step to etymology, and if ever and again we are amazed, we must remember that we are not ourselves so very long emancipated from the Philology that is not comparative. Nigidius is twice quoted on the letter D. Janus and Diana are the same, we are told, "with the addition of D which is often added to the letter I by way of adorning it (*causa decoris*) as in *reditur redhibetur* etc." (i. 8. 8). *Bidentes* means sheep two years old, representing *bidennes*, D being superfluously introduced to avoid hiatus, as in *redamare, redire* etc. (vi. 9. 6). April is from *Aphrilis*, from the Greek ἀφρός, with a reference by Romulus to the mother of Aeneas (i. 12. 8). The Ides are so called because we see the full moon (*videre*, compare the Greek ἰδεῖν, i. 15, 16). Artemis cuts the air and is properly Aerotemis (i. 15, 20), an old derivation quoted by Clement of Alexandria (668 P)[1].

Meantime what of literature, that we may vindicate the name from grammarians? With his treatment of Virgil I shall deal later. For the rest, the ordinary student need only turn to van Jan's index or Eyssenhardt's (which I think is the same, abridged to the reader's loss) to find himself in a new world, and, amid a multitude of obscure names which he does not know, he looks in wonder for those he does. Apart from Virgil and Cicero, where are the other familiar names? Where are Livy, Ovid, Tibullus, Propertius? They are not mentioned. Catullus and Horace have two references each. Of the "silver age," Silius, Statius, Valerius Flaccus and Tacitus do not occur; Persius only once, Juvenal three times, and Lucan once (to correct him). Hosts of forgotten grammarians and teachers are found but not Quintilian. Professor Nettleship explains this[2]. In the second century and onward interest in the Latin schools was lost for all literature after Virgil's day, and diverted to the prae-Augustan writers, and Macrobius is heir to this conservative or reactionary feeling. Ausonius has a pleasant little poem addressed to one of his professors, whose bent was in this direction. Victorius was assiduous in forgotten books and never read anything but what was obscure; worm-eaten, ancient parchments, prehistoric pontifical lore, anything and everything rather than Tully or Virgil[3]. For

[1] Etymology broke out in the epics of the day. Nonnus in his *Dionysiaca*, the longest of all Greek epics, explains that the Nile is so called from the new mud it brought with it (νέα ἰλύς, iii. 275); he derives Dionysus from Zeus and νῦσος ὅτι γλώσσῃ Συρακοσσίδι χωλὸς ἀκούει (ix. 20). Porphyry also uses etymology to elicit hidden truths from most unlikely quarters.
[2] *Essays*, i. p. 284 f. (on Nonius Marcellus).
[3] *Professores* 22.

Macrobius however all centres in Virgil. There is no attempt to appreciate or even to explain the other authors. They with Homer merely serve to illustrate Virgil. This word is from one author, that passage is copied from another.

The reader is surprised to find in the last book a good deal of what, for want of a better word, we may call science. It is certainly not systematic. Various guests propound to Disarius the physician questions prompted by their own fancy or some casual experience. In reality most of them come straight from Plutarch, who is of course not named. Is a simple or a varied diet better for the digestion? Disarius is for the former with a special caution against "mixing drinks" (vii. 4, 7), while Eustathius stands up stoutly for the latter. Why do women rarely get drunk and old men easily[1]? Is it because women's systems are moister or because they are warmer? Why do you become giddy if you spin round? Why is honey best when fresh and wine when old? Why is the ring worn on the finger next the little finger of the left hand? Egyptian anatomists say a sinew comes direct there from the heart (vii. 13, 8), but Ateius Capito, following the Etruscans, says the left hand is less used, and the particular finger neither too large nor too small, so the jewel is safer there than elsewhere. Why does game decay more quickly in moonlight than sunlight, and why does a brass knife stuck in it stop decay[2]? The answers to these and similar questions are astounding, but they come largely from Plutarch, and the scientists of the dialogue have a confidence about them, which reminds the modern reader of his own day.

There is a long discourse on the Roman calendar, but that was rather an antiquarian than a scientific subject, so Macrobius handles it fully and freely. He seems to have been much interested in Astronomy, of which we have a good deal in the Commentary, and here he is as clear and lucid as (apart from Physiology) he generally is. His system was that of his day and he really appears to have understood the subject, and what he has to say he sets forth easily and ably.

Macrobius and sometimes the guests lay down rules of manners,

---

[1] Petit, *op. cit.* c. ix. p. 98, mentions that this discussion was copied out by Abelard for Heloise. Macrobius took it from Plutarch (*Convivial Questions*, iii. 3), who implies that the question was asked by Aristotle but not answered. A splendid history for a triviality.

[2] I am told that the first part of this is a fact in dry hot Southern climates, but probably not in Italy nor in Greece. Hence it may be asked whence Plutarch got it. For the brass knife I have found no advocate.

which after all have a more permanent value than much of their
science. "Conversation at a banquet should be as pure in its
moral tone as attractive by its charm" (i. 1, 4). The narrator is
particular to emphasize that this is not a record "of meat and drink,
though they too were there in abundance and propriety" (i. 2, 12).
This point is repeated. Society has so far advanced that when it
reads the old sumptuary laws of the republic it does not know what
dish is meant by this or that term (iii. 17, 12), and is lost in
astonishment at "the slavish gluttony of that age" (iii. 16, 11).
"Peacocks' eggs, which used to sell at five denarii apiece, I will not
say they are sold cheaper to-day, they are not on the market at all"
(iii. 13, 2).

"Those centuries, which by their blood or their sweat won the
Empire," had no doubt their virtues, but their vices shock their
posterity. Times have improved—at whose banquet do you find
dancer or dancing-girl? Yet in those evil days sons of senators
and noble ladies danced and used castanets, and Macrobius cites
his authorities, and the unfortunate Sallust has his usual rebuke—
"a weighty critic and censor of other people's luxury" (iii. 13, 9)[1].

After all this, the "jokes" of book ii. strike the reader oddly.
"When moderation had put an end to the reasonable succession of
dishes (*castimoniam ferculorum*) and convivial mirth sprang up from
the tiny cups," Symmachus proposed "humour without impro-
priety" (*alacritatem lascivia carentem*). They are in turn to
produce the best jokes of famous men which they have found in
their reading—"a lettered lightness and learned quips." His own
first contribution and some of the others would certainly be relegated
to the smoke-room to-day. We have, after a series of miscellaneous
jokes, collections of witticisms of Cicero, Augustus and Julia—an
odd mixture of indecency and the handbook.

In the seventh book, however, the whole subject of tact at table
is discussed on the lines of Plutarch, who is closely followed[2]. The
first thing is to know your company, and then draw them out.
Men like to talk of themselves, but not wishing to seem vain prefer
to be asked to speak of their brilliant deeds in battle, their travels
in unknown lands, their afflictions in days gone by, "how they

[1] Against Macrobius the hostile critic will be able to cite Ammianus and
Jerome, while Claudian will furnish instances of enormous and tasteless
expenditure.

[2] *Quaest. Conviv.* ii. 1. It is interesting to note Macrobius' insertion of an
apposite line from Virgil (*forsan et haec olim meminisse juvabit*) after Plutarch's
quotation from Euripides (ὡς ἡδύ τοι σωθέντα μεμνῆσθαι πόνων).

successfully discharged the embassy, how they were presented to
the Emperor and most courteously received, and how, when the whole
fleet was boarded by pirates[1], they alone by their cunning or their
valour escaped" (vii. 2, 11).   Never ask a man a question before
people, unless you know he can answer it and answer it well, for
men do not like to confess ignorance (*ib.* 5).   But ask the hunter
about hunting, and if a religious person (*religiosus*) is there, let him
have a chance to tell "by what observances he has won help from
the gods, what results his ceremonies brought him, for they count
it a religious duty not to be silent about the benefits the gods give
them, beside liking to be thought favourites of heaven" (vii. 2, 13).
The reason given is Macrobius' own and suggests that his feeling
is not quite the same as Plutarch's, but if commentary is needed,
the inscriptions on the monument of Praetextatus and his wife
suffice[2].

One must be careful, we learn, in badinage not to hit too hard
and to beware of sore subjects.   On minor misfortunes—such as
baldness or a head shaped like Socrates'—a man may be quizzed,
but not on such grave ones as the loss of an eye.   The man who
jokes must not even in play charge a man with vices he has.   That
is "bad form," but it will not be amiss to tax a man of stainless
character with his immoralities, or to remind a wealthy man of his
creditors.   Above all the company and time and place must be
considered.   One may safely make game of a man in his wife's
presence for being uxorious, but some jokes one had better reserve.

As a model of bad manners Evangelus is exhibited.   He interrupts conversation recklessly, and contradicts grave and learned
gentlemen who reply with a smile which should serve as a correction
but does not.   He sneers at slaves and calls for wine and plenty of
it (*indulgere, flagrare vino* ii. 8, 4).   He insults the Greek guests
on the score of their race, their national loquacity and love of
display (vii. 5, 1 and 16, 1).   Contrasted with his conduct is the
uniform suavity and graciousness of the other guests toward him—
a silent lesson to Eustachius.

Morals and religion are touched on here and there.   Evangelus'
ridicule of the idea that the gods could stoop to care for slaves calls
forth from Praetextatus a speech in the slaves' behalf.   He pleads
in eloquent language (borrowed from Seneca, *Ep.* 47) their common

[1] Apart from the novels, which swarm with pirates, and one simile in
Claudian, I do not remember any other reference to them in the works of this
period, and these pirates are borrowed from Plutarch (*Qu. Conviv.* ii. 1, 3).
[2] See essay on Symmachus, pp. 163, 164.

humanity, their possible freedom and greatness of mind, their faithfulness and goodness; and supports his statements with historical
illustrations (from Gellius and elsewhere)[1]. Praetextatus also gives
a long discourse on the gods, shewing in turn how Apollo, Bacchus,
Mars, Mercury, Hercules, Serapis, Osiris, Pan, Saturn, Jove, the
Assyrian Adad and others are all equivalents of the Sun and of one
another. This was one part of the faith of later Paganism[2]. More
is said about it in the Commentary. It may be noted however
that in both works Macrobius writes rather from the point of view
of philosophy than of devotion. He has not the moral enthusiasm
of Plutarch, the fervent pietism of Julian or the mysticism of Hermes
Trismegistus. There is the chill of the pedagogue about him. The
equations of heaven are interesting to him and so are the rites of
old Rome. To judge from his treatment of the old religion, the
new was quite beyond his comprehension.

Almost all that a man needs to know he will find, according to
Macrobius, in Virgil—explicitly or by implication. This brings us
to a consideration of his work as a critic of Virgil—work for which
he is in large measure disqualified by his want of discrimination—
by what Gibbon calls "the blind superstition of a commentator[3]."
Like many before him and many more after his day, he found in
Virgil a pedant, an encyclopaedist. Virgil knew all learning (i. 16,
12), never went wrong (*Comm.* ii. 8, 1), was a master in priestly
lore (*S.* i. 24, 16) and delighted to introduce it into his poetry along
with astronomy, philosophy, and all sorts of gleanings from Greek
and Latin literature and oratory. It is Virgil's learning that appeals
to him rather than his poetry, and while there is much truth in
what he says of Virgil's felicity in using his knowledge of antiquity
and literature, it is absurd to make it, as he does, Virgil's chief
claim to distinction. Still he does not stand alone in this; he is
following a tradition. The excessive attention given to rhetoric in
the schools had so far perverted Roman taste that perfection of
language linked to wide information was all that was asked of a
poet. It is enough to read a book of Lucan to see this. How

[1] The equality before God of slave and freeman was a Neo-Platonic doctrine.
Synesius says (*Dreams*, c. 8, 1301 D) it matters nothing to God, which is the
Eteobutades and which the new-bought drudge Manes. Cf. his relations with
his own slaves (*Ep.* 145) who are treated as equals and love him as an elected
chief.
[2] So Gasquet in his interesting essay on Mithras (*Revue des deux Mondes*,
1st April, 1899), calls Macrobius "le théoricien par excellence du syncrétisme
païen. Ses Saturnales en sont le manifeste."
[3] Gibbon, ch. xxxii. n. 3.

many Roman poets find their highest eulogy in the word *doctus*?
To prove Virgil *doctus*, grammarians had for centuries busied themselves with the letter till they had forgotten the spirit. The
popularity of Statius, says Comparetti[1], proved the want of real
poetic feeling in Rome ; and in the three centuries between Statius
and Macrobius there had been nothing to quicken it. Here as elsewhere Macrobius held he was best serving the present by echoing
the past[2].

Of course Virgil is compared with Homer, but the criticism hardly
rises so high as Dryden's contrast of "majesty" and "loftiness of
thought." It is rather that Virgil, carried away, and sometimes
too far, by a desire to emulate Homer, imitates this, that and the
other passage or line ; and here he is superior, there equal and in a
third place inferior to his model. It is very systematically done,
for the *Aeneid* is taken book by book, and the parallels are pointed
out. There are no doubt flashes of light here and there, and good
points are brought out[3], but in the end the reader is not a whit
nearer a general judgment on the work of the two poets.

Virgil's knowledge of pontifical law is illustrated by the citation
of passages containing priestly word and phrase used in their just
and proper senses. Here Evangelus protests and cites instances to
prove Virgil was not universally careful in these matters. The
attempt is made to rebut the charge, but, though there is an unhappy break in the MSS, one has the impression that Virgil's
advocate is dealing with him as old-fashioned apologists did with
the Old Testament. The answers are too subtle, too clever. For
example, Evangelus quotes *Aeneid* iii. 21

caelicolum regi mactabam in litore taurum,

and cites Ateius Capito to shew that a bull is not sacrificed to Jove.
"Quite so," rejoins Praetextatus, "Virgil in view of the horror to
follow (the blood of Polydore) introduced the bull—a blunder, which
according to Ateius is expiable, and which is here deliberately
committed to lead up to the marvel" (iii. 10, 3—7).

[1] I may generally refer the reader to the first five chapters of Comparetti's
most interesting book on *Vergil in the Middle Ages.* Part II. c. 1 may be
consulted for the medieval view of Virgil as an outcome of that held by
Macrobius and his school.
[2] Perhaps he was, when men ranked Ausonius as equal to Virgil. How is it
that both Macrobius and Symmachus ignore Claudian?
[3] He remarks, *e.g.* (v. 16, 8) that Fortuna or Τύχη is a power unknown to
Homer. (See Rohde, *der Griechische Roman*, § ii. 4, p. 276, on the progress of
this "junge Göttin.") Macrobius following the "philosophers" takes a diametrically opposite view of her to that of Quintus.

An illustration may serve to shew his method of displaying Virgil's correctness. He twice quotes with the same explanation the line

interea magnum sol circumvolvitur annum

(*Aen.* iii. 284; *Sat.* i. 14, 5; *Comm.* ii. 11, 6). It refers to the period of Aeneas' wanderings and his arrival at Actium. Conington finds in *magnum* an ornamental epithet; Wakefield (cited by him) a reference to the feeling of an exile, which I think not unlikely in view of Virgil's constant recurrence to thoughts of exile. Macrobius explains *annus* as a revolution, *brevis annus* being that of the moon, *i.e.* a month, *magnus annus* that of the sun, *i.e.* so many lunar months *plus* some days. Thus *magnus* has no reference to Aeneas' exile, but is a technical term of Astronomy.

He prefers the Catalogue in the second book of the *Iliad* to Virgil's in the seventh *Aeneid*, because it is systematic, while Virgil forgets the map and mentions places as they occur to him, introducing elaborately warriors who never appear again, and forgetting others whose names should be there (v. 15, 16). Thus what is to modern readers the charm of the passage, Virgil's affectionate and intimate knowledge of Italy displayed as he lingers over this place and that, each with its memories of ancient glories of his people, of happy days he himself has known amid streams and woods and vineyards—all this goes for nothing; his geography is poor.

So much for Italy, and what of Rome?

Romanos rerum dominos gentemque togatum—

What has he to say about such a line? "Virgil appropriately used the epithet *gens togata* for the Romans, for Laberius used it in his *Ephebus: togatae stirpis;* and lower down *dilatatum est dominium togatae gentis.*" He is not concerned to speak of Virgil's conception of Rome giving peace and order to the world. He reads his poet carefully and comments on a thousand passages, but the great fundamental thought that fills and animates the work—*tantae molis erat Romanam condere gentem*—utterly escapes him. It was not so with all Virgil's readers of the day. This thought is caught by Prudentius and Claudian, and each in his own way developes it, but these men were poets and Macrobius was a commentator. The scribe is tithing mint and anise and cummin, and the greater matters of the law escape him.

Again, the *Aeneid* has been called the epic of human life.

More than in any Roman poet or indeed any poet of antiquity we
find in Virgil the sense of human limitations—"the pain of finite
hearts that yearn"—coupled with admiration for those who do their
proper work faithfully and manfully. Tennyson gives the truth of
the matter in his description of Virgil :—

"Thou majestic in thy sadness at the doubtful doom of human kind."

Macrobius, in illustrating Virgil's faithfulness to the canons of
rhetoric, picks out a series of passages to illustrate pathos, as he
does with the other emotions[1]. This is easy to do, but one might
almost say he is more conscious of the successful artifice than of the
depth of feeling. He judges the expression more as a telling appeal
addressed to an audience than as a poet's interpretation of human
life. The exquisite language charms him, but he is not greatly
moved by the sorrow and the love which animate it.

It may be doubted whether Macrobius really appreciated Virgil
as Augustine did. Thus Macrobius writes: "Virgil so far improved
on his model [Apollonius] (*elegantius auctore*), that the story of the
wantoning Dido, which everybody knows to be false, has passed for
true through all these centuries, and it is still popularly accounted
true, so that painters and sculptors and workers in embroidery employ
this theme as if there were no other. So greatly has the beauty of
the telling prevailed that all men, knowing as they do the chastity of
the Phoenician queen and well aware that she laid hands on herself
to save her fair fame[2], yet let the story pass and prefer to suppress
the truth, and allow that to be believed which the sweetness of the
poet has implanted in people's breasts" (*pectoribus humanis dulcedo
fingentis infudit, Sat.* v. 17, 5—6). St Augustine is not writing
about Virgil—heaven forbid!—but he remembers his introduction
to him. How he had hated the jingle of the school—"Two and two
make four"; and how he had loved the literature the grammarian
taught him—the tale of the wooden horse, the burning of Troy and
ipsius umbra Creusae! (Conf. i. 13, 22 and 20). And he had
"wept for Dido dead, because she slew herself for love, though
meanwhile I saw myself in all this dying away from Thee, O God
my life, and my eyes were dry—unhappy man! What could be
more pitiable than an unhappy man not pitying himself, and
weeping Dido's death which came of loving Aeneas, but not weeping

[1] See Comparetti, *op. cit.* p. 69: "While the rhetoricians in forming their
laws had quoted Virgil as their chief authority, Macrobius now praises Virgil for
having observed the laws of rhetoric."

[2] Cf. Aug. *Conf.* i. 13, 22, and Ausonius' epigram from the Greek, *Anth.
Plan.* iv. 151.

his own death which came of not loving Thee, O God?" (*Conf.* i. 13, 21). Both men know the tale is untrue, and one asks Why did I weep? the other, Why is it such a favourite with artists?

On the other hand, though Macrobius lacks the highest gifts of insight and inspiration, his work must be pronounced useful and interesting. On the lower plane which is more to his mind he has done good service in diligently collecting and gracefully presenting much valuable matter in illustration of Virgil. He shews us at once the tastes of the cultivated society of his day and the traditions of the best scholarship of the Empire. The weapons of the stone age are not perhaps very serviceable to-day but they have their importance, and so in other things a man, who will, even at the cost of the expression of himself, let us see vividly and clearly some former stage in the history of culture, is doing us good service. The faults we find in his work are largely those of his day and of his profession. If we to-day judge the grammarian almost as hardly as he judged the *litteratores*, those schoolmasters who won the scholar's contempt by trying to pass off their ignorance as omniscience; if even the higher work of the better teachers as shewn by Macrobius and Ausonius seems to us wanting in soul and feeling, we must remember Augustine's gratitude to the *grammaticus* who taught him Virgil. No doubt the great man thanks his teacher for much which he owes to himself, still there must have been quickening elements in the teaching. Augustine was surely not the only student, who wept for Dido, who was stirred to higher life and thought by such books as the *Hortensius*. We shall see that Macrobius in his own way believed in the things that are more excellent.

He had not Augustine's endowment,—his interest in everything, his delicate sensibility to impressions, his feeling and imagination, his passionate and emotional temperament, any more than his strength of mind, his spiritual nature and his determination to reach reality. Yet Macrobius was a man of feeling too, a good and affectionate father, as we can see from his address to Eustachius, and a conscientious teacher. There is, he says, no claim so great as a child's upon a parent, and no pleasure or pain so keen as the parent's according as he sees his labour of love for his child prosper or fail (*Sat.* i. 1, 1). He has read and studied for his son, and "all that I have" of history, literature, Greek and Latin, "is thine." We can read his feelings on friendship in the pictures he draws of the friends gathered at the Saturnalia. He has that mixture of amiability and a limitless readiness to take pains for those with whom he has been brought in contact, with the want of sympathy and even contempt for the unenlightened, the "outsider," which is too apt to be found in the professional teacher in every age.

To Macrobius' Commentary we owe the preservation of Cicero's *Dream of Scipio*, a part of the work *De Republica*. It is in some degree analogous to Plato's story of Er the Armenian. Scipio sees in a dream his father Paulus and his (adoptive) grandfather Scipio Africanus. He finds himself with them in the Milky Way, looking down upon the earth, which he thence realizes to be but a tiny portion of space, and the Roman part of it still more insignificant. The sense of infinite time is brought home to him, and he is asked, What is earthly glory[1]? A thing of narrow range and short duration. What then is man's work and end? The soul is divine and eternal, and his soul is the man—*mens cujusque is est quisque.* A good man's soul ascends from the prison house and chains of the body to the galaxy there to enjoy eternal life, but he must not hasten his departure, nor, without leave of him who assigned the station and the duty, abandon them. The soul must contemplate what is without and, while not cutting its connexion, must withdraw itself from the body in meditation. The best work a man can undertake is the welfare of his country. "That you may be the keener to guard the state, Africanus, know this : that for all who have saved, helped or increased their country, there is a fixed and definite place in heaven, where in happiness they may enjoy eternal life. For to that supreme God who rules the universe, there is nothing of all that is on earth more grateful than those gatherings and ordered societies of men (*coetus hominum jure sociati*) which are called states. Their rulers and saviours proceed hence and return again hither" (*Somnium* 3, 1).

This work Macrobius took as his text, and as sometimes happens the commentary is out of all proportion. It is here sixteen or seventeen times the length of the text. It is heavily weighted with digressions on every conceivable excuse. Without them it would be a better proportioned book, but certainly less interesting. So many subjects are handled and with such fulness of detail that the work has a substantive value of its own as a repository of popularized

---

[1] This line of reflexion recurs in Boethius' *Consolation of Philosophy*, ii. 7, in a passage recalling Cicero's story; and in a very different work, the *Life of Antony*, cc. 16, 17, it may be found again, pointing another moral—ascetic monachism, which is perhaps only an alternative route to the same goal in eternal life.

Neo-Platonism. As such indeed it had considerable use in the Middle Ages[1]. Myths (dealt with by Julian in his seventh *Oration*), dreams (the subject of a work of Synesius), numbers and their spiritual significances, the Milky Way, the horizon, eclipses, the moon, the motions of the celestial spheres, the stars, the origin of their names and the possibilities of their influencing or predicting the course of human life (a subject that much interested Augustine in his Platonist days)[2], the sizes of the sun and of the earth, and their distance from each other, the mapping of the Zodiac, the distribution of matter, the music of the spheres with incidental reference to the influence of music generally, the zones of the world and the antipodes, tides and their origin—all these themes are treated at length by Macrobius on pretexts arising from Cicero's little story. "Truly therefore we must pronounce that there is nothing more complete than this work, in which is comprised the whole range of philosophy" (*universa philosophiae integritas, Comm.* ii. 17, 17). In plain terms he is treating Cicero here as he did Virgil, though the *Dream* really does give him openings more strictly legitimate for the propagation of knowledge, which is usually borrowed but not always accurate[3].

I shall not follow him into his digressions, nor give in detail his discussions even of more vital matters, but I shall endeavour to sketch in outline the general results of his philosophy or, to give it the name it better deserves at this period of heathenism, his theology. Though a good deal of it is present in germ in Cicero, taken of

---

[1] St Thomas Aquinas cites it as his authority on Neo-Platonic teaching about the *primum ens*, and Abelard often refers to Macrobius—"no mean philosopher"—finding, *e.g.* an exposition of the Trinity in his God, νοῦς and *anima*. See Petit, *op. cit.* c. ix. and pp. 72, 79. Interest in Macrobius declined with the revival of the study of Greek, as befel with another Neo-Platonist, an even greater favourite in the Middle Ages, Boethius.

[2] Macrobius (*C.* i. 19, 20—27) seems to incline to the view of Plotinus (to whom he refers, *Enn.* ii. 3) that the stars like birds enable us to foresee, but do not themselves affect, our future. So Ammianus (xx. 1, 9) expounds augury, finding its ultimate cause in *benignitas numinis* and the divine interest in man. Porphyry (*de Abstinentia* iii. 5) says the gods if silent yet give warnings, which birds understand more quickly than men and then tell us as well as they can. "All things" says Synesius (*Dreams*, c. 2, 1285 D) "prophesy through all, since all are kin, that are in the one living creature, the universe." There are responses as between the chords of a lyre, and so conversely men can influence the gods by certain means, *i.e.* magic—a view Synesius later on renounced, as Augustine did all astrology (*Conf.* vii. 6, 8 and *C. D.* v. 1 f.). How great a feat it was to do this is shewn by Ammianus (xxviii. 4, 24)—"Many in Rome, who deny that there are higher powers in heaven, will not go out of doors, nor dine, nor indeed think it quite safe even to bathe, until they have carefully consulted an almanack and learnt where *e.g.* Mercury is, etc."

[3] The reader may be referred to Petit, c. v.

course from Greek thinkers, its development is Neo-Platonic, and it constantly points to its origin in the general teaching of Plotinus and his school[1].

How far Neo-Platonism by process of borrowing or of original reflexion reached its degree of likeness to Oriental modes of thought, this is hardly the place to discuss. But one thing at least in the Commentary stands out in marked contrast with the text. The heaven of which Cicero speaks is pre-eminently for patriots, servants of their country, for men of action in virtue of their life of political well-doing; with Macrobius the influence of Neo-Platonism is so strong that, though such men have a share in his heaven, they hardly enter it and in spite of their taking part in public life. It is no longer a help, it is a hindrance. We find this in other Neo-Platonists[2]. The hymns of Synesius, which are really prayers, ask for nothing so much as for freedom from anxieties and disturbing cares. When pressure is put upon him to become a bishop, his great dread is that this will drag him into the world, into affairs, and lessen and destroy the leisure and calm of mind essential to his spiritual life. It is playing with his own soul for other people's political and social necessities. He made the sacrifice, however, like the Spartan he was (*Ep.* 113).

The object of Macrobius' Commentary is to reinforce the doctrine of Plato and Cicero that there is a life beyond the grave— a doctrine in which he finds the very foundations of all morality and of society itself. The story of Scipio's Dream, like the myth of Er, is ridiculed, he knows, by the Epicureans, a flippant, loud-voiced and perverse school; but none the less it has "inexpugnable reason" behind it. Less emphasized perhaps but not less real is his aim to maintain the sufficiency of Neo-Platonism against Christianity as well as against Epicureanism, both being hated by his party[3].

In outline Macrobius' system is as follows. The universe is one vast whole, to be regarded in some sort as a temple (*C.* i. 14, 2) and

---

[1] Petit c. vi. discusses Macrobius' philosophy, finding that here, as in literary criticism, his work is second-hand. He gives other men's results as *dogmata*, without much insight of his own. It should be remembered that he is quite open about his dependence on "right thinkers," "Platonists," Plotinus, etc.; *e.g.* especially *C.* ii. 15, 2. "I do not forget myself so far, nor am I so ill inspired as of my own ability either to oppose Aristotle or defend Plato."

[2] Porphyry, *de Abstin.* i. 27, says he writes not for artisans, nor athletes, nor soldiers, nor sailors, nor rhetoricians, nor τοῖς τὸν πραγματικὸν βίον ἐπανελομένοις.

[3] Cf. Lucian's *Alexander* 25 and 38, an interesting anticipation of Julian's twin hatreds.

eternal (*C.* ii. 10, 9). God is the first and the origin of all things that are. By reason of the superabundant fertility of his majesty he created Mind (*mens* or νοῦς) from himself. From Mind came Soul (*anima*); thence bodies, stars animated by divine intelligences, and earthly bodies, human, animal and vegetable. Thus from the supreme god down to the lowest dregs of the universe (*ad ultimam rerum faecem*) runs a connexion, holding itself together by mutual links and never broken. This is Homer's golden chain, which he says God bade hang from heaven to earth. There is a real kinship between man and the stars[1] (*C.* i. 14, §§ 6, 7, and 15). The aim of his work is to shew that man is not only immortal but is god, the real man not being what is seen, but that by which the seen is ruled, his soul or *anima* in fact (*C.* ii. 12, 5 and 9).

Souls before they are ensnared by the desire for a body (*necdum desiderio corporis irretitae*) dwell in the starry region of the universe and thence sink down into bodies (*C.* i. 9, 10). I am not sure whether this is to be lamented or not. By Synesius and to some extent by Macrobius it is implied that this fall is not a happy thing altogether. Yet nature to continue animal life has put such love of the body into the soul that it loves its fetter and dislikes to leave it (*C.* ii. 16, 19). It is however in reality a fall[2], a death of the soul (*C.* i. 10, 17: 11, 1), but after all a temporary death (*ad tempus obruitur*, *C.* i. 12, 17)[3]. Much has been said by the ancients and many poetical descriptions put forth about things below, *infera*, hell or the grave. The body is the *infera* of the soul, σῶμα a body and σῆμα a tomb meaning much the same thing (*C.* i. 10, 9 ff. and 11, 3). There is yet another sense for *infera* as we shall see.

So the soul passes through the Tropics as through gates into this world (*C.* i. 12, 1—2), losing as it goes some of its memory of things above[4], "for if souls bore down into their bodies the memory

---

[1] Thus Synesius (*Ep.* 100) playfully says he thinks the stars must look down on him with kindly feelings as the only man in Cyrene who contemplates them with understanding. In *Hymn* i. 80—100, he sets the same doctrine forth in poetry of some beauty.

[2] Porphyry (*ad Marcellam* 5) calls it a fall, τὸ εἰς τὴν γένεσιν πτῶμα ὅσον καὶ οἷον ἡμῖν τῆς ψυχῆς περιέστη, though the gods do not forget us but are σωτῆρες. Naville (*Saint-Augustin*, p. 92) warns us that the analogy between this πτῶμα and Augustine's fall of man is much more apparent than real. The Neo-Platonist does not or should not attach the idea of sin to it.

[3] So Porphyry, *de Antro Nympharum* 10, cites Heraclitus, ζῆν ἡμᾶς τὸν ἐκείνων (sc. ψυχῶν) θάνατον καὶ ζῆν ἐκείνας τὸν ἡμέτερον θάνατον. Plotinus, *Enn.* iv. 83 ᾗ (sc. ψυχῇ) καὶ δέσμος τὸ σῶμα καὶ τάφος.

[4] So Synesius (*Dreams*, 1296 B) teaches that the soul is led to choose slavery by the gifts of matter (cf. ὕλα με μάγοις ἐπέδησε τέχναις, *Hymn*. 3, 574), as if contracting to be a slave for a term, and on entering bodily life it has to quaff a

of the divine matters of which they were conscious in heaven, there would be no difference of opinion among men about these things, but all drink oblivion in their descent, some in a greater and others in a less measure" (*C.* i. 12, 9). The soul then finds itself below, with some memory of heavenly things and a strong love of the body, and as it is ruled by the one or the other it rises or falls (*C.* i. 11, 11). Contempt for the world and a heavenward aspiration help it upward. Those alone are happy who live in the contemplation of things above (*superna*) and diligently seek after them and as far as may be imitate them [1] (*C.* i. 8, 3). Those who can escape public affairs, and purging themselves of the contagion of the body strive by flight from human things [2] to find their place among divine, have really advanced (*C.* i. 8, 8). For these may die to the world—"we use the word *dying* too, when the soul still domiciled in the body is taught by philosophy and spurns the allurements of the body and rids itself of the pleasant treachery of desires and all other passions [3]" (*C.* i. 13, 6). In such cases "conversation in heaven" may be reached, "for souls, who in this life free themselves from the fetters of the body by the death philosophy teaches, may, though the body yet lives, take their place (*inserantur*) in heaven and among the stars" (*C.* i. 13, 10) [4]. The universe is a temple of god; all the visible is his temple who is conceived by mind alone; to him as its founder

---

cup of Lethe. Pleasure (*Dio*, 1129 B) is the brooch (περόνη) that binds soul to body by divine arrangement. Cf. Porphyry, *de Antr. Nymph.* 16 δι' ἡδονῆς δεσμεῖσθαι καὶ κατάγεσθαι τὰ θεῖα εἰς γένεσιν... 22 δύο οὖν ταύτας ἔθεντο πύλας καρκίνον καὶ αἰγοκέρων οἱ θεολόγοι...τούτων δὲ καρκίνον μὲν εἶναι δι' οὗ κατίασιν αἱ ψυχαί, αἰγοκέρων δὲ δι' οὗ ἀνίασιν.

[1] Synesius (*Ep.* 139) cites with approval this teaching of Plotinus, phrasing it thus:—τὸ ἐν σαυτῷ θεῖον ἄναγε ἐπὶ τὸ πρωτόγονον θεῖον. So far do they go that Synesius (*Ep.* 137) maintains that right living, ὀρθῶς βιοῦν, is useful merely as a prelude to wisdom, προοίμιον τοῦ φρονεῖν.

[2] Cf. Plotinus, *Enn.* i. 6, 8; Porphyry, *ad Marc.* 10 τῇ μελετώσῃ (*i.e.* Marcella) φεύγειν ἀπὸ τοῦ σώματος.

[3] Porphyry, *ad Marc.* 7, on rising superior to pleasures. Cc. 12 ff. present a far loftier picture of right living than anything Macrobius says on the subject.

[4] He uses a phrase curiously recalling Christian hymnody when he speaks of the soul, after it has deserved to be purged from contagion, returning fully restored to the fountain of eternal life—*ad perennis vitae fontem restituta in integrum* (*C.* i. 12, 17). Boethius, *Cons. Phil.* iv. metre 1, has a beautiful little poem on the rising of the soul to the "dear lost land" (James' translation):

> *huc te si reducem referat via,*
> *quam nunc requiris immemor;*
> *haec dices, memini, patria est mihi,*
> *hinc ortus hic sistam gradum.*

Julian, *Or.* iv. 136 A, speaks of good men's souls ascending after death to Serapis, who saves them from γένεσις thereafter, and brings them to the intelligible world, κόσμος νοητός.

the highest worship is due, and whoever comes into this temple must realize he has to live the priest's life (*C.* i. 14, 2)[1]. The fruit of virtue lies in a good conscience (*C.* ii. 10, 2) but for the wicked there is the more awful meaning of hell, the *infera*. All that the poets have said is but parable; Phlegethon and Acheron mean but anger and sorrow, Styx whatever plunges men among themselves into the whirlpool of hate. The vulture is but the torture of conscience as it tears the guilty flesh, and with reminder of past sin lacerates the vital parts without ceasing, ever waking remorse anew should it seek to rest, never by any pity sparing itself—all in accordance with the law that no guilty man is ever acquitted by himself [Juvenal xiii. 3], nor can escape his own sentence on himself. So with the other penalties—the guilty ever seem to themselves on the brink of being overtaken by the ruin they deserve[2]. No, the insight of the *theologi* is not in vain (*C.* i. 10, 12—15).

This is the view of the Neo-Platonists. Synesius makes a somewhat playful allusion to it in a letter (32) about a bad slave whom he does not punish—"for his wickedness is sufficient punishment for the wicked." More seriously elsewhere he represents insensibility to evil, the absence of a desire to rise, as the last and worst state of evil[3]. So too says Augustine, with that note of experience which marks his theology, "Thou hast ordained, and so it is, that every disordered spirit is itself its own punishment" (*Conf.* i. 12, 19). The direct way in which he makes this law the law of God will strike the reader. It puts a different complexion on the doctrine at once. Later on he sums it up more briefly, though hardly more tellingly, *peccatum poena peccati*. (See *op. imp. c. Jul.* i. 44 f.)

Suicide Macrobius, avowedly following Plotinus[4], forbids on the

---

[1] Porphyry, *de Abstin.* ii. 49 ὁ φιλόσοφος καὶ θεοῦ τοῦ ἐπὶ πᾶσιν ἱερεύς: ii. 46 ἐν τῷ νεῷ τοῦ πατρὸς τῷ κόσμῳ τούτῳ. Synesius, *Ep.* 57, 1388 c ἔζων...ὥσπερ ἐν ἱερῷ περιβόλῳ τῷ κόσμῳ.

[2] The reader will remember the powerful lines of Persius iii. 35—43, his picture of the last stage of damnation *virtutem videant intabescantque relicta*, and the exclamation of the guilty *imus, imus praecipites*—a passage to which Augustine (*C. D.* ii. 7) refers with approval though he declares it was unproductive of effect in view of pagan stories of divine lust. Cf. Boethius, *Cons. Phil.* iii. m. 8.

[3] *Dreams*, 1293 D; cf. *Ep.* 44, 1372 A, an important letter on the whole question of retribution. Cf. the discussion of this in Boethius, *Cons. Phil.* iv. 4.

[4] Porphyry, *vita Plotini* 11, says he thought of suicide but Plotinus came to him and forbade him. Plotinus, *Enn.* i. 9 εἰ δὲ οἷος ἕκαστος ἔξεισι, τοιαύτην ἴσχει ἐκεῖ τάξιν, εἰς τὸ προκόπτειν οὔσης ἐπιδόσεως οὐκ ἐξακτέον. Petit, *op. cit.* p. 75, shews that Macrobius cites Porphyry's view (*de Abstin.* ii. 47) on the spirits of suicides as Plotinus', a slip he attributes to memory, though in view of Macrobius' methods one might suppose it due to an intermediary source. This whole passage on suicide is quoted by Abelard (Petit, p. 79).

ground that "since in the other life souls are to be rewarded for
the measure of perfection which they have attained in this, one
must not hasten the end of life while there is still a possibility of
further improvement. Nor is this idly said. For in the esoteric
discourses on the soul's return, it is said that those who sin
(*delinquentes*) in this life are like those who stumble upon level
ground, who can rise without difficulty; but souls that leave this
life with the stains of sins upon them are to be compared to those
who fall sheer down from a great and precipitous height, where
there is no power to rise again" (*C.* i. 13, 15—16). Link to this his
doctrine of the eternity of the universe and of the soul (*C.* i. 1, 7;
14, 20), and his picture is not unlike Prudentius' description of the
horrors of eternal hell[1]. On the other hand, heaven, he says, is
closed to all but perfect purity (*C.* i. 13, 19).

Such is Macrobius' presentment of the doctrines of the Neo-
Platonists. It is a creed of great moral elevation with many
elements of value. Definite and explicit he escapes the vagueness
that so often vitiates the teaching of his school, of Trismegistus, for
instance; while by skimming over the surface of things, as is his
wont, he seems to avoid the difficulties which a Plotinus presents.
Here at least Neo-Platonism is given in a form a plain man can
surely understand and readily put into action. What is wanting?

I will only ask the reader to consider two contemporary criticisms, if I may so call them both. On the funeral monument of
Praetextatus is given a list of his priesthoods and with it a more
impressive list of the mysteries into which he was initiated. What
had he to do with the rites of Bacchus and Eleusis, with Mithras
and the *taurobolium*, when such a simple faith as this was before
him? Or, to put it generally, why did theurgy so persistently dog
the steps of Neo-Platonism? Why was magic necessary to supplement philosophy? What is the meaning of the wistful prayerfulness
of Trismegistus, his desire for and belief in communion with a
personal God? Macrobius does not seem conscious of such things,
or, if he is, he rather inclines to disdain them (*Sat.* vii. 2, 13).

Augustine tells us how he read "certain books of the Platonists

---

[1] Prudentius, *Hamart.* 825—839. A little lower Prudentius describes the
upward flight of the purified soul after death, unhampered by the body, in
language which recalls these doctrines set forth by Macrobius. See too Synesius, *Ep.* 44, on punishment after death. Hermes Trismegistus (Ed. Bipont.
Apul. ii. p. 312) says guilty souls are condemned on an examination held by the
*summus daemon; ut in hoc obsit animae aeternitas, quod sit immortali sententia
aeterno supplicio subjugata.* This he says is more to be feared than physical
death.

translated from Greek into Latin," and was greatly helped by them. From them he gained the first hint for his solution of the problem of evil, with his doctrines of being and of order. Much that he there learned abode with him for ever, but he was not satisfied. The language in which he phrases his criticism is full of scriptural metaphors, and may strike the Classical student as oddly as the Scriptures did Augustine himself at first; yet in his own way Augustine has felt and is expressing the real weakness of Neo-Platonism.

"Those pages present not the image of this piety:—the tears of confession, Thy sacrifice, the troubled spirit, the contrite and humbled heart, the salvation of the people, the Bride, the City, the earnest of the Holy Spirit, the cup of our redemption. No one there sings: 'Shall not my soul be submitted to God? From Him is my salvation. For He is my God and my salvation, my guardian; I shall not be moved more' [*Ps.* lxii. 1—2, Septuagint]. No one there hears Him calling 'Come unto Me, ye who labour.' They disdain to learn of Him for He is meek and humble of heart. For Thou hast hidden these things from the wise and prudent and hast revealed them unto babes" (*Conf.* vii. 21, 27).

CHAPTER IX

ST AUGUSTINE'S *CONFESSIONS*

Factus eram ipse mihi magna quaestio.

Conf. iv. 4, 9

OF all men of the fourth century St Augustine is the most conspicuous[1]. It is not merely that in intellectual and spiritual endowment he eclipses his contemporaries, but Harnack is unquestionably right when he says that between St Paul and Luther there is none that can be measured with Augustine. He gave to Christian thought on God and man, on sin and grace, on the world and the church, an impulse and a direction, the force of which is still unspent. He shaped the Catholic theory of the Church, he gave the great Popes the idea of the City of God, of God's Empire, he was the father of the mystics, the founder of the scholastic philosophy of the Middle Ages, and above all the hero and master of the Renaissance and the Reformation. He gave the Catholic Church the baleful doctrine "Compel them to come in"; he gave Calvin the doctrine of Predestination and he was the only father from whom Luther really learnt.

---

[1] The literature on St Augustine is immense. I have used for the purposes of this essay Harnack, *History of Dogma*, section on St Augustine, and appendix on Neo-Platonism; also Harnack's separate lecture on the *Confessions of St Augustine;* J. Reinkens, *die Geschichtsphilosophie des hl. Aug.*; Boissier, *La Fin du Paganisme*, bk iii. c. 3 on the Conversion of St Aug. (also in the *Revue des Deux Mondes*, 1 Jan. 1888, vol. 85, pp. 43—69); E. Feuerlein, *Ueber die Stellung A.'s in der Kirchen- u. Culturgeschichte* in *Histor. Zeitschrift*, vol. xxii. (1869), pp. 270—313; Loofs, Art. on St Augustine in Herzog's *Realencyklopädie* (last ed.), vol. ii.; H. A. Naville, *St Aug., Étude sur le développement de sa pensée jusqu'à l'époque de son ordination*, Genève 1872; Mozley, *Augustinian Doctrine of Predestination;* and some other books which I have used incidentally. Last, but not least, I would mention the lectures (as yet unpublished) of my former colleague, Dr John Watson, of Queen's University, Canada, from whom I have had very great help.

But it is not with his theology or his philosophy or his influence on the Church that we have here to deal. For the present we are concerned with him as a man of letters, who with his wonderfully full and various nature entered into all the life of his time, and read the world and the heart of man as they had not been read before ; who after much hesitation became convinced that in the Church was truth and so to the Church made his submission, there to learn the way to God, in Whom at last he found rest for his soul. All this story is told in his *Confessions*, a book which among all books written in Latin stands next to the *Aeneid* for the width of its popularity and the hold it has upon mankind. It does not perhaps appeal to the same audience, it is not strictly a work of art, but it is as full of life and touches the heart as truly, though from a different quarter. It was a new departure in literature and stands at the head of a new school. It was in his own day the most widely read and liked of Augustine's works, and it is still printed and re-printed, translated and re-translated.

Its chief marks are truthfulness, observation and experience. Here is a man whom nothing escapes. Everything interests him, everything raises questions for him, and he must get to the root of everything. He studies himself, and relentlessly analyses his moods, his fancies, his ambitions, his feelings, his aspirations after God and his attempts to escape Him. He is not merely curious, for all these enquiries are related to one another, and all tend to the great questions : Who am I ? Why am I ? For whom am I ? What is the meaning and purpose of this complicated and even self-contradictory nature of man, of this disordered and confusing world ? At one time he tells us that he came near abandoning the search for the answers to these questions, so difficult were they, but he found its abandonment more impossible than its prosecution and persevered till he found what he sought. This inability of his to be content with no answer or a make-believe answer would have been remarkable in any age, but how much more in his own age, an age when the spirit of inquiry seemed to be saying farewell to mankind ? It was an age, too, when after centuries of rhetoric and tyranny mankind seemed almost as incapable of speaking the truth as of seeking it[1].

[1] The reader of the *Confessions* is every now and then reminded that Augustine was once a rhetorician. Such plays as that on *peritus* and *periturus* are far-away echoes from the school. This makes more significant the fact brought out by Mr E. W. Watson (*Classical Review*, Feb. 1901, p. 65), " Rhetorician as Augustine was, and master of several styles, he had a curious power of dropping his rhetoric when he undertook in homilies and com-

Told by another, the history of Augustine's development, of his complex life, his experiments (his own word) and observations in manners, morals and religion would have been interesting. Told by himself it has a unique value, as the record of a peculiarly rich life, a story of real experience, the drama of a soul's progress from error to truth, from uncertainty to rest in the love of God, in which every stage is won by struggle, where nothing is done by guesswork and everything has been tested in actual living, all set forth by the man who has been through it all and who can tell it with a charm, a power and an honesty rarely to be found together in any writer of any age.

He is observant, he is truthful, and he is affectionate. His nature was a large and genial one. He seems to have liked, to have loved, the men and women he met. He certainly won their love and kept it. His pupils in rhetoric became his disciples in thought and faith, following him over land and sea to be with him and to share his spiritual and intellectual life. It is this that makes his book what it is. The keen intellect is not quicker than the warm heart to detect the weakness of a wrong view of God and man. Intellect and instinct have each their strength and their weakness, and in Augustine they correct each other. Emotion cannot lead him where reflexion will not approve, nor can thought rest where heart is dissatisfied. He must be clear and he must be in contact with flesh and blood, so in turn he rises above Manichaeanism and Neo-Platonism. He must have a rational view of God, a God supreme and free from any taint of responsibility for evil, and yet a God Who knows and feels a man's inability to overcome evil by his own effort, a God Who knows the human heart at least as sympathetically as he does himself and does not love it less, in fact the God of grace. God is the origin of his life, and his life, properly understood, consists in returning to God, living in Him and enjoying Him[1], but here he rejects or supplements Neo-Platonism, for his experience has taught him that such life is impossible under the Neo-Platonic scheme of things with a remote God ; his heart cries out for a self-revealing God, Who will Himself come directly into relation with the heart of man and lift man into Himself. Thus his book is not

mentaries to interpret Scripture." I do not think it fanciful to find the same passion for reality underlying another fact which Mr Watson mentions. He quotes Norden, *Antike Kunstprosa*, to the effect that Augustine was the first to form his rhythms by accent instead of quantity.

[1] *Conf.* x. 22, 32 *Ipsa est beata vita gaudere ad te, de te, propter te; ipsa est et non est altera.* Cf. *de Beata Vita*, 35.

at all abstract, it touches life on the quick, and in the story of Augustine it mirrors the inarticulate movement of the old world from heathenism to Christianity, that moral, intellectual and spiritual dissatisfaction with other cults and philosophies which drew mankind to the Church.

He tells us the story of his career. He was born at Thagaste ; he studied there, at Madaura and Carthage ; he taught rhetoric at Thagaste and Carthage, at Rome and Milan, and then returned to Africa. A life more uneventful could hardly be conceived—no striking episodes, no great perils, a little illness, commonplace pleasures. Yet the story gives us vastly more insight into the society of the time than all the letters of Symmachus, with his splendid friends and his dangerous intimacies with Emperor and usurper. In the *Confessions* we are in the heart of a family, we see them as they see one another, we know their ideas and their aspirations, and we learn what they are reading and what they are thinking about.

Augustine was born at Thagaste on the 13th of November, 354. His father Patricius was on the whole a heathen, a man of a very kindly nature, but very quick-tempered[1]. His ideals were not perhaps very high, he enjoyed life[2] and he was anxious for his son to get on in the world. Monnica, Augustine's mother, was a well-trained, tactful, Christian woman. She had the sense, her son tells us, to recognize her husband's various humours, and so carefully avoided provoking him by word or deed when he was angry that she never had a blow from him, as certain of her acquaintance did from their own more amiable husbands. She was essentially a peace-maker and exercised a good influence on the "acid conversations" of the women of Thagaste. Monnica was the more positive influence in the home, and while Patricius by his good nature and love of pleasure set his son an example of taking the world comfortably and enjoying all it offers, her more strenuous and intelligent nature left a deeper and more lasting stamp on Augustine, though as usual the lighter ideal won the prompter response to its appeals. The early impressions of his mother's Christian faith and life were never effaced through all his years of moral and intellectual wandering. When he once began to reflect, nothing satisfied him that did not somehow bear "the name of Christ[3]," neither Cicero's *Hortensius*

---

[1] *Conf.* ix. 9, 19 *sicut benevolentia praecipuus ita ira fervidus.* People knew *quam ferocem conjugem sustineret Monnica.*

[2] *Conf.* ii. 3, 6 *gaudens vinolentia.*

[3] Cf. *Conf.* iii. 4, 8 on the *Hortensius* (cited on p. 193); v. 14, 25 *quibus tamen philosophis, quod sine nomine salutari Christi essent, curationem languoris animae meae committere omnino recusabam.* Cf. too vi. 4, 5.

nor the philosophy of the Academics.   We get a glimpse of the
family relations again, when Augustine tells us of his gratification
when Monnica on her death-bed told him that he had been a good
son (*pius*) and that she had never heard from his mouth a harsh or
rude word directed against her (*Conf.* ix. 12, 30).   At the same
time, he confesses that much of his conduct greatly troubled her.

Of his school-days Augustine has left us an interesting picture[1]
—the lessons, especially the Greek, which he found as tiresome as
other boys do, the rod, from which he prayed to be delivered,
and his general preference for play.   Sometimes he did not stick
to the truth, he pilfered from his parents' cellar either to eat
himself or to have something for his playmates[2], and sometimes
he did not play fairly.   Yet he had no mind to be imposed
on himself, and he was a bright, intelligent boy (*bonae spei
puer*, i. 16, 26), who waked the interest and hopes of those who
knew him.   For more advanced instruction he was sent to Madaura,
and after a year's interval he went to Carthage, "thanks more to the
spirit than the wealth of my father" (ii. 3, 6), who was however
aided by a rich fellow-townsman, Romanianus, for long Augustine's
steady friend.   There were many parents much richer than Patricius
who did no such thing for their boys, and people admired him for
it.   Of course it was not every father whose son was an Augustine.

Augustine was now sixteen years old when he went, as we
should say, to the university at Carthage[3].   It was a great
port with a famous history, a beautiful city with a great intermixture of population largely heathen, "a city of noise and
pleasure," says Boissier.   The boy had been captured by Virgil
and was an eager and quick student and did well in his studies.
But the same ardent nature that had felt the passion of Dido, and
the ambition that had once led him to take unfair advantages in
play, now led him astray.   His fellow-students were given to sensual

---

[1] See *Conf.* bk i. generally.
[2] One very interesting discussion in the *Confessions* (ii. 6, 12—9, 17) turns
on the question why he went with some boy friends to rob an orchard, though
his father had a pear-tree which bore better fruit, though he might freely have
taken from his father's tree, and though he did not want and did not eat
the stolen pears after all.   *Illa autem decerpsi tantum ut furarer...An libuit
facere contra legem, saltem fallacia quia potentatu non poteram, ut mancam
libertatem captivus imitarer faciendo impune quod non liceret ?...Et tamen solus
id non fecissem...Sed quoniam in illis pomis voluptas mihi non erat, ea erat
in ipso facinore, quam faciebat consortium simul peccantium...Risus erat quasi
titillato corde, quod fallebamus eos qui haec a nobis fieri non putabant et
vehementer nolebant.*
[3] *Conf.* ii. 3, 6; and iii. 1.

pleasures, and Augustine went with them. He heard them boast and boasted to excel them, though he confesses he did not do all he told them he did. The brutal amusements of the *eversores*, who overturned people in the streets, never appealed to him. His temptation lay another way. He "wandered in the streets of Babylonia and wallowed in the mud." Even before he came to Carthage his mother had thought it would be well to check his irregularities by marrying him to some one, but this was not pressed as it might spoil his career. Licentiousness, the theatre and pride— all these he deplores in later life, yet no one except his mother seems to have regarded his conduct as noticeably bad.

It has been pointed out that the wild period of Augustine's life cannot have been very long. He went to Carthage at sixteen, in the year 370, and he soon took to himself the woman with whom he lived in strict fidelity till they parted about 385. Their son was born in 372 and they called him Adeodatus, a significant name[1] for such a child. Augustine was obviously very fond of him, and, when he grew up a bright boy, not less proud. Even the Church at that time recognized monogamous concubinage, and this woman may have been a freedwoman or some one who could not be legally married to him. At all events Monnica received her and her child with Augustine[2]. Patricius had died in 371.

At the age of nineteen his mind was diverted to more serious things than the life of pleasure. Hitherto he had hardly thought. As a boy, on the occasion of some passing illness, he had asked for baptism, but when he very quickly recovered, it was deferred. It was generally believed that baptism washed away all previous sins and consequently that it was best administered, if possible, on the death-bed. People used to say, Augustine tells us, "Let him alone; let him do as he likes; he is not yet baptized." This course was followed in his own case and he regretted it[3]. However at nineteen he came upon a book of Cicero's, now lost, the *Hortensius,* and it

---

[1] Names such as *Deogratias, Deus dedit,* were not uncommon in Africa, being apparently translations of Semitic names like Mattathiah, Nathaniel and so forth. Augustine's words are worth quoting (*Conf.* iv. 2, 2): *servans tori fidem, in qua sane experirer exemplo meo, quid distaret inter conjugalis placiti modum, quod foederatum esset generandi gratia, et pactum libidinosi amoris, ubi proles etiam contra votum nascitur; quamvis jam nata cogat se diligi.* The last clause is remarkable and shews the man's character.

[2] See Loofs, art. Augustinus in Herzog's *Realencyklopädie für Protestantische Theologie,* 1897 edition, p. 261, and Council of Toledo (A.D. 400), canon 17 there cited. *Dict. Antt.* i. 526, art. *concubina.* Compare the somewhat similar case of Libanius and his son by a concubine, *Ep.* 983 (to Ammianus Marcellinus).

[3] *Conf.* i. 11, 17.

changed his life[1]. He now burned with incredible ardour for
philosophy, as Cicero had intended his readers should[2]. His prayers
and desires were changed. He longed to rise above the earthly and
reach God. It was not this or that school, but wisdom herself that
was the object of his aspiration—a disinterested passion for truth
awakened at last and conscious of itself. One thing gave him
pause ; the name of Christ was not there. So he turned to the
Scriptures to see what they were like and not unnaturally he was
disappointed. They seemed to him quite unworthy of comparison
with the dignified style of Cicero. In reviewing his life he explains
this. He at this time took a merely external view of the Scriptures—
acies mea non penetrabat interiora ejus[3]. Yet a new life had really
begun for him—the quest of truth. He had begun to be really
interested in religion, and to examine his own. He was dissatisfied
and now he fell in with the Manichaeans.

There are forms of religion which take a strong hold of the
popular mind, but are not so strongly represented in literature
as others which are less generally accepted. Stoicism for example
has far more literature than the popular cults of the early Empire.
Manichaeanism in like manner is much less accessible to the western
reader than Neo-Platonism, side by side with which it disputed the
field with Catholic Christianity in the fourth century. Of widely
different origin these religions had drawn nearer one another with
time. Manichaeanism had Christian elements, and Neo-Platonism
and Christianity had Oriental. All three had doctrines in common,
all three dealt with revelation, salvation and immortality.

Mani, who died about 277 A.D., blended in his religion elements
drawn from Persian Zoroastrianism, from Syrian Gnosticism, from
Christianity and perhaps from Buddhism. His system turns on the
origin of evil, which he thus explained[4]. There are two eternal

---

[1] *Conf.* iii. 4, 7 *librum quendam Ciceronis*. The fashionable reading seems
now to be *cujusdam* for *quendam*. I have not gone into the ms. evidence, but
the genitive seems to me a foppishness of which Augustine surely ought to have
been incapable. His *Aeneae nescio cujus* (i. 13, 20) is not very happy, but this
is worse, to say nothing of the ingratitude. He quite honestly says *Virgilius* in
i. 14, 23.
[2] Cic. *de Div.* 2. 1, 1 *cohortati sumus ut maxime potuimus ad philosophiae
studium eo libro, qui est inscriptus Hortensius*.
[3] *Conf.* iii. 5, 9.
[4] See Gustav Flügel, *Mani, seine Lehre u. seine Schriften, aus dem Fihrist
des Abû'lfaradsch Muḥammad ben Isḥak al-Warrak*, Leipzig 1862—especially
pp. 86 to 105 for a translation of the surviving fragments of Mani's original
teaching. Naville, *op. cit.* ch. II. pp. 19—28, has also a very good and clear
account of Manichaeanism and its appeal to Augustine. I am indebted here as
elsewhere to Dr John Watson.

principles or substances, the one good and light, the other evil and
dark, and the universe is the result of their mixture. Light and
dark are here not symbols but actual descriptions. Each of these
principles involves the same confusion of spiritual and material, of
the physical phenomena of nature and the facts of the moral order.
Each has five elements—the world of light falling into gentleness,
knowledge, understanding, mystery and insight corresponding with
the gentle breeze, the wind, light, water and fire and contrasted
with the elements of the kingdom of darkness, viz. mist, burning,
the hot wind, poison and darkness. The world of light overlay the
world of darkness, and out of the latter came Satan to storm the
former[1]. The King of the Paradises of Light produced the Primal
Man (Christ, not Jesus), and arming him with the gentle breeze, the
wind etc , sent him to fight Satan, who was armed with mist and
burning and the rest. Satan triumphed over the Primal Man, who
was however rescued by the King of the Paradises of Light, but not
without a certain confusion of the elements. Thus fire and burning
are involved in each other, mist and water,—good and bad mingled.
Of these mingled elements the visible universe was made by command of the King of the World of Light, in order to their separation.
The moon and sun were created to take part in this work, the moon
drawing to herself elements of light (*e.g.* from a body at the time of
death) and passing them to the sun[2], who in turn passes them
onward and upward, till at last good shall be separated from evil,
the latter massed below in a pit covered by a stone as large as the
earth. The blooming of a plant and the aspiration of a soul are
alike the disentangling of particles of light, while the eating of a
plant[3] or the generation of a new life[4] means their re-imprisonment.
Hence asceticism is necessarily a part of the Manichaean religion.
Mankind are apparently descended from Adam and Eve, whose family

[1] Flügel, *op. cit.* p. 87. Aug. *Conf.* vii. 2, 3 refers to this war of the powers.
Cf. v. 10, 20 cited below.
[2] When the moon is waxing, she is gathering light, and when waning she is
transmitting it to the sun.
[3] Mani's followers were grouped into two main classes, the higher and the
ordinary (*auditores*). If vegetable food were eaten by the latter, light was
imprisoned in the process, but not if eaten by the former. To obviate starvation a portion might be given to a man of the higher grade and the hearer
might eat the rest. Cf. Aug. *Conf.* iii. 10, 18 *quae particulae summi et veri Dei
ligatae fuissent in illo pomo nisi electi sancti dente ac ventre solverentur;* and
iv. 1, 1 *escas de quibus nobis in officina aqualiculi sui fabricarent angelos et deos
per quos liberaremur.*
[4] See Aug. *de Mor. Manich.* ii. 18, 65, the reason of the boasted Manichaean
chastity (which had once impressed Augustine) was *ne carni anima implicaretur.*
See Naville, p. 83.

history is terribly complicated by mythology and the intervention of archons and Cain's two daughters by Eve, Worldly-Wisdom and the "daughter of Avarice." Man is of Satan's creation, but owing to the imprisoned particles of light he too is of mixed nature, not wholly evil nor wholly good.

Mani rejected the Old Testament as the work of the devil. With his view of chastity he could not approve of the patriarchs on any terms. Jesus he set among the prophets, though His flesh was only a phantom and His crucifixion only apparent—a type of the general crucifixion of a portion of the Primal Man upon matter. Jesus had foretold the coming of the Paraclete who should clear His teaching of Jewish interpolations, and Mani was himself the Paraclete. In this case, as Augustine thought later on, it was a pity that his astronomy was incorrect[1].

The question of evil was very much before the minds of men in Augustine's day. Synesius, for example, wrote a book on Providence to explain that the triumph of evil is only temporary. Here then was a system which, it might be said, looked the facts well in the face and gave a plausible explanation of them. It recognized man's dual nature, and relieved man of the responsibility for his own sinfulness[2], while it relieved God of the responsibility for the general existence of evil in man and in nature[3]. Here was a system which made the most magnificent promises of knowledge[4], and rescued a thoughtful man from the necessity of accepting the immoralities and anthropomorphisms of the Old Testament—serious difficulties

[1] *Conf.* v. 5, 8 *Spiritum sanctum consolatorem et ditatorem fidelium...personaliter in se esse persuadere conatus est. Itaque cum de coelo ac stellis, et de solis ac lunae motibus falsa dixisse deprehenderetur...cum ea non solum ignorata sed etiam falsa tam vesana superbiae vanitate diceret ut ea tanquam divinae personae tribuere sibi niteretur.*

[2] *Conf.* v. 10, 8 *Adhuc enim* (he is speaking of his life in Rome while still more or less a Manichaean) *mihi videbatur non esse nos qui peccamus sed nescio quam aliam in nobis peccare naturam. Et delectabat superbiam meam extra culpam esse; et cum aliquid mali fecissem non confiteri me fecisse.*

[3] *Conf.* vii. 14, 20 *Et quia non audebat anima mea, ut ei displiceret Deus meus, nolebat esse tuum quidquid ei displicebat. Et inde ierat in opinionem duarum substantiarum.* Cf. v. 10, 20 *Et quia Deum bonum nullam malam naturam creasse qualiscumque pietas me credere cogebat, constituebam ex adverso sibi duas moles, utramque infinitam, sed malam angustius, bonam grandius.* He feels Omar's difficulty but he would have repudiated Omar's explanation as blasphemy:

> O thou, who Man of baser Earth didst make,
> And ev'n with Paradise devise the Snake:
> For all the Sin wherewith the Face of Man
> Is blacken'd—Man's forgiveness give—and take.

[4] *Conf.* vi. 5, 7 *illic temeraria pollicitatione scientiae credulitatem irrideri.* Cf. *De Utilitate credendi* i. 2 *quis non his pollicitationibus illiceretur, praesertim adolescentis animus cupidus veri.*

which Augustine greatly felt[1]. It saved him from bowing to the authority of the Church and from believing what he could not understand[2], by appealing to his reason, his love of truth and his common sense. At the same time it professed and could exhibit a certain ascetic holiness—if asceticism is holiness.

Augustine, as we have seen, had been quickened to the search for truth by the *Hortensius*. He had found the Old Testament morally unsatisfactory besides being deficient in style and charm. The Church was committed to it, he thought, teaching that God had hands and feet, and holding up the patriarchs as virtuous men. Anxious to be free and to be right intellectually, he was also beginning to be conscious of his own moral failures, which he would not attribute to God but for which he did not wish to blame himself. But here was a door of escape. Manichaeanism recognized the facts he had himself been feeling, and gave an explanation so far acceptable to his reason and, he says, to his vanity. And it did more. He was already revolting from the self-indulgent and sensual life he had been leading and recognized the contrast between his own conduct and character and the chastity and holiness of the Manichaean ascetics. He also found among them the "name of Christ[3]," for Mani accepted Christianity, and after purging it of its errors, exhibited the true faith of the Gospel, or at least he said so. Here then were Christ's name, holiness and philosophy. So he joined the Manichaeans and though he was never more than a "hearer" he was an ardent adherent and a proselytiser[4]. He was required not to worship idols, not to use magic and not to kill animals, but he was not required to break with his mistress.

It is interesting to find that Monnica, who had been distressed before about his irregular life, now debated with herself whether she

[1] *Conf.* iii. 7, 12. The Manichaeans asked him *utrum forma corporea Deus finiretur et haberet capillos et ungues; et utrum justi existimandi essent qui haberent uxores multas simul et occiderent homines et sacrificarent de animalibus. Quibus rerum ignarus perturbabar.* iii. 10, 18 *irridebam illos sanctos servos et prophetas tuos.*
[2] Julian (*ap.* Greg. Naz. *Or.* iii. p. 97 β) sneers at the Christians on this score; ὑμῶν ἡ ἀλογία καὶ ἡ ἀγροικία, καὶ οὐδὲν ὑπὲρ τὸ πιστεῦσον τῆς ὑμετέρας ἐστὶ σοφίας.
[3] *Conf.* iii. 6, 10. He speaks of the Manichaean use of Christ's name: *viscum confectum commixtione syllabarum nominis tui et Domini Jesu Christi et paracleti consolatoris nostri Spiritus Sancti :* the syllables merely, not the real thing.
[4] *Conf.* iii. 12, 21 *quod...nonnullis quaestiunculis jam multos imperitos exagitassem.* iv. 15, 26 *dicebam parvulis fidelibus tuis...garrulus et ineptus ; cur ergo errat anima quam fecit Deus.* Later on (*Conf.* v. 10, 19) he speaks of his *pristina animositas* in maintaining Manichaeanism.

ought to allow her heretic son to continue in the house with her. She was reassured by a dream in which an angel told her she should yet see her son "standing where she did"; nor was she disturbed by Augustine's endeavour to shew that it meant she too would be a Manichaean[1]. She tried to induce a bishop to reason with him, but the bishop, who had been brought up as a Manichaean and knew all about the system and who seems also to have known Augustine, refused to engage him. "Let him alone," he said, "he will find out by reading[2]." When Monnica wept and was importunate, he bade her "believe it impossible that the child of those tears should be lost."

Augustine was at the time professor of rhetoric in Thagaste, but a friend's death upset him so much that he left his native place and went to Carthage in or about 376. This friend had followed Augustine into Manichaeanism, but had been baptized while ill and unconscious. When, on his rallying, Augustine had laughed about this baptism, expecting him to be as ready to laugh himself, he suddenly fired up and bade him cease such talk. It had a great effect on Augustine, which was probably heightened by the friend's death of a recurrence of the fever. "My heart," he writes, "was darkened by this sorrow; and everything I saw was death...I became a great question to myself and I asked my soul why it was sad and why it troubled me so much; and it knew nothing to answer me... Weeping only was pleasant to me, and had succeeded my friend in my affection[3]." When he bade himself hope in God, his God was "a vain phantasm, his own idle imagining." For he tells us several times that while he was a Manichaean he thought of God as "an infinite, luminous body" (iv. 16, 31), "surrounding and pervading creation, infinite in every direction," as a vast sea might hold a vast sponge (vii. 5, 7), "a bright mass of material substance[4]." Life was painful to him, and death was terrible[5], so he left his native place where everything suggested his friend, and went to Carthage.

He was very busy reading and thinking. At twenty years of age, he tells us, he read Aristotle's *Categories* and understood the book without a teacher. The exercise was no doubt useful, but

---

[1] *Conf.* iii. 11, 19—20.
[2] *Conf.* iii. 12, 21 *ipse legendo reperiet.*
[3] *Conf.* iv. 4, 8—9. "Grief fills the room up of my absent child."
[4] *Conf.* v. 10, 19 *cum de Deo meo cogitare vellem, cogitare nisi moles corporum non noveram (neque enim videbatur mihi esse quidquam quod tale non esset)...* 20 *massa lucidissimae molis tuae.*
[5] *Conf.* iv. 6, 11 *taedium vivendi et moriendi metus.*

after all his chief energies were not directed to Aristotle. "His remarks on this work," says Dr Watson, "shew that he was not able, in his pre-occupation with new problems, to appreciate the aim of Aristotle in this analysis of the main elements by which being is characterized. The use he made of it was to apply to his Manichaean conception of God, as an infinitely extended substance, the categories which for Aristotle were simply the most general modes of determining things. In this external application to a foreign matter of predicates accepted on authority we have the beginning of a false method, which afterwards played so large a part in Scholasticism." It is well to notice what weight Authority carried universally in this age. The reader may for example be referred to Julian and Macrobius as instances of men who lived by Authority and *dogmata*.

Augustine was also exercised in another line of inquiry which would seem less likely to have been profitable but perhaps really aided him more. Manichaeanism was fatalistic and it boasted an astronomy of its own. It set the primal man in the sun, the mother of life in the moon, and the primal elements of life in the twelve stars. While, like a good Manichaean, Augustine would have nothing to do with magic, the case was different with astrology and he became very much interested in it; in its "mathematicians" and "books of generations." His friends, especially an eminent physician, Vindicianus, and the young Nebridius, argued against all this divination, urging that it rested on deceit and its occasional successes were the result of accident (iv. 3, 4—6). He was at last cured of this passing interest by an experiment. A rich and eminent man, Firminus, had been born at the same moment as a slave of his father's, and their horoscopes were carefully taken, and though these entirely coincided, the freeman and the slave had had a very different experience of life (vii. 6, 8).

But the matter did not rest here, for Augustine had been making considerable researches for himself into Astronomy[1] and found that "secular science" gave an accurate account of solstices, equinoxes and eclipses and so forth. He laments that the astronomers had too often not found the Lord of the universe, but he was none the less impressed with the fact that they had discovered much and could predict to an hour an eclipse many years beforehand, while on comparison the voluminous writings of Mani proved full of fables

---

[1] *Conf.* v. 3, 3—6.

and gave no account of the science which he could understand. He was uneasy about this, but he waited till he could be clear[1], and he had long to wait, for it was not for nine years that he met the great Manichaean preacher Faustus[2]. Faustus at last came and Augustine found him charming, but alas! "it was exactly what *they* always say, that he prattled, only more agreeably." He had learnt by now, he says, and had learnt it, though unconsciously, from God, that a thing is not necessarily true because eloquently said, nor false because the sounds the lips utter are harsh, nor on the other hand is rough speech always truth nor eloquence always falsehood. He came to closer quarters with the preacher, and found that his training had been quite ordinary and his reading slight, and that he could not solve Augustine's difficulties. However Faustus was honest—"he knew he did not know these things and was not ashamed to own it; he was not one of those many chatter-boxes I had suffered under, who tried to teach me and said nothing. He had some sense (*cor habebat*)...so I liked him better" (v. 7, 12). So Faustus "without wishing it or knowing it" began to release him from the snares of Manichaeanism, for he now despaired of ever disentangling Mani's doctrines.

All the argument was not on the Manichaean side. A certain Helpidius declaimed against them in Carthage with some effect on Augustine, for he brought them matter from the Scriptures which was hard to meet and "their answer struck me as weak." All they could say—and even that only secretly—was that the New Testament had been falsified in the interests of the Jewish law (v. 11, 21). Nebridius too used to propound a difficulty. Supposing, he said, that when the darkness attacked the light, the God of light had refused to fight, could the darkness have injured the light or not? If it could, then the God of light was subject to violation and corruption—an intolerable position, for Augustine, as we saw, became a Manichaean to maintain the integrity of God. If on the other hand the darkness could not hurt the light, the Manichaean system was absurd, for why should there have been a war at all? or the defeat of the Primal Man? or the consequent intermixture of some of God's substance with natures not made by Him? or the need of any redemption at all[3]?

---

[1] *Conf.* v. 5, 9: note his reservation of judgment—*nondum liquido compereram* whether Mani's astronomy could be explained.

[2] Harnack remarks that the story of Faustus is the one touch of humour in the *Confessions*.

[3] *Conf.* vii. 2, 3. *Jam diu ab usque Carthagine* gives us a useful date.

But Augustine was testing Manichaeanism in another way, for
he was finding out by experience that it had little aid to offer
toward living aright. For with Augustine the moral side of things
was as important as the intellectual. The problem of the origin of
evil was always with him ; he must explain why it was he did what
was evil. In other words he was conscious of sin, and could not
escape the thought of his own guilt. He had upon him the fear of
death and future judgment, a fear which haunted him through all
his changes of opinion (vi. 16, 26). His doctrine that sin is its own
punishment, like others of his doctrines, rested on experience. He
had been drawn towards the Manichaeans by their chastity, but
Manichaeanism failed to make him pure.

Thus Manichaeanism had proved to have little comfort for him
in the hour of bereavement ; it had lost credit with the exposure of
the folly of astrology ; its astronomy had been demonstrated to be
nonsense ; its whole foundation was imperilled by the dilemma of
Nebridius ; and it had failed to give him the moral strength he had
hoped from it to rise above the life of sense.

All this was not reached quickly. He was for years a Manichaean, and meanwhile he taught at Carthage. He took part in a
poetic contest in the theatre (iv. 2, 2) and was crowned as victor by
the proconsul (iv. 3, 5). He read assiduously, and wrote his first
book, *De Pulcro et Apto*, a book he was highly pleased with at the
time, but after twenty years he was content to have lost sight of it[1].
But he did not care for Carthage now. He was older and a professor.
Even as a student he had not liked the *eversiones*, and now he hated
the reckless violence with which students not his own would invade
his classes. Discipline there was none. Even in Rome students
from Africa had a bad name. At home they committed outrages
with an insensibility that astounded Augustine, and rendered themselves liable to correction by the law. But "custom was their
patron," and allowed them to fancy they escaped unpunished because
their only punishment was the "blindness of their action," whereby
"they suffer far more than they inflict[2]." To escape this atmosphere
of disorder Augustine resolved to go to Rome, and to Rome he
went, though it cost him a lie to get away from his mother (383).
She came to him later on at Milan. At Rome he was at once

[1] *Conf.* iv. 14, 23 *libenter animo versabam...et nullo collaudatore mirabar;*
and 13, 20.
[2] *Conf.* v. 8, 14 *cum ipsa faciendi caecitate puniantur*—in consonance with
his general view: *Jussisti enim, et sic est, ut poena sua sibi sit omnis inordinatus
animus*, i. 12, 19.

overtaken by illness and was befriended by another Manichaean *auditor*. But university life in Rome had its own drawbacks. The students cheated him of his fees[1], and he was glad to obtain an official post as teacher of rhetoric at Milan, on the recommendation of Symmachus (385).

Here we may pause. He was still friendly with the Manichaeans, but really in revolt against their religion on the grounds which we have seen. For the moment he despaired of reaching truth and leant to the scepticism of the Academics. He had revolted from the Church and now Manichaeanism failed him. Each stage had left its mark on him. Even his wild life at Carthage had not been without its use, for he had learnt painfully and in himself how real a thing is evil. He had been wakened by Cicero to be serious. The Scriptures had repelled him, and though he deplored his long years in Manichaeanism, even there he was on a higher plane than before. He had found real weaknesses in what he believed to be the Christian position, and he had to escape or transcend them When Monnica wept over him, he was not in so perilous a case as she supposed. His mind saw more while it saw less than hers, and when he came back to the Christian faith he retained the real gains of his years of separation. He had become a Manichaean because he believed in the real goodness and greatness of God, in the value of truth for itself and in purity of life. The pursuit of these ideals had brought him through Manichaeanism, a stronger man for his years of experiment and perseverance, and though now for the moment he despaired of ever achieving truth and the knowledge of God, and indeed believed them to be unattainable, he yet did not doubt their value. Happiness was to consist in these ; that they could not be reached did not alter the fact. Even this mood contributed to his growth, for, since his mind was essentially positive, he could not rest here, and the double conviction (for his scepticism was dogmatic) that God really exists and that man cannot of himself know Him, led him to attach the more importance to the Christian doctrine of the self-revelation of God. There were however intervening stages, which we must consider.

When Augustine reached Milan, he was very kindly received by Ambrose. It may be a fair inference from the text that Symmachus had written to Ambrose, as we know he occasionally did, or it may be that Ambrose naturally gave a kindly welcome to a new professor

---

[1] *Conf.* v. 12, 22.

of marked ability. Augustine in return liked him, and went to hear him preach, chiefly out of curiosity to see if his eloquence were equal to his reputation. The subject-matter he disregarded, but he was delighted by the style, which, while it had not so much liveliness or charm as Faustus', shewed more education[1]. But he could not help incidentally noticing what Ambrose said, and in spite of himself remarked how truly as well as how eloquently he spoke, and then how well he managed to maintain positions Augustine had thought indefensible, solving one difficulty after another out of the Old Testament. Augustine realized that there was more to be said for the Church than he had supposed, and now the balance stood even between Christianity and Manichaeanism, and he began to look for something by which to prove the latter false. It was against the system of Mani that its doctrines about nature were wrong. It stood in the way of the Church that Augustine had not yet conceived of the spiritual nature of God, nor satisfied himself on the origin of evil. It was against the Academics that they knew nothing of the name of Christ. So till he found some certain goal Augustine resolved to become and remain a catechumen in the Church of his parents[2].

The difficulties of the Old Testament vanished under Ambrose's application of the allegoric method. " The letter killeth, but the spirit maketh alive " was a favourite text with the bishop. The method was not his own, but had long been used by the Church in the interpretation of the Bible, just as the Greeks used it with Homer. Porphyry's explanation of the Cave of the Nymphs is perhaps a fair example. It may be remarked that Augustine thus owed his next step to an unsound method, and no doubt this is true. The historical method is modern and is sounder, but the allegoric method for all its immediate unsoundness really enabled an earlier generation to reach, as conveniently for its particular mental habits, the same fundamentally sound conclusion that the real value of the Old Testament is after all its spiritual content and that all else is in the long run immaterial. Augustine's estimate of Scripture was completely changed. He now found in it wonderful mysteries which he had never suspected, and he began to accept its authority. As man is unable to find truth by pure reason and needs such authority (this was the outcome of his scepticism), he reflected that God would never have given so excellent a guide had

---

[1] *Conf.* v. 13, 23.　　　　[2] *Conf.* v. 14, 24—25.

He not meant men to seek Him and to believe in Him through its agency. If certain things had to be taken on trust, he reflected that in ordinary life the things so taken are innumerable, and that if none of these were so accepted, we should do nothing whatever in life (vi. 5, 8).

Meantime Augustine still had worldly ambitions—office, gain, marriage. He had to deliver a panegyric to Valentinian II.—most of which he says was false, though of course the falsity would be applauded by the listeners who knew as well as he did that it was false. That day he saw on a Milan street a beggar, drunk, jocular and happy, and he compared himself with him. Both sought one goal—temporal happiness. A few small coins secured it for the beggar—not the true joy, however, but Augustine felt he himself reached neither the one nor the other with all his toils and ambitions. The beggar was free from care ; he was not, and yet he would not change with him[1]. He was thoroughly dissatisfied with himself and in the dark. "How long will this go on?" was a question he and his friends often asked (vi. 10, 17). Life was wretched, death uncertain. "If it steal suddenly upon us, how shall we go hence ? and where must we learn what we have neglected here ? Or will it not rather be that we must pay the penalty for our negligence?" Would death end all? This was against the authority of the Christian faith. "Never would so much be done for us by God if the life of the soul were ended with the body." Then why not seek God and the truly happy life ? But the world and its honours and pleasures were sweet He disliked the idea of the celibate life, which holiness then implied ; he felt it would be beyond his strength and he knew of no other strength (vi. 11, 18—20). His mother urged him to marry and he arranged to do so. He said farewell to the mother of Adeodatus, but only to replace her with another. The fear of future judgment was heavy upon him. "I grew more wretched, and Thou drewest nearer. Thy right hand was near me ready to lift me from the mire and wash me, and I knew it not."

He still was troubled by his materialistic conception of God, "and my heart vehemently cried out against all these phantasms of mine." He felt forced to believe he was really a free agent, that when he wished or did not wish a thing, it was himself and not another who had the feeling and that there lay the reason of his sin.

---

[1] *Conf.* vi. 6, 9.

But who had made him so? How should he be responsible? Who set this root of bitterness in him? If the devil, whence was the devil? If the devil were an angel once good, whence had the devil the evil will that changed him? Nebridius' dilemma made it hard to suppose evil came from matter, for that seemed to limit God's omnipotence (*Conf.* vii. 3, 4—5). The question tortured him. "Thou with a goad in my heart wast pricking me on to be impatient till Thou shouldst be a certainty to me by inward vision."

Help came to him from Neo-Platonism[1]. Some one gave him Victorinus' Latin translation of some Platonic works, either Plato or Plotinus. Here Augustine found a way of escape from both his intellectual difficulties. In Absolute Being he found a better account of God than in the infinitely diffused luminous body he had always hitherto imagined. But of Absolute Being the human mind cannot properly conceive, and Neo-Platonism bridged the gulf by a series of emanations. First came Intelligence, the κόσμος νοητὸς or intelligible world, the perfect image of the Absolute. From this came the World-Soul, the image of Intelligence, and like it immaterial, deriving its illumination from Intelligence which interpenetrates it, while it is in contact with the phenomenal, all souls being part of it. From the World-Soul is the corporeal or phenomenal world, further still from Absolute Being, yet not evil, but rather absolutely good so far as it actually is, though of course defective in being in proportion as it is removed from Absolute Being[2]. Where then is the materialistic God? He at least has disappeared as a contradiction and an absurdity, and with him has gone a burden from Augustine's mind[3]. Evil too is now less perplexing. He sees now that evil *is* not really anything, it is not-being, failure to be[4]. It is not therefore the creation of God. It lies in will and inclination, since everything is good so far as it is capable of being, so far as it is[5]. Evil is turning away from God and the intelligible world which comes next Him.

[1] See *Conf.* vii. c. 9 to the end of the book generally. Harnack refers to these chapters as the best account of Neo-Platonism in the Fathers.
[2] *Conf.* vii. 11, 17 *et inspexi cetera infra te, et vidi nec omnino esse nec omnino non esse; esse quidem quoniam abs te sunt; non esse autem quoniam id quod es non sunt. Id enim vere est quod incommutabiliter manet.*
[3] *Conf.* vii. 10 on God as *supra mentem meam lux incommutabilis*, iii. 7, 10 (of his Manichaean days) *et non noveram Deum esse spiritum.*
[4] *Conf.* vii. 12, 18 *ergo quaecumque sunt, bona sunt; malumque illud quod quaerebam unde esset, non est substantia, quia si substantia esset, bonum esset.*
[5] *Conf.* vii. 16, 22 *et quaesivi quid esset iniquitas, et non inveni substantiam; sed a summa substantia te Deo detortae in infima voluntatis perversitatem.* Note here that *substantia* is not the equivalent of the English *substance* but the usual Latin rendering of the Greek οὐσία, *essence.*

Hence, as he says, the soul that disregards the divine order of the universe, the disordered soul, is its own punishment by its loss of real being in the very turning away from God. This appealed to his experience, for he had himself found evil-doing prove its own punishment[1]. God's nature and the question of evil thus grew clear to him in Neo-Platonism.

But there was more to be done. Augustine had found the inadequacy of human effort to achieve holiness, to turn to God and rise into His nature, and he realized that nothing else will lead to happiness. The questions now came, how was man to come into contact with God, and how did God reveal Himself to man? Plotinus answered the second question by pointing to the emanations, the first by a virtual abandonment of philosophy and recourse to ecstasy. Man, by entering into his own mind and abstracting himself from all else, can obtain under happy circumstances an immediate intuition of the Absolute Being, can leap by a bound into mystical unity with it. Porphyry tells us in his life of Plotinus how often his master achieved this happy vision. This latter doctrine appealed very strongly to Augustine as the language of his *Confessions* shews[2].

Augustine now, as he says, saw the "fatherland of peace" from the summit of a forest-clad mountain afar, but it was another thing to find the road there (vii. 21, 27). "I saw a way of gathering strength adequate to enjoy Thee, but I did not find it till I embraced the mediator between God and men, the man Christ Jesus" (vii. 18, 24). So far he only thought of Christ as a man of excellent and incomparable wisdom, one miraculously born of a virgin, to shew thereby that the temporal should be despised, and one who by his divine interest in us seemed to have merited the authority of a teacher (vii. 19, 25). The Divine Word he had found in the Neo-Platonic Intelligence, which was in the beginning with God, by which all things were made, which darkness could not comprehend, but the Incarnation and all it involved he had not found (vii. 9, 13). So, though the divine beauty attracted him upward, his own weight, the carnal habit, pulled him back (vii. 17, 23). He began to read St Paul and found in him, as was not unlikely, a great deal of coincidence with Neo-Platonism, and something of his own experience. "O miserable man that I am! who shall free me from the body of this death?" was an utterance of

---

[1] *Conf.* i. 12, 19.

[2] E.g. *Conf.* vii. 10, 16 *admonitus redire ad memet ipsum intravi in intima mea*, ix. 10, 23 *venimus in mentes nostras et transcendimus eas.* A fuller account of this is given in vii. 17, 23. Cf. Plotinus, *Enn.* iv. 8, 1.

the heart, for which the Apostle had an answer, but hardly the Neo-Platonist (vii. 21, 27).

He was at last certain of God's eternal and incorruptible essence, and longed now to be "not more certain of Thee but more stable in Thee" (viii. 1, 1). Yet though he had found the good pearl and should have sold all he had and bought it, he hesitated (viii. 1, 2). In fact, he found he did not want to break with the life he saw to be lower. The new will to live in God and enjoy Him was not strong enough to overcome the old and perverse will. From the perverse will had risen lust; from the service of lust came habit; from the failure to resist habit, it had become necessity. Not only so, but he found he liked the necessity more than he had supposed. He wished to be saved from himself, but his prayer, if put honestly, would have been, "Give me chastity and continence, but not now." He was afraid his prayer should be quickly heard and he should be healed from his disease, which he wished to be sated rather than extinguished. He knew himself at last. His difficulty had not been so entirely intellectual as he had supposed ; it was really a moral failure.

It was in the doctrine of the Incarnation that he at last found strength to rise above this conflict of wills, to break "the violence of habit." The Neo-Platonic God did not after all reveal himself ; he was remote and the series of emanations did not bring him nearer. The Word of the Neo-Platonists was not the Christian Word, but one emanation in a series of others, and it did not declare God's inner being. If man wished to reach God, he had to do it for himself. The supreme God did not apparently care for the individual man, he did not really love man, he did not forgive sins nor give the power to rise above sin. But the Church, inculcating a doctrine utterly repellent to heathen philosophy, preached the Incarnation and the Love of God. For the colourless and indefinable Absolute Being it set forth a God, who Himself cared for the individual (iii. 11, 9), loved him and gave His Son for him to the death of the cross (vii. 9, 14). The Church taught that in that Son God forgave sin and dissolved man's hostility to Himself (v. 9, 16), and that to those who would receive that Son God gave the power to become the sons of God, through belief in His name (vii. 9, 13)[1].

---

[1] He finally crystallizes the thought of the Christian's dependence on God in the expression *Da quod jubes et jube quod vis* (x. 29, 40). It was this phrase which attracted the attention and criticism of Pelagius, thus leading to the

To believe all this was a great tax on the philosophic mind, but here came in the authority of the Church with that of the Scriptures. It offered a doctrine without explanation, without reconciling it with current philosophy, and demanded its acceptance. Human pride might rebel, but in the long run the heart must make the surrender, when after long "tossing in experiments" (*nos volvimur in experimentis*) it found nowhere else the power to overcome sin. The Church was thus the voucher for the Gospel as a result of its long years of experience. For so long as it had been in the world, it had uniformly been solving the problem of holy living. It accounted for this by the doctrine of the Incarnation, which was to the philosophic thought of heathendom blasphemous and unintelligible, inconsistent in a word with the whole trend of ancient philosophy and with all its conceptions of God. There was apparently no common basis for discussion, until experience was consulted. Augustine accepted the experience of the Church as confirmed by his own. He believed without understanding, and of course at once began anew to reconstruct his philosophy to accommodate his new experience. No wonder it lays so much stress on sin and grace.

At the last it was the story of *Antony* that completed Augustine's conversion. A tale of an unlettered Copt, triumphing by divine grace over evil in forms which Augustine had found irresistible, because attractive, this little book had stirred mankind, and the scholar saw how "the unlearned rise and seize heaven, while we with our learning without sense wallow in flesh and blood." Torn this way and that, ashamed and aspiring, he heard from behind him the mutterings of the flesh, and before him he saw the Church, "serene and gay with an honest happiness," surrounded by pure men and pure women of every age. He seemed to hear the Church saying to him: "And can you not do what these do and these? Or do they do it of themselves and not in the Lord their God? The Lord their God gave them to me. Why do you stand in yourself—and yet do not stand? Cast yourself on Him; fear not, He will not withdraw Himself and let you fall. Cast yourself on Him without a care; He will receive you and heal you" (viii. 11, 27). As in great perturbation he lay under a tree in the garden, he heard a child crooning "*Tolle, lege; tolle, lege.*" We get an indication of the man's temperament in the process of thought through which

great controversy between Augustine and Pelagius. The strength of Augustine's position in the controversy was that he had experience behind him and spoke from a knowledge of man's nature and of sin, which Pelagius entirely lacked, while on the other hand he had proved the inadequacy of Pelagius' theory. The doctrine of Grace follows naturally on the story unfolded in the *Confessions*.

he at once went. The words were unusual; he had never noticed a child's game in which the refrain occurred, and the childish jingle impressed him the more. Not all men would have caught the words at such a time or have had Augustine's store of observation of childhood[1]. He remembered then how Antony had found an oracle in a chance verse of Scripture, and he thereupon opened the epistles of Paul at a venture and lit on the words "Not in riotings and drunkenness, not in chambering and wantonness, not in strife and envying; but put ye on the Lord Jesus Christ and make no provision for the flesh in concupiscence" (*Romans* xiii. 13, 14). He accepted this as a divine message to himself, and took the course the Church had seemed to urge and surrendered himself to God (viii. 12, 28—30).

He very soon gave up his work at Milan, and withdrew for a while to a country house at Cassisiacum with a group of friends, including his mother and his son[2]. Apart from studies of Virgil and other literary subjects, their time was chiefly occupied by discussions, which were taken down by a shorthand reporter, and are still extant. In these his language is not so avowedly Christian as in the *Confessions*, for he is still trying to couch the new thought in the old terms, but the new thought is there and if not yet fully developed it is still Christian. From Cassisiacum he returned to Milan and was there baptized by Ambrose at Easter (387). His mother had seen him "standing where she did," and when shortly afterwards she died at Ostia she died content.

Augustine's return to Africa and the great work he did there as bishop of Hippo lie beyond our present concern. I have tried here to follow the course of Augustine's thought up to his conversion, to the exclusion of nearly everything else. This is perhaps an injustice to the *Confessions*, which, as I said above, give a vivid picture of the external as well as the spiritual conditions of his life and are enriched by reflexions gathered from ten years of Christian experience. The sum of this experience is given in the first chapter, and is as it were the keynote of the book; "Thou hast made us for Thyself, and our heart is restless until it rest in Thee."

[1] Similarly I feel there is something significant in the confession he makes that a lizard (*stellio*) catching flies, or a spider throwing its net round them, will absorb him (x. 35, 57). *In quam multis minutissimis et contemptibilibus rebus curiositas quotidie nostra tentatur?* Everything however, as I said, points in one direction. *Num quia parva sunt animalia ideo non res eadem geritur? Pergo inde ad laudandum te creatorem mirificum atque ordinatorem rerum omnium.*

[2] The best account of the conversations at Cassisiacum is given by Boissier, *op. cit.*

CHAPTER X

CLAUDIAN

We've drunk to our English brother
(And we hope he'll understand).

KIPLING

IT seems that both Virgil and Horace were invited to write a great epic on the deeds of Augustus, and both declined the task. Virgil, as we read in the third *Georgic*, thought of it, but he gave up the theme as unsuited to poetic treatment. Horace instead wrote the Emperor an epistle on literary criticism, though he would have preferred, he alleges, to have told of lands afar, of rivers, of tower-crowned peaks and barbarian realms, of wars waged the world over, and of peace with honour thence resulting. Probably he would not, and his true reason was as in Virgil's case the perception that the historian's task and the poet's are different. The poet's function is the interpretation of life and is ill fulfilled when he is fettered to historical narration, and especially ill when he is forced to play the panegyrist. And we may be sure that if Augustus asked for history, he wished for panegyric.

But on one occasion Horace wrote as he was asked to write, and the first six odes of his third book were the result—a splendid series of poems dedicated to the reformation of Roman society. We find in them as it were incidentally the deification of Augustus, but the work owes little to Imperial direction, for it is the outcome of the poet's life and thought. The minor interest, the Imperial purpose, sinks into its proper place and is lost in the genuine inspiration that the poet drew from sources beyond an Emperor's sway. Virgil in the same way though with more enthusiasm introduces Augustus into his epic of the life of man, but the interest of the *Aeneid* does not lie in the foreshadowings of the Emperor, nor perhaps in the adventures of his forerunner and archetype, but in the poet's treatment of human sorrow and human quest, of all that is heroic and pathetic in the common lot of all men. Thus round the name of Augustus grew a literature, of which, whatever he may have thought, he is really not the centre. The patron may prompt, he may suggest and he may pay, but the poet creates, and there is hardly any relation between their activities. When a Virgil and a Horace found scant inspiration in Augustus, what could a poet find in an Emperor like Honorius? in a soldier, whether patriot or adventurer, like Stilicho? Yet the poetry of Claudian, flecked though it be by much that is unworthy, is still poetry. There is about it much to fascinate and charm the reader, who will take the trouble to learn the poet's mind. Stilicho is after all not very interesting, a striking figure perhaps and a great man, but not so unique that Roman history cannot shew a score like him. As for Honorius, a more uninteresting character is hardly conceivable, unless it be his brother Arcadius, but perhaps even he is not such a complete nonentity[1]. To discover the source of Claudian's charm and the force which, in spite of Stilicho and Honorius, has made his work immortal, is the object of this essay.

First, however, a word or two must be given to his own story. He suddenly appears a ripened poet in 395 and after nine years of great fertility as suddenly disappears in 404. Dismissing the question whether he is the Claudian of whom Evagrius speaks[2], we find a certain reference to him in Apollinaris Sidonius[3].

> ......*Pelusiaco satus Canopo*
> *qui ferruginei toros mariti*
> *et Musa canit inferos superna....*

Here, beside emphasizing what I cannot but feel to be his greatest work, the later poet confirms the Egyptian birth of Claudian, which is clear from one or two passages in his poems, passages in which it is hard not to find something of that affection for a distant birthplace which no prosperity in another land can quite overcome. Whatever be the real purpose of the *Deprecatio*, there is this note in the last lines :—

> *Audiat haec commune solum longeque carinis*
> *nota Pharos, flentemque attollens gurgite vultum*
> *nostra gemat Nilus numerosis funera ripis*[4].

---

[1] Zosimus, v. 12, says Eutropius the eunuch owned Arcadius as if he had been an ox, κυριεύων καθάπερ βοσκήματος.
[2] *Hist. Eccles.* i. 19, p. 274.
[3] ix. 271. Suidas, too, speaks of Κλαυδίανος Ἀλεξανδρεὺς ἐποποιὸς νεώτερος, a contemporary of Arcadius and Honorius.
[4] *Minor Poems*, 22 (39), 56—59.

Pharos, known afar of ships, and the Nile and Alexandria may seem strange substitutes for Sirmio or Mantua, but for Claudian they have the same power. Elsewhere in a little idyll on the Nile, he writes,

Felix qui Pharias proscindit vomere terras[1],

a line Virgilian in sound and sentiment. I have dwelt on this Egyptian origin, for it gives added significance to his love of Rome. Neither Catullus nor Virgil was less a Roman for loving Sirmio and Mantua, nor was Claudian for remembering Pharos.

His name, Claudius Claudianus, is hardly an index of his race. It need not imply Latin stock, for Ammianus was Greek and his name was Latin[2]. On the other hand Gaul was full of Celts with Greek names, Aetherius, Pelagius, Potamius, Evagrius, Euanthius. His extraordinary mastery of the Latin hexameter, which would have been remarkable at any date and seems a miracle in the days of Ausonius and Paulinus, has led some to suppose him the son of Latin speaking parents, and his father, it is suggested, may have been a government official in Egypt. But I doubt if this theory be necessary. St Augustine[3] tells us of a man of his own day, who though a Syrian and bred to Greek rhetoric had become eventually a famous teacher of Latin eloquence, so brilliant that to him, though a stranger, Augustine dedicated his first work. Hierius' writings, if he left any, have not reached us, but the most splendid Latin history after Tacitus was the work of the Greek soldier Ammianus.

Whatever his origin, Claudian's first attempts in poetry were in Greek, and it is debated whether the two extant fragments of a Greek *War of the Giants* be his. He treated the theme in an independent Latin poem and has more than one allusion to it beside. The Greek piece is not unworthy of these, but it opens questions into which I cannot here go. The Greek epigrams attributed to him are slight and one implies acquaintance with Nonnus, every line being decorated with a borrowed plume. They, too, may be dismissed, and we must content ourselves for the present with his own statement that he first wrote, or perhaps published, Latin poetry in the year of Theodosius' death and Probinus' Consulship, 395 A.D.

---

[1] *Minor Poems*, 28 (47); *Nilus* 1. Another reminiscence is his account of the electric fish in 49 (46).

[2] Apollonius of Tyana was very indignant to find Greeks decorating themselves with Latin names—Lucullus and Fabricius for example. See Philostr. *V. Apoll.* iv. 5, and Apollonius' 71st letter.

[3] *Confessions*, iv. 14.

Romanos bibimus primum te consule fontes
et Latiae accessit Graia Thalia togae¹.

He refers to his Panegyric on the brother consuls Probinus and
Olybrius, which however has none of the marks of a first attempt.
The beauty and purity of his diction and metre tell of long
acquaintance with the greatest of the Latins, and M. Boissier may
be right when he suggests that his youth, spent far from lands
where Latin as the vulgar tongue had lost something of its earlier
grace, may by throwing him back on the writers of the older days
have contributed to his mastery of the language of Virgil and
Lucan. In the same way, he says, the French of the *émigrés*, who
returned from the solitudes of America, had the ring of the old
literary style of the previous century².

He soon became one of the circle of Stilicho's dependents, an
event happy perhaps for his fortunes but lamentable for his genius.
(*Non enim uno modo sacrificatur transgressoribus angelis.*) In 400
he writes of having been away from Rome on his staff for some five
years³. Possibly there is a rueful tone in his insistence on the
self-denial of Stilicho, which makes his visits to the capital so rare
and so short⁴. He had consolation however, for, apart from other
rewards, which he must have received though he says little of them,
a letter from Serena⁵, the wife of Stilicho, won him a bride, a lady
of North Africa, presumably rich, for the letter served him instead
of "herds and fields and a palace." Whatever were the date of
this marriage, he seems to have had throughout an interest in
African affairs, which may imply some connexion with the country.

In a society where Ausonius had passed for a poet, Claudian
became more deservedly popular. He is in many ways a lively
exponent of the views of the Roman nobility, political, social and
religious. As early as 396, in the preface to his Panegyric on the
Third Consulate of Honorius, he speaks of being in some sort
delegated by mighty Rome to address the Emperor⁶. Three years
later, "Behold" he says to himself "the glory and majesty of the
Roman Senate and the men in whom Gaul rejoices. In every land

¹ *Minor Poems*, 41 (42), 13.
² *La Fin du Paganisme*, ii. 238.
³ *Praef. Cons. Stil.* iii.
⁴ *Cons. Stil.* i. 116 *adsiduus castris aderat, rarissimus urbi.*
⁵ *Minor Poems*, 31, 43 *tua littera nobis | et pecus et segetes et domus ampla fuit. | Inflexit soceros.*
⁶ *Praef. iii. Cons. Hon.* 15:

me quoque Pieriis temptatum saepius antris
audet magna suo mittere Roma deo.

I am heard and the ears of the world listen[1]." In 402–3, in the preface to his *Gothic War*, he announces that his earlier triumphs have won him a statue of bronze, granted by the Emperor at the request of the Senate, so that he is at once read and seen in the midst of the forum[2]. The same honour was afterwards given to Sidonius Apollinaris. It may perhaps have meant less in Rome than it would in London, for we learn that in the fifth century, even after Alaric's capture of the city, it could boast 3,785 bronze statues[3]. The inscription for Claudian's statue may be found in the Corpus of Latin Inscriptions, and it does not fail in extravagant eulogy. Some doubt has been cast on this inscription and on the reliability of Pomponius Laetus who first copied it, but Orelli and Mommsen accept it, and Gesner gives the testimonies of two more scholars who saw it. It is now said to be at Naples[4].

No poem of Claudian's can be dated with any certainty later than the year 404, and after that date we know nothing whatever of him He may have retired to Africa, free, in virtue of his wife's dowry, from the necessity of composition. Stilicho fell in 408, and by an ingenious combination of two of the minor poems a pretty legend has been created[5]. An epigram turning on Manlius Theodorus and an unnamed "man of Pharos," who is identified with one Hadrianus, may be thus rendered :—

> Day and night will Theodore
> Snore and sleep and sleep and snore;
> Egypt's son, the other way,
> Plunders sleepless night and day.
> Romans, your supplications make
> That this may sleep and that may wake[6].

A longer poem bears the title *Deprecatio ad Hadrianum*[7] and it is

[1] *Praef. Paneg. Manlio Theod.* 7 :

> culmina Romani majestatemque Senatus
> et, quibus exultat Gallia, cerne viros.
> omnibus audimur terris mundique per aures
> ibimus.

[2] *Praef. B. Goth.* 7 :

> sed prior effigiem tribuit successus aenam,
> oraque patricius nostra dicavit honos ;
> adnuit hic princeps titulum poscente senatu...
> ...legimur medio conspicimurque foro.

[3] See Gregorovius, *History of the City of Rome in the Middle Ages* (translation), i. 79.
[4] I am indebted to Dr Hodgkin for this correction.
[5] See Gibbon, iv. 64, but compare Hodgkin, *Italy and her Invaders*[2], i. 730.
[6] *Minor Poems*, 21 (80).   [7] *Minor Poems*, 22 (39).

thence supposed that on the death of Stilicho Hadrianus proceeded to avenge himself on the poet. But some manuscripts give *ad Stilichonem* for *ad Hadrianum*, which address, though obviously absurd, for Stilicho was not an Egyptian, leads one to suppose that both names are mere conjectures, the insertions of copyists. A good case may moreover be made for the view that the poem is not strictly serious. Another *Deprecatio* is clearly playful. Claudian (shall we say?) has criticized the poetry of a great man—well, Homer and Virgil are both criticized, but neither of them was a quaestor, so Claudian will henceforth applaud everything, and every line shall have its *'sophos!'* [1]

Claudian is chiefly famous as a panegyrist, though for myself I feel that he has stronger claims to fame. Still among the Roman panegyrists he stands foremost. We have a number of panegyrics in prose addressed to various Emperors from Trajan to Theodosius— works graceful in language and elegant in execution, but not literature. They have a certain value for the historian in the facts they display or conceal, and for the student of Roman society in the light they cast on the relations of the ruler and the ruled, but no one, I imagine, would ever read them for pleasure. Adulation may be less unpleasant in verse than in prose (" the truest poetry is the most feigning "), but a poet who attaches a serious value to poetry is reluctant to hymn Augustus or any other monarch. Claudian had his reasons for doing it. And however it may have seemed to his first readers, to-day the mythical element in his poems lessens still further the risk of our assuming that everything he says is literally felt by him. As it is, there is far too much that to us seems utterly insincere: yet while no doubt much of it really is so, we must allow for the difference time has made. With the progress of centuries the divinity that hedges a king has grown less and less, but in Claudian's day many factors tended to shroud the Emperor in a shining mist of glory. For three hundred years the Imperial tradition had grown stronger and stronger. Emperors might be madmen or savages, they might be set up and overthrown by armies or murdered by slaves, but none the less the sacred omnipotence of the Emperor became more and more an object of awe. Diocletian enhanced this by transforming the court and the monarch at once. The Emperor became a Sultan, whose person was kept from the vulgar gaze, and the court a hierarchy of splendid

[1] *Minor Poems*, 23 (74).

officials. The conception of sovereignty had been orientalized. The awful power and hardly less awful mystery of the Emperor may well have dazzled the mind of the subject, and perhaps it was really the world's interest to keep up the illusion. There had been far too many insurrections. So Claudian may have felt more than we suppose, though, as I have said, there is much in his work that he could not have felt and much that he ought not to have felt.

Let us take one or two of Claudian's panegyrics for closer study, and first one not addressed to an Emperor. One of the greatest of Roman nobles, one of the wealthiest and most successful of them, was Petronius Probus. He is typical of many of the officials of his times, and Ammianus[1] gives an amusing account of him. "He was a man known to the Roman world at once for his high birth, his influence and his enormous wealth, and throughout nearly the whole extent of that world he owned estates, whether justly or not is no matter for my poor judgment[2]…And just as the finny tribe driven from their native element cannot long breathe upon earth, so he would waste away if he held no prefecture." In 373 he proved himself quite incapable of meeting a serious emergency at Sirmium and incurred the rage of Valentinian, but he recovered[3]; and outlasting Valentinian and his family, he was in 395 a man of such importance as to make Theodosius wish to attach him to his interests. Never before had the two consulships been held simultaneously by brothers, not members of the reigning family, but in 395 Probinus and Olybrius, the sons of Probus, were consuls together. It was a great event and had to be celebrated[4].

Claudian was able to offer something congenial to the occasion, and though he is hardly as explicit as Pindar in such matters, we may find his inspiration in his praise of Probus :—" Not his to hide his wealth away in caves of night nor doom his riches to darkness; but more bounteous than the rain, it was his wont to enrich countless throngs of men. Nay, one could ever see his gifts streaming as from a cloud. The nations swarmed to his house in throngs ; poor they entered, rich they came away. That lavish hand outdid the

---

[1] xxvii. 11. Probus was a Christian and was buried in St Peter's, where his tomb stood till the fifteenth century when Pope Nicholas V. removed it. Gibbon, iv. p. 73, n. 20; Seeck, *Symm.* p. civ.

[2] *Juste an secus non judicioli est nostri*—a favourite phrase of his. (xxviii. 4, 14.)

[3] See Amm. Marc. xxix. 6, 9, and xxx. 5, 4—10.

[4] Ausonius (*Ep.* 12 = 16) had volunteered to play Choerilus to Probus' Alexander, and his verses may be said to have attained the standard he proposed. In all probability, however, he was dead by this time.

streams of Spain in its flood of golden gifts." The same thing is
said about him by Ammianus, but there is a difference. Claudian
does not mention the source of this river of gold, but we may gather
from Ammianus that such streams rose in the provinces and contributed to the Empire's decay. But we must not mar a splendid
scene with such reflexions, for does not Theodosius say : " Under
his rule we saw the western land rise with all her weary tribes to
new life[1] "?

So much for Probus. Proba might be Modesty itself come from
heaven, or Juno turning to Argos to receive gifts of incense ;
Greek and Latin records alike fail to shew her peer—in a word, she
is a worthy wife for Probus. The sexes strove to produce their
best and behold ! Probus and Proba, the perfection of each[2], and
their sons alone outdo them. As the Roman matron of old made
garments of wool, Proba prepares the *trabea*, the consular robe, for
each of her consul-sons, "and shining vestments of the thread the
Seres shave from the slender twigs, gathering the leafy fleeces of the
wool-clad forest "—in other words, of silk[3]. The frequent mention
by Claudian of silk and of exquisite and elaborate embroidery is one
indication of the change that has come over Roman taste in art and
poetry.

This, then, is the subject of the poem—to oblige a rich and
noble place-hunter Theodosius makes his two sons consuls, not an
event of any permanent import, for the consulship was an office
involving much glory and no duties whatever, it was a mere
courtesy title. What does Claudian make of it? When Theodosius had overcome Arbogast and Eugenius, Rome, personified as
a goddess[4], seizes the moment to shew her gratitude to Probus.
Impetus and Panic yoke her winged chariot of war and she leaps on
it habited like Minerva. "For she brooks not to bind her flowing
hair with bands, nor wear on her neck the woman's twisted chain.

[1] 163.   [2] 177—204.
[3] Compare Amm. Marc. xxiii. 6, 67. "Working the product of the trees with
constant application of water, as it were fleeces of a sort, from the down and
the moisture they comb out a substance of the most delicate fineness, and
spinning this they make silk, for the use hitherto of nobles but nowadays of
the meanest without any distinction." Prudentius, *Ham.* 288, says much the
same. Their common sources may be Virgil, *Georgics*, ii. 121, and Pliny, *N. H.*
6, 17.
[4] Claudian is fond of personifying Rome; cf. *b. Gild.* 16; *vi. Cons. Hon.*
356, etc. The same is done by his contemporary Prudentius, *adv. Symm.*
ii. 648, where Symmachus led the way. The Christian poet's Rome is as
complimentary to the Emperors, but has certain things to say of more importance.

Her right side is bare, her snowy arms uncovered, and one bold
breast appears ; a gem holds fast her flowing garb, the knot that
bears her sword shews gleaming purple on her white bosom. Valour
and beauty meet, and fair modesty is armed with stern terror, and
over her threatening helmet falls the tawny shade of blood-red
plumes. Her shield with its dread light challenges the sun, that
shield whereon Mulciber had shewn all his various art might do—
here is set the paternal love of Mars, and Romulus and his brother ;
here the kindly river and the strange nurse ; the Tiber is wrought
in amber and the boys in gold ; the wolf is of brass and the gleaming
Mars is adamant."

I have given this picture at length, for it is significant in many
ways. To his love of Rome I shall return, but for the moment I
speak of his method. There is a notable difference between Virgil
and Claudian in their view of poetry. Virgil's method is that of
suggestion ; it is that of appeal to the heart, and it requires something from the reader, as music does from the listener. Claudian
on the other hand leans more to painting than to music, appealing
rather to the eye. Thus he lingers fondly over his work, seeking to
bring before the eye the presentment of his conception by massing
colour upon colour, making his picture splendid as one of Honorius'
toilets. The reader *sees* in Claudian's case and *feels* in Virgil's.
Throughout, it would appear that the Roman's weakness had been
to seek beauty through decoration, and Claudian is decorative as
Virgil is not. Yet it must be understood that his hand is that of a
master. His standard is lower than Virgil's, and his work must be
judged from a different point of view. It is not equal to Virgil's in
execution, even allowing for difference of conception, but of its kind
it is successful—that is, of course, when it is not injured (as this
poem is) by the things for whose insertion his patrons paid him

Rome then, in the poem, seeks Theodosius and finds him by
the river Frigidus, resting after his victory. He addresses her as
"kindly goddess, Mother of Laws, whose sway is wide as the sky,
who art the Thunderer's bride [1]," and asks why she has come. She
tells him of the two youths she has bred, peers of Decii and Metelli,

---

[1] *Pan. Prob. Ol.* 126:

> o numen amicum,
> dux ait, et legum genetrix longeque regendo
> circumfusa polo consors et dicta Tonantis.

It is interesting to see throughout that Claudian's pride in Rome rests on her
laws and her eternity. So too Prudentius, *c. Symm.* i. 455 *domitis leges ac jura
dedisti gentibus.*

of Scipios and Camilli ; learned and eloquent, and grave beyond
their years, and asks that they may be consuls, "so may the
Scythian Araxes own our rule, and the Rhine on either bank ; so
may the towers of Semiramis[1], their Median defenders fallen, dread
our standards ; so may Ganges in wonder flow on from Roman town
to Roman town." Theodosius consents, the city rejoices and Proba
sets to work at her son's finery. The poem closes with another
picture. From the island in the Tiber, where stood a palace of the
family, the river god himself watches the triumphal procession of
the new consuls awhile in the silence of joy, and then he speaks.
He challenges the Spartan Eurotas to shew such a pair of brothers,
predicts a year of peace that recalls the promised bounties of
Nature as foretold in some eclogue of Virgil, and summons all the
rivers of Italy to rejoice with him. A few final lines follow, addressed to the new year by the poet and laden with the delights of
the several seasons, and the poem ends

> te variis scribent in floribus Horae
> longaque perpetui ducent in saecula fasti.

All this divine machinery is set in motion—Rome, Theodosius
and the Tiber all take action—for the sake of two obscure young
nobles. *Parturiunt montes.*

Take now the panegyric addressed to Honorius on his fourth
consulship. This is a greater event surely, and yet a year later
Synesius writes to a friend and, speaking of this date, says
Aristaenetus was consul, "for I do not know who was his colleague[2]." The poet begins with the pomp of the consular procession,
and passes thence to tell of Honorius' family, of his grandfather
Theodosius, who pitched his camp amid the frosts of Caledonia, and
the Orkneys were drenched with Saxon blood and Thule was warm
with Pictish gore, while glacial Ireland mourned heaps of Scottish
slain[3]—of his father Theodosius, to whom the suppliant purple
came[4], and who alone of men at once deserved and was invited to
rule, of his wars against barbarian and tyrant, and of his victories,

---

[1] May we not compare "planting the banner of St George on the mountains
of Rasselas"?
[2] *Ep.* 133. After 400 or so, one consul was named in the West, another in
the East. But here is a proof of the division of the world.
[3] Compare *Cons. Stil.* ii. 247 for these three curses of Britain—Scot, Saxon
and Pict. *Populi bestiales Pictorum* is long afterwards the phrase of Eddi,
St Wilfrid's biographer.
[4] *Ultro se purpura supplex obtulit*, 47.

which taught men that there are gods and gods ready to help, *praesentes docuere deos.* (He does not say, however, that the last usurper Eugenius had pointedly favoured paganism, and that Theodosius' victory was a crushing blow for the *dei* of the old religion.) They were victories, to win which was to prove the existence of divine justice ; and the use Theodosius made of them was blessing to the conquered—*profuit hoc vincente capi*[1]—love and loyalty sprang up in response. " Glorious in such lineage wast thou born, at once into life and majesty, no stain of private station upon thee....Thy mother laid her down on gold ; with gems bedight she brought thee forth on a bed of Tyrian dye[2] ; it was a palace that shrilled with the cries of august childbed......One day gave thee life and gave thee empire ; a consul in thy cradle, the year that bore thee bears thy name."

So after a babyhood of greatness we come to Theodosius' advice to his son, a passage of great interest. It can hardly be supposed that Claudian was favoured with the confidence of Theodosius, and Honorius, a dull boy of fourteen, was not likely to have remembered the long speech his father is said to have delivered. We must give the credit to the poet for a lesson " that might," says Gibbon, " compose a fine institution for the future prince of a great and free nation. It was far above Honorius and his degenerate subjects[3]." It may seem strange that the poet should use such freedom, yet contemporary parallels may be found. Julian wrote two Greek panegyrics on Constantius, in which he set forth views on true kingliness very like Claudian's. Synesius addressed some advice to Arcadius on the right policy for the empire at the moment, which of course was not taken. His speech too shews a number of points of contact with Claudian's work. It is not to be supposed that these men have influenced each other, but rather that all three are presenting anew the results of philosophic or quasi-philosophic speculation on monarchy gathered from the past. Much of their exhortations is inapplicable to the ruler of so large a state. Claudian is perhaps after all the most practical of the three for once. He shewed considerable delicacy and tact in putting his advice into Theodosius' lips. Elsewhere too he has preferred this indirect method.

---

[1] A line Rutilius seems to have imitated or recollected, when in addressing Rome he says of the conquered peoples *profuit invitis te dominante capi* (i. 64).
[2] Cf. Synesius, *de Regno*, 11 A, quoted on p. 326.
[3] Gibbon, iv. 22.

Much of the passage, it may be said, recalls the platitudes of Polonius, yet these parts no less than the rest have their value. Under all the sycophancy of the age there still lived something of Roman dignity, and the *Roman* character of the Empire is more than once quietly emphasized[1].

"If the tiara of the Persian rose on thy brow, thy high birth were enough for thee; but far other is the lot of the rulers of the Roman court. On worth, not birth, must thou lean, worth that is mightier and more useful linked to a mighty destiny. Learn thou then for mankind what each must learn for himself. Prometheus formed man's nature of three elements, one divine (*mens*)[2], the others mortal, and they are ever at strife, and man's work is to keep them in harmony. Rule far and wide through farthest India; let the Mede, let the soft Arab, let the Seres (Chinese) adore thee; if thou fear, if thou cherish base desire, if thou art led by anger, thou art a slave[3]. Thou canst not be lawful ruler of the world till thou art monarch of thyself[4]. Think not of what is lawful, but of what will be becoming, and let the thought of honour reign in thy heart. Remember thou dost live before the gaze of the whole earth, thy deeds lie open to all men, for the fierce light that beats upon a throne suffers naught to remain hidden (*nam lux altissima fati occultum nihil esse sinit*); rumour enters every secret place and lays bare the inmost corner. Above all things be kind (*pius*), for while in all else we are outdone, clemency of itself makes us equal to the gods. Be not suspicious, nor false to thy friends, nor greedy of praise. Not men at arms, nor a hedge of spears, are such a rampart as love[5]. Dost thou not see how all this fair universe itself is held together of love, and the elements unbound of force conspire together for ever[6]? Do thou play the citizen's part and the father's; love thyself last (*tu consule cunctis non tibi*)[7]; be thy prayers for the State and not thyself. First do thyself what thou biddest

---

[1] *iv. Cons. Hon.* 213—351. I have condensed the passage.

[2] Cf. Synesius, *de Regno*, 6 B, νοῦς to be king, and all within ἀστασίαστον διάγειν, etc.

[3] Syn. *Regn.* 6 ὀχλοκρατία τῶν παθῶν. Boethius too (*Cons. Phil.* iv. m. 2) has a little poem on this.

[4] Syn. *Regn.* 6 ἑαυτοῦ βασιλεύειν. Cf. Dio Chrys. *de Regno, Or.* i. 14.

[5] Syn. *Regn.* 9 καὶ τίς ἐχυροτέρα βασιλεία τῆς ἔρωτι τετειχισμένης; 14 B εὔνοια... βασιλέως ἐστὶν ἰσχυρὸν φυλακτήριον. Julian, *Or.* i. 48 A εὔνοιαν...τῷ βασιλεύοντι ἐρυμάτων ἀσφαλέστατον. Dio Chrys. *Or.* i. 3 τίς δὲ φρουρά κτὲ...κρείττω τῆς ἀπὸ τῶν εὐνοούντων φυλακῆς;

[6] Boethius, *Cons. Phil.* ii. m. 8, 13 *hanc rerum seriem ligat* | *terras ac pelagus regens* | *et caelo imperitans amor;* and iv. m. 6.

[7] Syn. *Regn.* 14. The king to be λειτουργὸν τῆς βασιλείας. Cf. Dio Chrys. *Or.* iii. 55, 56, 62.

others; the people will hearken when they see the ruler obey himself, for the world forms itself after the pattern of its king and
naught moulds it so much as his life[1]. No scorn, no pride; I have
not given thee Sabaeans long taught to be slaves; I have not made
thee lord of Armenia, nor do I yield thee the Assyrian race, ruled
by a woman. Romans, who long have ruled the world, hast thou to
rule[2], Romans, who brooked not Tarquin's pride nor Cæsar's laws
(*jura*). Long will the glory of Trajan live, not by his conquests,
but because he was kind to his own country."

Instructions somewhat in the style of Nestor follow on war, but
when the lad asks to accompany his father on his march against
Eugenius, he is bidden stay at home and read history, and a list of
thirteen great examples is given him.

Claudian now calls on Theodosius, who had risen to heaven to
become a star, to look down and see his hopes for his son fulfilled,
thanks to Stilicho, for Stilicho is almost inevitable whatever the
subject. He gives a list of Stilicho's German triumphs and then
turns to the Greek campaign of 396, and here we may well pause
to consider another aspect of Claudian's poetry—the defence of
Stilicho.

The story of the Greek campaign may be thus summarized. In
395 Alaric was laying waste Thrace and Macedonia, and Arcadius
summoned Stilicho to protect Constantinople and the East. Almost
as soon as Stilicho reached Thessaly, he was bidden to return with
the western troops, but to send back to their proper headquarters the
eastern forces which Theodosius had led westward against Eugenius.
He obeyed. Alaric unhampered marched into Greece and ravaged
the country, but Stilicho reappeared and blockaded him on the
plain of Pholoe (396). And then, already at Stilicho's mercy, he
escaped, went on plundering and was bought off by the government of Constantinople with the military command of Illyricum.

Two great questions arise. How came Stilicho so readily to
obey the order to return to Italy? How came Alaric to escape
from Pholoe? The same happened again at Pollentia in 402. On
the answer to these questions depends our estimate of Stilicho.
Zosimus (v. 7) says he was so busy with dissipation that Alaric
eluded him at Pholoe. "I say nothing," writes Orosius[3], "of King
Alaric with his Goths, often conquered, often hemmed in, and

---

[1] Julian, *Or.* ii. 88 c ἐξομοιοῦσθαι πρὸς τὸν ἄρχοντα τὰ τῶν ὑπηκόων.
[2] Tacitus puts a similar sentence in Galba's mouth, *Hist.* i. 16.
[3] Orosius, vii. 37, 2 *saepe victo saepe concluso semperque dimisso.*

always allowed to escape." Heathen[1] and Christian alike seem to
have mistrusted him, and the controversy about Pholoe and
Pollentia has lasted to our day, Dr Hodgkin acquitting him[2] and
Mr Bury bringing him in guilty.

But our concern is with Claudian. These are the facts to be
explained for his patron; what does Claudian do? Gibbon[3] characterizes his account as "curious circumstantial flattery"; "as the
event was not glorious it is artfully thrown into the shade." Mr
Bury[4] commits himself and calls it "an absolutely false and mis-
leading account, which no allowance for poetical exaggeration can
defend." The act of obedience is glorified with a fine phrase[5]. The
Greek affairs he alludes to once or twice, always rapidly and without
condescending to particulars, once hinting at a supposed treaty
made from Constantinople. To Pollentia he gives more space, and a
vast flood of declamation about historical parallels, which are not
parallel, covers or tries to cover the fact that, for whatever reason,
Alaric had not been crushed. One seems to see that there was
hostile criticism in Rome, which the poet is trying to silence by
special pleading. Mr Bury holds that on this and on other occasions the utterances of Claudian were direct manifestoes suggested
by his patron, while M. Boissier[6] shrewdly doubts whether Stilicho
always meant quite so much to be said as is said. Men thought
Stilicho wanted to make his son Eucherius Emperor, beginning by
marrying him to Honorius' sister[7]. Now Claudian says nothing
about the ultimate design, but he does hint at the possible marriage.
The union never took place, and M. Boissier thinks that Claudian
has here exceeded his instructions.

To return to our poem. The Greek affair is vaguely got rid of
in fourteen lines, and we resume the blessings of Honorius' reign,
which are very significant. If the recommendations we have seen
addressed to him seem to hint at the violence of Valentinian, the
uneasy suspicion of Valens and the savage temper of Theodosius,
what are we to say when we read this? "We are ruled by judges

[1] The most ferocious attack is made by Rutilius (ii. 41 f.), who accuses
Stilicho of burning the Sibylline books, and calls him worse than Nero: *hic
immortalem mortalem perculit ille, | hic mundi matrem perculit ille suam.*
[2] Perhaps a Scots verdict of "Not proven" is nearer Dr Hodgkin's view.
Can it be his troops would not push their kinsmen on the other side to extremi-
ties? Cf. Syn. *Regn.* 14.
[3] iv. 27 n.
[4] *L. R. E.* i. 74.
[5] *In Ruf.* ii. 249 *non est victoria tanti ut videar vicisse mihi.*
[6] *F. P.* ii. *l.c.*
[7] Orosius says this and the idea probably did not originate with him.

we know, and enjoy the blessings of peace and of war. No sword
hangs over us; there are no butcheries of the nobility; no accusa-
tions are forged against the common folk; the exile is not thrust in
sadness from his native land; the wicked additions to continuous
taxation cease. Thy treasury does not grow rich on the losses of
thy subjects[1]." Yet how like his father the Emperor grows!
Quantus in ore pater radiat! He can wear his father's helmet
(*jam patrias imples galeas*) and is very athletic and warlike.
Historians have remarked that later on he forsook riding for feeding
poultry, and life through had a profound sense of the value of the
sacred life of an Emperor. The poem closes with pomp, procession
and splendour[2], with a brilliant spectacle and a prophecy of an
extended frontier.

What does the poet mean by this poem? He means no doubt
to flatter the Emperor and defend Stilicho, for doing which he was
paid; but when he glorifies Rome's victories over the Goths, when
he magnifies the true Roman character in language that should
remind his readers of their great past, of a day when the Roman
faced and overthrew greater foes than Alaric, is he not doing more?
And does he not so atone for his hireling work and rise into real
significance?

Beside panegyrics and panegyrical histories Claudian wrote in-
vectives. These were directed against the two successive ministers
of Arcadius, Rufinus and the eunuch Eutropius, the enemies of
Stilicho and therefore of the true Rome on the Tiber. The world
was too happy, and a council in Hell was called to deal with the
matter. Various plans were discussed, but on the proposal of
Megaera (rhetorically described) it was decided not to make war on
heaven, but to send among men Rufinus, a nursling of the Fury, so
well trained by her that he can outdo her in her own arts. She
hailed him from his native Elusa in Aquitaine to Constantinople,
where, insatiate as the sea, by extortion of every kind he amassed
infinite riches. Here let me leave Claudian to quote Zosimus, who,
while confirming his story, makes an interesting addition: "Every
kind of villainy throve in the cities, and all the wealth of all the

[1] ll. 491 ff.
[2] "Royalty, followed by the imperial presence of ambassadors, and escorted
by a group of dazzling duchesses and paladins of high degree, was ushered with
courteous pomp by the host and hostess into a choice saloon, hung with rose-
coloured tapestry and illuminated by chandeliers of crystal, where they were
served from gold plate." There is more than a little common to Claudian and
the author of *Lothair*.

world flowed into the houses of Rufinus and Stilicho, while poverty
in every place invaded the houses of those who had but lately been
rich. Yet the Emperors saw nothing of what was going on, but
only decreed whatever Rufinus bade and Stilicho[1]."
Rufinus of course came to a bad end. It was believed he had
inspired the order which sent Stilicho so precipitately home in 395.
Stilicho's speech to his soldiers on that occasion is well done by
Claudian—

> *flectite signa duces. redeat jam miles eous.*
> *parendum est. taceant litui, prohibete sagittas.*
> *parcite contiguo—Rufinus praecipit—hosti[2].*

The eastern troops bade Stilicho farewell after the manner of Lucan,
marched off, were reviewed by Arcadius and concluded the review
by tearing Rufinus in pieces. "The *dissection* of Rufinus, which
Claudian performs with the savage coolness of an anatomist[3]," may
be paralleled by some of the martyrdoms of Prudentius. Detail is
not spared. It was horrible and it permitted a list of members, and
both of these features lent themselves to rhetoric. Such was the
evil legacy of Lucan and his school[4].

The irony, the rhetoric and the swing of this poem impress
every reader, but there are other points of interest in it. It begins
with a debate as to whether or no there is evidence for believing in
Providence[5]. "For when I saw the laws of the ordered universe,
bounds fixed for the seas and paths for the rivers, the alternation of
light and darkness, then I inclined to think that all is decreed by
the council of God, who has bid the stars move by rule, the crops
grow in their seasons, Phœbe in her changes shine with the borrowed
light and the Sun with his own, who has set shores for the waves
and poised the earth in mid air. But when I saw mankind wrapped
in such darkness, the guilty long enjoying gladness, and the good
afflicted, religion in its turn was shaken and like to fall." The
punishment of Rufinus however, he continues, has settled his doubts
for ever. In the same way Synesius demonstrates at greater length
the truth of an effective Providence by his "Egyptian story" of
Aurelian and Gainas' revolt, and actually says that the rule of
"Typhos" had driven belief in Providence from the minds of men[6].

[1] v. 1. [2] *In Ruf.* ii. 217.
[3] Gibbon, iv. 13. It is not an invention of Claudian's. Cf. Zosimus, v. 7.
[4] Quintilian, x. 1, 90 *Lucanus...magis oratoribus quam poetis imitandus.*
[5] An exordium pronounced beautiful by Gibbon, vol. iv. p. 14, n. 33.
[6] See esp. *de Prov.* ii. 1 ἤδη τῆς ἀνθρώπων γνώμης ἐξερρύηκε δόξα προνοίας.

The descent of Rufinus into hell, at the close of the second book, is drawn with vigour. The ghosts of his victims swarm about him like the wild bees round the shepherd who is robbing their nest. It is a hell where the distinctions of earth are lost, no dignity survives and the king stripped of his empty title rubs shoulders with the beggar. The guilty are condemned to bear the forms of beasts for three thousand years, but Rufinus is too bad for hell. "Cleanse the home of Pluto. Whip him across Styx, across Erebus; give him to the void abyss, below the night of the Titans, below the furthest Tartarus, below Chaos itself, where lie hid the foundations of Night: there, plunged headlong, let him pant, while the stars wheel through heaven and the winds lash the shores of the sea[1]."

The invective against Eutropius, the eunuch made consul, is in much the same style—the tone very often recalling Juvenal—

omnia cesserunt eunucho consule monstra.

This old slave, set free because worthless—*contemptu jam liber erat* —his *aides-de-camp*, the fuller and the cook, his council of war, eaters of peacocks and parrots, and the Senate of New Rome, the "Greek Quirites," who fondle and kiss the creased cheeks of the "old woman," are all drawn with the perfection of hatred and of skill.

Once more we have an indirect contribution to Imperial policy in the words of the Fury to Tribigild, urging him to imitate Alaric: "To-day, who breaks treaties, is enriched; who keeps them is a beggar. He, who laid waste Achaea and but lately ravaged Epirus unavenged, rules Illyricum…Thee too let them fear; let them admire thee guilty, whom they have spurned while loyal. Sated with spoils and prey, when it is thy pleasure thou shalt be a Roman" (ii. 213).

This was a criticism of the helpless government, not undeserved and certainly well and guardedly delivered. Claudian however as a statesman was as ineffectual as Synesius, and his homilies and his ironies despite his art achieved nothing. But I need not linger over the poem, as I think its general character will be clear.

Here let me pause before discussing matters of deeper interest to consider Claudian's style and manner. Something of his spirit may, I hope, have survived translation in the passages I have quoted.

---

[1] Thus in Syn. *de Prov.* ii. 3, 1269 c, Typhos is to be ἐν Κωκυτῷ as a παλα- μναῖον καὶ Ταρτάριον δαίμονα along with the Titans and Giants.

His handling of the hexameter is brilliant and powerful, in some
points very different from Virgil's, but different too from Lucan's.
He avoids with a curious sensitiveness those minor licenses Virgil
uses[1]; and though he goes further than Lucan in his use of the
hephthemimeral pause, on the whole his verse is not so monotonous,
though rhetorical.

His debt to earlier poets is great and manifold. Words, phrases
and ideas are often borrowed, and very often manner. Yet his
indebtedness does not affect his independence. As an example of
Lucan's manner one citation will suffice. He is speaking of Rufinus'
mutilation—

> jacet en! qui possidet orbem
> exiguae telluris inops et pulvere raro
> per partes tegitur nusquam totiensque sepultus[2].

Of Juvenal's,

> exterret cunabula discolor infans[3].

The opinion has been held that his use of Virgil is different from
that made by Prudentius, and in some respects this is true. He
never, for example, approaches such annexation as

> Christe graves hominum semper miserate labores[4],

but his language constantly recalls Virgil in word and phrase and
rhythm[5].

---

[1] A few details may be given. Spondaic hexameters. 5; Leonine, 6; double
disyllabic ending, 6; double monosyllabic ending, 7; monosyllabic ending, 4;
quadrisyllabic ending, 5; hiatus, 1 (*heu ubi*); irregular quantities, 2 (*hic* and
conubiale); rhyming couplets, 1;—a very short list for some seven or eight
thousand lines. The spurious poems attributed to him may be condemned
at a glance for their false quantities and roughness. How they came to be
called Claudian's I cannot understand. One further small point may be
mentioned in this connexion. A heavy ending of a particular type—the pen-
ultimate word four long syllables and one short—is much affected by him.
The form *tempestatumque potentem* occurs some twelve times in the *Aeneid*,
perhaps oftener but not very much oftener. It is not much used by Lucan.
I have counted ninety-eight examples in Claudian. I believe it is due to the
influence of rhetoric, though the long roll of the movement is better fitted
for prose.
[2] *Ruf.* ii. 452. For a passage inspired by Lucan, see the story of the
"Thundering Legion" in *vi. Cons. Hon.* 335—350.
[3] *B. Gildon.* 193.
[4] Prud. *Psych.* 1. Cf. *Aen.* vi. 56.
[5] A short passage may shew how much he can borrow. In the poem on the
War of Gildo the two Theodosii leave heaven to visit the dreams of Arcadius
and Honorius and the passage shews Claudian's study of the *Aeneid*, particularly
(here) of the fifth book. A table will make this clear.
306 *dum vita maneret.*   *Aen.* v. 724 *dum vita manebat.*
309 *respice fratris conubium.*   *Aen.* iv. 275 *spes surgentis Iuli respice.*

While many of these coincidences may seem accidental, and some the inevitable diction of the epic poet, still it is clear that Claudian has assimilated Virgil. If likeness of form be not enough, clear kinship is shewn by such passages as the hell of *In Rufinum* ii. and the sixth *Aeneid*, and by the treatment of country life. Still it may, I think, be admitted that in tone he is nearer Lucan or Juvenal.

He can never resist the opportunity to make a list, and on several occasions he digresses into strange paths of geography— *e.g.*, the situation, boundaries and aspect of Phrygia (*In Eutrop.* ii. 238—273), of Sicily (*R. P.* i. 142—178), of the prefectures of the Gauls and of Italy (*Paneg. Manl. Theod.* 41—57 and 198—204). Even his list of the forces sent against Gildo is not as bad as Lucan's list of Pompey's legions (*Phars.* vii.). Other lists are:— Thirteen Roman worthies (*iv. Cons. Hon.* 400), the philosophical schools (*Paneg. M. Theod.* 70—83), Victory's five possible abodes in heaven (*Cons. Stil.* iii. 202), and many more.

He is apt to fall into exaggeration and other forms of false taste. Venus addresses Maria, the daughter of Stilicho and the wife of Honorius, and, after specific mention of nine several charms, concludes, "If Bacchus in love could adorn heaven with his bride's wreath, why are there no stars for a garland for a fairer maid? Nay, already Bootes frames thee starry crowns, and for Maria's honour heaven brings forth new constellations[1]." Theodosius addresses his last words to Stilicho, commending to him the young Honorius; "then with no further word, even as he was, he left a path of light upon the clouds and entered the orb of the Moon,"

315 *ille licet* (beginning a line).	*Aen.* xi. 440 (the same).
315 *praetentis Syrtibus.*	*Aen.* vi. 60 *praetentaque Syrtibus arva.*
318–9 *in omnes aequalem casus animum.*	*Aen.* ix. 277 *comitem casus complector in omnes.*
320 *inveniet virtute viam.*	*Aen.* x. 113 *fata viam invenient.*
323–4 *commissa profanus ille luet.*	*Georg.* iv. 454 *magna luis commissa.*
325 *longo...sermone.*	*Aen.* i. 217 *longo...sermone.*
326 *castumque cubile.*	*Aen.* viii. 412 *castum servare cubile.*
327 *Tyrio...ostro.*	*Georg.* iii. 17 *Tyrio...ostro.*
328 *carpebat...somnos.*	*Aen.* vii. 414 *carpebat nocte quietem.*
329 *per somnia,* a ghost speaks.	*Aen.* v. 636 *per somnum.*
330 *tantane...fiducia* (also *b. Get.* 380).	*Aen.* i. 132 *tantane...fiducia.*
331 *care nepos.*	*Aen.* vi. 682 *carosque nepotes,*
	and the ghost vanishes in the Virgilian style.
348 *adflatus vicino sole refugit.*	*Aen.* v. 739 *me saevus equis Oriens adflavit anhelis.*

Add a number of single words used in Virgil's way 321 *ultro*, 326 *fusus* (of sleep).

[1] *Epithalamium,* 271.

and so on his way past star after star, each quarter of heaven contending for the honour of his presence—" O glory of the sky as once of earth, thee thine Ocean welcomes when weary to thy native flood, and Spain doth bathe thee in the waves thou knowest so well[1]." When Honorius hunts, "gladly will the beasts fall to thy spear, and the lion rejoicing in his *sacred* wounds will welcome the shaft, prouder in his death[2]." When Honorius marries Maria, the poet says to Stilicho, "More, even more, we all admit we owe to our lord, that he is thy son-in-law, unconquered hero[3]!" Some of his utterances on the same marriage pass belief. Again, when, at a length of 130 lines, he sets Diana and her nymphs to collect wild beasts (elephants it seems excepted) to be shipped to Rome for Stilicho's triumph[4], one feels to-day a certain disproportion between means and end. Still there is a value in the passage as shewing the mind of the time, attested likewise by Prudentius. Lastly, when Aethon, the steed of Aurora who (*qui*) puts the stars to flight, longs to be ridden by Honorius[5], one feels that Lucan's famous appeal to Nero not to overbalance the universe when he takes his seat among the gods, has been very nearly equalled.

On the other hand his descriptions are strong and his pictures striking. His similes (some ninety-seven in number) are often happy. Rufinus, among the soldiers, "shut in on right and left, stood spell-bound by the shouts of the armed ring around him, even as a wild beast, that has but lately lost its mountain home, an exile from the towering forests, and condemned to the games of the arena, bounds wildly in. The man shouts to it and awaits with poised spear. But the beast trembles at the din, and head in air looks round upon the benches of the amphitheatre and marvels at the hissing of the throng[6]." Another interesting simile describes Alaric after Pollentia; "even as a pirate bark, that has long cruised the seas and laid waste the ships, falls full of guilty wealth upon a great trireme of war, which she has mistaken for a prey; and oarless, her wings of canvas torn, her helm and rigging broken, she is tossed by wind and wave the plaything of the sea, till at last she pay her penalty to the deep she has wronged[7]." Alaric, deserted

---

[1] *iii. Cons. Hon.* 162, 175. A magnificent way of saying the star sets in the West. Theodosius was a Spaniard. Dr Hodgkin should be read on this.

[2] *Fescen.* i. 13. The lion reminds one of the wounded pigeon in *Lothair* that fluttered over a paling from a terrier, that it might die by a ducal hand.

[3] *Epithal.* 335.   [4] *Cons. Stil.* iii. 237—369.

[5] *iv. Cons. Hon.* 561.   [6] *Ruf.* ii. 394.

[7] *vi. Cons. Hon.* 132.

by some of his Goths, is compared to an old man of Hybla, whose
bees have swarmed ; he clangs cymbals all in vain, and, wearied by
the bootless noise, gives over and laments the faithless swarms and
empty hives[1]. Again, in view of the story of the Rape of Proserpine, there is an impressiveness in the simile of the path of Venus.
"The path shone as the goddess trod, even as a comet of dire augury
crosses the heaven in fire and blood, ruddy with ominous import ;
the mariner sees it to his sorrow, and the folk to their hurt, for the
menace of its streaming light speaks of storm for ships and foemen
for cities." Another simile, no new one, tells of the starry sky,
where the moon outshines the stars, but an added touch makes it
new. The point turns on brightness, but the poet adds the silence
of night.

tacitam Luna regnante per aethram.

It is clear that a poet, whatever he be told or paid to write, can
write nothing of any value that does not come from the heart—
denn es muss von Herzen gehen, was auf Herzen wirken soll—whatever moreover the subject assigned him, he will write what he must
write. The poet, like the Hebrew prophet, has a burden, he can do
nothing but what is *given* him. It has nothing to do with
patronage. In the poetry of Claudian we find two noble conceptions, overlaid and marred, it is true, in some measure by uninspired
work, by rhetoric and adulation, yet noble still—the eternal
grandeur of Rome and the beauty and sufficiency of the old
religion. Both of these call for study.

To begin with Rome. In the brilliant apologetic of Tertullian
and the sober homilies of Afrahat we find the opinion, that Rome
is to last as long as the world lasts. But as yet to Christians
Rome was not an object of love ; they had not seen beyond the
"scarlet woman" the majestic queen of the Church. It was the
heathen who at this time felt for her the passionate enthusiasm of
the Christian of the middle ages, though already a Prudentius has
visions of a Christian Rome, and the pilgrims cross the bridge of
Hadrian[2]. To the heathen, however, she was dear not so much for
what she was to be as for what she was and had been. The associations of ten centuries were about her ; the wealth, the culture, the

---

[1] *vi. Cons. Hon.* 259.
[2] Boissier, *F. P.* ii. 253, remarks that Claudian and his friends, by maintaining the imperial destiny and sacred character of Rome, were really con-
tributing to the growth of a papal Rome. I feel however that their influence
may easily be over-estimated.

art and the faith of the world had gathered to her. She summed up the history of mankind. She had been and was still "mother of laws" and giver of peace. Justice between man and man and amity between nations were her gifts to the world, and her visible splendour and prosperity were the seal of the world's happiness. She was the chosen city of the gods; god after god had forsaken his native home for Rome, had brought his people under her sway and made it clear that Rome and heaven stood together. And now a new faith had risen, and the first Emperor to forsake the old gods had also forsaken the old Rome, and had made at once a new heaven and a new earth, a new heaven that knew not the gods of his fathers, and a new Rome that flouted the old. The cause a man loves he loves the more when it is attacked. So the heathen loved Rome the more for the menace of Christian Constantinople, and in Claudian's poetry we read this love. Honorius is the Emperor of the true Rome (though alas! he did indeed live at Ravenna); he had begged Rome of his father rather than Constantinople, says Claudian. Stilicho was the saviour of Rome. Thus the extravagant eulogy of these men means more than might appear at first sight. The pageantry and pomp he delights to describe are Rome's, they are the symbols of her greatness.

Let us take as our starting-point the greatest word spoken in Stilicho's praise:

> *nihil in tanto circum terrore locutus*
> *indignum Latio*[1].

"Amid all the terror that stood around he said no word unworthy of Latium"—this was written by an Alexandrian Greek and written of a Vandal. The situation was very different, but the spirit is that of the men who thanked the defeated Varro that he had not despaired of the Republic.

"Look," he cries to Stilicho, "look around upon the seven hills, that challenge the sun's rays with their gleam of gold, upon the arches hung with spoils, upon the temples that tower to the clouds and all the fabric of so many triumphs. What thou hast wrought, what a city thou hast saved, measure thou with eyes of wonder[2]." The seat of the Empire is as peerless as itself.

When Stilicho had won the victory of Pollentia and Alaric at all events withdrew, Claudian apostrophizes Rome. "Rise, venerable

---

[1] *Cons. Stil.* i. 294.   [2] *Cons. Stil.* iii. 65.

mother, and free from care trust the favour of the gods. Away with craven fears of old age. City eternal as the sky, iron fate shall touch thee then and only then, when nature makes new laws for the stars[1]." Into the lips of a Gothic counsellor of Alaric, he puts the words: "If it be truth our fathers tell, none who was so mad as to attack this city in war, returned triumphant in his guilt. The gods fail not their home; thunderbolts, men say, are hurled on the foe afar, and the fires of heaven guard the walls, whether it be the gods or Rome herself that thunders[2]." The poem closes with the words posterity shall read at Pollentia. "Here laid in Italian soil are the Cimbri and the valiant Goths, slain by the great captains Stilicho and Marius. Learn, foolish peoples, not to despise Rome."

From the city we pass to the Empire

> *tanto quaesitum sanguine, tanto*
> *servatum, quod mille ducum peperere labores,*
> *quod tantis Romana manus contexuit annis*[3].

These are the words of a "provincial," of one of the conquered perhaps. What did the Empire mean to him? There is in the third book of *Stilicho's Consulship* a passage which, in spite of one or two weak spots, really reaches a high level of patriotism and inspiration—a stirring appeal to his countrymen to be worthy of their past. Note in particular the reference to Hannibal with whom he elsewhere compares Alaric. In this tacit contrast of present and past we can surely read what Rome was to this poet of her later days[4].

"Nought grander on earth does the sky embrace. The eye cannot comprehend her extent, the heart her beauty, nor the voice her praise. With the lustre of her gold she rivals the stars she touches. Her seven hills recall the zones of Olympus. Mother of arms and laws, she spreads her rule over all mankind, the first to give them law. She it is who from narrow bounds spread to either pole, and starting from a little home reached forth her hands with the sun. Battling with destiny, while she waged countless wars at once, laid hold on the towns of Spain, besieged the towns of Sicily,

---

[1] *b. Get.* 54. *Urbs aequaeva polo.*
[2] *b. Get.* 506—511.
[3] *In Ruf.* ii. 50. Compare Prudentius, *Symm.* ii. 550:

> *non fero Romanum nomen sudataque bella*
> *et titulos* tanto quaesitos sanguine *carpi.*

[4] *Cons. Stil.* iii. 131—170.

brought low the Gaul on land, the Carthaginian on the sea, she never bowed to blow; no whit was she affrighted by wound, but her voice rose stronger after Cannae and the Trebia[1], and when the flames girt her round about and the foe was at the wall, she sent her armies to the distant Iberians, nor was she stayed by Ocean, but embarked upon the deep and sought the Britons in a world remote for a fresh triumph. This is she who alone took the conquered to her bosom and cherished all mankind alike, as mother not as queen, and called them her sons whom she had conquered, and bound them to her afar by bonds of love. To her rule of peace we owe it that the stranger is at home in every land, that men may dwell in every clime, that it is but sport to visit Thule and the furthest shores; that we may range from Rhone to Orontes; that we are all one people. Nor shall there ever be an end to Rome's sway. Other realms luxury with its crimes and pride with its hatreds brought low. So the proud Spartan overthrew Athens and fell in turn to Thebes; so the Mede from the Assyrian, and the Persian from the Mede took the power. The Macedonian crushed the Persian, himself to yield to the Romans. She stands grounded on the Sibyl's oracles, inspired by the rites of Numa. For her Jupiter wields the thunderbolt; her Pallas shields with the Gorgon; hither brought Vesta her secret flame, and the tower-crowned Mother of the Gods her mysteries and her Phrygian lions."

And yet there are ominous signs of what is coming. The Empire is weaker, the Goths grow stronger and do more and more mischief, and with loss of territory the number and the rapacity of the officials grow[2]. More ominous still, his "gods" have said to Alaric (who by the way was Christian, if Arian)

penetrabis ad Urbem.

Claudian may make merry over this prophecy fulfilled at the river Urbis (the Borbo)[3], but the divine pressure was still on Alaric, as he told the hermit, and to the City (*Urbs*) he came[4].

And Constantinople? "Look," he says, "at the Senate applauding (Eutropius), those nobles of Byzantium, those Greek Quirites!

---

[1] I may be permitted to quote these lines, which after the battle of Colenso I felt represented English sentiment as truly as they do the Roman feeling of 216 B.C.:

> *nunquam succubuit damnis et territa nullo*
> *vulnere post Cannas major Trebiamque fremebat.*

[2] *In Eutrop.* ii. 590 *rectorum numerum terris pereuntibus augent.*

[3] *b. Get.* 555.   [4] Sozomen, ix. 6.

O people worthy of its Senate ! O Senate worthy of its Consul[1]!"
"The ruler of the East, the destined consul, combed a mistress'
locks[2]." "Nobles," he says, "wont to scorn Rome and admire their
own abode—which may the Bosporus overwhelm[3]." His crowning
insult is the enumeration of the "founders" of New Rome—Byzas,
Constantine and Eutropius[4]. From many of his expressions we can
clearly see the growing severance between East and West. Apart
from his Roman sympathies, his Alexandrian origin would contribute to his dislike of Constantinople. Alexandria hated Constantinople, and to such an extent that Egypt did not care to battle
against the Saracens, but surrendered to them at once. The hatred
was racial and afterwards religious.

We come now to the question of religion. "An exquisite poet
but a most stubborn heathen[5]" says Orosius of Claudian, when
he quotes a line or two from which he carefully eliminates the
heathenism. Augustine gives the same account of him—"the poet
Claudian, though a stranger to Christ's name[6]." One likes to think
that Christians read and enjoyed him in spite of a difference of
view. For Claudian was pronounced in his adherence to the old
religion. No doubt it may be said, and it has been said at least
often enough, that the gods in his poems are even more avowedly
ornamental than in the *Aeneid*. Yet while Orosius and Augustine
made a strong point of the bloodlessness and completeness of
Theodosius' victories because they were God-given, it is surely not
merely for decorative purposes that Claudian gives all the glory to
the gods of old Rome. It has been remarked[7] that there is also a
significance in his invocation of Victory (*Cons. Stil.* iii. 205), in view
of the battles that had been fought about the statue of the goddess
and its removal from the Senate House.

His direct allusions to Christianity are as scant as might have
been expected from a man of culture of the old faith. It was a
point of style to ignore the new religion. He has one or two sneers
for the "Egyptian oracles" on which Eutropius rested, oracles

[1] *Eutrop.* ii. 135.   [2] *Eutrop.* i. 105.
[3] *Eutrop.* ii. 339.   [4] *Eutrop.* ii. 83.
[5] Orosius, vii. 35 *poeta quidem eximius sed paganus pervicacissimus.*
[6] Augustine, *C. D.* v. 26 *poeta Claudianus quamvis a Christi nomine alienus.*
[7] Boissier, *F. P.* ii. 244. I believe this critic is nearer the truth when he says of Claudian's attitude to Christianity, "il y songe toujours," than M. Beugnot (cited by Milman on Gibbon) who talks of "his extraordinary indifference." As to Victory, see the famous *relatio* of Symmachus and Ambrose's reply (*Epp.* i. 18), and the two thoughtful and courteous books of Prudentius *adversus Symmachum*.

supposed to be those of the Egyptian hermit John, whom Augustine tells us Theodosius consulted[1]. But the epigram addressed to the military commander (duke) Jacob is his only direct mention of saint and scripture, and surely suffices to shew his mind.

> By the threshold of Peter, the ashes of Paul,
> My verses, duke Jacob, misquote not at all;
> So the saints from the Alps the invaders repel;
> So Susanna the chaste lend her forces as well;
> So Thomas be with you instead of a shield;
> So Bartholomew go as your squire to the field;
> So whoever shall swim the chill Danube to fight,
> Like the horses of Pharaoh be lost to your sight;
> So the sword of your vengeance lay Gothic hordes low;
> So the blessing of Thecla add strength to your blow;
> So your guest by his death yield the glory to you;
> While the bottles outpoured shall your dryness subdue;
> So your hand ne'er be stained by the blood of a foe;
> Those verses, duke Jacob, I pray you, let go.

Point is added to the opening of this little piece by the fact that the basilica of St Paul had been begun by Theodosius and was finished by Honorius, and bore the inscription

> *Theodosius coepit perfecit Honorius aulam*
> *Doctoris mundi sacratam corpore Pauli*[2].

No wonder Orosius says *paganus pervicacissimus*, when Claudian wrote as he did under the shade of this church, newly dedicated by his Emperor[3].

As men are influenced by their environment, I had the curiosity to note all passages in which I could find anything that looked at all like specific knowledge of the scriptures. Had he any knowledge of them? "Pharaoh's horses" answer yes. But did they make any impression on him? I give a list of these passages, which, liberally interpreted, might be referred to some scriptural parallel.

---

[1] Augustine, *C. D.* v. 26. *Praef. Eutrop.* ii. 39 and *Eutrop.* i. 312. Soz. vii. 22.

[2] See Gregorovius, *City of Rome*, i. 100, and the famous poem of Prudentius on the churches of Saints Peter and Paul and their pilgrims. (*Peri Stephanon*, 12.)

[3] In triumphing over Eutropius he speaks of the *pias aras* (the Christian church) where the eunuch took sanctuary.

Ruf. ii. 442—54. The fall of Rufinus and the movement of hell to meet him.

Isaiah xiv. 12. How art thou fallen from heaven, Lucifer— Hell from beneath is moved for thee.

Ruf. ii. 474. A hell without class distinctions and an examination of lives.

Rev. xx. 12, 13. (More probably Neo-Platonic, cf. *Hermes Trism.* (ed. Bipont.) p. 312.)

Cons. Stil. i. 84. *Tunc exultasse choreis astra ferunt.*

Job xxxviii. 7.

vi. Cons. Hon. 523. Simile of mother preparing bride for her husband.

Isaiah lxi. 10.

Laus Serenae 94. *Omina non audet genetrix tam magna fateri | successusque suos arcani conscia voti | spe trepidante fovet.*

Luke ii. 19.

R. P. ii. 94 of flowers : *Parthica quae tantis variantur cingula gemmis | regales vinctura sinus.*

Matthew vi. 29. Solomon in all his glory.

To these let me add parallels Dr Hodgkin suggests :

b. Get. 625—632. · Alaric's mother wanted Roman ladies as slave girls.

Judges v. 28—30. The mother of Sisera.

Exordium to *In Rufinum* i.

Psalm lxxiii.

In Ruf. ii. 249—50. *Non est victoria tanti*, etc.

Prov. xvi. 32.

None of these is very convincing. Claudian *may* have known something of the Christian scriptures, but I doubt if it was very much. One striking coincidence with Christian language I believe to be accidental. In one of his pieces of embroidery he introduces the child it was hoped the Empress Maria might bear—a child, however, never born. *Sacri Mariae partus*[1] is his phrase, and it has a strange suggestion to our ears, which I do not think it had at the time. The Christian thought of the day had not reached that point of view, and it would not occur to Claudian, and perhaps hardly to his Christian readers, that the words might be taken in another sense than that meant.

[1] *Cons. Stil.* ii. 342. Almost everything connected with an Emperor is *sacred*, even the wounds his hunting spear makes. Even in business prose Symmachus, reserving cases for the Emperor's decision, refers to it as *sacrum oraculum*. Brockhaus, *Prudentius*, pp. 252, 294, brings out the fact that, in spite of the stress laid by Catholic archaeologists on representations of the Virgin in Christian art, the language and tone of Prudentius are decidedly against the theory that she yet received any special honours ; she is still a *Nebenfigur*. So Gregorovius, *Rome in the Middle Ages*, i. 103. The cult of the Virgin was as yet not officially recognized in the 4th century.

But whatever heathens may have thought or wished, it was inevitable that their beliefs must be affected by the presence of Christianity. The Reformation caused the Counter Reformation and thus affected the Papacy. The Disruption in Scotland in 1843, by creating the Free Church, gave new life to the Established Church. So heathenism is not the same after as before the dissemination of Christianity. Too much stress may be laid on this, it is true, for there was a general revival of religion contemporaneously with the spread of the Gospel, which aided it but is hardly to be traced to it. Marcus Aurelius doubted but sacrificed. In Apuleius we may first read the general drift of this revival. Juvenal has indeed a curious hint of the future faith of heathenism, when he writes of the gods *Carior est illis homo quam sibi*, but the acceptance of this as the great feature of the old religion comes later.

At the end of the fourth century heathen thought in the West has reached a genial if rather shallow optimism, whose cardinal doctrine is what Ammianus calls *benignitas numinis*[1], the kindliness of the divine. It is the philosophy of Omar Khayyam's pot, whose conclusion to the debate on the potter is

"He's a good fellow, and 't will all be well."

We have seen how Claudian held that the universe rests on love[2], and that mercy makes us like the gods while in all else we are inferior[3]. Elsewhere he dilates further on Mercy, the eldest of the gods, the guardian of the universe, who ended chaos and brought the world into light, who chooses man for her temple, and teaches peace, forgiveness, gentleness, "after the example of the heavenly Father (*aetherii patris exemplo*), who, though he shakes the world with his thunder, directs his shafts upon the rocks and sea monsters, and sparing of our blood uses his bolts upon the woods of Oeta[4]." Thus the problem of the seeming aimlessness of heaven's judgments is solved. The warm springs of the Aponus are a witness to heaven's goodness. "Who dare ascribe such services to Chance? Who denies that the gods ordained all this? The great Father (*ille pater rerum*), who allots the aeons to the stars, when he gave

[1] Amm. Marc. xxi. 1, 9.
[2] *iv. Cons. Hon.* 284 *Nonne vides operum quod se pulcherrimus ipse mundus amore liget.*
[3] *iv. Cons. Hon.* 277 *sola deos aequat clementia nobis.* It sounds like a correction of Lucretius if he really was still read.
[4] *Cons. Stil.* ii. 6—28. Cf. Synesius, *Ep.* 31.

the sacred first beginnings of heaven gave thee, and pitying our frail tenure of our form bade earth give forth streams of healing, and the waters that should stay the stern distaffs of the fates gushed forth upon the hills[1]." Retribution is the lesson of Rufinus' fall, while on the other hand heaven rewards the good, for he tells the story of the so-called Thundering Legion "whether Chaldean strains with magic rite thus armed the gods, or, *as I think*, the character of Marcus won all the care of the Thunderer[2]." The sum of his criticism of the Universe may perhaps be given in these words of his, "Nature has given to all to be happy if a man but know how to use the gift[3]."

In the *Rape of Proserpine*[4], Claudian is telling again the story that had charmed mankind for a thousand years, but I seem to find even in the fragment of it, the three books which are all we have, elements of the poet's own. His tale is incomplete but it is yet instinct with beauty and sorrow. The atmosphere is not that of the Homeric hymn to Demeter. It could not be. It more nearly recalls Apuleius' story of Cupid and Psyche in its richness of colour and prettiness, the humanity of its gods and its suggestions of some deeper meaning. The whole story seems re-conceived, and the new treatment differs from the old, much as a fairy tale of Andersen's differs from one of Grimm's collection. The wistful imagination of the modern has read something of himself and his day into the legend of divine sorrow.

It opens not very well. Pluto's rhetorical rage at being without a wife seems ludicrous, when the Fates at once intervene with the words, "Ask Jove and thou shalt have a wife." But when we come to Ceres and Proserpine it is very different. Fearful of losing her child, Ceres hides her in Sicily and then goes to visit Cybele in Phrygia. Venus is sent by Jove to Proserpine, and to disarm suspicion takes with her the virgin goddesses Pallas and Diana; yet her path gleams like a comet's trail of boding, for Venus in Claudian, as in Apuleius, is a somewhat malign figure. They find

---

[1] *Minor Poems*, 26. *Aponus* a medicinal spring near Padua, cf. Lucan vii. 193. Cf. Amm. Marc. xxi. 1, 9, on augury, which *benignitas numinis* grants to mankind to help them through the world.

[2] *vi. Cons. Hon.* 349 *seu, quod reor, omne Tonantis | obsequium Marci mores potuere mereri.* Is this a quiet correction of the common Christian legend?

[3] *In Ruf.* i. 215 *Natura beatis | omnibus esse dedit si quis cognoverit uti.*

[4] The reader may be at once referred to Mr Pater's essay on *The Myth of Demeter and Persephone* in his *Greek Studies* for a genuinely sympathetic account of this poem. On one point I differ from him, for I cannot prefer Ovid's story of the two goddesses.

her at her embroidery "the description of which" says Mr Pater "is the most brilliant of his pictures, and, in its quaint confusion of images of philosophy with those of mythology, anticipates something of the fancy of the Italian Renaissance." Let me give it in Mr Pater's translation.

" Proserpina, filling the house soothingly with her low song, was working a gift against the return of her mother, with labour all to be in vain. In it, she marked out with her needle the house of the gods and the series of the elements, showing by what law, nature, the parent of all, settled the strife of ancient times, and the seeds of things disparted to their places; the lighter elements are borne aloft, the heavier fall to the centre; the air grows bright with heat, a blazing light whirls round the firmament; the sea flows; the earth hangs suspended in its place. And there were divers colours in it; she illuminated the stars with gold, infused a purple shade into the water and heightened the shore with gems of flowers, and, under her skilful hand, the threads, with their inwrought lustre, swell up in momentary counterfeit of the waves; you might think that the seaweed[1] flapped against the rocks, and that a hollow murmur came creeping over the thirsty sands. She puts in the five zones, marking with a red ground the midmost zone, possessed by burning heat; its outline was parched and stiff; the threads seemed thirsty with the constant sunshine, on either side lay the two zones proper for human life, where a gentle temperature reigns; and at the extremes she drew the twin zones of numbing cold, making her work dun and sad with the hues of perpetual frost. She paints in, too, the sacred places of Dis, her father's brother, and the Manes, so fatal to her; and an omen of her doom was not wanting; for, as she worked, as if with foreknowledge of the future, her face became wet with a sudden burst of tears. And now in the utmost border of the tissue she had begun to wind in the wavy line of the river Oceanus, with its glassy shallows; but the door sounds on its hinges and she perceives the goddesses coming."

Next day the three goddesses go forth with many nymphs to gather flowers which Zephyr has made grow to greet her in a lovely scene. It should be noticed here, as Mr Mackail has remarked, that Claudian's treatment of nature leans to the old method, the rhetorical, the Alexandrine, and is very different from Ausonius' work in the *Moselle*. Here once more Claudian is essentially

---

[1] Mr Pater's "sea-wind" seems a misprint of his editor's in view of Claudian's *algam*.

decorative. Proserpine, interested beyond her comrades, plucks and twines, and "crowns herself without thought—a fatal augury of her wedlock." The ground rocks and Pluto appears and bears her off, his horses plunging at the light. The goddesses Diana and Pallas would rescue her, but a pacific clap of thunder forbids. As he drives, Pluto tries to console his bride, but not quite as he does in the Homeric hymn when her return to earth is threatened. "Count not the daylight lost. We have other stars, and thou shalt see a clearer light and marvel yet more at the sun of Elysium...... Nor shalt thou lack grassy meadows, where lapped by gentler Zephyrs fadeless flowers breathe......Thou shalt rule rich Autumn and ever be blest with yellow fruits......Purpled kings shall come to thy feet, mingling with the throng of poor folk. *Thou* shalt condemn the guilty; *thou* shalt give rest to the good." (*Tu requiem latura piis.*) Not so the Homeric hymn, but "Thou shalt have vengeance of such as do thee wrong, whosoever shall not all their days do thee honour with sacrifices." The conception is very different. It is not merely the contrast between the vindictive and juridical spirit of Greek and Roman, but between the earlier and the later days. "Rest for the good" had perhaps never been such an object of desire.

Again, the descent of Proserpine into hell is new and strange. The souls gather to meet her, thick as autumn leaves, many as the waves or the sands, as the god drives home his bride, "suffering a smile to play on his lips, and unlike his wonted self." The pale region rejoices and the nations of the buried triumph. The eternal night permits less palpable darkness. The penalties of the damned are relaxed, and death keeps holiday. One has seen something like this before, though it was not in the classics, but in the apocryphal gospel, which tells of another descent into hell and the rejoicing of the dead. Did Claudian think of it, or is it the same instinct which gave rise to the apocryphal story asserting itself again?

With the third book we come to Ceres, the *Mater Dolorosa*, as she has been called, of heathenism. Jove summons the gods and explains the design behind his action. To waken mankind from the sloth and lethargy of the golden age, he has let it pass away— not that he envies man, for gods may not feel ill-will nor do hurt— but want must be nurse and breeder of all good. Yet under the change Earth complains of her sterility. So he has brought this grief upon Ceres, and it is decreed that she wander over sea and land in yearning sorrow, till in joy for learning how to find her daughter she give corn to men, but none of the gods must help her. Thus a moral purpose is given to the old story it hardly knew before. Aeschylus has shewn us the divine sufferer for mankind, who paid a cruel penalty for the blessings he had given them, but here is one whose sufferings are the very means towards the blessings to be given. They are involuntary, but underlying them is a great divine design.

Ceres, moved by strange dreams, returns to Sicily and finds the empty house, and as she crosses the desolate hall she lights on the web her daughter was embroidering, over which the spider is weaving his web. Yet she wept not nor mourned; only she prints kisses on the fabric, and gathers up the work-things her daughter's hands had touched and presses them to her bosom for her. This episode is Claudian's own. The introduction of the spider busy at what had been the daughter's labour of love, and the contrast, suggested but not pictured with its "sorrow's crown of sorrow," mark Claudian's highest level of poetic feeling[1].

The old nurse (like the nurses in the tragedies) tells her tale, which is a little too pretty perhaps for epic; and we hear Ceres call out on the gods, angry and distraught; and then when they answer not, sad and downcast, she prays at least, as a mother would, to know her daughter's fate:

> *hoc tantum liceat certos habuisse dolores.*

The poem closes with a striking picture of her standing at night upon Etna, torch in hand, while the light falls upon the waters far and wide.

So much we have of a poem, in which I think it is not hard to see a deeper vein of thought than we find in the poet's panegyrics. He is not playing with his theme as Ovid played with it, but he reads in it a moral significance. How he would have worked this out we cannot

---

[1] It may seem harsh to be critical at this point, but though the idea be beautiful, the expression of it seems to me to fail. Granted that the whole poem is left unfinished and that this passage may be unrevised, it still shews the marks of Claudian's habitual haste. There is a want of meditation about the verses. They are not a final expression, but seem more like a rough note for future use:

> *Divinus perit ille labor, spatiumque relictum*
> *audax sacrilego supplebat aranea textu.*

The *spatium relictum* differs little from conversational prose of shop or work-room, and the adjectives *audax* and *sacrilego* are by no means inevitable. They are weak in fact. Put alongside this almost any similar passage of Virgil— *ignarum Laurens habet ora Mimanta*—and Claudian's weakness will be felt. I have emphasized this, because this is a sort of crucial passage where a poet *must* rise if he can.

say, for like Proserpine's embroidery it is for ever unfinished. Still we may not be far astray in holding that he means to justify the ways of God to men. Of course his work here is not free from the defects it shews elsewhere. It bears marks of haste and cleverness and rhetoric, but still the poem has undeniable dignity and beauty.

Liceat certos habuisse dolores! This later Paganism was amiable and on the whole cheerful. It had left behind the essential hopelessness and sadness of Virgil, and was happy and contented in makeshift truth. It did not go below the surface very much. It was not vitally concerned with realities, but dealt with dreams and memories and hopes. Thus it wanted that depth of feeling and conviction which come from contact with life, and the robuster minds turned away. For those who really thought, who really felt the weariness and darkness of the world, paganism, even though reinforced by Neo-Platonism, had neither consolation nor hope. It was not solid enough. Augustine, speaking of his sorrow as a young man at his friend's death, writes: "The burden should have been laid on Thee to be healed; I knew this, yet I would not and I could not, for when I thought of Thee, *Thou wast not to me anything firm or solid.*" The dreams of Claudian, like those of Julian, were beautiful, and some perhaps were true, but they lacked the *certum* Augustine sought and mankind with him. *Volebam enim eorum quae non viderem ita me certum fieri ut certus essem quod septem et tria decem sint.*

Historians may debate the value of this or that statement of Claudian's, and with reason. But they must admit his evidence on the general conditions of the life of his day. Its pageants and circuses and splendours, its magnificence and flunkeyism, its desolation and wretchedness, he brings vividly before us. The Goths in Greece and in Phrygia seem to haunt us, even when we are most confidently assured that the Empire is saved and that its frontiers will be wider than ever[1]. For his pictures of Gothic devastation seem not to be so overdrawn as those are which shew us the smiling and glorious Rome under Stilicho's wing. If he suffered, and he certainly did suffer, as a poet by undertaking the literary defence of Stilicho, it was not all loss, for Rome—the Rome he loved—in her glitter and her misery, stands before us in his gorgeous series of panegyrics as she could scarcely else have done.

---

[1] Here for example is a tell-tale phrase—*solo poterit Stilichone medente | crescere Romanum vulnus tectura cicatrix, Cons. Stil.* ii. 204.

CHAPTER XI

Dic tropaeum passionis, dic triumphalem crucem.

Cath. ix. 83

EVERY man is influenced to a greater or less extent by his age and his contemporaries, and we must understand these if we would understand the man. His thoughts will be guided by those of his time, for whether he agree or disagree, whether he lead or follow he will think of what other people are thinking around him.

Prudentius was born in the middle of the fourth century, in the midst of a cluster of great men. Jerome and Ambrose were born in 340, Chrysostom in 347, Prudentius in 348, and Augustine in 354. Prudentius was thirteen when Julian ascended the throne and made the last attempt to galvanize heathenism into life, and by his failure shewed the world that its day had passed. Athanasius, a household name in every Christian land, died when Prudentius was between twenty and thirty. He was thirty when the Goths won their first great victory in 378 at Adrianople. He lived to see Rome herself the Christian centre of a Christian world, and perhaps died *felix opportunitate mortis* before she too fell to the conquering Goth when Alaric sacked Rome in 410. It was a century of great movements and great men—interesting from its dark beginning with the persecutions of Diocletian, Galerius and Maximin to its end. It was the century when, triumphant over foes without, as Prudentius loves to emphasize, the Church had her first great world-wide fight with foes within to secure that victorious Christianity should not prove after all another form of heathenism. The councils from Nicaea onward mark the progress of the struggle. And all the time there was this dark cloud of

barbarism threatening in the North—a terrible background for all
this carnal and spiritual warfare.

Christianity, as we have seen, had won the day and had won
the world. It was no longer perilous to be a Christian and the
world rushed into the Church. We picture to ourselves an Athanasius and an Augustine as types of the age, but a far more typical
man is the great semi-Arian ecclesiastical diplomatist and politician
Eusebius of Nicomedeia. The world had swarmed into the Church
and taken the sacraments, but the result could have been prophesied. The tone of Christian living and thinking grew lower and
lower. Even before now heathen influences had deeply coloured
much of the best Christian thought, but now the dye is unmistakable. The priesthood had grown great, thanks to St Cyprian
and his followers; it now grew greater still. Saints and martyrs
took the place of eponymous heroes and demi-gods—a change for
the better perhaps, for they were less immoral, but scarcely an
improvement on primitive Christianity. Eastern and Western
alike had elevated the Supreme God to such a height that He was
out of reach of the universe, and now they began to introduce
the martyrs to bridge the gulf. And with the martyrs came their
relics, the tales of their passions, their tombs and their images,
pilgrimages to see all these wonders, and prayers at the shrines.
We shall find all this in Prudentius, and we must remember that
he was a Spaniard and in Spain began the worship of pictures[1].
Simultaneously came in from outside heathen notions which turned
the simple rites of the early Church into mysteries. Let any one
read St Ambrose on baptism and contrast him with St Paul, and the
change in Christian thought will be felt. And with all this came a
lower tone of Christian living, and the gladiatorial games (not ended
till after Prudentius' death, and the subject of more than one
honourable appeal made by him) and the races and the theatres
(*privatum consistorium impudicitiae*) divided with the churches
and the martyrs' shrines the interests of mankind, and as is usual
in such cases took more than their share.

Of all this and of the heresies with which the Church, especially
the Western Church, had to contend, we find abundant evidence
in Prudentius. Like most Western Christians he had little aptitude

---

[1] See Dale, *Synod of Elvira*, pp. 292, 295. This Council met about 306 A.D.
and already found it necessary to forbid the use of images and pictures in the
churches. Pope Damasus, whose energy in this direction was epoch-making,
was also a Spaniard.

for theological speculation and was intensely practical. Accordingly with the rest he adopted the Nicene Creed as the final statement of Christian truth, and except by accident turned neither to the right hand nor to the left.

Prudentius was born in 348, probably in the Spanish town of Caesaraugusta or Saragossa[1]. " His early age wept under the cracking rods[2]," he tells us, and leaves us to infer what other elements there had been in his education. Probably, like most other boys, he studied the two great subjects of the day—grammar and rhetoric. Ausonius, his contemporary (310—393), the poet of Bordeaux, wrote a series of poems on his professors and it appears that most of them were grammarians or rhetoricians. Both would use the same text-book—Virgil. In every school of the Latin world *haerebat nigro fuligo Maroni*, and as the grime gathered on Maro's page the grammarian drew from it all the lessons letters can give— grammar, prosody, style, archaeology, philosophy, history, religion, and what not? But while the rhetorician taught the youth to write replies for Dido, he did not teach them the real meaning and value of Virgil, as Macrobius' works plainly shew. Still Virgil left his mark on this age of Latin literature too. They wept for Virgil's Dido if not for the rhetorician's, and echoes of his music passed into their verse. World and Church alike loved him and canonized him in their own ways.

Juvencus, an elder Spanish contemporary of Prudentius, alludes in the preface of his Evangelic History to *Minciadae dulcedo Maronis*, and the same sweetness shaped Prudentius as a hundred passages in his poems shew. Over and above his Virgil, he learnt his Bible to such an extent, that M. Boissier finds rather more of it in his poems than he thinks will be readily intelligible to modern

[1] Tarraco and Calagurris have also been named as the poet's birthplace, but opinion is generally in favour of Caesaraugusta. See Sixt, *die Lyrischen Gedichte des A. Prud. Clemens*, p. 3, n. 1, where it is discussed at length. Brockhaus, *Aur. Prud. Clem.* p. 15.

[2] It is curious to find both that St Augustine (*Conf.* i. 9, 14) should have a good deal to say about the rod, a subject to which he devoted much ineffectual prayer in his boyhood to his parents' amusement; and that Ausonius (*Ep.* 22, 29), in a letter designed to encourage his grandson, should give him a positively tingling list of a whole armoury of scholastic implements, memories perhaps of more active days. Elsewhere Prudentius gives a more particular account of the hatefulness of school-life in the crowning martyrdom of the schoolmaster Cassianus. It is not written, like Ausonius' description, from the teacher's point of view, and the general conclusion seems to be in ll. 27, 28:

> *doctor amarus enim discenti semper ephebo,*
> *nec dulcis ulli disciplina infantiae est.*

readers¹. At a later period in life he seems also to have studied the apologists and perhaps others of the fathers. The influence of Tertullian is particularly conspicuous in his works².

On boyhood followed the toga of manhood, and taught him to lie, he tells us, and wanton lust and selfish indulgence defiled his youth. This may be poetical license. His language reminds one of St Augustine's *Confessions*, yet the question may fairly be raised whether the poet had really a loose and ill-governed youth to deplore like the saint (though injustice has been done to Augustine here, as Loofs shews), or whether a highly sensitive conscience, like Bunyan's, led him to over-estimate his youthful depravity. When he speaks of learning to lie, *falsa loqui*, it should be remarked that he is only using the common Christian description of the study of rhetoric³.

Though he speaks of *militia* he was probably not in the army, but in the civil service, of which the word is sometimes used⁴. He rose to be twice a magistrate of noble cities, dealt out Roman law to the good, and was a terror to evildoers, and was finally honoured by the Emperor and awoke to find a snowy head convicting him of old age. He was fifty-seven, he tells us, and his tone has suggested premature age. He looks back on his past life with regret, honourable as it had clearly been, and asks in sadness, "What useful thing have I done in all these years?" He then says he will now begin life in earnest. He will, he tells us, write hymns day and night, war against heresies and unravel the catholic faith, trample under foot the sacred things of heathenry, do despite to Rome's idols, hymn the martyrs and praise the Apostles.

Accordingly some have supposed his poetical work to belong to the latter years of his life, untouched till he was fifty-seven! But apart from the fact that he knows nothing of Stilicho's fall in 408, which would seem to limit his activity to a short period,

---

¹ Boissier, *La Fin du Paganisme*, ii. 115 "ces récits nous étant devenus moins familiers."

² See Brockhaus, *Aurelius Prudentius Clemens in seiner Bedeutung für die Kirche seiner Zeit*, c. 8. I shall have to refer again to this excellent monograph.

³ Cf. Paulinus to Ausonius (*Ep.* x.), God's light is obscured:

> quam vis sophorum callida arsque rhetorum et
> figmenta vatum nubilant,
> qui corda falsis atque vanis imbuunt
> tantumque linguas instruunt.

Similarly St Augustine in his *Confessions*, e.g. iv. 2, 2.

⁴ *E.g.* Aug. *Conf.* viii. 6, 15, of an Agens in Rebus. Sixt however (p. 5) believes he was in the army, against Brockhaus and Puech.

we can certainly date his second book against Symmachus 403 A.D.
—*i e.* two years earlier than the date he himself gives for his
preface. It is surely more reasonable to assume he wrote this
preface on the completion rather than the inception of his book
of collected poems.

First, however, let us see what had been achieved by his
predecessors in Christian verse. The extraordinary poems of
Commodian, written in hexameters which suggest *Evangeline* quite
as much as the *Aeneid,* would hardly have been counted as
literature at all by cultured people. In fact it seems it was not for
such readers that they were intended[1]. We are told that Tertullian
wrote poems and Cyprian too, but the best editors group their
several poems as spurious works, and in three cases the same
piece appears amongst the pseudonyma of both fathers. More
genuine works are those of some men roughly contemporaries of
Prudentius. Damasus, Pope 366 A.D., wrote neat Ovidian verse
on Jerusalem, some hymns on the saints, a couple of acrostics
on our Lord's name, and a large number of poetical inscriptions
for the Catacombs, which under his care were becoming great
centres for pilgrimages. There are moreover some dull and rather
halting hexameters on Genesis (a fatally attractive theme at this
period), which have been attributed to Hilary of Poitiers, though it
is now believed they are not his work. I come now to two more
important poets. "Juvencus the presbyter," says St Jerome (*Ep.*
lxx. 5), "in the reign of Constantine, set forth the history of our
Lord and Saviour in verse, and was not afraid to submit the
majesty of the Gospel to the laws of metre." Juvencus was a
Spaniard, a fellow-countryman of Damasus and Prudentius. His
harmony of the Gospels is a quiet and very neat piece of work,
holding to the original with extraordinary closeness. His metre
is most monotonous if correct. But such works have little interest,
however successful. St Ambrose of Milan wrote hymns for the
Christian day in iambic dimeters, one of them noble in its simplicity, the others simple but hardly noble. These hymns were an
epoch-making innovation; but Ambrose, if more serviceable as a
hymn-writer, is by no means equal to Prudentius as a poet.

Prudentius is after all the first really great Christian poet,

---

[1] What pleasure was there for ears trained in Virgil in two such lines as
these? (*Carm. Apol.* 942):

> *nec mortuos plangunt nec lugunt more de nostro,*
> *exspectantque vitam resurrectionemque futuram.*

towering over his fellow-Christians as Claudian did over the heathen. It is not easy to-day to realize his significance, so familiar are we with the union of Christian thought and poetry. Prudentius lived in a day when men clung to old ways and old themes, and he displays a certain independence and even originality in daring to strike out a new path in literature. He broke away from tradition, took an unfamiliar subject, and triumphantly shewed mankind that it was capable of poetic treatment.

He is as strongly Roman in feeling and instinct as Claudian himself, if possible more Roman than Claudian. He is as proud of Rome's history, her victories and her lawgiving, her heroes and patriots. He too has stood in the long succession and has had his share, as Claudian never had, in the ruling of the Empire, and the temper of the man of affairs clung to him. All he does has the Roman mark upon it—it is all directed to some practical end[1]. But he is a Christian, and if possible he is a Christian before he is a Roman. Ausonius passed for a Christian, but Prudentius, in every line of his work, proclaims his faith and serves his Church with all the energy of his being. It was the age of the victorious Church, mistress of the Roman world, and not yet seriously dreading the heathenism and savagery of the German. Prudentius writes with the consciousness of victory. The cross is the triumphal emblem of the *labarum* and has very little suggestion of suffering about it. Yet the victory was not quite complete. Heathenism lived on in a stubborn minority, and was ready to reclaim many from among the Christian majority on slight provocation[2].

Prudentius must from a child have heard many a tale of martyrdom. The five edicts of persecution from 303 to 308 must have fallen in his grandfather's, if not in his father's time, and Prudentius had at the most receptive time of boyhood lived through the reign of Julian (*Apoth.* 449), for whom it is interesting to find he had like St Augustine a not unkindly feeling[3]. Conse-

---

[1] Cf. his question when he reviews his life; *quid nos utile tanti spatio temporis egimus?* This is the old Roman ideal of *utile.* Cf. Horace, *Epp.* ii. 1, 163, the Roman inquired *quid Sophocles et Thespis et Aeschylus utile ferrent.*

[2] Augustine, *Enarr. in Psalm. xcviii.* 2 *magis remanserunt idola in cordibus paganorum, quam in locis templorum.*

[3] Cf. *Apoth.* 450 *me puero, memini, ductor fortissimus armis | conditor et legum, celeberrimus ore manuque | consultor patriae...perfidus ille Deo, quamvis non perfidus orbi.* Julian as a man of action, a soldier, a lawgiver, appealed to Prudentius, who would have cared little for his philosophy.

Augustine, *C. D.* v. 21 *apostatae Juliani...egregiam indolem.* For Augustine, never a civil servant (unless as professor at Milan, perhaps), and writing after

quently he has a good deal to say about idolatry, and if much
that he says was said before by Tertullian and others, still we
must not think it did not need to be repeated, or that our poet
was fighting a dead issue. And again, heresy called for attention.

We do our thinking so much in compartments that we do not
always realize to what extent things are mixed in this world. We
read of Julian, Valentinian, Stilicho, and we read of Athanasius,
Jerome and Augustine, but we do not always properly correlate
the spheres in which they moved. Prudentius was the contemporary of them all, and in a measure entered into the life of
them all. He saw the Roman world as a whole still, though
there were already signs of the ultimate cleavage of East and
West. Various questions rose in his mind. Why had God so
markedly throughout all these centuries subdued people after
people to Rome, and welded the world into one[1]? Long ago
Virgil had seen mankind under Roman sway, and in Prudentius'
own day Claudian was writing nobly of Rome's imperial destiny,
for he saw the Roman world a world of Romans, and he was
himself the symbol of his age, a Roman poet of Egyptian birth and
Greek education.

> *Haec est in gremio victos quae sola recepit,*
> *humanumque genus communi nomine fovit,*
> *matris non dominae ritu; civesque vocavit*
> *quos domuit nexuque pio longinqua revinxit.*
>
> *Cons. Stil.* iii. 150.

But Claudian's reason would not satisfy Prudentius. The true reason
lay outside Claudian's range.

Prudentius rises to the problem in the very spirit of St Paul.
He sees that the object of the unification of mankind under the
sway of Rome was the unification of mankind under the sway of
Christ. There was to be one earthly and one heavenly empire,
the one in order to the other; mankind was to be one in Rome
that it might be one in Christ. Christ was the author of Rome's
greatness for Himself. This was a new idea.

Alaric's capture of Rome, it was impossible to have Prudentius' feeling for Rome
and the Empire. He had to find God's ideal state elsewhere.

[1] Not everybody asked such questions. Cyprian, for example (*Quod idola
dei non sunt*, 5), is content to say *regna autem non merito accidunt sed sorte
variantur.*

Felices, si cuncta Deo sua prospera Christo
principe disposita scissent! qui currere regna
certis ducta modis Romanorumque triumphos
crescere et impletis voluit se infundere saeclis.

Adv. Symm. i. 287.

Vis dicam quae causa tuos Romane labores
in tantum extulerit? quis gloria fotibus aucta
sic cluat, impositis ut mundum frenet habenis?
Discordes linguis populos et dissona cultu
regna volens sociare Deus, subjungier uni
imperio quidquid tractabile moribus esset,
concordique jugo retinacula mollia ferre
constituit, quo corda hominum conjuncta teneret
religionis amor: nec enim fit copula Christo
digna nisi implicitas societ mens unica gentes.

Adv. Symm. ii. 582.

O Christe numen unicum,
O splendor, O virtus Patris,
O factor orbis et poli
atque auctor horum moenium:

qui sceptra Romae in vertice
rerum locasti, sanciens
mundum Quirinali togae
servire et armis cedere:

ut discrepantum gentium
mores et observantiam,
linguasque et ingenia et sacra
unis domares legibus.

Steph. ii. 413.

Hoc actum est tantis successibus atque triumphis
Romani imperii; Christo jam tunc venienti,
crede, parata via est.

Adv. Symm. ii. 618.

It follows then that heathenism is an obstacle to God's designs, but not the only one. When the fighting is at an end in the *Psychomachia* and every vice is vanquished, a new enemy is discovered within the ranks of the victors—Discord or Heresy, and the names of Photinus and Arius occur *immanes feritate lupi*[1].

---

[1] Curiously enough this is Prudentius' only reference to Arius. The West was as yet little troubled about Arianism. Justina and the Germans were the only Western Arians of any importance. As a general rule the heretics Prudentius attacks are those against whom Tertullian has supplied him with ammunition.

Heresy has to share the fate of Idolatry, Lust, and other enemies, and then the temple of God is built within the soul. So in the case of the world Heresy mars God's intended unity, and must be done away. To what this led we see in the case of a younger contemporary, Nestorius, the bishop of Constantinople, who asked the Emperor to give him earth clear of heretics and he would assure him of heaven in return. Fate's revenges are interesting. Nestorius was an arch-heretic ere he died. Prudentius is very far from such violence, and would use no force with heretic or heathen. In fact he would not use violence even with idols, but cites with evident approval the decree of Theodosius that as works of art they are to be preserved—the workmanship of great artists, fairest ornaments of our land[1].

We may now turn to the works of Prudentius and pass them in rapid review. All of them are practical. His theological poems are directed to the end of presenting the true faith to his fellow Christians in an attractive form and at the same time clear of error. The *Daily Round* (or *Cathemerinon*) displays the same ethical tendency—employing abundant Scripture to make all aspects of our life conform with our Lord's, each action recalling His, for as He redeemed us by sharing our life, we rise by associating His own with ours.

Beginning then with the two theological poems, the *Hamartigenia* and the *Apotheosis*, we find Prudentius displays remarkable ease and grace in handling well and poetically subjects which appear difficult and unpromising. He shews great skill in the vivid illustration of abstruse doctrines, and by glowing language, range and insight he achieves passages of distinction and elevation. His theology, if not original, is at least intelligent, though as I have said he occasionally slips a little one way or the other from the true Athanasian position. These poems have been pronounced to be his best, and the poet has been compared with Lucretius for the enthusiasm and the poetic feeling with which he presents his views[2].

The *Hamartigenia* deals with the origin of evil and with

---

[1] *c. Symm.* i. 502; cf. *Steph.* ii. 481. See Gregorovius, *Rome in the Middle Ages* (translation), i. 61, 76—7. *Cod. Theod.* 16, 10, 8 *aedem in qua simulacra feruntur posita, artis pretio quam divinitate metienda, jugiter patere publici consilii auctoritate decernimus.*

[2] See Brockhaus, *op. cit.* p. 165, who prefers these Hexameter poems; and Boissier, *F. P.* ii. who gives the higher praise to the lyrical poems (p. 107), but compares the others with Lucretius (§ 3).

Marcion and his two gods, following mainly the lines of Tertullian's first two books against Marcion. If Marcion will maintain *dividuum regnare Deum*, Nature at least knows but one God. If two Gods, why not more? *Si duo sunt igitur, cur non sunt multa Deorum millia?* One of Marcion's gods is author of evil and of the Old Testament, and maker of man and the universe, but he is more a devil than a god. *Inventor vitii non est deus.* And then we have the story of Satan's revolt and his envy of man, of man's fall, and nature's corruption, the consequence of that fall. It is a striking passage of some length, tracing the painful and shameful results of man's first sin, and exhibiting the general depravation of the senses, though at the beginning it was otherwise, for God saw His work that it was good (214—251). Then after a good deal of further discussion, and a prodigious parable from nature turning on the life-history of the viper[1] which illustrates sin being its own eventual punishment, we have the great question, Why does God permit evil?

> *si non vult Deus esse malum cur non vetat?*   (641)

And the familiar and perhaps only answer:

> *non fit sponte bonus cui non est prompta potestas*
> *velle aliud   *   *   (691)
> *probitate coacta*
> *gloria nulla venit sordetque ingloria virtus.*   (694)

Man has a free choice, and so we come to lines which recall Browning.

> *Nunc inter vitae dominum mortisque magistrum*
> *consistit medius: vocat hinc Deus inde tyrannus*
> *ambiguum atque suis se motibus alternantem.*   (721)

No, when the fight begins within himself
A man's worth something. God stoops o'er his head
Satan looks up between his feet—both tug—
He's left himself i' the middle.

There follow illustrations from Lot and Naomi's daughters-in-law and bird catching, with an allusion to the Two Ways— that wonderful parable, popular from the days of Hercules' choice, and in Prudentius' hands reminding one of Bunyan's Hill Difficulty

[1] This may be found in part in Pliny, *N. H.* x. 62. The young vipers eat their way out of their mother, so killing her. Thus 'sin, having conceived, bringeth forth death.' Plutarch (*Ser. Num. Vind.* end) quotes this viper as Pindar's.

and its alternatives. And so to pictures of Heaven and Hell, which may be rendered into English as follows :

> Then, of foreknowledge, did the Father set
> Murk Tartarus to burn with streams of lead.
> Pitch and bitumen fill the infernal sluice,
> Sunk deep in darkling hell. Beneath he bade,
> Deep under Phlegethon's malignant wave,
> The greedy worm to live and prey on guilt
> Perpetual. For He knew Whose breath had given
> Immortal life to this our bodily frame,
> A soul from His own lips, that cannot die,
> Nor climb again the sphere, from whence it came,
> Once sin-stained, but must sink within th' abyss
> That burns for ever. Like immortal years
> To worm and flame and punishment He gave,
> That, as the soul should never die, the pang
> Should know no death. The tortures waste and feed
> Their food eternal. Death itself forsakes
> Their ceaseless groanings, and bids live and weep.
>
> But, far remote, in fields of Paradise,
> The prescient Majesty to spirits pure
> Assigned rewards, to them that know not guilt,
> That look not back upon Gomorrha's fall,
> But fled with eyes averted from the gloom,
> The wrath to fall upon a wretched world.
> And first with easy flight they reach the stars,
> Whence came God's breath to move the new-made man.
> For since the downward weight of life no more
> Burdens, nor any bond of iron clogs,
> The glowing spark with speed reclimbs the air,
> And scales the sky anew, glad to forsake
> The limits of the alien prison-house.
> Her child, new come from exile, Faith receives
> To her maternal breasts, and bids enjoy
> Heaven's pleasures, and recount the many toils
> Known in this caravanserai of flesh.
> There on a couch of purple, soft reclined,
> It tastes the sweetness of eternal flowers
> And quaffs the nectar on its bed of rose.
> While for the rich, whose smoke goes up afar,
> Who thirst for water and the rains of heaven,
> For all their prayers, it cannot put a hand
> To the parched palate to allay the flame.
> But marvel not, the blessèd and the damned
> Far, far apart are held, and th' interspace
> Spreads vast between the spheres of bad and good.

(824—866)

Here are elements from different sources, never mingled before, but at least a new realm has been found for Christian art. The poem ends with the prayer for a mild sentence upon the poet at the last.

In the *Apotheosis* we have to do with a series of heretics who misrepresent our Lord's nature. First of all the Patripassian is confounded with references to the manifestations of Christ in the Old Testament—the common property of the defender of the faith from Justin Martyr's days—though as usual Tertullian is Prudentius' more immediate inspiration. Then comes Sabellius, who despoils God of Fatherhood by not allowing the Son. Gods are many, but does any idolater really believe Jove or dog-faced Anubis occupies the supreme throne? Consult *barbati deliramenta Platonis*, and despite cocks owed to Aesculapius, the philosophers conclude their arguments with one god[1]. Christ was at once God and man. It is only in Christ we understand Rome's history.

Then the Jew has his turn and is confronted with *legis in effigie scriptum per enigmata Christum*, and our poet grows eloquent as he demands to know in what literature Christ is not now famous: all the languages of Pilate's inscription proclaim Him;

Hebraeus pangit stilus, Attica copia pangit,
pangit et Ausoniae facundia tertia linguae;   (379)

and he rehearses the triumphs of the cross among Scythians, Goths, Moors, and the world over, and the silencing of the world's oracles, Delphi, Dodona, Ammon and so forth, at the birth of Christ, adding a tale of his boyhood, how the heathen rites of Julian were baulked by a German page who wore a cross[2]. The exiled Jew is being punished for the death of Christ. With this he turns to the Psilanthropists—Homuncionites or Mannikinists as he calls them—and confronts them with our Lord's miracles, for which he goes by preference to St John's Gospel, as that one of the four which most clearly sets forth the deity of Christ. He discusses the nature of the soul, which is made and not begotten by God, yet is not corporeal (*in corpore discas rem non corpoream*) as was supposed

[1] This flout at the philosopher is in Tertullian's vein, who mocked but studied. Prudentius perhaps had no Greek. Neither had Augustine nor Ausonius very much. The Greek titles of the books may be a fanciful imitation of Virgil.
[2] Brockhaus, p. 23, ingeniously makes the boy a German on account of his hair—*e cuneo puerorum flavicomantum.*

by many in his day, *e.g.* by Augustine in earlier life. In this connexion he drops at least one memorable line,

sed speculum deitatis homo est. (834)

Lastly he deals with the Docetists who held Christ was a phantasm, and really strikes out a fresh thought and a noble one.

Et quid agit Christus si me non suscipit? aut quem
liberat infirmum si dedignatur adire
carnis onus, manuumque horret monumenta suarum? (1020)

These lines may be paralleled by Browning's

I never realized God's birth before—
How he grew likest God in being born.

Tantus amor terrae, he continues, *tanta est dilectio nostri.* So much for the purely theological works of Prudentius.

We now come to his book *Peri Stephanon* or *The Crowns*— a set of fourteen hymns to martyrs, of very various metres and merits. Many of the Saints are Spanish, so many as to give confirmation to the statement of his own Spanish origin. Others he had found on his travels—painted in sacred pictures in churches, commemorated by local usage, or told of in Damasus' inscriptions. Thus he chiefly depends on verbal as against written traditions, and a curious confusion hangs about his stories here and there. Notably this is the case with Romanus and more strangely still with Cyprian, for he has patched together incongruous legends to the exclusion of real facts, actually confusing the great Cyprian of Carthage with the converted magician Cyprian of Antioch. In those hymns specially describing martyrdoms the general scheme is a confession, torture and a miracle, but after all it must be confessed that martyrology is generally a dull subject, and the poet who deals with it is destined to repeat himself like a Poet Laureate who makes birthday odes, and to charm as little. Prudentius however did his best, for he had a Spaniard's love of the Saints and a great enthusiasm for them, and he introduced some new features not all of which are successful. In places his rhetorical training shews itself very clearly.

The best of the hymns is perhaps the second, to St Lawrence, a Spaniard and an archdeacon, who suffered at Rome under Decius.

The complaint is made by the Praefectus Urbi that the Church is hoarding wealth and hunting legacies :

> *et summa pietas creditur*
> *nudare dulces liberos:*

charges if not already true soon to be so. Lawrence has three days to produce this wealth, and then brings forward a crowd of pensioners, *ne pauperem Christum putes*. He is then committed to the "gridiron," and thence utters a remarkable hymn from which I have already quoted. He foresees (no doubt with the aid of the poet's retrospect) a Christian Rome and a Christian Emperor who will close the temples and keep as works of art what now are idols. The hymn ends with a picture of the lights of the Senate, sometime Luperci and Flamens, kissing the thresholds of martyrs' shrines, while afar beyond Alps and Pyrenees the Spanish poet sees the saint in heaven and implores his grace.

> *Audi benignus supplicem*
> *Christi· reum Prudentium.*

One or two of the hymns border on the grotesque through the exaggeration of the poet, who has, as M. Boissier says, *le goût de l'horrible*. He is apt too to be carried away by admiration for the un-Christian mania for martyrdom which led many early Christians to insult their neighbours and provoke authority—to the great peril of the Church, which condemned this unnecessary and dangerous zeal[1]. The story of St Eulalia, a child martyr of Emerita, is told trippingly in a dactylic metre, roughly the first half a Virgilian hexameter, which we also find in Ausonius[2]. *Germine nobilis Eulalia* was a sadly precocious child who would be martyred, in very truth a *torva puellula*. She insulted the praetor, declaimed at large on idolatry, spat at the unhappy magistrate who was really very gentle with her, kicked over the idols and thuribles, and so achieved a martyrdom, the details of which a Spanish and rhetorical poet could hardly be expected to spare us[3]. The story

---

[1] See Dale, *Synod of Elvira*, p. 30. This Spanish Council (about 306) forbade voluntary and aggressive martyrdom within a decade (say) of Eulalia's exploit. It is interesting, in this connexion, to note first, that St Theresa in 1522, while still a little girl, had a similar childish ambition to be martyred by the Moors, which was happily frustrated, for she grew to be one of the most useful and sensible women in Spain; and second, that Eulalia's name is still familiar in Spain, being borne to-day by one of the King's sisters.

[2] Sixt (p. 30) finds in the metre (as well as in the story) "etwas schwärmerisches" and a certain "stürmisches Ungestüm."

[3] Compare Claudian's "dissection of Rufinus" as Gibbon calls it. Boissier, *F. P.* ii. 122, compares the Tragedies of the Spaniard Seneca.

of St Cassianus the schoolmaster, delivered over for death to his schoolboys, is amusing; but while Prudentius took a pleasure in a rhetorical elaboration of it he also felt it seriously, for when he saw a picture of it all at Forum Cornelii on his way to Rome, he was moved to prayer. His prayer was granted, and he wrote this poem in grateful memory of it. One of the poems (iv.) is a *tour de force*, perhaps in imitation of Martial's little epigram (i. 62), on the towns of Italy and Spain and their literary glories, but for poets Prudentius puts saints. The cities appear before Christ on the Judgment-day bringing their saints, and Caesar-augusta, the poet's own town, surpasses them all with no less than eighteen martyrs crowded into sapphic verse—a great achievement, but scarcely poetry. The worst poem of the collection, as a work of art, is the martyrdom of St Romanus. The poet has made the mistake of developing the usual confession of a martyr into an elaborate polemic against heathenism along with an exposition of Christianity. These are drawn mainly from Tertullian, and are witty and effective in their way, but forensic rather than philo-sophic. They are also quite out of place and terribly delay the action. The saint in a speech of two hundred and sixty lines denounces heathenism, and even when his tongue is cut out, he talks on for hundreds of lines more. A ridiculous episode in this poem is that of another lamentably precocious child, who knows a good deal too much Theology and Physiology for his seven years, and who, when a familiar remedy fails

> (*pusionem praecipit
> sublime tollant et manu pulsent nates*),

is put to death, while his mother sings a psalm to encourage him. Romanus was a real historic character, but Eusebius' account of his martyrdom (*M. P.* 2) is more reasonable. A poem on St Hippolytus[1] gives an interesting account of the Catacombs, which had become under Damasus' care a centre of interest for Christian pilgrims, and with their traditions and pictures greatly influenced Prudentius. The hymn to St Peter and St Paul, with descriptions of their churches in Rome, is interesting and valuable as con-temporary evidence on these famous places then recently built.

It is quite clear that the poet shares the popular view of the Christian church of his day as to the saints. He had not the

---

[1] The catacomb of Hippolytus was found by de Rossi in 1881, but the picture which inspired Prudentius' poem has not survived. Sixt, p. 35.

uneasiness of Augustine, but after all the Christian faith meant
more to Augustine in spiritual and intellectual implication than
to any of his contemporaries[1].

The *Psychomachia*, which perhaps in view of the likenesses
it presents to Bunyan we may translate *Holy War*, has been
pronounced the richest of his works in colour and brilliance.
It was the most widely read of them all in the Middle Ages, which
means a good deal, for Prudentius was then one of the most
popular authors. No one was more universally read and imitated,
and no books, with the exception of the Bible, were so abundantly
provided with Old High German glosses as the *Daily Round* and
the *Peri Stephanon*. This book however has also great significance
from its influence on medieval art[2].

The book may be considered from two points of view. It may
represent the progress and victory of virtue in the individual soul,
and no doubt it does, but it also suggests the victory of the faith
in the Roman world. The vices described are especially those
characteristic of Rome. Pride, for example, plumes itself on
military glory, and has the greatest scorn for the various unwarlike
and unmanly virtues of peaceful Christianity (ll. 237—9). Luxury
"coming from the West" (clearly Rome) has all the air of that
Roman luxury and licence described by Jerome and Ammianus
Marcellinus (ll. 310 ff.). Avarice "doffs the arms of hell and
transforms herself to fairness ; she becomes a Virtue, stern of mien
and garb, whom they call thrift (*frugi*), who loves to live carefully
...and calls theft and covetousness by a sweet name, forethought
for the family" (ll. 551—563)—*i.e.* Avarice is the crowning virtue
of the Sabine farmer of the good old days.

The War is a series of single conflicts between Virtues and
Vices, in which the former invariably win. Lust is overcome by
Modesty by the virtue of the Virgin birth of our Lord :

> *inde omnis jam diva caro est quae concipit illum ;*   (76)
> *majestate quidem non degenerante per usum*
> *carnis sed miseros ad nobiliora trahente.*   (80)

Patience waits for Anger to fall of itself. Pride stumbles into

---

[1] Aug. *de moribus eccl. cath.* 34, 75 *Novi multos esse sepulchrorum et pictura-*
rum adoratores ; novi multos esse qui luxuriosissime super mortuos bibant et epulas
cadaveribus exhibentes super sepultos seipsos sepeliant et voracitates ebrietatesque
suas deputent religioni...nec mirum est in tanta copia populorum.

[2] See Brockhaus, pp. 36, 165 n., and Schmitz, *Die Gedichte des P. und ihre*
Entstehungszeit, p. 9.

a pit (which had been dug by Deceit), after reviling Humility and her sister graces ;

Justitia est ubi semper egens, et pauper Honestas.

Luxury, gorgeously described as she rides to the fray, comes nearer winning the day, but is overthrown by Sobriety, who displays the *Vexillum sublime crucis,*—a favourite theme with Prudentius, who has a pride in referring to the Cross, especially as a symbol of the victory of Christianity. It is the triumphant cross of the *labarum*, the monogram ☧ which Constantine made Rome's standard, to which the dragon-flags, so often to be found in Claudian and Ammianus and elsewhere, have had to bow[1]. It may seem strange to us that he has so little to say of the cross in its relation to Christ's death, in its theological significance, or as an emblem of Christian suffering.

Lastly, as I have said, Heresy is slain by Faith and torn in pieces as the soldiers tore Rufinus in Claudian's poem. Then, after eulogies on peace, recalling St Paul's chapter on Charity (ll. 769—787), a temple is built to the design of the Apocalypse, with gates and jewels as there described. Altogether it is a bright and interesting work, though one is startled to find how Homerically the Virtues treat the fallen Vices.

The *Cathemerinon* or *Daily Round* is a collection of hymns for the Christian's day, made more various and instructive by long but acceptable and often impressive digressions into Christian doctrine and Scripture story, which are often only very loosely, if at all, connected with the immediate theme, and are further developed in the same way themselves. Thus the hymns are not adapted for singing in church, like those of Ambrose, which were clearly their original inspiration, and the influence of which is visible in them, especially in the first two. Prudentius however does not seem to have meant his poems to be sung in church by common worshippers, but to be read by persons of more or less education. Yet while none of them has apparently ever been sung at length, most of them have contributed to Christian hymnology, for passages have been taken from them and used as hymns. The Roman breviary contains about a dozen of these abbreviated hymns, three for example being carved out of Prudentius' twelfth. The

---

[1] See Claudian, *In Ruf.* ii. 363 f.; Amm. Marc. xvi. 10, 7 (an elaborate description) and compare Prud. στεφ. i. 35, 6. For the *labarum* see Prud. *Symm.* i. 487, and Lactantius, *M. P.* 44. See Brockhaus, 73 n. On the cross Neander, *Church History*, iii. 405 (Bohn).

famous hymn to the Holy Innocents, *Salvete flores martyrum,* and
the equally famous *Jam maesta quiesce querella* have thus been
taken from Prudentius' poems for Epiphany (xii.) and for the Burial
of the Dead (x.).

For poetic touch and thought, for delicacy and brightness, the
Daily Round ranks with the best of Prudentius' work.   Quotations
and abstracts never do a poet full justice, but they must suffice.
The hour of lighting the lamps would hardly seem a promising
theme for a hymn.   But Prudentius strays very happily to the
burning bush, and thence in Moses' company to the Red Sea and
the desert and the fiery pillar, and draws from it all very skilfully
a parable of Heaven.   There are one or two odd little touches in
the piece, *e.g.* even spirits *sub Styge* have holiday on Easter Eve[1] ;
candles and lamps are described with some detail and grace, and
classed as God's gifts—a pretty thought—for artificial lights are
given us

> *ne nesciret homo spem sibi luminis*
> *in Christi solido corpore conditam.*   (*Cath.* v. 9, 10)

When he writes a hymn (vi.) for sleep-time, he tells of Joseph
interpreting dreams in prison and of St John on Patmos.   The
sign of the cross on brow and heart before going to bed will keep
one safe from evil dreams and evil demons.

The hymn "for all hours" is a remarkably graceful poem in
trochaic tetrameters, setting forth Christ's glory as shewn by the
fulfilment of prophecy in His earthly life.   Sprung from the Father's
heart before the world was, He is Alpha and Omega, creator,
redeemer and judge.   His birth of the Virgin, His Miracles, told
briefly one by one and with vigour, and lastly and chiefly His
Descent into Hell are sung in turn.   It is not the suffering so
much as the triumph of the Cross which the poet emphasizes.
While sun and stars in our sky hide themselves, He bursts the
bars of Hell and with yellow light floods the caves of death.   The
wiles of the Serpent have been in vain, his poison fails him, he
drops his hissing neck.   The fathers and the holy ones rise with
joy, leave the tombs, and follow Christ as He rises a victor to
the tribunal of the Father, bearing back the peerless glory of

---

[1] This hymn has been held to refer specially to the Easter vigil, a view not
without some plausibility, but the poet makes no definite reference to it, and
some antiquarians maintain it was not a practice of his day; Brockhaus,
pp. 87—8. Sixt, p. 11, holds that the hymn was not written for the vigil but
that the poet after his digressive manner touches on it in verses 137—140.

His passion to heaven, from whence He shall come yet again as Judge. This Second Coming still held the minds of men, and Prudentius tells of it in the hymn for sleep-time (v. 81—100), and yet again in that for the Nativity (xi.), with something of the majesty of the *Dies Irae* itself.

Peccator, intueberis
celsum coruscis nubibus,
dejectus ipse et irritis
plangens reatum fletibus.

Cum vasta signum bucina
terris cremandis miserit,
et scissus axis cardinem
mundi ruentis solverit;

Insignis ipse et praeminens
meritis rependet congrua,
his lucis usum perpetis,
illis gehennam et tartarum.

(*Cath.* xi. 101—112)

The descent into Hell is the subject of a striking hymn of Synesius, and is told in still more impressive prose by an unknown Greek writer, whose work is now imbedded in the so-called *Gospel of Nicodemus*[1]. But the Last Judgment seems to have appealed far more to the Latin than to the Greek mind, as no one need be told who has read the terrible last chapter of Tertullian's *de Spectaculis*. And Tertullian, one might almost say, was as much Prudentius' " master " as he was Cyprian's.

A few stanzas from the hymn " Before Meat " (iii.), translated into English as closely as adherence to the original metre will allow (the original is of course not rhymed), may give some impression of the poet's manner of treating his subjects in his various lyrical poems, though this one is not his strongest. The grace of the Latin must not be expected.

Cross-bearer, kindly one, giver of light,
Maker of all things, and friend of most worth,
Born of the Word, of immaculate birth,
Equal of old with the Father in might,
Ere there was heaven or ocean or earth.

[1] See the abstract on pp. 378—381.

Come, for salvation is found in Thy smile,
Come and behold with beneficent gaze,
Giving us peace, as the bountiful rays
Stream from Thy face, that our banquet the while
Lit by Thy presence may be to Thy praise.

Come, Lord, for nothing without Thee is sweet,
Pleasure is none, there is nothing save gall,
If Thy good favour, O Christ ! Thou recall,
Savoureth nought of our drink or our meat—
Faith be the sanctification of all.

God be it still that we taste in each dish,
Christ in the cup may our spirits descry :—
Matter or mirth—the light jests as they fly—
All that we are, every act, every wish,
Be by the Trinity ruled from on high.

What would I now with the spoils of the rose ?
Wherefore the fragrance of odours outpoured ?
Ours the true wine, the ambrosia, flows ;
Faith is the nectar the Christian heart knows,
Borne to us straight from the heart of the Lord.

Not for light ivy, sweet Muse, calls the time,
Erewhile the garland thou wontest to wear ;
Thread with the dactyl a coronet fair,
Weaving a mystical chaplet of rhyme,
Bind with the praise of the Saviour thy hair[1].

What shall a soul of such origin ask,
Born to the aether and child of the light ?
Where shall it find it so worthy a task,
Praising its Maker, His gifts to recite—
All the soul's music the theme shall unite.

He, it is He, to us all things doth yield,
Rulers of all He hath framed us to be ;
All that the earth or the sky or the sea
Bears in the flood or the air or the field,
These He made mine ; for Himself He made me.

Birds the dark craft of the fowler ensnares,
Whether the gin be his wile or the net,
Or the limed twigs for his quarry be set ;
Once the winged creatures alight unawares,
Caught in the tangle no freedom they get.

---

[1] This stanza has been cited as evidence for the supposition, *a priori* most probable, that Prudentius had served his apprenticeship in poetry on themes which were not distinctively sacred. Sixt, p. 21.

Lo ! through the waters with fold upon fold
Nets sweep the wandering swarms of the main ;
Whipped from the stream the fish struggles in vain,
Ne'er shall it make the fell hook loose its hold ;
Pleasure the silly mouth sought and found pain.

Lavish the bounty the rich acres bring ;
Ours the full ears of the cornland's increase,
Ours the luxuriant vineyards that fling
Tendril and twig forth to cluster and cling :
Ours the green olive the nurseling of peace.

God of His bounty in Christ giveth all,
All things are ours, all our wants he supplies ;
Far be from us the fell hunger that cries
Asking the death of the ox of the stall,
Lusting for flesh though the life-blood should fall.

Be the fierce banquet for races untamed !
They may eat flesh, who in savagery live ;
Never 'mid us be such cruelty named !
Lettuce and bean for our feeding were framed,
Guileless the banquet the garden shall give.

From the banquet of innocence the poet passes to the garden
of man's innocence, and tells of Adam and Eve and the serpent ;
of the fall of man and the virgin birth of Christ. Let it be enough
that man has once fallen ; now let temperance preserve him, for
there is another life and we shall rise again because Christ has risen.

The *Dittochaeon* is a series of quatrains designed to explain
sacred pictures in some church or churches. They have some
importance in the history of Christian art but not of literature.

We come lastly to the great work *Against Symmachus*. From
Augustus' day onward a statue of Victory had stood in the
Senate House, and at every meeting of the Senate an offering was
made to it. But on his visit to Rome in 357 Constantius had
image and altar removed. Julian restored them. Twenty years
later Gratian removed them again in 382. The heathen members
of the Senate presented to him a petition for the restoration of
the altar and the goddess, but were refused admission to his
presence. This rejection was due to the Christian Senators, who
through Pope Damasus communicated with St Ambrose. When
Gratian was killed by Maximus, they made a further appeal in
384 to Valentinian II. Symmachus presented their case in a
speech which survived and was so greatly and so generally admired,
that Ambrose, after prevailing on the Emperor to decline to take

action, felt obliged to write a reply. Victory once more took her place during the rebellion of Arbogast and Eugenius (393) and was removed by Theodosius on his overthrowing the usurpers (394). This altar was thus the standard of paganism, which could hardly indeed hope to recapture the world but had a sentimental feeling for retaining this last emblem. Even in 400 and again in 404 Claudian was at special pains in his poetry to emphasize that Victory was a goddess and one to whom Rome was deeply indebted. So vital was the controversy. Symmachus' petition was still read and admired, and offered a fair opportunity for attack. Even later than this, beginning in 410 after the fall of Rome, Augustine thought it worth while to spend years on the last great refutation of heathenism, the *De Civitate Dei*, and to commission Orosius to compile his history of the world's calamities to shew that the effect of Christianity had been to lessen them.

Symmachus' petition may be very briefly analysed. He pled for the restoration of the altar to the goddess, even though she were but a name (*numen* and *nomen*), and of various immunities to priests and vestals, which had just been taken away. It was not a question between this and that religion. Everyone to his taste and custom in religion. Every nation had its tutelary genius, and Rome had hers. Let not antiquity go for nothing. The great mystery of life could hardly be discovered by one line of search. Rome personified pled for her old usages, for the Vestals and their due, out of gratitude if for no other reason. In fact, famine and disaster marked heaven's disapproval—not, of course, of the Emperor's new religion, but of the neglect of the old religion.

To this St Ambrose made a vigorous reply. The old rites had not, as alleged, defended Rome—from Hannibal and the Gauls, for example. Rome personified resents her victories being put down to aught but her valour. She is not ashamed to be converted in her old age. As for the great mystery God's voice reveals it to us. Contrast seven Vestals with the multitude of Christian virgins. Heavy burdens lay on Christian priests who must surrender their taxable property on ordination, while the wealth of the Church was the revenues of the indigent. Why had the famine been so slow in following its cause? As for antiquity everything advanced; agricultural methods were bettered; man himself grew; even Rome had adopted foreign rites. The temples never helped Pompey, Cyrus or Julian, victory being more a matter of legions than religions—the bishop here anticipating Napoleon.

In 404 Prudentius published his two books of hexameters on the same theme. Boissier is right in saying the world was not fully converted and men of letters were still heathen in their libraries, and that a literary presentment of Christianity was still sighed for by Christians of education[1]. Ambrose's reply was not after all a match for the eloquence of Symmachus in the eyes of people of taste, though he had out-manœuvred the orator with the Emperor.

Prudentius begins by saying Plato's dream of philosophers for kings is realized in Christian Emperors, and proceeds to exhibit the heathen Pantheon, as Tertullian had done before. Heathenism is so long-lived because of early training, and he has a fine passage on the heathen associations of childhood and growing years opening out with further initiation into pagan rites. For a thousand generations Superstition was unchecked, and the tiny heir of the house trembled and worshipped whatever his hoary grandsires displayed for his veneration. He drank in error with his mother's milk ; his first food was the sacred meal, his earliest sight the sacred candles and the family gods growing black with holy oil. As a little child, he saw the image of Fortune with her horn, and his mother pale at her prayers before the sacred stone ; and he too would be lifted by his nurse to kiss it in his turn. To it he made his baby prayers. Without the house he saw the gods laurel-crowned on days of festival and gala-days, and above all he was taught to worship Rome (*c. Symm.* i. 197—214).

He assails the gladiatorial games, and narrates the story of Theodosius' homily to the Senate after the fall of Arbogast and of the Senate's conversion[2], and how *sua secula Roma erubuit,* and finally tells Symmachus that to a Christian Emperor he owes his rise in the world. So much for the first book. It is interesting throughout to remark the kindly and respectful way in which Prudentius always speaks of Symmachus. Courtesy is not always the mark of Christian controversy in the fathers.

In the second book he repeats Ambrose's points about victory won by *labor impiger, aspera virtus,* about progress and other

[1] At the beginning of the century Lactantius made the same complaint, *Instit.* v. 1 *Haec inprimis causa est cur apud sapientes et doctos et principes hujus seculi scriptura sancta fide careat, quod prophetae communi ac simplici sermone ut ad populum sunt locuti...adeo nihil verum putant nisi quod auditu suave est ; nihil credibile nisi quod potest incutere voluptatem. nemo rem veritate ponderat sed ornatu. non credunt ergo divinis quia fuco carent.*

[2] Zosimus, iv. 58, says none of the senators was converted, but then Zosimus did not wish them to be and Prudentius did.

things, but adds much of his own which is better and undreamt
of by Ambrose. Once more he approximates to Browning :

> *nonne hominem et pecudem distantia separat una?*
> *quod bona quadrupedum ante oculos sita sunt: ego contra*
> *spero.*

> Progress, man's distinctive mark alone,
> Not God's, and not the beasts' : God is, they are,
> Man partly is and wholly hopes to be.

If there is no future, he continues in fine declamation, let us eat
and drink and break every law at once. Where Symmachus introduced Rome as speaking, Prudentius introduces God Himself telling
of man's creation, end and resurrection, and pleading for a temple
of mind not marble. Curiously enough, here as elsewhere, Prudentius does not mention truth as belonging to the spiritual
temple. He makes great game of the genius of Rome, and of
immigrant gods—some of whom Claudian had recently held up
as Rome's guardians (p. 239).

> *Non divum degener ordo*
> *et patria extorris Romanis adfuit armis.*   (535—6)

To allow this was treason to Rome—it diminished her glory.

> *Non fero Romanum nomen sudataque bella*
> *et titulos tanto quaesitos sanguine carpi.*   (550—1)

Rather it was God who had made Rome for His own ends, that
Rome might make mankind one, and so prepare the way for Christ.
Rome too is personified, congratulating herself on having sloughed
off her former taints, on being free from danger from the Goths,
through Christ and His servants,—the Emperor and Stilicho, who
had just won the victory over the Goths at Pollentia[1] (402). The
Gauls had once captured Rome despite her gods, but now she
knows the Goths only by the hearing of the ear, and (vividly
drawn by the poet) she bids the Emperor climb the triumphal car
and come to Rome with Christ beside him.

As for the many ways to the great mystery, one is right if
rough and hard, and the others are wrong if pleasant, and his
language recalls Hesiod. The famine! nobody goes to the Circus

---

[1] Was Pollentia a victory? Claudian's contemporary explanations to prove
that it was have made it seem doubtful. That it was a Roman defeat, as the
Goths have claimed, Prudentius' words prohibit our supposing.

hungry! and he concludes with an entreaty for the abolition of the gladiatorial shows—

> *nullus in urbe cadat cujus sit poena voluptas*[1]. (1125)

It is interesting to compare the panegyric written almost at the same time by Claudian for Honorius' sixth consulship. There we have a splendid procession with cataphracts (armoured cavalry) and dragon-standards and all that is gorgeous. But for *huc Christo comitante veni* we read of "winged Victory, guardian of the Roman toga, coming herself to her shrines"—a tacit defiance to those who had driven the goddess from the Senate. We find a grand equestrian display in the Circus, but no such plea for mercy for the wretched as that with which the Christian poet crowns his poem.

This rapid sketch must suffice for the works of Prudentius, but a few points of style remain to be considered. He has been harshly criticized for the characteristic faults of his training, and of his age. He has confessed that he received a training in rhetoric and that he had been an advocate. He had the resultant weaknesses. In his polemics against heathenism, the poet is sometimes subordinated to the advocate, who has taken his brief from Tertullian and drives home his points with the same keen, but hardly poetic, energy. He urges as it were the conviction of the gods on charges which involve heavy penalties under Roman law. The immorality and sensuality attributed by legend to the gods rather than the fundamental weaknesses of the Pantheon are attacked. Again, he still suffers, like Claudian and others of his contemporaries, from rhetoric. All the rhetoric-bred poets declaim from Lucan onward. They cannot break loose from the school. They lack imagination and balance, and are carried away by language. Prudentius does not always know when to leave off. One or two examples will serve. A common taunt against the heathen gods is that they betrayed their own lands to Rome. This is how Prudentius sets it.

> *Juppiter ut Cretae domineris, Pallas ut Argis,*
> *Cynthius ut Delphis, tribuerunt omine dextro.*
> *Isis Nilicolas, Rhodios Cytherea reliquit,*
> *venatrix Ephesum virgo. Mars dedidit Hebrum;*
> *destituit Thebas Bromius, concessit et ipsa*
> *Juno suos Phrygiis servire nepotibus Afros.*

> *Adv. Symm.* ii. 489.

[1] Compare Wordsworth:—

> Never to blend our pleasure or our pride
> With sorrow of the meanest thing that feels.

When speaking of the way which does not lead to the great mystery and of its ramifications, he spends seventeen lines in detailing some thirteen forms of heathenism—the worship of Bacchus, Cybele, etc. Again the Star in the East outshone the Zodiac, and we have some twelve lines describing how each of nine signs was affected, and the sun too   Contrast Horace's moderation when Astrology tempted him to prolixity. The jewel gates of the New Jerusalem at the end of the Holy War take fifteen lines, as jewel after jewel is invoiced. He actually adds the price of one of them, which had cost Faith a thousand talents.

But this is not all. For besides what may be called relevant overloading, we have overloading which is irrelevant. Prudentius could tell a story and could not refrain. So we have plentiful digressions into stories, interesting and well told, but aside from the main theme. They are generally Biblical. Brockhaus finds an excuse for the Biblical digressions in the plea that Prudentius wrote for the instruction of educated Christian people and under the influence of Christian art, selecting for poetic treatment especially those stories which were painted in catacomb and church. These were in his own mind and he knew they would be familiar to his readers. "'Tis the taught already that profits by teaching."

Though his *sententiae* are often crisp and clear, he has a tendency at times to draggle—whether from exuberance or from impatience of correction. Claudian is superior to him in precision and edge.

While in hexameters Prudentius seems fairly strong, in argumentative passages, like Lucretius and Juvenal, he is almost bound to drop into ending lines with quadrisyllables or pairs of disyllables—especially when he expounds the Trinity—and the effect is not happy. His quantities, though generally, are not always classical—Greek diphthongs and long vowels being often shortened, *e.g. rhomphaealis, haeresis, Paraclitum* ; and short vowels lengthened, *e.g. charisma, catholicus* (too tempting a word metrically), *sophia.*

His spondaic hexameters are fairly numerous and not very impressive. They are more like Juvenal's than Virgil's. His pentameters are weak. I do not find his alliterations very dignified or always very musical.

On the other hand, he is a master of narrative clear-cut and effective. His language is often graceful and pointed, and he brings out his thoughts well. His prologues, for example, are excellent.

Metrically he has some redeeming qualities, which it is well to recognize. His hexameters are varied and easy, and his elisions frequent enough to relieve monotony without producing roughness. He is in this respect a wonderful contrast to Juvencus, whose lines are all alike and all lacking in elision. In fine, if Prudentius' hexameters lack the highest finish (as it must be confessed they do), they are still telling and vigorous and hang well together. He employs, besides, a considerable number of lyrical metres and handles them like a master. Many of them are Horatian, and the rest may be paralleled in contemporary poets.

I have already remarked that the critics are divided in their preferences, some preferring his work in the style of Virgil and Lucretius, others his lyrical poetry, and both parties can say a good deal for their views. In other words, the poet has been successful in both styles. The more one studies his contemporaries the more one admires him. Spiritually and intellectually he far outstrips the heathen poets, and in poetic insight, grace and mastery of his material he is far above the Christians.

Of his indebtedness to previous poets, particularly to Virgil, much might be written. I will content myself with remarking that I have found a number of direct imitations, or perhaps echoes, of Juvenal; one or two cases of the influence of Propertius and Lucan; some of Lucretius; and rather more of indebtedness to Horace. To Virgil his debt is naturally very much greater. He knew him well as scores of passages shew. Some are cases of undisguised pilfering[1] : *e.g.*

Christe graves hominum semper miserate labores.	*Psych.* 1.
Phoebe graves Trojae semper miserate labores.	*Aen.* vi. 56.

Others are more honest reminiscences or echoes :

Martis congressibus impar.	*Psych.* 549.
impar congressus Achilli.	*Aen.* i. 475.
ad astra doloribus itur.	*Cath.* x. 92.
sic itur ad astra.	*Aen.* ix. 641.

Others again would be less marked if not so numerous, *e.g.* such phrases as *Psych.* 40 *gramineo in campo*, 41 *fulget in armis*, 49 *adacto transadigit gladio*, which are Virgil's : others less conspicuous are metrical parallels if the phrase may be allowed : *e.g.*

funalis machina.	*Psych.* 866.	*fatalis machina.*	*Aen.* ii. 237.
femina provocat arma virum.		*Steph.* iii. 36.

[1] Sixt however goes too far, I think, when he calls the *Psychomachia* "almost a cento." Compare *Aen.* vi. 640 with Catullus lxiv. 39, for a loan as patent.

Again there are instances of what I may call deliberate quotation :
e.g. when Theodosius comes to Rome as a Christian victor and
the Empire becomes Christian:

> *denique nec metas statuit, nec tempora ponit ;*
> *imperium sine fine docet, etc.*   *Adv. Symm.* i. 542.

This same Virgilian influence is found in very many Latin poets,
and is not at all extraordinary when we remember that Virgil is
the one book which has never yet been out of the schools since
Tucca and Varius published the *Aeneid.*

One source of inspiration, from which we might have expected
him to draw, he ignores. The poetry of the Psalter was lost to
him. From the historical books of the Old and the New Testament,
from Paul and the Apocalypse he borrowed incidents, ideas and
pictures, but the Psalms and generally the Prophets he ignored.
The Prophets were unintelligible, the Psalms were uncouth, and
persons of education shrank from them. Even Ambrose's recommendation of Isaiah failed to make Augustine read him through.
For the Psalms, Augustine tells us of his enjoyment of them as
a marked proof of his change of feeling.

"In what accents did I speak to Thee, my God, as I read
the psalms of David, those faithful songs and sounds of piety
that exclude the proud spirit... What accents did I utter to
Thee in those psalms, and how was I inflamed toward Thee by
them, and kindled to recite them, if possible, the world over,
against the pride of mankind" (*Conf.* ix. 4, 8).

Jerome says much the same (*Ep.* xxii. 30). "So with a mind
to read Tully, I used to fast. After a long night of watching,
after tears which the memory of my former sins brought from my
inmost being, I would take up Plautus. If ever I came to myself
and began to read the Prophets, the rough language grated on
me." It took an angel with a scourge, he says, to correct his too
classical taste. So that we need not be surprised if Prudentius
ignored the Psalms and studied Virgil, as even Jerome did after
his celestial flagellation. But surely it was a bad sign that the
education of the day should prevent men of culture from recognizing
the real worth through the rough translation.

We have seen something of the Spaniard with his national
love of and pride in the Spanish saints, his interest in martyrdoms
and his devotion ; of the Roman proud of his Roman citizenship,
jealous of his country's honour lest it be usurped by false gods,

and above all bound up in a Christian Rome and its mission;
of the man of letters, the poet, the artist; one side of him remains—
and that may best be set forth in his own words, in the poem which
may be taken as the epilogue to his whole collection. When we
have seen the whole man, and have studied him all round, and
in relation to his times, we cease to think of the points strange
and even grotesque to-day, but feel that here is a true man.

> Gifts for God the Father wrought
> To Him true, pure, and holy spirits offer;
> Gifts of honest mind and thought,
> The riches of a heav'n-blest life they proffer.
>
> Wealth another man may bring,
> The needs and sorrows of the poor relieving;
> I, alack, can only sing,
> Swift Trochee and Iambus interweaving.
>
> Scanty holiness is mine,
> Nor can I help the needy, rich alms flinging;
> Yet will deign my Lord Divine
> To lend a Father's ear to my poor singing.
>
> In the mansion of the great
> Stand needful furnishments in rack and trestle;
> Gleams the gold and silver plate,
> The bowl of polished brass and earthen vessel.
>
> Wrought of precious ivory
> Or carved of oak—or simple elmwood platters—
> What their nature, so each be
> Meet for the Master's use, it nothing matters.
>
> There are uses for them all,
> Great cost or small is not of use the token.
> Me within my father's hall
> Christ found: He came and found me old and broken.
>
> Yet has Christ a need of me,
> Though but a moment's space I have my station;
> Earthen vessel though I be,
> I pass into the Palace of Salvation.
>
> Be the service ne'er so slight
> God owns it. Then whatever Time is bringing,
> This shall still be my delight
> That Christ has had the tribute of my singing.

CHAPTER XII

SULPICIUS SEVERUS

Caelestem quodammodo laetitiam vultu praeferens.

Vita Martini 27

When the priest sees himself vanquished by the prophet, he suddenly changes his method. He takes him under his protection, he introduces his harangues into the sacred canon, he throws over his shoulders the priestly chasuble. The days pass on, the years roll by, and the moment comes when the heedless crowd no longer distinguishes between them, and it ends by believing the prophet to be an emanation of the clergy.

This is one of the bitterest ironies of history.

PAUL SABATIER, *St Francis of Assisi*, p. xv[1]

In the Christian movement as in most other movements of mankind two tendencies display themselves in constant reaction and interaction, the tendencies to make the group and the individual the unit of life. Great conceptions underlie them both. The one is that of a society ordered and organized, part answering to part, and all parts of one majestic whole, a great imperial system embracing mankind, every man in his proper sphere, star differing from star in glory but all moving harmoniously on their several orbits. The other is that of a life resting on communion with God, a life each man must live for himself (for in this relation no intermediary is tolerable or possible), a life dependent on no system or organization but above and beyond the reach and scope of systems and their makers, for the wind bloweth where it listeth and so is every one that is born of the spirit. Both conceptions, it may be said, can be held by the same mind at once, and perhaps under ideal circumstances they are not incompatible, but where the

---

[1] References are made to the translation by Louise Seymour Houghton.

circumstances are not ideal there is apt to be a preference given
to one as against the other, and the result is often extravagance
and reaction.

The story of the Church is full of these alternate reactions.
St Paul, if any man, stood for the freedom of the individual to
live his own spiritual life, and St Paul wrote the Epistles to the
Corinthians, for he could not approve an individualism run mad
and unshackled. Ignatius to correct the disorders of Docetism
laid stress on episcopal order, and thence came the Catholic Church,
and within a century reaction came under Montanus who pled for
the emancipation of the Holy Spirit from the yoke of the bishop.
Half a century later, when the Roman bishops had denounced
Montanism and the Church system was crystallizing, the persecution
of Decius started the same conflict over again between the order of
the Church and the purity of Christian life, and Novatianus made a
stand for holiness, though here the Catholic principle asserted itself
and he organized the great Puritan Church of the Novatians. With
the triumph of Constantine came the triumph of the Church, the
Nicene and the following Councils, and the age of Court bishops
and metropolitans, when the Church was deluged by a secular
society, when bishops fought for creeds and richer sees, when
spiritual arms were reinforced by material and the victories of faith
were changed for those of George and Damasus, whose followers
made him Pope at the cost of one hundred and thirty-seven lives.
Reaction might have been expected and it duly came. It was at
this time, we are told, that the monastic communities of the
Egyptian god Serapis were converted to Christianity, and simultaneously there appeared in the same regions and among men of
the same race, the Coptic race, the earliest Christian monachism.
Antony and Paul are nowadays dismissed very properly from
history to the realm of fiction. But at all events now was the day
when Christians began to take to the desert to seek there that
perfection and holy living they found impossible in the Church life
of the cities. If the movement began with the Copts, it did not
end with them. It spread the world over. And then reaction,
for the monks, the individualists of the Church of the day, and
wild and extreme ones too, began very soon to organize, and we
read that in the Egyptian deserts the first of virtues was obedience
to the Abbot under any and every circumstance—a virtue, experience would shew, of somewhat doubtful worth. Later on St Benedict
organized the monks of the West. With each fresh outburst of

spiritual life there followed a new order. Friars were the sign of a
revolt against the monasteries, as they had been and were against
the bishops, for the religious orders were subject to the Pope and
independent of the local episcopate[1]. The Reformation was a great
revolt of the individual against bishop and monk and friar, and
when it imposed English prelate and Scotch presbyter on the
Church, George Fox led a great revolt against both, as later on
John Wesley did likewise in spite of himself. Both organized fresh
societies, with very different degrees of individual freedom in thought
and worship. Here it would be well to halt, though it should be
remarked in the case of all these movements that, while they
represent the desire for higher life, there are rarely wanting men
whose character might give ground for believing that revolts and
secessions are unnecessary for the maintenance of Christian piety,
or, at all events, that nowhere is there a monopoly in holy living.

The fourth century witnessed a great change, startling and
almost dramatic, but yet neither so astonishing nor so great as
might seem at first sight. It was, at least to those who can look
back upon it and what preceded it, inevitable. Persecution is a
clumsy method, and it had failed to crush Christianity, which, it
was also clear, was proof against all the social, moral and intellectual attacks the old world could bring against it, and possessed
too of an assimilative force which drew to it steadily, if slowly,
the best minds and hearts. The change was inevitable, and yet
it was by no means so great or complete as it looked. A great
many among the millions of the Empire were not keenly interested
in the question of cult, where conduct was free from interference,
and a conventional and occasional settlement of accounts might
be made as conveniently with the God of the Christians as with
any other, provided He, like the other gods, would leave his
worshipper free in the intervals. When all is said, the religions
of the ancient world were largely, were chiefly, external—sacrifices,
lustrations, purifications and other magical rites, and to change
from them to a magical Christianity meant not very much after
all. The change to spiritual Christianity was a very different
matter, but that was not always consequent upon the other.
Beside these nominal Christians, there were many more honest

---

[1] Cf. A. V. G. Allen, *Christian Institutions*, "Monasticism never lost its
inner mood of antagonism to the episcopate; its history is a record of conflicts
with bishops, of rivalries and jealousies, of defeats and victories, till the Reformation."

heathen who went their quiet way, bowing to the storm and content if allowed to walk in the old paths without let or hindrance.

If the world was more Christian, the Church was certainly more heathen. It had lost many of its best spirits in the persecution of Diocletian, and the new recruits by no means made good the loss. The laity were more pagan, and the clergy and bishops were pagan too in heart, more worldly and less spiritual. While the Church, particularly in the East, was busying itself about the definition of its fundamental truth, less attention was paid to the common virtues, and the bishops rivalled the eunuchs and the freedmen of the palace in love of power and wealth and in the questionable means they took to secure them. The episcopal office suffered for not being the post of peril. The protest of the laity was monachism. While their guides in things spiritual fought for pomp and place, they looked after their own spiritual interests, and found, as we read in Sulpicius Severus, that in general they had most to fear (after the Devil and his more invisible legions) from the bishops. Ammianus, the fairest of historians, had hard things to say of the great bishops, yet his charges are more than confirmed by the devout Churchman. One Athanasius, one Ambrose, and one Augustine mark the century, while there were many of the type of Damasus, Ursacius and George[1].

Beside the desire to satisfy spiritual cravings, there was perhaps another inducement to embrace the monastic life in that *praesentium fastidium* we find in Sulpicius. The Roman power in the West was nearing its end. Taxation, war, rebellion, extravagance and slavery had exhausted the Empire, and men turned from the City of Destruction to realize the City of God in the desert and the cell. In such times of stress the common expressions of the religious instinct are felt to fail and men crave for closer access to the divine.

St Martin (c. 336—c. 400) was a Pannonian who entered the army at the early age of fifteen, was baptized at eighteen, and at twenty got his discharge from Julian, then Caesar, and betook himself to the monastic life. He was not an educated man, and, as we may see, he was terribly credulous and superstitious, but he was a great force in Gaul, his adopted country. His kindness, his dignity, enhanced rather than lessened by his mean garb and

[1] Even these men had their excellences. George was a scholar, or at least had amassed a library which Julian coveted, and Damasus was the antiquarian who opened the Catacombs to the pilgrims.

humble ways, his shrewdness, his language, his seriousness, and
the awful gravity and the quiet joy[1] he drew from communion
with Christ in a life of prayer and imitation, gave him an influence
and a charm which drew to him the suffering and the sinful, and
a power that on more than one occasion proved more imperial
than an Emperor's.   He became bishop of Tours, though against
his will, for it had not been his purpose to be ordained[2].   But
Hilary of Poictiers, to whom he at first attached himself, failing
to make him a deacon, made him an exorcist, and later on he was
captured by a stratagem and consecrated whether he would or no.
The bishops were unwilling to do it, but the laity would not be
denied and an accidental *sors Biblica* clinched the matter.   The
most strenuous of the bishops was one Defensor, and a mistake was
made in the lesson whereby the words were read, "Out of the
mouth of babes and sucklings thou, hast perfected praise, because of
thine enemies, that thou mayest destroy the enemy *et defensorem.*"
Martin was "un saint un peu démocratique" as M. Boissier says,
and he ended, as he began, the poor man's bishop, just as St Francis
long afterwards led a spiritual movement rising from the common
people and recognized by them as their own[3].   And Francis also
refused to become a priest.

Such a man was magnetic, and amongst others he drew to him
Sulpicius Severus, the subject of this essay.   We do not know
much of Sulpicius' life, probably because there is little to know.
Gennadius, who includes him in his list of ninety-nine famous men
which he made to supplement St Jerome's, only gives us one fact
which we could not gather from his own writings and the thirteen
letters addressed to him by Paulinus of Nola, and to that fact
I shall have to return.

Sulpicius was born in Aquitaine about the year 363 (according
to Reinkens), probably of good family, for he had at Bordeaux the
best education his times could give, he became a pleader and he
made a great marriage[4].   His wife was of a wealthy family which

---

[1] *Nemo unquam illum vidit...maerentem, nemo ridentem; unus idemque fuit
semper caelestem quodammodo laetitiam vultu praeferens* (*Vita Mart.* 27).   We
read a somewhat similar account of Marcus Aurelius:—*Erat enim ipse tantae
tranquillitatis ut vultum nunquam mutaverit maerore vel gaudio, philosophiae
deditus Stoicae* (*Hist. August. M. Antonin.* 16)—the difference will be noted
however.

[2] For an interesting account of this reluctance to be ordained, still a formality in the Coptic Church, see Stanley, *Eastern Church*, Lect. VII.

[3] Sabatier, *St Francis*, p. xvi.

[4] See Paulinus, *Ep.* v. 5 (to Severus) *in ipso adhuc mundi theatro, id est, fori
celebritate diversans, et facundi nominis palmam tenens...divitiae de matrimonio*

could boast a consul. Of her we know nothing, unless from his grief at her early death and his lifelong affection for her mother Bassula, evidently a woman of fine character and kindly nature, we may conjecture, "like mother, like daughter." His wife's death, while he was still a young man with a father living, altered the current of his life[1]. He had given signs of rising in his profession, but "from his Tullian letters," to borrow the phrase of Paulinus[2], he turned to "the preachings of the fishermen," and "the silence of piety." In less extraordinary language, he turned to St Martin for advice, and the Saint advised him to quit the world[3]. This he did, as Paulinus also had done, cheerfully, gladly, and without regret, though it would seem his father resented his action. He settled down (about 393) to the life of a monk on some land of his at Toulouse, selling all else[3]. We need not expect much incident in such a life, but one or two little details appear. As M. Boissier remarks, "dans le dévot et le moine le lettré survivait." The man of letters had necessities the illiterate among the monks knew not, and we read of amanuenses, whom he owed to the kindness of his mother-in-law[4], and who, he playfully insinuates, as if in private duty bound, supplied her with advance copies of whatever he wrote. His phrase implies that these men were slaves, and, in the *Dialogue*[5], Gallus who has been "teased" (*fatigare*) by him on "Gallic edacity" retorts with some good-humoured banter about "somebody" whose ungrateful freedman ran off without however making his master very angry, and Sulpicius replies that but for so and so "I should be very angry." It is an interesting sidelight on monastic life, but no

---

familiae consularis aggestae...post conjugium peccandi libertas et caelebs juventas. So *ib.* 6, 7, references to eloquence. All of which may illuminate his comparison of his friend to the Queen of Sheba (§ 2).

[1] Paulinus, *Ep.* v. 6 *respuens patrimoniorum onera ceu stercorum, merito socrum sanctam omni liberaliorem parente in matrem sortitus aeternam, quia caelestem patrem anteverteras terreno parenti, exemplo apostolorum relicto patre in navicula fluctuante, scilicet in hujus vitae incerto cum retibus rerum suarum et implicatione patrimonii derelicto Christum secutus...Piscatorum praedicationes Tullianis omnibus [e] tuis litteris praetulisti. Confugisti ad pietatis silentium, ut evaderes iniquitatis tumultum.* (7) *O vere Israelita!*

[2] Was it a case of sudden conversion? Paulinus, *Ep.* v. 5, says *repentino impetu discussisti servile peccati jugum*, and if this is what he means, it fits in with much else we know of Severus, but Paulinus loves to shroud his meaning (when he has a meaning) in words—*juvat indulgere sermoni*, he says. He was Ausonius' pupil.

[3] Paulinus, *Ep.* xxiv. 3 *nec in reservatis praediis possessor et perfectus in venditis.*

[4] *Ep.* iii. 2 *notarios meos...qui in jus nostrum ex tua potissimum liberalitate venerunt.* Cf. Paulinus, *Ep.* v. 6, for Bassula's generosity *socrum sanctam omni liberaliorem parente.*

[5] *Dial.* i. 12.

one who has read his delightful works will grudge Sulpicius his amanuenses[1].

He was the literary exponent of the movement of which St Martin was the prophet, and he shared in the ill-will that attended his master. More than once we hear of episcopal dislike and perhaps a little mild persecution. At the beginning of the *Dialogue*, Postumian asks after some years of absence whether the bishops are still the men they were when he went away[2]. Sulpicius bids him not ask, for they are no better, and his one friend among them, who was his one relief from their vexatiousness, is rougher than he should be. We get another glimpse at this unpopularity of Sulpicius in one of Paulinus' letters, where the writer presses Sulpicius to come and visit him, for one reason urging that by being absent for a while he will still the voice of jealousy[3].

The same letters cast some little light on Sulpicius' life. The earlier ones repeatedly invite him to Nola, but he never went. Twice, he writes to Paulinus, he meant to come but was stopped by illness[4]. By and by it is pretty clear he does not intend to visit his friend at all. He jokingly wrote that he was afraid Paulinus' generosity would soon leave him too poor to repeat the invitation[5] —a jest which plunged Paulinus into a flood of declamation about faith, ending in the happy thought that perhaps after all Sulpicius had been playful rather than faithless. Sulpicius did a good deal of travelling, it would appear, in Gaul[6], but he was content to be represented in Italy by his servants and his annual letters[7].

When engaged on his *Chronicle*, Sulpicius wrote in 403 to Paulinus for aid, particularly on some points of doubtful chronology[8], but Paulinus had to confess he was unable to help him. History was seemingly too solid a study for the pupil of Ausonius, but he did the best he could and passed on his friend's letter to Rufinus. In place of information he sends a declamation on the Emperor Theodosius and some hymns he had written to St Felix.

---

[1] From the letters of Paulinus, it is clear Sulpicius had still *pueri* to carry letters, etc., *e.g. Ep.* v. 1 *pueris tuis sancta in Domino tibi servitute conexis;* xxvii. 3 *famulis conservus.* Paulinus was rapturous about the loan of a cook, an expert in vegetarian *cuisine* and an adept at the razor (*Ep.* xxiii.), a lad therefore very like Samson.

[2] *Dial.* i. 2, 3 *an isti omnes quos hic reliqueram sacerdotes tales sint quales eos antequam proficiscerer noveramus?*

[3] Paulinus, *Ep.* v. 13 *zeli fuga qui maxime conspectu aut vicinia aemulae conversationis accenditur.*

[4] Paulinus, *Ep.* v. 8.

[5] Paulinus, *Ep.* xi. 12.

[6] Paulinus, *Ep.* xvii. 4.

[7] Paulinus, *Ep.* xxiii. 2, xxviii. 1.

[8] Paulinus, *Ep.* xxviii.

Over and above the letters, other courtesies passed between them. Sulpicius sends a camel's hair cloth to Paulinus, who acknowledges it in a rambling letter[1] about camels and the analogy of the camel and the needle's eye to salvation by the cross of Christ, and returns a tunic of lamb's wool made by a saintly lady, Melania, and presented to Paulinus by her on her return from a twenty-five years' residence at Jerusalem. He hoped Sulpicius would value it the more for his having worn it a little first. By and by[2] Sulpicius asks for a portrait of Paulinus, who is very reluctant (or would have it seem so) to send it, but we may surmise it was sent, for a little later we read that in a baptistery Sulpicius has been building he has painted on the walls St Martin and Paulinus[3]. His correspondent is obviously highly pleased, but feels it his duty to make a long and rhetorical protest. At Sulpicius' request he sends him a series of verses to inscribe on the walls and something far more precious— *part* of a fragment of the True Cross brought home by St Silvia of Aquitaine[4]. The Cross, he explains, permitted these souvenirs to be taken from it without suffering a loss of bulk. Melania appears again as sending a choice selection of ashes and other relics.

Paulinus' letters are insufferably long and trivial, with one or two exceptions. While here and there amid his endless moralizings we find a stray fact of interest, the correspondence has this value that, beside showing the respect men had for Sulpicius' character, it brings out by contrast his brilliance and worth as a man of letters. The two men had had much the same training, had made the same surrender and lived the same life; but there the likeness ends.

Now and then Sulpicius speaks of himself. Writing to one Aurelius, a deacon[5], he speaks of himself sitting alone in his little cell, "and the line of thought came to me which so often occupies me, the hope of things to come and disgust for the present, the fear of judgment and the terror of punishment; and what follows these thoughts and is their cause, the recollection of my sins, made me sad and weary." His story of Martin's discourse and his obvious approval of it shew his own temper. "His talk was ever, how we should leave the seductions of the world and the burdens of the age to follow the Lord Jesus free and unhampered: he would

---

[1] *Ep.* xxix.   [2] Paulinus, *Ep.* xxx.
[3] Paulinus, *Ep.* xxxii.   [4] Paulinus, *Ep.* xxxi. 1.
[5] Sulp. Sev. *Ep.* ii. 1.   For the thought cf. Paulinus, cited on p. 124; and Prudentius, p. 267.

instance the most splendid example of the present day set by the famous Paulinus, who by abandoning great wealth and following Christ had been almost unique in these times in fulfilling the gospel precepts. *He* was the man we should follow! *he* was the man to imitate! he would exclaim; and the present age was happy in possessing such a pattern of faith and virtue, since, as the Lord advised, he, though rich and possessing much, had by selling all and giving to the poor, made possible by his example what was impossible[1]." We have seen Sulpicius did as much, and most people will prefer him at once as a robust character and a pleasant writer.

For this brings us to his literary work, and throughout it runs the glad note. Sin might sadden him, and bishops worry him, but the dominant character of his work is its joyousness and brightness. A gentle humour plays about it ever and again, and grace and delicacy are its constant marks. For it seems established that the cheerfullest and sunniest of men are those who for a great cause make a great renunciation. So through Sulpicius, as through Prudentius, we find a vein of quiet happiness, whatever their subject, in striking contrast with the unhappiness and violence of so much of the heathen literature of the Empire. In the pages of Montalembert's *Monks of the West* we find very much the same glowing joyousness, for the author, if he had not the critical qualities that make a historian, was in love with his subject and caught the spirit of the early Gallic monasticism. The same note, but with the historical gift, marks Sabatier's *Francis of Assisi*.

Sulpicius' prose style is admirable for its ease and fibre[2]. The schools had taught him Cicero and Virgil, and he had assimilated more than their roll and cadence. Ausonius, Paulinus and Symmachus had had the same training, had learnt and loved the same authors, and they wrote smoothly and fluently enough, but their work is very bloodless—they say nothing, and they say it with infinite meandering. Sulpicius is the well-girt writer; his style follows his theme, is earnest, playful or impassioned with his

---

[1] *V. Mart.* 25. It was polite of Sulpicius to write this of his friend, who returns the compliment by perpetually professing to be a very poor creature by comparison. *E.g. Ep.* v. 7: Sulpicius blazes *septena Domini candelabra*, while Paulinus is *sub modio peccatorum*. The jumble of scripture is characteristic of Paulinus.

[2] Jerome (*Ep.* 125, 6) speaks of the high state of education in Gaul. His correspondent, Rusticus, was, however, sent on to Rome *ut ubertatem Gallici nitoremque sermonis gravitas Romana condiret.* Cf. Claudian, *iv. Cons. Hon.* 582 *Gallia doctis civibus.*

thought, never draggles, never wearies. Here and there slips in a
happy phrase from Virgil, with the utmost aptness and naturalness
—the snake charmed by the lads of an Egyptian monastery *quasi
incantata carminibus* caerula colla *deposuit* (*Dial.* i. 10, cf. *Aeneid*
ii. 381). Of Martin's preaching we read that he groaned in spirit,
infremuit nec mortale sonans *praedicabat* (*Dial.* ii. 4, cf. *Aeneid* vi.
50). Once more, he bids Postumian on his return to Egypt to find
somewhere on the shore the grave of Pomponius, *ac licet* inani
munere *solum ipsum* flore purpureo *et suave redolentibus* sparge
graminibus (*Dial.* iii. 18, cf. *Aeneid* vi. 885)[1]. Once he quotes a
line of Statius without precisely naming him—*utimur enim versu
scholastico, quia inter scholasticos fabulamur*[2]—much as a modern
might in conversation quote a line of Shakespeare more for play-
fulness than because of a rigid relevance. Remarkable too, as
instancing his care for the purity of his vocabulary, is his apology
for the verb *exsufflare*, which he must use though *parum Latinum*
to express his thought[3].

The excellence of his style is remarked by most of his critics,
M. Boissier finding in him the typical charm of French literature,
but the criticism of Gibbon will help us best to the next point for
consideration. He alludes to the narration of "facts adapted to
the grossest barbarism in a style not unworthy of the Augustan
age. So natural," he continues, "is the alliance between good
taste and good sense that I am always astonished by the contrast[4]."
Sulpicius has indeed an almost unbounded credulity. It must be
recognized, before we judge him, that modern science is, after all,
very modern, and that while we are emancipated from much crude
superstition to-day, much still remains in odd corners of minds by
no means uncultured, and that after all it is possible to pay too
high a price for the extinction of superstition. At all events we
must judge Sulpicius by the standard of his time, and, not to go
back to Tacitus and his phoenix and Vespasian's miracle, so sane a
man as Ammianus has a wistful regret for portents "which occur
still but are not noted," while a century or so later Zosimus, the
bitter critic of Christianity, can seriously attribute the decay and

---

[1] Cf. also *V. Mart.* 22 and *Aeneid* vii. 338.
[2] *Dial.* ii. 10. Does he mean an "example" from a grammar?
In one of his letters (xxii.) Paulinus rallies him about Virgil, citing a letter
of his ending with a Virgilian quotation (*Aen.* iii.) and giving at length another,
a very racy one about a cook for the monastery, where he uses the Plautine *lar*
for "home."
[3] *Dial.* iii. 8.
[4] *Decline and Fall*, iii. p. 376 n.

decrepitude of the Empire to the neglect of Constantine to hold the
secular games.   These men were heathens.

There are not wanting signs that men of his day found some
of Sulpicius' stories hard to believe.   We have one notice of a
man who told St Martin himself that "what with empty superstitions and ridiculous delusions he had come to dotage and
madness," but as a brace of devils were seen chuckling and ejacu-
lating "Go it! Brictio!" to encourage him, we may discount this
critic's views[1].   More important is another passage in the third
book of the *Dialogue*[2], where Sulpicius interrupts his narrative with
a little piece of apologia, which, if it somewhat mars the art and
verisimilitude of the piece, illuminates the character of the author.
A good many (*plurimi*) are said to shake their heads (*nutāre*) about
what has been said in the second book.   "Let them accept the
evidence of men still living and believe them, seeing they doubt my
good faith.   But if they are so very sceptical, I protest they will
not even believe them.   Yet I am astonished that any one who has
even a faint idea of religion would be willing to commit such a sin
as to think any one could lie about Martin.   Far be such a suspicion
from any who lives under God; for Martin does not need the support
of falsehood.   But the truth of the whole story, O Christ!
I pledge with thee, that I have not said nor will say anything but
what I have either seen myself or learnt on good authority,
generally from Martin himself.   But even if I have adopted the
form of a dialogue, that variety in my story may prevent monotony,
I profess I am religiously making truth the foundation of my
history.   I have been obliged at the cost of some pain to make this
insertion on account of the incredulity of some people......Believe
me, I am quite unstrung and beside myself for pain—will not
Christians believe in those powers of Martin which devils acknow-
ledged?"   This inset makes the conclusion of the piece remind us a
little of Virgil's wounded snake in its rather unsuccessful attempt to
proceed as if nothing had happened, but it has its value.   With
other passages it establishes Sulpicius' honesty.   It is therefore
worth while to consider how it is he can believe so much that is
incredible to us.

I have said, we must allow for his living in a very unscientific
age, an age, too, when the refined scepticism of Roman society
in Cicero's day and the blatant atheism of Lucian and his kind

[1] *Dial.* iii. 15.   [2] *Dial.* iii. 5.

had been made well-nigh impossible by that reaction toward faith, which is seen in Neo-Platonism, in the rapid spread of Christianity and in the general revival of religion which began in the second century and was so pronounced in the third. Men were ready to believe much, and where this is the case, there is actually less tax upon credulity. For there is a certain amount of evidence that some diseases, mainly of the mental or hysterical order, may be cured by the exercise of faith in the sufferer. Nothing helps a patient very much who firmly believes he is going to die, whose mind is made up to it, and the converse is true too. Let the sick man conceive the belief that the practitioner or the saint can cure him and is doing it, and in some cases this belief will cure him. But for this Notre Dame de Lourdes and Ste Anne de Beaupré in Quebec might earn less gratitude. Now Martin was an ignorant man, though a man who had great power with men in virtue of his character and personality, and he believed he could heal disease by prayer and faith, and that this faculty was but the fulfilment of Christ's promises. Sulpicius says, and it is not improbable he is presenting Martin's view, as well as his own, that to doubt these miracles of healing, etc., is to diminish the credibility of the gospel, "for when the Lord himself testified that such works as Martin did were to be done by all the faithful, he who does not believe Martin did them, does not believe Christ said so[1]." Perhaps the logic is not above suspicion, but it is clear that it was held Martin's miracles were proven no less by the words of the gospel than by ocular evidence. Thus Martin believed he could work miracles, and no doubt he did effect cures, and he had a strange influence over men and animals, which to-day might be called hypnotism, or some such fine name, and was then called miracle. If Martin's evidence was not enough, there was the witness of the people healed. While we may admit they were the better for his treatment, we have no kind of guarantee that their diagnosis of their own maladies was at all more likely to be sound than the pronouncements of ignorant people on their complaints to-day. To an untrained observer, however, the evidence of the worker of the miracle and the subject of it, supported by the inherent probability of its happening in view of what the gospel said and the reflexion that it might very well happen in any case, would be overwhelming. We may then pronounce some of the miracles to be actual instances of cures effected, and some to be cures of imaginary diseases,

[1] *Dial.* i. 26.

some the results of mere coincidence, some the ordinary everyday
order of events, and all greatly coloured by ignorance and childlike
faith[1].

Visions[2] are more easily explained as they depend on the
evidence of an individual and neither require nor obtain corroboration. Ignorance again will explain some, and overstrung nerves
others, while emotion and a touch of poetry or a tendency to
imagery will help in nearly every case. In many of Martin's
visions a certain spiritual insight is implied. For example, on one
occasion the devil appeared to Martin at prayer, attired in purple
with diadem of gold and gems, and boots wrought with gold, with
serene countenance and glad mien, and proclaimed himself to be
Christ descended from heaven and rewarding Martin with the first
sight of himself. The Saint was silent. "Martin, why hesitate to
believe when you see? I am Christ." "No," said Martin, "the
Lord Jesus did not say he would come with purple or diadem.
I will not believe Christ has come, unless it be in the garb and
form under which he suffered, unless he bear upon him the marks
of the cross (*stigmata crucis*)." Thereupon the devil vanished.
Here his asceticism helped him; but at the same time it should be
remembered that the millennium and the second advent were much
in the thoughts of Martin and his school. To this, however, we
must recur.

It may be regretted that Sulpicius on turning to the religious
life should have taken as his guide so rude and untrained a thinker
as Martin, rather than some more cultured man like Augustine.
But we must realize that it is by no means unusual for men of
refinement and education to be fascinated by the unpolished
directness and rough vigour of a leader, a prophet, from among
the people. Apart from this however, there is little doubt that
Martin with all his limitations was the best and most spiritual,

[1] George Fox (1649) at Mansfield-Woodhouse quieted an insane woman by
speaking to her. "The Lord's power settled her mind and she mended," when
a doctor and many people about her, "holding her by violence," had failed.
"Many great and wonderful things were wrought by the heavenly power in
those days; for the Lord made bare his omnipotent arm, and manifested his
power to the astonishment of many, by the healing virtue whereof many have
been delivered from great infirmities, and the devils were made subject through
his name; of which particular instances might be given, beyond what this
unbelieving age is able to receive or hear." It may be added that America
swarms with groups of "Christian Scientists," "mind-healers," "faith-healers,"
and the like, who achieve cures of disease now and then by means they only
partly understand, and then generalize with an extraordinary and pathetic
courage.
[2] *Vita Martini*, 24.

the most practically and consistently holy, of the Christian leaders of Gaul; and manliness and godliness are perhaps after all not outweighed by ignorance of physical science[1].

If Sulpicius is not to be followed in his opinions on medicine and nature, in his judgments of men he is sterling and sound. He saw the great man under the uncouthness of Martin, and he realized how terribly lacking were others among the bishops of Gaul. Like his master, he is fair-minded and fearless. Let us take three examples. Into the great controversy about Origen and his orthodoxy, we need not go. It was in the East one of the burning questions of the day, utilized for political ends by the unscrupulous Theophilus, a successor to Athanasius in the see of Alexandria. It crops up in Postumian's account of his Eastern travels in the *Dialogue,* and whether we say Sulpicius is putting his own views into Postumian's mouth or publishing Postumian's idea in his own work, the conclusion, which is reached after independent study of the books in question, is that, whatever the authorities may say, while there is some doubtful teaching in them, there is undoubtedly much that is good and useful.

Again, when he reviews the life and character of Maximus the British usurper who slew Gratian, and after some five years of Empire (383–388) was overthrown by Theodosius, Sulpicius is remarkably careful to give him credit for good qualities which men were not concerned to discover in a fallen rebel. He was "a man whose whole life deserved honour, had it been possible for him to refuse the diadem set upon his head by the soldiers in mutiny, or to abstain from civil war; but Imperial power (*magnum imperium*) cannot be refused without danger nor upheld without arms[2]." This is a most just criticism, and in it is the explanation of much of the history of the third and fourth centuries. Many a man had in self-defence to embark on civil war. It was a necessity of military despotism.

Elsewhere[3] he says, that while Maximus "had done many fine acts he was not enough on his guard against avarice, except that

---

[1] Philostratus' *Life of Apollonius of Tyana* has marvels and miracles far beyond Martin's, and Macrobius' wonders of science (*Sat.* vii.) reveal what men educated in the physics of the day could and did believe. I do not know that either falls much short of St Alphonso Liguori's *Glories of Mary*, published in English not so long ago with the commendation of Cardinal Manning.

[2] *Dial.* ii. 6. This judgment curiously coincides with that of Orosius vii. 34, 9 *Maximus vir quidem strenuus et probus et Augusto dignus nisi contra sacramentum per tyrannidem emersisset.* Contrast Ausonius, p. 121, n. 3.

[3] *Dial.* iii. 11.

the necessities of monarchy, in the exhaustion of the treasury by
former rulers and his own immediate expectation of civil war ever
impending, afford an easy excuse for his providing support for his
power in any and every way."

Maximus had a great regard for Martin, and his queen was
really extravagant in her admiration of him This was seen in
the strange affair of Priscillian, where once more the fairness and
reasonableness of Sulpicius appear. Priscillian was the founder
of a small sect, of a Gnostic type, Sulpicius says. In 1885 the
German scholar Schepss discovered a manuscript of the fifth or
sixth century, containing some treatises and other matter, which,
though anonymous, he and other scholars attribute to Priscillian
himself. For the first time the heretic has been heard on his own
account, and the reader may be referred to his works in the Vienna
Corpus, vol. xviii., and to the monograph of Friedrich Paret. Our
present concern is rather with the civil than the theological significance of the story, and with the attitude of Martin and Sulpicius
toward the heretics[1].

Two bishops had joined Priscillian and had consecrated him.
But the bishops of Spain and Gaul set themselves to bring about
the extinction of the sect by persecution and the sword. The
matter was brought to the Emperor Gratian who issued an edict
against the new sect. Priscillian made overtures for an interview
with Damasus and Ambrose, but when neither of them would see
him he got a court official, Macedonius, to use his influence and
have the edict withdrawn. The death of Gratian followed in 383,
and in 384 a synod of Burdigala (Bordeaux) condemned Priscillian,
who took the unusual step of appealing to the new Emperor. The
case came to Maximus and the bishops cried for the surety of blood.
Here Martin intervened—it was enough, he said, and more than

---

[1] St Augustine, *Ep.* 237, deals with the sect's false scriptures, and especially
with a hymn supposed to have been spoken by Christ. This hymn is to be
found entire in the *Acts of St John*; see M. R. James, *Apocrypha Anecdota*,
2nd series. I quote the fragments Augustine cites:

salvare volo et salvari volo:
solvere volo et solvi volo:
......generari volo:
......saltate cuncti.
plangere volo, tundite vos omnes:
ornare volo et ornari volo:
lucerna sum tibi, ille qui me vides:
janua sum tibi quicumque me pulsas:
qui vides quod ago tace opera mea:
verbo illusi cuncta et non sum illusus in totum.

enough that they had been pronounced heretics by the bishops and
driven from the churches: it was a cruel and unheard of sin that a
secular judge should hear an ecclesiastical case[1]. He won a promise
from Maximus that no blood should be shed, "but afterwards the
Emperor was depraved by the bishops and turned away from milder
counsels," and Priscillian and others were put to death. That
some of these people, the earliest examples of Christians slain by
Christians for opinion's sake, were women, a professor's widow and
daughter from Bordeaux, excited great indignation[2]. It would seem
that Maximus, like another usurper in France, was bidding for the
support of the Church[3].

The bishops were successful and now thought of going further
and having a commission sent to Spain to arrest and try heretics.
The assize would have been a bloody one, for their leader Ithacius
was a man, says Sulpicius, with no moderation and nothing of the
saint about him, extravagant, talkative and gluttonous. "He had
reached such a pitch of folly as to be ready to include under the
charge of Priscillianism all holy men, who had either a love of
reading or a habit of fasting." The *studium lectionis* as a mark of
heresy might pass for a phrase of Erasmus. Elsewhere he says it
was clear that scant distinctions would be made, as the eye was
a good enough judge in such cases, for a man was proved a
heretic rather by his pale cheeks and his poor raiment than by his
belief[4].

Martin once more appeared—deeply grieved for the crime
committed, anxious about the crime preparing. He would not at
first communicate with the bishops, whom he not unjustly regarded
as guilty of Priscillian's murder, but when Maximus made his
communion the price of the stoppage of persecution he gave way.
But he felt he had lost spiritual power by so doing, as he had
previously done by being consecrated bishop, and thereafter he kept
studiously away from every gathering of bishops. Ambrose also
broke off all connexion with Ithacius and Ursacius.

Now throughout this strange story it is remarkable how clear
and definite is Sulpicius' judgment. He has no sympathy with
Priscillian's views, far from it, but he is moved to horror and indignation by the conduct of the bishops. Maximus in some measure

[1] *Chron.* ii. 50.
[2] Cf. Pacatus, *Paneg. Theod.* 29, cited on p. 111.
[3] Richter writing in 1865 drew an elaborate parallel between Maximus and
the eldest son of the Church. (See Hodgkin, *Italy and her Invaders*, i. 443.)
[4] *Dial.* ii. 4.

he excuses, and he points out that "not only was the heresy not crushed by the killing of Priscillian, but strengthened and spread further. For his followers, who had formerly honoured him as a saint, afterwards began to worship (*colere*) him as a martyr. The bodies of the slain were taken back to Spain, and their burial celebrated with great pomp, and to swear 'by Priscillian' was counted the most binding of oaths. But amongst the orthodox (*nostros*) there blazed a ceaseless war of quarrels, which after fifteen years of dissensions could not yet be ended." All, he says, is confusion as a result of the quarrelling, the lust and the greed of the bishops, and "meanwhile the people of God and every good man are treated with shame and mockery[1]." So in the thirteenth century "the priest," says Sabatier, "is the antithesis of the saint, he is almost always his enemy."

We may now pass to a short review of the works of Sulpicius, which fall into two divisions—his writings on St Martin and his Chronicle.

The *Chronicle*[2] is an epitome of Scripture history, supplemented by a rapid survey of the ten persecutions of the Church (a numeration for which he is one of the earliest authorities), a glance over the Arian controversy and a rather fuller account of the Priscillianist troubles. It is plain that the interest of the work grows greater toward the end, for an epitome will generally lack freshness. But in this case there are one or two things to be said. First of all, the epitome is written in Sulpicius' usual style. It is clear and lucid, and though short and concise does not give too strong an impression of scrappiness. There is something of a classical flavour here and there, and it strikes one as odd to read of Jacob's burial, *funus magnifice curatum*, or of Moses', *de sepulcri loco parum compertum*. The phrases somehow do not suggest the Pentateuch. He has a keen eye for chronology, on which he is at issue with Archbishop Ussher to the extent of some sixteen centuries[3]. After repeated difficulties with one figure after another in his authorities he concludes: "I am sure that it is more likely

---

[1] *Chron.* ii. 51.

[2] This is the only work of Sulpicius precisely dated. He brings his work to a conclusion in Stilicho's consulship, 400 A.D. (ii. 9 *omne enim tempus in Stiliconem direxi.*) Martin's life and the first letter seem to have been written before Martin's death, which was sixteen years after his second visit to Maximus. Maximus reigned from 383—388, but must have left Gaul *about* 386. Reinkens puts the publication of the *Life* after Martin's death, that of the *Dialogue* in the year 405, supposing Sulpicius to have died shortly after the year 406.

[3] *Chron.* i. 40.

that the truth has been lost by the carelessness of copyists, especially when so many centuries have intervened, than that the prophet should have erred. Just as in the case of my own little book I expect it will befall that, by the carelessness of those who transcribe it, things will be spoiled about which I have not been careless." He keeps his story wonderfully clear of typology, only once, I think, going so far as to remark a type, Deborah, it seems, being a prefigurement of the Church. Where necessary, he reinforces his story with material from secular historians, though he is careful to explain that he regards their standing as very different. In this way he has preserved for us a passage of Tacitus, otherwise lost, on the destruction of the temple by Titus. He makes some shrewd remarks on the effect on Christianity of the destruction of Jerusalem by Hadrian, and the resultant removal of the servitude of the Law from the freedom of the faith and of the Church.

It is remarkable how abruptly he passes from Isaiah[1], merely mentioning his name, while he recommends the careful study of Ezekiel, whose prophecy is "magnificent, for the mystery of things to come and of the resurrection was revealed to him[2]." But when he comes to Daniel he devotes to him a number of chapters and gives an interesting interpretation of Nebuchadnezzar's dream. In the feet of iron and clay was foretold the Roman Empire which is to be divided (*dividendum*) so as never to cohere again. "This has even so come to pass, for the Roman world is not administered by one Emperor, but by several who are always quarrelling by war or faction. Finally the mixture of clay and iron, whose substances can never cohere, signifies the destined incompatible intermixtures of mankind, for the Roman territory is held by foreign tribes or rebels, or is handed over to them when they surrender and make what passes for peace, and we see in our armies, our cities and provinces admixtures of barbarous nations, chiefly Jews[3], who dwell among us but do not however adopt our ways. And the prophets tell us that this is the end." He complains that men will not

[1] St Augustine confesses that he too, at least before his baptism, found Isaiah too hard, *Conf.* ix. 5, 13. *Verum tamen ego primam hujus lectionem non intelligens, totumque talem arbitrans, distuli repetendum exercitatior in dominico eloquio.*
[2] *Chron.* ii. 3.
[3] See authorities quoted by Seeck in an interesting note in his *Gesch. des Untergangs der Antiken Welt*, p. 328, ll. 30, 31; note Salvian, *de gub. Dei*, iv. 14, 69, there cited, for an attitude toward Syrians in Gaul closely like that taken in America toward the Jews. Add Rutil. Namat. i. 383—396. It is one of the most astonishing things to realize how many Syrians and Armenians, apart from Jews, go to the New World to make money by peddling and return to Asia.

believe in those parts of the vision which still remain to be fulfilled, in spite of the fulfilment of it all so far. I have spoken before of the millenarism of the school of Martin and this is one more instance of it.

The *Chronicle* had a curious fate, for after the invention of printing it was used as a manual of history in schools for a century and a half, and at one time incurred the ignorant suspicions of the authorities of the Index[1].

His other writings deal mainly with St Martin. His *Life of Martin* is a model of biography though it has too many marvels for the taste of to-day[2]. He supplemented it with three letters on his great leader, and from these we learn that it was written before Martin's death, which comes upon us as a surprise ; for one would never judge from its style that its subject was living. It may indeed have been revised, but this is mere conjecture.

In the *Dialogue* he continues the same subject, though he prefixes to it an account of the monks of Upper Egypt. The interlocutors are three—himself, Gallus, a Gaul from the North, and Postumian, like himself an Aquitanian. Postumian begins with the story of his travels, how he sailed to Carthage and worshipped at St Cyprian's tomb, how bad weather gave him a glimpse of a curious little Christian community of shepherds in the desert, how he went to Alexandria when the famous quarrel about the Tall Brothers was at its height, and thence how he went to Bethlehem and stayed with St Jerome, and to the deserts of the Thebaid and saw all manner of holy men. Some of his tales are a little saddening. When obedience is carried to such a pitch that one foolish man at the bidding of another will spend two years in carrying water a mile to water a walking-stick, one feels there is some fundamental error in the system. The holy man, who lived alone on Mt Sinai for years and years, and by God's blessing did not know he was naked, who ran from his fellow men, and when at last

---

[1] Symonds, *The Renaissance in Italy*, vol. vi. p. 221, "Sigonius, a Vatican student, was instructed to prepare certain text-books by Cardinal Paleotti. These were an ecclesiastical history, a treatise on the Hebrew commonwealth and an edition of Sulpicius Severus. The manuscripts were returned to him, accused of unsound doctrine and scrawled over with such remarks as 'false,' 'absurd.' "

[2] Even Paulinus deviates into relevance (*Ep.* xi. 11) to say of this *Life: historiam tam digno sermone quam justo affectu percensuisti. Beatus et ille pro meritis qui dignum fide et vita sua meruit historicum.* The *Life* was done into hexameters in the 5th century by Paulinus of Périgueux, and in the 7th by Venantius Fortunatus. Probably the original prose will be preferred by most readers.

he deigned a word to one explained that angels will not visit him
who dwells with other men, might, I am afraid, to-day be counted
as merely insane. The pleasanter tales tell of wild beasts tamed
and making friends with solitary hermits, though one fears that
the tale of the grateful lioness who sought a holy man's aid to give
sight to her blind cubs, and presented him a day or two later
with the skin of some rare animal, may seem to fall short of
probability.

When Postumian's travels are told, Gallus tells of St Martin
and manages to eclipse point by point the marvels of the desert
with the miracles of Gaul. It has been remarked that these stories
are put by Sulpicius into the mouth of his Celtic friend as if with
the intention of suggesting that they are not to be taken quite
literally, but his digression in the third book (to which I have
alluded) seems to make this view impossible.

One of the most interesting things in the *Dialogue* is the naïve
account of the wonderful success of the *Life of Martin*[1]. It was
Postumian's "companion by land and sea, his fellow and comforter
in all his pilgrimage," and he found it before him wherever he went.
Paulinus had introduced it to Rome, where it sold like wildfire
to the vast delight of the booksellers. It was already the talk of
Carthage when Postumian got there. At Alexandria nearly everybody knew it better than Sulpicius himself. It was spread all over
Egypt, and Postumian brought a request from the desert for a
sequel. Sulpicius hopes that the *Dialogue* may do as well as the
Life[2].

Several general features remain to be remarked in the works
of Sulpicius. To his belief in miracles and visions I have already
referred. With this, I think, we should associate his millenarian
views. They too seem to be due to St Martin. It is a curious
thing how often a belief in the speedy return of Christ goes with
a revival of the religious life, a Nemesis one might perhaps say of
literalism, almost of materialism, shadowing the development of the
spiritual.

His earliest reference to the subject is in the *Life of Martin*.
A false prophet, Anatolius by name, appeared in Gaul[3], and another
simultaneously in Spain. The latter began by being Elias and then

---

[1] *Dial.* i. 23. Paulinus in one of his letters (xxix. 14) tells how he read the
Life to the very saintly lady Melania and others. The lady was much interested
in lives of holy men.
[2] *Dial.* iii. 17.   [3] *V. Mart.* 23.

proceeded to be Christ, and actually got a Spanish bishop to admit his claim and worship him as God[1]. Sulpicius continues, "A good many brethren also told us that at the same time there had risen in the East a person who proclaimed that he was John. From all this we may conjecture, when so many false prophets appear, that the coming of Antichrist is at hand, and that he is already working in them the mystery of iniquity."

The whole of this line of thought betrays at this early date as ever since the influence of the books of Daniel and Revelation, and in point of fact Martin and Sulpicius were nearer the original than their successors, for they realized that Nero was portended by the latter book[2]. Martin said that Nero would subdue ten kings and become Emperor in the West, Antichrist in the East. Each would start persecution, Nero in the interests of idolatry, Antichrist seemingly of Judaism, for he was to rebuild the Temple[3], enjoin circumcision and claim worship as Christ. There was to be civil war between them, as so often between West and East, and Nero should fall and Antichrist reign, till the man of sin should be crushed by Christ's coming. Antichrist was in fact already born, had reached boyhood even, at the time of Martin's speaking, eight years before Sulpicius wrote his *Dialogue*, "so take thought how near at hand are the things men dread as still in the future[4]."

In the *Chronicle*, Sulpicius says less, perhaps because more was unfitting *in hoc tam praeciso opere*. All he says is that Nero was "a very fitting person to inaugurate the persecution of Christians[5], and perhaps he will yet be the last to carry it out, for it is believed by many that he will come in person before Antichrist[6]." But we need not go further into the subject, for the dangers of the interpretation of prophecy are obvious, and there is little pleasure to be derived from the contemplation of the errors and eccentricities of good men.

---

[1] *V. Mart.* 24.

[2] For stories of false Neros see Tacitus, *Hist.* i. 2; ii. 8, a pretender about the year 70; and Suetonius, *Nero*, 57, apparently another twenty years later. Dio Chrysostom, *Or.* xxi. 10 (*de Pulchritudine*) οἱ δὲ πλεῖστοι καὶ οἴονται (that Nero lives), καίπερ τρόπον τινὰ οὐχ ἅπαξ αὐτοῦ τεθνηκότος, ἀλλὰ πολλάκις μετὰ τῶν σφόδρα οἰηθέντων αὐτὸν ζῆν.

[3] Is this a far away memory of the Emperor Julian's attempt to rebuild it?

[4] *Dial.* ii. 14. Jerome on Ezekiel xxxvi. (Migne, col. 339 B) alludes to these views—δευτερώσεις, a Jerusalem of gold, the restoration of the Jews etc., as lately upheld by *Severus noster in dialogo cui Gallo nomen imposuit*.

[5] Cf. Tertullian on Nero, *Apology* 5. *Sed tali dedicatore damnationis nostrae etiam gloriamur*, etc.

[6] *Chron.* ii. 28.

I have alluded more than once to the ill-will between the monks
and the bishops which was not lessened with time, though ever and
again a monk was made a bishop. Sometimes like St Martin he
would remember his calling, but not always, for Sulpicius has much
to say about monks losing their heads on being ordained or consecrated, and conceiving passions for building, for maintaining great
establishments and travelling with ease and magnificence with
multitudes of horses and servants[1]. Again and again he protests
against luxury and display and more serious vices among the
bishops and clergy. They have forgotten, if they ever knew, that
Levi received no share in the land of Canaan; at least one would
suppose so from their eagerness for acquiring property in land[2].
Prudentius says much the same, only more ingeniously, for by a
little anachronism, involving a century and a half, he puts into the
mouth of a dead and gone persecutor the words

> *et summa pietas creditur*
> *nudare dulces liberos*[3].

But worse still was their habit of consorting with spiritual
sisters[4]. This was no new story, and perhaps it will never be old.
Cyprian long ago had written against the practice, and Jerome
fulminated against it still. He was himself the friend and adviser
of many women, and many of his letters to the nun Eustochium
and other ladies survive[5]. There seems to be a perennial fascina-
tion about the clergy for spiritually-minded women, but surely,
Sulpicius felt, monks have renounced feminine society and nuns
masculine. Scandals occurred oftener than so strait a school cared
to see them, and we find it told with pride how Martin but once in
his life allowed a woman to minister to him. But "as the grammarians
do, we must consider place, time and person[6]," and it was the queen
of Maximus and her husband was present. One very scrupulous

[1] *Dial.* i. 21.
[2] *Chron.* i. 23. *Non solum immemores sed etiam ignari.* Note his conclusion
as to the meaning of their rapacity; *quasi* venalem *praeferunt sanctitatem.*
[3] *Steph.* ii. 83—4.
[4] Two Councils at least in the 4th century condemned this consorting with
syneisaktoi and agapetae. The 3rd Canon of the Council of Nicaea, and the
27th of Elvira both forbid it. "Spiritual brothers" and "sons" are mentioned
by Gregory of Nazianzus and Jerome. See Dale, *Council of Elvira*, p. 200. On
the better aspects of this matter the reader may consult Sabatier's interesting
chapter on St Clara in his work on St Francis of Assisi.
[5] *Nosti puellares animos his rebus plerumque solidari, si se intelligant curae
esse majoribus,* he says (*Ep.* 7, 4)—a very worthy reason for very extraordinary
letters to be written to a girl of seventeen or eighteen.
[6] *Dial.* ii. 7.

virgin point-blank refused to see Martin himself, for though thaumaturge and bishop it could not be disguised that he was after all a man[1]; and Martin praised her for her modesty. Well indeed might Gallus say that if we were all like Martin, we should not so much discuss the *causas de osculo:*—"But after all we are Gauls[2]."

One mark of the monastic movement was its new relation with nature, a new interest in birds and beasts, a new love for them. Pet birds and dogs the old heathen world had known, but now man and animal met on more equal terms of freedom, and we read already of wolves and lions who were friends of the Egyptian monks. Martin, himself, does not seem to have been intimate with any animal, still we hear of him saving a hare from some hounds, and there is a curious parable from nature recorded, not, it must be said, a very happy one. The seagulls that flew up the Loire and caught the fish were, he said, a type of the powers of evil seeking the human soul. It reminds one of Bunyan's *Book for Boys and Girls*, and its odd expositions of natural things. On the sacred trees of the heathen Gauls Martin waged relentless war, hewing them down by grace of miracle in spite of protest.

We now come to the last story told of Sulpicius, which, I should say, I find strong reason for doubting. Sulpicius, as we have seen, renounced the world and its allurements to become a monk, to live the life best adapted, as men thought then, to the quest of holiness. The thought of sin was often in his mind, his life in fact was a hand to hand battle with sin. Now in the west, among men of his own blood, rose a teacher with a new doctrine of sin—Pelagius. It may seem odd to find a Celt, a British Celt, with a Greek name, but we find quite a number of Greek names among the Gallic and Spanish monks in Sulpicius' pages[3]—Eucherius, Euanthius, Aetherius and Potamius, and a Briton Pelagius was. Into Pelagianism we need not enter, but certain features should be remarked. Faith is not enough to save a man; it must be reinforced by works, by conduct, by watchfulness; and a man's will-power, aided by grace (which is

---

[1] On the other hand when Martin slept in a vestry of the church at Claudiomagus, on his departure there was a rush (*inruerunt*) of virgins into the room, to kiss the spots where he had sat or stood, and to divide up the straw on which he had lain. *Dial.* ii. 8.

[2] *Dial.* ii. 8.

[3] The Celt carried his fancy for a little Greek so far, that in Irish MSS. we are apt to find stray Latin words written in *Greek* character. The Greek names may, perhaps, be illustrated by the habit native converts in India have of giving their children English names.

won by his good inclinations), and supported by good works, may
secure him a pure life, not indeed free from temptation, but from
sin.   Underlying all this there was to begin with a protest against
the worldliness and evil living of professing Christians, though the
logical outcome of the system was really to underestimate sin.   But
for the time it was urged that a low standard was not inevitable ;
the highest was attainable, if proper means were taken.   The proper
means meant the monastic life generally.

This view of the possibilities of Christian living was a monk's,
a Celtic monk's, and from what we have seen of Sulpicius, it will
not be altogether surprising to read in Gennadius that he adopted
Pelagius' position[1].   Millenarism and an over-hasty idea of achieving
sinlessness not uncommonly go together and it may be that Sulpicius
became a Pelagian.   Gennadius wrote a refutation of the heresy,
which is lost, and he might be supposed to know who were its leading
adherents.   He adds, however, that Sulpicius ultimately realized he
had made a mistake and renounced his error, and in his repentance
abjured speech for ever, "to expiate by silence the sin he had
contracted by speech."   Whether we believe all this to be true or
not[2] depends on whether we accept Gennadius' story, but it must be
admitted it is not inherently impossible.   It would be sad to think
of this most genial and gentle of men ending his days in the agony
of remorse and silence, but even if he did, it does not lessen the
value of his delightful works.   Probably, however, the story is a
mistake, the invention of stupidity.

Reviewing the life of Sulpicius, it may seem to us strange that
a man of good family and culture should so surrender himself to the
guidance of a man his inferior in everything society valued, should
surrender above all his judgment and accept so much that would
appear contrary to reason, to sense and to experience.   Yet, after
all, it is not a very rare phenomenon.   Our own day has seen a

[1] Gennadius, *Vir. Ill.* 19.
[2] More and more I incline to think that this story—*silentium usque ad
mortem tenuit*—is, after all, a mere misunderstanding of Paulinus' phrases
*confugisti ad pietatis silentium ut evaderes iniquitatis tumultum. Mutescere
voluisti mortalibus ut ore puro divina loquereris et pollutam canina facundia
linguam Christi laudibus et commemoratione ipsa pii nominis expiares (Ep.* v. 6).
Gennadius mentions (c. 49) that Paulinus wrote *ad Severum plures epistulas,*
nor is this his only allusion, and he obviously depends for all his other statements on these letters and on Sulpicius himself.   List-making is a poor trade,
and such a blunder is not very improbable.   Paulinus Petricordius (of Périgueux)
a contemporary of Gennadius (469—490) who did Severus' *Martin* into an epic
of six books, speaks of him with admiration, but no hint of this story.   See
Book v. (1052 c, Migne).   Reinkens, without discussing the origin of Gennadius'
story, dismisses it as untrue.

similar renunciation of everything by a man of letters, a member of the English House of Commons, who at the word of one he believed inspired of God, left all to work on a farm and sell strawberries on a train, still retaining a buoyant cheerfulness. Whatever we may make of his teaching, we cannot but respect the spirit of Laurence Oliphant.

It may, however, be said, that while Sulpicius' problem is the constant problem of mankind, his solution is not satisfactory. Though many things in his day made it attractive to men of a religious temper, it none the less rested eventually on a fundamentally false philosophy, a wrong explanation of the world, the old Oriental mistrust of matter and of the body. Over and over again since Sulpicius' day this mistake has been exposed, error, as Augustine says, proving in all sorts and kinds of strange ways its own punishment, revolting against its own consequences and exposing itself. But if the monastic solution of the problem of holy living will not satisfy mankind in the long run, it must not be forgotten that a debt of gratitude is due to the men who had the nobility of character to venture all on the experiment. That it failed proves their judgment was unsound, but it does not affect the fact that they thought such an experiment worth while.

CHAPTER XIII

PALLADAS

O wedding-guest! this soul hath been
Alone on a wide, wide sea;
So lonely 't was that God himself
Scarce seemed there to be.

THE great note that distinguishes Christian from heathen
literature is its fundamental gladness. On the surface it may
seem sad at times;

hora novissima, tempora pessima;

but there is a deep-rooted consolation in the thought, terrible
though it be, that follows;

imminet arbiter ille supremus.

This at least implies distinctions drawn between what is good and
what is bad, a moral supremacy in the world of One who is of
purer eyes than to behold iniquity, and therein the value of life and
of holy life. The absence of any certainty that life has a permanent
value is the canker at the heart of heathenism.

It is hard to understand aright the heathenism of the Roman
world. It calls for sympathetic treatment, if we are to read its
spirit as well as its words. Underneath its varying moods is the
same weariness, the same restlessness, that shews itself to-day under
moods very similar. There is the quest for certainty which is
not to be found. In reason some men sought it and their conclusion was an uncertainty that grew more and more uncertain and
unhappy. Others turned to religious revival and looked to Cybele,
to Isis, to Mithras, to any god and every god, and found perhaps
more comfort than the others, but hardly, if they thought, more

certainty.   It is worth while to study these lines of inquiry in some
typical minds, until in Palladas at the end of the fourth century we
reach the final conclusion to which Greek thought came.

The Latin poets of the last century B C. are so largely influenced
by Greek thought, and the Latin habit was so commonly to look to
results rather than to follow methods, that we can gauge by the
words of the Roman much of the thought of the world.

Lucretius preaches with fervour the wisdom of Epicurus.   The
gods have no existence, except as shadowy beings who live afar,
as little concerned with us as men in an undiscovered island.
There is no hell, no hereafter.   No man need shudder at death,
since in death he will not feel the loss of wife or children, for he
will be resolved into elements, which will immediately recompose
into something else, something quite distinct from the man they
lately formed.   Hence with no higher powers above him, and no
future world before him, man can rid himself of that religious dread,
which spoils and poisons all his happiness.   He can dismiss the idle
terrors of death and enjoy life.   This was on the whole a dangerous
theory.   It was one thing in the mind of Lucretius, but quite
another in the more commonplace minds around him.   If it was
not to lead to mere self-indulgence, more self-control and more
thought were required than were possible for ordinary people.
But there were other considerations of perhaps even more importance.

For there is another side to all this.   If a man die, he is free
from desire to see his dear ones, but what of them?   Theirs is
"the pain of finite hearts that yearn."   Tennyson remarks that no
poem of farewell to the dead written to-day can have the terrible
pathos of Catullus'

> atque IN PERPETUUM *frater ave atque vale.*

In perpetuum!   If we are to be merry, we must have no brothers,
then, or not feel it if they die.   Yet who would not rather choose
"the poet's hopeless woe"?

In Horace we find the thought of death as constantly introduced
as in *The Earthly Paradise.*   How far Lucretius directly influenced
him, this is not the place to discuss, but it was upon the Epicurean
theory that Horace lived—on the whole.   He is not consistent.
He is for enjoying the present, but his views of enjoyment undergo
a change, and as he grows older and his pleasures purer, he seems to
grow less satisfied with himself and his theory of life.   He betrays a

sense of failure; effort and all a man can do for himself are not enough, and placid and clean Epicureanism proves inadequate.

Contemporary with these men were Virgil and Tibullus, who have a good deal in common. Tibullus harks back to the gods of the countryside. Speculation may have its charms for others, they are not for him. He will stand quietly and gladly in the old ways, very largely insensible to the currents of philosophic thought. But Virgil is a greater mind. His is a greatness that grows on the reader who will read him much and with love. He had been caught by the spell of Lucretius, by the glory and majesty of the knowledge of Nature and her ways—

felix qui potuit rerum cognoscere caussas—

he too loved the quiet life that Horace sang, but he knew the sorrows of the human heart even better than Catullus knew them. Ever and again we hear the note of sorrow in his music, of sorrow that will not be assuaged though Pallas or Lausus, Creusa or Dido be resolved into insensate atoms, each instinctively swerving in search of others to combine with to form another fortuitous concurrence, which shall have to learn the same gamut of woe to as little purpose. Life after all involves more than atoms. It carries with it deep seated affections and tender yearnings, which must either imply the reunion of Dido and Sychaeus, of Anchises and Aeneas, or else wrap man's existence in deeper and blacker sorrow. Before the eyes of Love hovers

ipsius umbra Creusae,

and the poet turns from the cold and really, if not superficially, loveless life Lucretius required, and exclaims

fortunatus et ille, deos qui novit agrestes.

It is the revolt of the feelings of the man against the logic of the thinker—significant as coming from a disciple, who was also a sufferer and a poet. This testimony of heathenism (one can hardly write the word of Virgil) to the unsatisfactoriness of Epicurus' godless atoms is remarkable.

It is not surprising to find, when a Virgil revolts, that for common people atheism was inadequate. It appeals indeed to man at his lowest—Ovid was probably an atheist—but let the recollection of better things come to the voluptuary and he casts his atheism aside for devotion. Sacrifice, lustration, initiation and all

kinds of ritual flourished alongside of the atheism of the early
Empire.

As time went on, the sadness of heathenism deepened. Lucan
may be glib enough and prove by an epigram that the fall of the
Roman republic means the non-existence of gods[1], and Persius may
be quite happy in a young and innocent life with the view that all
that is needed is effort and purity follows, without much reference
to heaven. But the second century saw the pendulum swing away
from atheism into superstition. The world was growing too unhappy to be atheist, and the gods came back from exile and brought
strange friends with them[2]. Their votaries had cast them out, and
now recalled them and "kissed again with tears." Some might
mock, but most worshipped, and among the doubters were devotees.
Three great names stand out in literature at the century's end,
Lucian, Marcus Aurelius and Apuleius.

Lucian, a Syrian Greek of Samosata, was a scoffer in grain. He
might be serious at times, but never reverent. His position was
sceptical. There were riddles of life, but no man could ever guess
them—why try? The gods were excellent butts for flippant wits,
and nearly as good were the philosophers, the preachers and teachers
who would not practise what they taught others. His humour is of a
type not unfamiliar to-day. To jest at the scriptures and wittily to
insinuate that a teacher of Christianity is probably a hypocrite,
possibly a rogue or certainly a fool, may still please some minds.
It is not very fresh by now, but perhaps in Lucian's day it was more
novel; perhaps, too, such mirth had a shade more truth about it.
Still I feel that they exaggerate who attribute much weight to
Lucian and his school in the downfall of paganism. Flippancy is
not so fatal to a Pantheon as moral dissatisfaction, and in so
religious an age Christianity grew because it offered men a higher
ideal itself, and not because scoffers laughed at the ideas of God
and Truth and every other thing that made for righteousness.

Perhaps the most read book of the age is the diary of Marcus
Aurelius—in many ways the saddest of all books. Its manliness
and purity, its high ideals and earnestness, make more pathetic that
haunting uncertainty and want of rest, which one feels throughout
it. The theory of life is so obviously only a working hypothesis,

[1] See vii. 454.
[2] Chassang, *Histoire du Roman*, p. 400: "Vers le premier siècle de l'ère
chrétienne, la fureur de la magie s'empara de tout le monde païen." Compare
the works of Philostratus, especially his *Apollonius of Tyana*, and Lucian's
Lover of Falsehood and *Alexander*.

unverifiable at best. Whenever doubt clouds religion, men will turn
to Marcus and see in him perhaps the highest level reached by the
religious temper that seeks truth but cannot be sure of finding it.
He is no atheist, no sceptic perhaps, but he looks for heavenly
guidance and is not conscious of receiving it, and so he makes his
own way sadly as well as he can. Yet from the story of his life we
learn that this thinker, this speculator, emancipated as we might
suppose him from common weakness, sacrificed perhaps more than
any other Roman Emperor. If he was not to attain light from the
gods, it was not to be for want of asking it. So doubt and devotion
went hand in hand in sadness.

Apuleius in after days passed for a magician; indeed men
accused him of magic while he lived, but I mention him in order to
compare his immortal book with one of Lucian's, one at least attributed to Lucian by many people. The *Golden Ass* (a much better
title than the *Metamorphoses* and one which has St Augustine's
sanction) is either modelled on Lucian's *Lucius, or the Ass*[1], or more
probably both are drawn from a common source. Both deal with
witchcraft, and introduce us to a hero, Lucius, who by meddling with
a sorceress' boxes transforms himself into a donkey and in this form
has a series of wonderful adventures. The *Golden Ass* follows one
by one the episodes of Lucian, enlarging and digressing very
admirably, and giving us a wonderful panorama of provincial life,
its humours, comedies, tragedies, and above all its perils. There
are woven into it stories after the manner of Boccaccio[2], and of
the *Hundred Mery Tales*, adventures with brigands and soldiers
alike dangerous to honest folk, the exquisite tale of Cupid and
Psyche, and in a word *quidquid agunt homines Asini farrago libelli*.
But the significant thing is that at the end Apuleius entirely departs
from Lucian. In Lucian the human donkey runs into a procession
by accident and, finding a priest carrying roses, eats them and is a
man again. In Apuleius he escapes to the sea-shore and delivers
himself of a long and careful prayer to a goddess of many names and
prays her for release. She comes to him in a dream, and acknowledges his prayer, telling him that the many names are indeed all
her own, but her truest name is Isis, and she directs him to meet the
procession, when the priest, instructed by her in a similar dream,

---

[1] See Chassang, *Histoire du Roman*, pp. 401, 402.
[2] The tale of the cooper, for example, is common to Apuleius and Boccaccio.
How far does such a fact affect the value of such tales as evidence of the
manners and morals of an age?

will tender him the roses. So it befalls, but while Lucian ends his
story with one more obscene incident to cap all, Apuleius shews us
Lucius a converted character, intent on nothing but initiation and
undergoing no less than three special introductions to the Mysteries
as a mark of divine favour. And what did he learn by it all? "I
approached the confine of death; I trod the threshold of Proserpine;
I was borne through all the elements and returned. At midnight
I saw the sun flashing with fair light. The gods of the lower world
and the gods of the world above I drew near unto, and I adored
them from close at hand[1]." So ends in initiation and divine
revelation the most amusing, the most brilliant and the most
Aristophanic of all books in Latin.

This is significant. There were instincts in man too strong and
too profound to accept a negative conclusion or no conclusion at all
to the great quest. Lucian might mock, and Marcus hesitate; the
mass of men must believe something. The pity of it was that they
found nothing better to believe in than Isis and Mithras.

We are apt to forget how much paganism was left in the fourth
century. It was not clamorous but quiet and content as a rule to
be left alone. There were some writers, honest heathens, who said
nothing one way or another about their tenets. Others found their
interest in gentle retrospect and old association, their faith a
sentimental cherishing of ancestral tradition. But the stronger
spirits went further, and were absorbed and illumined by a
revived, or rather perhaps a new, heathenism, different in many
ways from the old heathenism of Greek and Roman, different too
from that of Phrygian and Egyptian. It appealed to the individual
as did the latter, but otherwise, for it went deeper than lustration
and sacrament. It was a faith that appealed to reason, emotion
and imagination, a blend of everything congruous or incongruous,
philosophy, theosophy, mysticism, magic, ritual, trance, asceticism,
what not. One of the most conspicuous of the adherents of this
new religion is Julian, the more faithful an exponent of it for not
being an original thinker. He betrays clearly what we feel must
have had a great deal to do with the revival from long before—the
influence of Christianity. His grand scheme of the Catholic Church
of Hellenism has been discussed elsewhere. Its failure was the
death-knell of heathenism. The latest and grandest of all attacks
on Christianity was a fiasco, and thinking men must have realized
it. And so they did; and in the unhappy Palladas we have one

[1] Apuleius, *Met.* xi. 23.

who saw the old order pass away giving place to none, and his bitter hopelessness is the last dark mood of dying heathenism. Its consolations were gone. The exhilarating atheism of Lucretius, weighed and found wanting by Virgil, was impossible. The moral enthusiasm of Persius, unconscious of weakness, and the moral purpose of Marcus, painfully aware that he is not sure of anything, were out of the question for the Alexandrian scholar, who could find no base to build on and would not build without a base. Apuleius and Julian might draw comfort from Isis and from Mithras, but Palladas could not find support in gods who could not support themselves. As for Lucian's flippant scepticism, the times forbade it. Sceptical a man might be, but the burden of life was too heavy for flippancy. So it may repay us to study for a little the work of Palladas.

In the Greek Anthology, that wonderful garland of the flowers and weeds of fifteen centuries of literature, his is one of the most frequent names, so frequent indeed as perhaps really to affect the colour of the whole. An epigram among the Greeks was at first an inscription, and, as almost anything might be inscribed, it came to designate roughly anything written in verse, whether in one line or a dozen, dealing with any and every conceivable subject. Hence in the Anthology, beside inscriptions for tombs, for statues and paintings, and dedicatory verses for shrines, we have a highly miscellaneous collection of criticisms of life and literature, remarks on Providence, Chance and the vagaries of Destiny, "quips and cranks and wanton wiles," jibes, flouts and sneers of every type of humour and sometimes of no humour at all. The earlier epigrams have the calm equipoise of all Greek art, rhythm and thought in harmony; but as we come to later writers, the epigrams tend more and more to resemble those of the Romans, who set the fashion for ourselves, and held that an epigram like the apocalyptic scorpion should wear its sting in its tail. Naturally a degeneration set in, when poetry yielded place to point and pun, and the epigram was gradually abandoned by the poet to the versifier.

Palladas[1] has been called, rather cruelly, *versificator insulsissi-*

---

[1] I only know of one allusion to Palladas in ancient literature. An epigram of a conventional character exists, in which the writer gently deprecates being compared with Palladas (or Palladius, as the exigencies of verse require). I think it will be seen from the epigrams to be quoted that neither in virtue of his inspiration nor his music was Palladas the man to found a school. Is it impossible that Claudian, a fellow-citizen and contemporary of his, means Palladas, when he writes *Sic non Tartareo furiarum verbere pulsus | irati relegam carmina grammatici*?

mus. He is partly to blame for this, even if it is a little hard. On the same subject he will make epigram after epigram, though his theme be at best as trivial as his lines. His verse is apt to be lumbering, and he will repeat the same thought without adding materially to the force of its expression. Somewhat lacking in grace, he does not always achieve point, and sometimes when he does the point is poor. Yet Palladas must and will be heard. We have one hundred and fifty of his epigrams, and we have no reason to believe that these were all he wrote, yet of them we might sacrifice a half or two-thirds without any substantial loss.

The greater number of these little poems deal with one subject, and the spirit in which he writes of it, his savage insistence, and the terrible humour with which he clothes and reclothes his one idea in one startling garb and another, gloomy and grim, command attention for him. The melancholy and the misery of life, the vanity and vexatiousness of things are his constant burden. Of all Greek writers he is most like Theognis. We must bear in mind however that it is not always easy to say for how much of the work that bears his name Theognis was responsible. And at all events Theognis, whatever he may have disbelieved, had a saving faith in gentlemen, in birth and breeding, which may not be so satisfying a faith as some, but has fine elements nevertheless. Palladas had not that faith; possibly there were not many Greek gentlemen left in the fourth century. Over and above his atheism he has a highly developed disbelief in man.

Society in Alexandria in Palladas' day is perhaps best known to the English reader in Kingsley's novel *Hypatia*. If heathenism was exhausted and had nothing to offer the weary soul, Christianity as a spiritual system could hardly have been attractive when presented by such men as the bishops Theophilus and Cyril. When honest heathen thought ill of Athanasius, what can they have thought of his successors? and if the rulers of the Church were such, what was to be expected from officials like Orestes? and there were worse men than Orestes, as we may read in the pages of Ammianus Marcellinus.

Hence we need not be surprised at the tone of Palladas about society, about great men and their toadies. Rulers with pleasant manners, he says, are generally thieves; and honest rulers generally have nasty manners[1]. Gold is a terror to possess, and anguish not

---

[1] *Anth. P.* ix. 393.

to possess[1]. The rich are insolent, and if they deviate into politeness their compliments—dinners[2], presents or what not—are usually
the refinement of insult. Zeus himself, if he were poor, would be
treated with outrage. There is just a possibility that Palladas may
have been soured by waiting in vain for promotion. At any rate an
epigram speaks of years of wretchedness and literature, and the
final descent into Hades of a Councillor of the Dead. Did
promotion come too late to be enjoyable? the point is a small one and
does not greatly matter. The main thing is, that society was rotten.

Palladas was a grammarian, a student and a teacher of the
ancient literature of Greece, still every whit as precious and
absorbing as it had ever been. It is astonishing to us to realize
what delight men took in the form, quite apart from the spirit, of
Greek literature. Now Palladas does not seem to take delight in it
at all. A man may—many men do—lament the miseries of a
profession freely chosen and not really distasteful; it is a form of
humour, perhaps of modesty; but at all events the scholar and the
artist are apt to take a joy in their work, to feel enthusiasm for
what they are doing, and what other men have done before them.
In no republic is there so much loyalty as in that of letters, but it
is difficult to discover in Palladas a line that implies delight in his
work. One or another of his epigrams about it may well be ironic,
but the general impression is of a yoke borne without much love.
Here and there he speaks of selling his books[3], for Syntax is the
death of him—not an unpardonable feeling surely—but we find him
out when he deals with Homer. Even here he displays no feeling
for the greatest of Greek poets. He uses him freely, and abuses
him as freely. His great discovery is that Homer was a misogynist.
Circe points a moral to keep good company[4], and the general gist of
both *Iliad* and *Odyssey* is that woman is a failure.

> All women, good or bad, are snares,
> All deadly, Homer's self declares:
> Men die for Helen's sin: like waste
> Attends Penelope the chaste.
> Thus springs from woman, good or bad,
> An Odyssey, an Iliad[5].

[1] *Anth. P.* ix. 394.　　　　[2] *Anth. P.* ix. 377, 484, 487.
[3] *Anth. P.* ix. 171, 175.　　[4] *Anth. P.* x. 50.
[5] Πᾶσαν Ὅμηρος ἔδειξε κακὴν σφαλερήν τε γυναῖκα,
σώφρονα καὶ πόρνην ἀμφοτέρας ὄλεθρον.
ἐκ γὰρ τῆς Ἑλένης μοιχευσαμένης φόνος ἀνδρῶν,
καὶ διὰ σωφροσύνην Πηνελόπης θάνατοι.
Ἴλιας οὖν τὸ πόνημα μιᾶς χάριν ἐστὶ γυναικός·
αὐτὰρ Ὀδυσσείῃ Πηνελόπη πρόφασις.　　*Anth. P.* ix. 166.

Women provoke Palladas, or perhaps he is only jesting. Still one feels he jests too much and with tools of too sharp an edge. The married grammarian comes in for several epigrams, generally as the husband of a shrew. Perhaps this is the best of them:

> An Iliad of wrath I read;
> An Iliad of wrath I wed;
> Too much of wrath for one poor life,
> Wrath of Achilles, wrath of wife[1].

Woman is the anger of Zeus[2]—given to man in wrath, to balance the blessing of fire[3]. Zeus himself has a sad life of it with Hera, and has had to kick her out of heaven more than once; Homer tells us that.

One more epigram and we can leave that wearisome *Iliad*.

> Achilles' wrath, to me the direful spring
> Of beggary, I a poor grammarian sing.
> Ah! would that wrath, ere I starvation knew
> Had with those other Danaans slain me too:
> That Helen and Briseis both might be
> Rapt from their lords, I came to beggary[4].

A *non sequitur*, but what of that? There is many a *non sequitur* in misery.

Before passing on to his more general reflexions on life, it may be well to give a few instances of his humour when he is in a lighter mood. Even here he does not lack a certain pungency, nearer perhaps to Martial than to the Greeks of the earlier days when epigrams were at their best.

---

[1] Μῆνιν οὐλομένην γαμετὴν ὁ τάλας γεγάμηκα,
κ αὶ παρὰ τῆς τέχνης μήνιδος ἀρξάμενος.
ᾤμοι ἐγὼ πολύμηνις, ἔχων τριχόλωτον ἀνάγκην,
τέχνης γραμματικῆς καὶ γαμετῆς μαχίμης.
Anth. P. ix. 168.

[2] *Anth. P.* ix. 165.

[3] *Anth. P.* ix. 167. Cf. also x. 55 and 56 on the woman question and note the almost brutal bitterness of the line εἰ σώφρων ἐστὶ γυνή τις ὅλως.

[4] Μῆνις Ἀχιλλῆος καὶ ἐμοὶ πρόφασις γεγένηται
οὐλομένης πενίης γραμματικευσαμένῳ.
εἴθε δὲ σὺν Δαναοῖς με κατέκτανε μῆνις ἐκείνη,
πρὶν χαλεπὸς λιμὸς γραμματικῆς ὀλέσει.
ἀλλ᾽ ἵν᾽ ἀφαρπάξῃ Βρισηΐδα πρὶν Ἀγαμέμνων
τὴν Ἑλένην δ᾽ ὁ Πάρις πτωχὸς ἐγὼ γενόμην.
Anth. P. ix. 169.

I chid my belly for foul treason,
And made it list to words of reason;
Belly below and mind atop—
Why can't their foolish wrestling stop[1]?

A happy thought, not ill put perhaps, but very far from the high-water-mark of Greek poetry. It lacks grace and shews the heavy hand of the versifier. Here is another rather neater.

Daphne the snub-nosed Memphis danced,
And Niobe danced he;
A stock indeed his Daphne was,
A stone his Niobe[2].

The joke was however common property, such as it was. The following has a little more originality.

So lazy is Pantaenetus that he
In fever prayed he never more might rise;
He bettered, though, and "Thence we all may see
"In Heaven's deaf ears," he vows, "no succour lies[3]."

He looks out on life, takes a broad survey of it—its starving teachers, rich churls, villain rulers, successful murderers[4] and quarrelsome wives—its freaks, its topsy-turveydoms and general irrationality, and his conclusion is irritation, disgust and unhappiness. The only power worth considering is Chance or Fortune, a feminine personification with every feminine vice as he loves to emphasize.

[1] Νηδὺν ἀναίσχυντον στιβαροῖς ἤσχυνα λογισμοῖς,
σωφροσύνῃ κολάσας ἔντερον ἀργαλέον.
εἰ γὰρ ἔχω τὸν νοῦν ἐπικείμενον ὑψόθι γαστρός,
πῶς μὴ νικήσω τὴν ὑποτασσομένην;
Anth. P. ix. 170.

[2] Δάφνην καὶ Νιόβην ὠρχήσατο Μέμφις ὁ σιμός,
ὡς ξύλινος Δάφνην, ὡς λίθινος Νιόβην.
ib. xi. 255.

[3] Οὕτως ἔστ' ἀργὸς Πανταίνετος, ὥστε πυρέξας
μηκέτ' ἀναστῆναι παντὸς ἐδεῖτο θεοῦ.
καὶ νῦν οὐκ ἐθέλων μὲν ἐγείρεται, ἐν δέ οἱ αὐτῷ
κωφὰ θεῶν ἀδίκων οὔατα μεμφόμενος.
ib. xi. 311.

[4] *Anth. P.* x. 53, If murderers thrive—well! Zeus rules, and he would have murdered Kronos, had Kronos been a mortal. But cf. ix. 378, a murderer saved by Serapis from a falling wall for the gibbet.

Nor rhyme nor reason tyrant Fortune knows;
　Mere random whims dispose her vagrant course;
Bad men she leans to and the good o'erthrows—
　The more to flaunt the might of senseless force[1].

Our life's a slave that runs away,
　And Fortune is a courtesan;
We needs must laugh to see their play,
Or else must weep to mark alway
　The worthless is the happier man[2].

Life is the toy of Fortune, and can tell
Of piteous change; now all goes ill, now well;
　Some like a ball come down and then go up,
And some have fallen from the clouds to hell[3].

Life is a dangerous voyage; storm-winds fling us
　Where worse than shipwrecked mariners we lie;
Chance, the one pilot of man's life, will bring us
　Chance knoweth where as o'er the seas we fly.
Some meet good weather; others ill have found;
All make the common anchorage underground[4].

And if all these cheerful statements are true? What can a man
do in a world where forethought is waste of time?

Get riches, and what then? the coffin's lid
　The company of thy coffer will forbid;

---

[1] Οὐ λόγον οὐ νόμον οἶδε Τύχη, μερόπων δὲ τυραννεῖ
　τοῖς ἰδίοις ἀλόγως ῥεύμασι συρομένη.
μᾶλλον τοῖς ἀδίκοισι ῥέπει, μισεῖ δὲ δικαίους,
　ὡς ἐπιδεικνυμένη τὴν ἄλογον δύναμιν.
　　　　　　　　　　　　　　　Anth. P. x. 62.

[2] Ἂν μὴ γελῶμεν τὸν βίον τὸν δραπέτην
　Τύχην τε πόρνης ῥεύμασιν κινουμένην,
ὀδύνην ἑαυτοῖς προξενοῦμεν πάντοτε
　ἀναξίους ὁρῶντες εὐτυχεστέρους.
　　　　　　　　　　　　　　ib. 87.

[3] Παίγνιόν ἐστι Τύχης μερόπων βίος, οἰκτρός, ἀλήτης,
　πλούτου καὶ πενίης μεσσόθι ῥεμβόμενος.
καὶ τοὺς μὲν κατάγουσα πάλιν σφαιρηδὸν ἀείρει,
　τοὺς δ᾽ ἀπὸ τῶν νεφελῶν εἰς Ἀίδην κατάγει.
　　　　　　　　　　　　　　ib. 80.

[4] Πλοῦς σφαλερὸς τὸ ζῆν· χειμαζόμενοι γὰρ ἐν αὐτῷ
　πολλάκι ναυηγῶν πταίομεν οἰκτρότερα·
τὴν δὲ Τύχην βιότοιο κυβερνήτειραν ἔχοντες,
　ὡς ἐπὶ τοῦ πελάγους ἀμφίβολοι πλέομεν·
οἱ μὲν ἐπ᾽ εὐπλοΐην, οἱ δ᾽ ἔμπαλιν· ἀλλ᾽ ἅμα πάντες
　εἰς ἕνα τὸν κατὰ γῆς ὅρμον ἀπερχόμεθα.
　　　　　　　　　　　　　　ib. 65.

Add wealth and time subtract; and what remains?
Life not an hour the longer for thy pains[1].

Is it not the same lesson that we learn from Omar?

Some for the glories of this world and some
Sigh for the prophet's Paradise to come;
Ah! take the cash and let the credit go,
Nor heed the rumble of the distant drum.

Taking the cash and letting the credit go commonly means eating
and drinking, especially drinking, and so Palladas teaches.

Eat thou and drink, and shut thine eyes to woe;
Belike the dead no stomach-ache will know;
Twelve children buried, Homer lets us see,
Her appetite was left to Niobe[2].

Why toil in vain and strive against the star
    That marked your birth with its controlling presence;
Give way and quarrel not with things that are—
    Accept your fate in silent acquiescence—
Or rather catch at joy; be your employment
To steal a march on Fate and taste enjoyment[3].

If this course of life is a failure, there is always death to fall
back on, and once death is passed there is no sorrow left[4].

Living in Alexandria Palladas must have been in constant
contact with Christians—and such Christians! Riotous monks and
courtier bishops were not the best preachers of the faith, but one

---

[1] Πλουτεῖς, καὶ τί τὸ λοιπόν; ἀπερχόμενος, μετὰ σαυτοῦ
   τὸν πλοῦτον σύρεις, εἰς σορὸν ἑλκόμενος;
   τὸν πλοῦτον συνάγεις δαπανῶν χρόνον· οὐ δύνασαι δὲ
   ζωῆς σωρεῦσαι μέτρα περισσότερα.

Anth. P. 60.

The triple pun of the Greek I am afraid I have failed to represent.

[2] Ἔσθιε πῖνε μύσας ἐπὶ πένθεσιν· οὐ γὰρ ἔοικεν
   γαστέρι πενθῆσαι νεκρόν· Ὅμηρος ἔφη.
   καὶ γὰρ ὁμοῦ θάψασαν ὀλωλότα δώδεκα τέκνα
   σίτου μνησαμένην τὴν Νιόβην παράγει.

ib. 47.

The reference is to the *Iliad* xxiv. 602 Νιόβη ἐμνήσατο σίτου.

[3] Τίπτε μάτην ἄνθρωπε πονεῖς καὶ πάντα ταράσσεις
   κλήρῳ δουλεύων τῷ κατὰ τὴν γένεσιν;
   τούτῳ σαυτὸν ἄφες, τῷ δαίμονι μὴ φιλονείκει·
   σὴν δὲ τύχην στέργων, ἡσυχίαν ἀγάπα.
   μᾶλλον ἐπ᾽ εὐφροσύνην δὲ βιάζεο, καὶ παρὰ μοίρην
   εἰ δυνατὸν ψυχὴν τερπομένην μετάγειν.

ib. 77.

[4] *Anth. P.* x. 59.

feels here and there in his work a hint of some knowledge of Christianity. For example; everything that lives can feel anger, and may not I with an angry word requite him who does me an ill deed[1]? Again, he hints at possibilities after death, and his language, though it may be called vague, seems to recall Christian eschatology. Body, suffering of soul, Hades, burden, destiny, fetters and tortures;—and then freed from the body to face an eternal God—φεύγει πρὸς θεὸν ἀθάνατον[2]. God he takes to be a philosopher, not promptly angered by blasphemy, but taking his time to prepare punishment for bad and tiresome men. What again does this mean?

> Weep not, nor faint: how short a life we know!
> Short beside that to be, there's no denial;
> Till the worm breed and to the grave you go,
> Break not your spirit, while as yet on trial[3].

Add to these indications his very plain-spoken epigram on the monks. We read of communities of them in the Thebaid two or three thousand strong. Well may he ask, "If solitaries (μοναχοί), why so many? So many, how solitaries[4]?"

In 391 the Christians led by the Archbishop and the Governor destroyed the Serapeum at Alexandria, the most famous and sacred of temples[5]. The tables were turned. Palladas has one or two mysterious epigrams on the superlative folly of not being friendly with the favourites of God, which of course may be taken in more ways than one, but this on seeing an image of Hercules thrown out somewhere is noteworthy and unmistakable.

> On the cross-roads I saw Jove's brazen son,
> That once had worship but his day seems done;
> "Ah! guardian god!" in bitter rage I say,
> "So long unconquered thou art fall'n to-day!"

---

[1] *Anth. P.* x. 49.   [2] *Anth. P.* x. 88.

[3] 'Ρίπτε γόους, μὴ κάμνε, πόσον χρόνον ἐνθάδε μίμνων,
    ὡς πρὸς ἐκεῖνον ὅλον τὸν μετὰ ταῦτα βίον.
    πρὶν τοίνυν σκώληκα βαλεῖν τύμβοις τε ῥιφῆναι,
    μὴ δαμάσῃς ψυχὴν ζῶν ἔτι κρινομένην.
                                        Anth. P. x. 78.

[4] *Anth. P.* xi. 384. The references to Judgment to come might be Neo-Platonic.

[5] See Rufinus, *E. H.* ii. 22—24; Socr. v. 16, 17. On the threatening fall of paganism in Egypt, the Latin translation of Hermes Trismegistus (ed. Bipont. Apul. vol. ii. pp. 307—309) may be consulted.

By night he came to me and smiled, "My friend!
"Know, to the tempest ev'n a god must bend[1]."

Enough commentary is supplied by the epigram on the Olympian
dwellers at Marina's house who have turned Christian and need
fear no melting-pot or bellows[2]. Gods were melted down and
became very common articles in those days, as an epigram shews,
the sense of which is clear though the text is corrupt.

> A smith, a most discerning man,
> Turns Love into a frying-pan.
> Why 'most discerning,' you inquire?
> How close are frying-pan and fire!

With gods turning into pots and pans, men may well bow to the
tempest, but it will hardly make them happy to do so. When
Palladas sees the muddle of life, his conclusion is "hatred of everything," μισῶ τὰ πάντα, and, whether he refer to a Greek or a
Christian Providence, he sums all up so:

> If care will avail you, then care and prepare;
> But why care for yourself though, if Providence care?
> Yet 'tis Providence makes you or care or forbear,
> For Providence cares that you've cares and to spare[3].

His one enthusiasm was oddly enough for a woman. Hypatia,
the more famous daughter of the philosopher Theon, was one of the
most conspicuous figures in Alexandria. A Platonist of the school
of Plotinus, she lectured publicly, and pupils gathered from every
quarter. She mingled freely with the rulers, and for her splendid
dignity all men respected and feared her. She was a great friend
of Orestes the prefect, and in Church circles they said she kept him
from making friends with Cyril the bishop. Some hot-heads, led
by one Peter, a reader, conspired, watched for her, tore her from her
chariot and dragged her into the Church called the Caesareum. They

---

[1] Τὸν Διὸς ἐν τριόδοισιν ἐθαύμασα χάλκεον υἷα,
τὸν πρὶν ἐν εὐχωλαῖς νῦν παραριπτόμενον.
ὀχθήσας δ' ἄρ' ἔειπον· 'Αλεξίκακε τρισέληνε,
μηδέποθ' ἡττηθείς, σήμερον ἐξετάθης.
νυκτὶ δὲ μειδιόων με θεὸς προσέειπε παραστάς·
καιρῷ δουλεύειν καὶ θεὸς ὢν ἔμαθον.

Anth. P. ix. 441.

[2] ix. 528.

[3] Εἰ τὸ μέλειν δύναταί τι, μερίμνα καὶ μελέτω σοι.
εἰ δὲ μέλει περὶ σοῦ δαίμονι, σοὶ τί μέλει;
οὔτε μεριμνήσεις δίχα δαίμονος, οὔτ' ἀμελήσεις·
ἀλλ' ἵνα σοί τι μέλῃ, δαίμονι τοῦτο μέλει.

ib. x. 34.

stripped her of her raiment, and did her to death with potsherds, and then after tearing her limb from limb they picked up the fragments and burnt them. This, says the historian whom I have been paraphrasing, brought no small shame on Cyril and the Church of Alexandria, for murders and fights and the like are utterly alien to such as have the mind of Christ[1]. This was in 415 and this is the only fixed date we have in Palladas' life. "When I see thee," he says to her, "I worship thee and thy discourses, seeing that the home of the maiden is with the stars. For thy practice is with heaven, holy Hypatia, beauty of language, pure star of philosophy[2]."

Deaths like this shocked the Christian conscience and may well have deepened in men like Palladas the feeling that Chance and brute Unreason ruled the world. One is tempted to wonder whether she was in his mind when he wrote

> We are but fattened as men fatten swine,
> Death the one guest that on us all shall dine:
> Now this, now that, as he may list, he slays,
> And never recks of reason or design[3].

Hypatia's death however was not needed to shew mankind that the old order was dead. Palladas knew it and it added to his load of bitterness. We Greeks, he says, are men already burnt upon the funeral pyre: ours are the buried hopes of dead men, for all the world is upside down to-day[4]. Elsewhere he laments

> O men of Hellas, but that men still deem
> Us living, we are dead. Alive we seem,
> But, lit on such misfortune, if we live,
> Or seem, life dead, to live—'tis but a dream[5].

---

[1] Socrates vii. 15.

[2] "Ὅταν βλέπω σε προσκυνῶ καὶ τοὺς λόγους,
τῆς παρθένου τὸν οἶκον ἀστρῷον βλέπων.
εἰς οὐρανὸν γάρ ἐστι σοῦ τὰ πράγματα,
Ὑπατία σεμνή, τῶν λόγων εὐμορφία,
ἄχραντον ἄστρον τῆς σοφῆς παιδεύσεως.
                                    Anth. P. ix. 400.

I sometimes wonder whether ix. 508 may not also be addressed to Hypatia.

[3] Πάντες τῷ θανάτῳ τηρούμεθα καὶ τρεφόμεσθα
ὡς ἀγέλη χοίρων σφαζομένων ἀλόγως.
                                    ib. x. 85.

[4] *Anth. P.* x. 90.

[5] †Ἆρα μὴ† θανόντες τῷ δοκεῖν ζῶμεν μόνον
Ἕλληνες ἄνδρες συμφορᾷ πεπτωκότες·
ὄνειρον εἰκάζοντες εἶναι τὸν βίον,
εἰ ζῶμεν ἡμεῖς τοῦ βίου τεθνηκότος.
                                    ib. x. 82.

Palladas in spirit is the last of the heathen. He had ceased to
take joy in the old, he hated the new. Life was all wrong and the
Greek world was infinitely weary. Heathen literature might throw
out branches still here and there, as a tree will throw out branches
though its roots are not healthy. Literature was at its last. The
old religion was worse than dead; it was discovered for an idle
thing. Philosophy[1], scepticism and atheism gave no comfort but
proved an apple of Sodom, and heathenism was in a word death in
life[2]. There were, as Palladas says, those who kept up a semblance
of life, pretended to be alive, dreamt they lived, but men who
thought and men who saw knew they were dead. The day of old
Hellas was done. Her inheritance passed to the Church, and part
was incorporated in the common life of Europe and part wrapped up
in a napkin till the Renaissance. Nothing of value is permanently
lost, and it is not very necessary to bewail the lost Hellenism. The
attempt to revive it, without heeding the ten centuries that had
passed, was unhappy, for the world can never be heathen again, and
all that was essential and permanent in the mind of the Greek still
lives. But none the less, if we need not sorrow over Hellenism,
they at least may claim compassion who could conceive of no other
light of life, and when it failed found themselves in the horror of
thick darkness.

[1] Even before he became a Christian, Synesius admitted that Philosophy
was in danger of dying out, unless supported by the Emperor's example; ἐπεὶ
νῦν γε, ὡς ἠμέληται, κίνδυνος ἀποσβῆναι, καὶ μετὰ μικρὸν οὐδ' ἐμπύρευμα λείπεσθαι
βουλομένοις ἐναῦσαι, though, of course, Philosophy will always flourish in heaven
(*de Regno*, 22).

[2] Probably the acme of bitterness and horror is reached in the epigram
Anth. P. x. 45. "It is good to know the truth for the truth" perhaps, but is it
all the truth?

CHAPTER XIV

SYNESIUS

οἰκεῖον ἀλήθεια Θεῷ, ᾧ διὰ πάντων ἀναίτιος εἶναι βούλομαι.

Ep. 105, 1488 A

EVERY reader of Pindar and Herodotus remembers Battus the stammerer, and how he founded the Dorian colony Cyrene, and established there a dynasty to grow rich on the products of a land with three seasons and to win chariot-races at the Pythian games. Already we can see the characteristic features of the land which are permanent in its history. A land of flocks and herds, of wheat and wine, of roses and silphium, a land of hunting, and above all a land of horses. Pindar shews us the nymph Cyrene "as she struggled alone, without spear, with a terrible lion," and Nonnus, the last great poet of the Greeks, once more calls her "the slayer of lions." As for the horses, Herodotus says, rightly or wrongly, that it was from the Libyans of this region that the Greeks adopted the four-horse chariot, and Callimachus, her great poet (cited by Strabo), calls his country "blest in her steeds" (εὐίππου πατρίδος). "Cyrene grew great," says Strabo (c. 837), writing about the beginning of our era, "by the virtue of her land; for it is the best of all lands in breeding horses and is blest in its fruits." Again in Synesius it is the same. In his youth he was scolded for "being mad for arms and mad for horses beyond what was fitting," and when he is to be made bishop he sighs to think that "his dear dogs will never go a-hunting more." Modern travellers tell us of pictures of hunting scenes still preserved in the monuments of Cyrene and of the abundant opportunities for the chase the country still offers.

The dynasty of Battus and Arkesilas passed away, and Greek democracy ran its course in Cyrene. Wars with Carthaginians and Persians ended with Persian control. Taught by experience, the

Cyrenians yielded without a blow to Alexander, and under his successors Cyrene belonged to Egypt—a doubtful blessing to the Ptolemies, for it was too far away to become one with Egypt and so near as to be a splendid vantage-ground for rebel and pretender. Prof. Mahaffy says it was a sort of Ireland to Egypt. Ptolemy Apion left the land by will to the Romans in 96 B.C. Under Augustus it was a senatorial province—a sure sign of its peacefulness.

Now another aspect of Cyrenian life comes before us. As in Egypt, so in Cyrene, the Ptolemies had deliberately encouraged the settlement of large numbers of Jews—who might develope commerce and begin denationalization In the New Testament we find the Cyrenian Jews no inconsiderable element of the Dispersion and strongly represented at Jerusalem, where they shared a synagogue with the Alexandrians. It was "a man of Cyrene" who carried the Cross. Josephus now and again refers to his countrymen at Cyrene, recording among other things how they got a charter permitting them to send freely their "sacred money" to the Temple. But the most striking episode in the Roman history of Cyrene was the rising of the Jews against Trajan, when they killed, it is said, two hundred thousand Gentiles. As the Roman forces would probably exact ample vengeance for those thus butchered, the loss in population to Cyrene must have been enormous. Whether the land suffered with the rest of the Roman Empire from the great plague, which "filled the world" under Marcus Aurelius, we are not told. In any case the depopulation from which the Empire was universally suffering (Jews excepted) was probably helped forward by this outbreak, and all hope of recovery lost.

Ammianus, speaking of the province in his day, mentions Cyrene first in his list of towns—"an ancient city though now deserted, which the Spartan Battus founded." The last blow to the town had been dealt when Apollonia, in Strabo's times its port, was made independent. The haven Phycus, of which Synesius often speaks, and where his brother lived, was insignificant, and with the trade the prosperity passed away. "Cyrene," says Synesius, "a Greek city, with an ancient and honourable name, hymned a hundred times by the wise of old; but now she is poor and downcast, a great ruin in need of the Emperor's aid, if her fortune is to be at all worthy of her ancient history" (*de Regno* c. 2).

That ancient history, ἀρχαιολογία, and the hymns of the wise were part of the consciousness of this last great Cyrenian. Pindar's poetry was only part of the retrospect. Callimachus and his successor at the Museum, the great geographer Eratosthenes, were both Cyrenians, and among philosophers Carneades, the founder of the Third Academy, and Aristippus, who gave his country's name to the Cyrenaic school[1]. The last two, curiously enough, alone are mentioned by Synesius—"the famous land of Cyrene was once inhabited by a Carneades and an Aristippus, but now by a John and a Julius" (*Ep.* 50). But the peculiar pride of Synesius was in his ancestry—"from Eurysthenes who led the Dorians to Sparta down to my father my pedigree is carved on the public monuments" (κύρβεσιν *Ep.* 57, 1393 B). Elsewhere he goes still further back—"the public monuments of Cyrene shew the succession from Herakles to me" (*Catastasis* i. 1572 B). It was no empty boast. On the eve of battle he writes to his brother, "I am a Laconian by descent and I know the message the magistrates sent Leonidas, 'Let them fight as if to die and they will not die'" (*Ep.* 113). Elsewhere he prays that such glory (κῦδος) may be given to his deeds as will befit the ancient fame of Cyrene and of Sparta (*Hymn* 5).

Two hundred and fifty years intervene between the Jewish revolt and Synesius' birth, during which we hear but little of Cyrene. Then for some fifteen years we know the land as never before, and after that we only hear now and again of its gradual downfall[2]. In 616 Chosroes invaded it and in 647 the Arabs. Its conquest by the latter followed that of Egypt as an immediate consequence, and to secure it the Greek race and Greek civilization were blotted out in accordance with Saracen policy. To-day it is occupied by strolling Arabs.

The writings of Synesius are extremely interesting. "A man of many and wandering thoughts," to use Mrs Browning's description of him[3], whatever he may be thinking about at the moment, he can express with ease and with charm. It will hardly be expected that such a man can be original or profound, but after all it is a great deal if a writer is delightful. Yet he is more than that. To

---

[1] We may also count Sabellius here. Socrates (i. 5, 2) calls him a "Libyan." On the other side, diametrically opposed to him, we may reckon Arius' two loyal bishops, Theonas of Marmarica, and Secundus of Ptolemais, Synesius' future see (Socr. i. 9, 4).

[2] Procopius tells of Justinian's attempts at restoration. He repaired the aqueducts of Ptolemais and fortified two monasteries to the south (the expression recalls Synesius' statement of his home's situation) to check the barbarian inroads.

[3] Is it Sophocles in her mind, *O. T.* 67 πολλὰς ὁδοὺς ἐλθόντα φροντίδος πλάνοις ?

the historical student he is valuable on several grounds—for the picture he gives of the Empire battling with its Goths within and more savage barbarians without[1], for the insight his letters allow into the daily life of a Roman province, its pleasures, scandals, anxieties and dangers, travel, sea-faring, business and agriculture, for his illustration of the process by which Neo-Platonism and Christianity ran into each other, for hints on the difficulties of a modest bishop and for one more example, the happiest of all, of the education and literary taste of his age. On all of these points a good deal might be said, but I shall in general confine myself to the first three, grouping what I shall have to say mainly, but not rigorously, according to the chronology of his life.

Synesius was born somewhere between or near the years 365 and 370. As neither father nor mother is mentioned as alive in any of his writings, it is assumed that they died when he was still young, leaving him and his sister Stratonice perhaps to the care of an elder brother Euoptius, for whom Synesius had always the deepest regard and affection. His boyhood, as we have seen, was a thoroughly healthy one, given over to arms and horses—to hunting in fact, the Macedonian ideal as opposed to Greek athletics. Athletes were in poor repute now, and Porphyry set them down among the stupid classes. Leisure and a "waveless" calm of disposition were Synesius' ideals from boyhood (*Ep.* 57, 1388 A), but never mere laziness or unprofitable inertia. A life without disturbance was needful for the intercourse of the soul with God. It should be distinctly understood from the outset that this was throughout his idea of religion or philosophy, for with him they are one. Confusion will be avoided if we remember that both before *and after* becoming a Christian he uses the language of Neo-Platonism almost invariably in speaking of serious things.

He went to Alexandria to study philosophy under Hypatia, to whom he was devoted ever after. Nor was she the only friend he made there, for to others of her pupils and the members of her circle he became warmly attached. To Herculian he writes that there is a special bond in the fact that "we both saw with our own eyes and heard with our own ears the true exponent of the mysteries

---

[1] It should be remarked how little he is conscious of the Western half of the Empire—few Greeks indeed were—*e.g.* he did not know that the Emperor Honorius was consul in 404 (*Ep.* 133), and though he outlived the event he gives no hint of having heard of the capture of Rome by the Goths in 410. He must however have known of it.

of philosophy" (*Ep.* 137). He also made the acquaintance of another circle, which was Christian and with which his relations were eventually to be closer. But perhaps Hypatia still came first. To her he sent his books, to have her approval before they were published (*Ep.* 154), and she alone could tempt him to leave his native Libya, where he was born and where his fathers' graves were still in honour (*Ep.* 124), though he did not leave it even for her.

From Alexandria he returned home, and very soon (about 397) was sent to Constantinople on an embassy to the Emperor to procure some remission of taxation for the "poor and downcast" Cyrene. His birth, his position as a country gentleman, and his brilliance would explain the selection of so young a man. A greater contrast than that between Cyrene and Constantinople could hardly be imagined. Here, if anywhere, leisure of mind should have been impossible.

In 330 Constantine had founded his new Rome on the Bosporus with the enforced aid of "the wealth, the labour and all that yet remained of the genius of obedient millions." Where the art of the day failed, antiquity supplied its place, and works of art were removed from the cities of Greece and Asia to adorn the capital and the magnificent buildings that studded its two thousand acres. But it did not depend on ancient art alone; it was a city of blazing splendours, splendours of Emperor and bishop and minister. But more interesting to a man of Synesius' quick mind must have been the great personages of the city—the eunuch Prime Minister Eutropius, whose picture has been drawn for ever by Claudian; the Gothic captain Gainas, sometime the agent of Stilicho in the murder of Rufinus; the Frank or half-Frank Empress Eudoxia, gorgeous in her toilets and violent in her hatreds; Aurelian, the leader of the patriot or at least anti-Gothic party, a man unlike some of his rivals in being able to mention a father who had merited and attained distinction; the new metropolitan (398), the saintly and ascetic Chrysostom, greatest of preachers and most honourable of bishops; the infamous opponent of Aurelian, whoever the man may have been whom Synesius calls "Typhos"; and last and least significant of all the Emperor, the dull, heavy-eyed and "bovine" Arcadius.

Synesius attached himself to the party of Aurelian, but three years elapsed before he secured the end for which he came—"three evil years lost to my life!" In the meantime he saw and bore his part in a series of strange movements—the fall of Eutropius[1] before the hatred of Gainas and Eudoxia, the revolt of Tribigild sustained if not suggested by his countryman Gainas, the subsequent attempt of Gainas on the capital, the exile of Aurelian brought about by Gainas and his restoration after the expulsion, defeat and death of the Goth, and perhaps the overture of the ruin of Chrysostom begun by Theophilus the bishop of Alexandria. Into all these events we need not go, but Synesius' famous speech and his mysterious book on Providence in history call for our attention.

The speech was delivered in 399 before the Emperor, when Aurelian was Praetorian Prefect. Tribigild had already revolted in Phrygia or was on the point of doing so, while Gainas was still supposed to be acting against him for the Government.

The speech itself is pronounced by Volkmann to rank with the best public speeches of the orators and rhetoricians of the period, and another critic, Krabinger, calls it his best work. But what most impresses the reader is not its ease or its grace, but its extraordinary courage. Synesius himself said of it some years later that he had harangued the Emperor with more boldness than any Greek had ever done before, and even if the speech was touched up in places by him before publication, it is clear that if it at all represents what he said his boast is well founded[2].

Is there a hearing, he asks, for philosophy, for plain, honest speech without flattery? If there is, he will discuss kingship. Who is the true king? (The Greek word used for Emperor is βασιλεύς, and odd as it may seem is echoed in the *rex* and *regius* of Symmachus[3]. This of itself shews how times had changed.) The true king is he who lives for his people's good, who realizes his responsibility as the representative, in some sort, of Divine providence, who grounds his character on piety and bids mind overthrow "the democracy of the passions" and be king within him, who will

---

[1] This and the revolt of Tribigild may also be read in Claudian's two books against Eutropius, "a very elegant and spirited satire, which would be more valuable in an historical light if the invective were less vague and more temperate" says Gibbon. But at least some of the actors are named.

[2] A number of points of contact with Claudian (*iv. Cons. Hon.*) and Julian (*Or.* ii. 86, etc.) may be noted in this speech. Perhaps something is owed by them all, directly or indirectly, to the *Cyropaedeia*, and by Synesius a little to Dio's Orations on Kingship. Julian more than the others bids the Emperor live in close relations with the divine.

[3] Claudian goes further—*nunc Brutus amaret vivere sub regno* (*Paneg. Manl. Theod.* 163, Justice herself is speaking), and *nunquam libertas gratior extat quam sub rege pio* (*Cons. Stil.* iii. 114), the last a sentiment anyone may endorse who has lived on the borders of a great republic.

be a man among men and count love the surest foundation for a kingdom. From the ideal he turns to the actual and finds it wanting. In many directions the Empire is threatened.

The conceptions of kingship have been orientalized (c. 10)[1]. "Nothing has done the Empire so much harm as the pomp and circumstance with which they surround the king as if with hierurgy and mystery." "The fear, that you may become men if you are frequently seen, keeps you close prisoners, besieged by yourselves, neither seeing nor hearing anything that may develop practical sense, with no pleasures but those of the body and of those the most sensual, such as touch and taste give,—living in fact the life of a mollusc. So long as you disdain manhood, you can never reach the perfection of manhood." The courtiers are "microcephalous," and the stupider, the better courtiers. The Emperors "are all purple and all gold, covered with gems from barbarian mountain and sea, shod with them, girt with them, hung with them, brooched with them, couched on them[2]." They are made a spectacle of all hues and colours, like peacocks, and have brought on themselves "the Homeric curse—a coat of stone." The common earth must be sprinkled with gold dust for their tread. Like lizards which will only peep out now and then in the sunshine, "you keep to your chambers for fear men should find you out to be men." The contrast between the real and the ideal is at least vivid enough.

The second great danger to the Empire is the enormous number of Goths in the army. They are untrustworthy and cannot be expected to be Roman in feeling. "Themis herself, the goddess of counsel, and the god of war I think must veil their faces, when the man in skins leads the men in cloaks, and when one of them doffs the fleece, dons the toga and takes counsel with the Roman magistrates about affairs, sitting conspicuously beside the consul perhaps, while the proper people sit below him. And when they are outside the council-chamber, it is not long before they are back into the sheepskins[3] and laughing at the toga among their clansmen, because, they say, it does not let you handle your sword easily" (c. 15). Gothic soldiers and generals in the army, Gothic slaves in the houses—how long will it be before there is an uprising—another Spartacus? No, let none but Romans serve in the army, turn out

---

[1] So Lactantius, *M. P.* 21.

[2] So Claudian, *iv. Cons. Hon.* 585 ff. *asperat Indus velamenta lapis* and so forth, but in admiration.

[3] Cf. Claudian on Alaric's council, *b. Get.* 481 *crinigeri sedere patres, pellita Getarum curia.*

the Goths and make them helots. He alone can have peace who is
strong enough to injure the man who would harm him[1].

Soldiers and money-lenders oppress the people. Taxes wear
them out, and who can help them but the king? The provincial
governors are chosen—not for their merits but for their wealth. A
man raises money somehow, buys a governorship, and looks to repay
himself. Hence the governor's residence is a shop for the selling of
justice (τὸ ἀρχεῖον δικῶν πωλητήριον c. 21)[2].

The remedy for everything lies with poor Arcadius. He must
develop his soul with philosophy, his body with martial exercises.
His troops must know him in person and not merely from his
picture. He must remit taxation in response to embassies from his
cities. He must get rid of flatterers and choose wise and experienced
advisers (Aurelian and his friends no doubt), and with their aid rise
to be an incarnate Providence.

Synesius had recognized the bad symptoms—no difficult task—
but the disease was deeper than he saw. The fault did not lie with
Arcadius, who was the creature of his environment. The easy
remedy of Synesius was therefore inadequate. Charming and fresh
as his speech was, it was too old-fashioned. It shews the old Greek
disdain for business and trade, and a thoroughly claustral ignorance
of the strength of human passions and the terrible vitality which
the parasites of a state always possess. Arcadius with a wave of
the hand is to do with the political world what Julian tried to do
with the religious—πάντα δ' ἔναλλα γένοιτο.

Events moved on, in spite of the speech. The prophecy about
the Goths came true. Gainas joined hands with Tribigild and came
near being master of Constantinople, but his plans mysteriously
miscarried. The story of it all is told by Synesius in his book on
Providence.

This is a strange work. "It is a tale of ancient Egypt. But

---

[1] One may compare the last episode of Ammianus (xxxi. 16, 8)—the
treacherous murder of all the Goths in Roman employ beyond the Taurus
by orders of a commander who had early news of the disaster of Adrianople
(378). "By this prudent plan being carried out without noise or delay, the
eastern provinces were rescued from great dangers," says the historian, with
a coolness that astonishes some of his readers. See Seeck, *Untergang der Ant.
Welt*, c. vi. "die Barbaren im Reich," esp. p. 407 notes. *Hist. Aug. Claud.* 9, 4
*impletae barbaris servis Scythicisque cultoribus Romanae provinciae...nec ulla
fuit regio quae Gothum servum triumphali quodam servitio non haberet*—this
a century before Synesius was born.

[2] Claudian in praising Stilicho is carried away and makes a strange revela-
tion; *nec te gurges corruptior aevi | traxit ad exemplum, qui jam firmaverat
annis | crimen et in legem rapiendi verterat usum* (*Cons. Stil.* ii. 116).

the Egyptians are a subtle people.   So perhaps, tale as it is, it may
riddle something more than a tale, seeing it is Egyptian.   But if it
is not a tale, but a sacred discourse, it may be better worth reading
and writing."   It is at once a philosophic romance, a demonstration
of Providence, and an allegoric picture of the present.   Taurus
king of Egypt has two sons, the good Osiris and the bad Typhos.
These represent Aurelian and his opponent, whom we only know
from here and so cannot name, and the story tells in effect the
events of 397–400 in Constantinople.   Synesius himself appears in
it as a certain person with a "rustic" breeding in philosophy, an
admirer of Osiris and more "rustic" than ever when he fell, for he
held by his fallen friend.   The first book was written at the time of
the events, and the second after the happy ending, and the whole,
the narrative of the fall and restoration of a minister, is to prove
the doctrine of Providence.

There is a providence in the fall of a sparrow, but it seems
strange to a modern reader that a matter of a minister is so
important as this.   Yet Claudian avows he felt doubtful of
Providence till Rufinus' fall re-established his faith.   A similar joy
shines in Symmachus' pages on the death of Maximinus—"it is a
pleasure to live, one does not regret having been born" (*Ep.* x. 2).
All these discussions may be taken as indications of the deep importance which the question of the origin of evil had in the thought
of the day.   It is not, why has this bad minister been allowed such
power ? but why have the many, of whom he is but one, been
tolerated by the Gods ? and, in fine, why is there evil at all in the
world ?   Synesius explains things much as Porphyry does (*de Abstin.*
ii. 39, 40).   Evil demons, says Porphyry, besides bringing plague
and drought, work through men's passions and produce wars and
factions, till (worst of all) men really believe all this misery and
confusion is due to the Best God—a mistake actually shared by
some philosophers.   As a matter of fact, Synesius explains, the
great and good Gods endow man with a certain amount of power
and set him to battle for himself, "a divine soul among demons,"
and when his power is exhausted and a fresh start required by the
confusion of the whole fabric, they will intervene in due time, but
they must not be disturbed by man on petty pretexts.   If men will
but accept this view, they will not think that the visitation of God
and the exercise of energy (ἀρετῆς) conflict.

Gainas met a miserable end, and Aurelian returned and was
made consul, so Providence justified itself.   One wonders where the

Emperor was throughout this story, for he is not mentioned. Volkmann sees in this the author's prudence, Chassang (*Histoire du Roman*, p. 295) the Emperor's insignificance, and to this latter view I incline. In any case the conspicuous absence of Arcadius is something of a comment on the speech on kingship. There is no place for him whatever in a story of his reign. There was hardly more in the events themselves.

At last a happy decision was given to the case of Cyrene, and Synesius was able to leave Constantinople, where he had made many friends and found admirers for his prose and his verse. Their opinion of him may be inferred from the great speech, which was clearly the manifesto of the party. He with them had to face serious risks in the evil days, and so acute was his peril at one time that he found himself praying in the Christian churches, Neo-Platonist as he was [1]. However his dreams brought him warnings, which enabled him to come safely through all. From Constantinople he went to Alexandria and the story of his departure is characteristic. He writes to his friend Pylaemenes thus (*Ep.* 61):

"Here is a big rug of Egyptian make, not the thing to be spread under a bed, but to be a bed all by itself. Asterius the stenographer [2] saw it and asked it of me, when I had to sleep in front of the great offices. I promised I would leave it behind for him as a parting gift. For I could not give such presents while I still had to battle with the snow of Thrace. So I send it now, for I did not leave it then. Please give it to him with my apologies, which you can support with your own testimony, if you remember the time when I left. We were having earthquakes—many in the day, and the people were falling to prayer, many of them flat on their faces, for the ground was rocking. At that, I thought the sea safer than the land—the open sea. So I started at a run for the harbour, without a word to any one, except poor Photius—and to him I only gave a shout from afar and a wave of the hand to say 'I'm off.' And he said never a word to my friend Aurelian, consul as he was, though to the assistant [3] Asterius he did make my apology. That was what befell then."

[1] He tells us so in *Hymn.* 3, 448; he prayed "in the temples to the acting gods whom thou hast crowned with angelic rays." Δρηστῆρες θεοί, active or labouring gods, *i.e.* agents of the supreme God, who, himself remote like an Emperor, entrusts activities to subordinates. Synesius is thought to mean the saints. In any case his action and his description are remarkable.

[2] The stenographers were made part of the civil service by Constantine, and grouped as we see from this letter (lower) in symmories. See *Dict. Ant.* s.v. *notarius*.

[3] Reading and translation are here alike doubtful.

The letter concludes with directions for finding the stenographer, "a Syrian, with a dark complexion and a lean face, and of average height." From Alexandria Synesius returned home to Cyrene. His brother he left in Alexandria, where perhaps he had lived since first the two of them came to study. His voyage homeward was adventurous and he has left us a lively account of it in a letter (*Ep.* 4) written to his brother on the way. It is a long letter, but I will quote part of it, as it illustrates Synesius in some of his various minds and moods as *The White Squall* does Thackeray. It shews his vivacity and his habit of playful exaggeration, but also betrays the curious influence of the sophistic training of the day in some traces of artificial simplicity and in the scholastic interpretation of the line of Homer. How far superior he is to the school can be seen by anyone who will read a page of Achilles Tatius or a so-called letter of Aristaenetus.

"We loosed from Bendideion in the early morning and barely by the afternoon passed Myrmex Pharios; and twice or perhaps three times the ship touched bottom in the harbour. That to begin with seemed a bad omen, and the wise thing would have been to leave a ship that was unlucky from the very start. But I was afraid that, if I deserted, you would all call me a coward. So

'not yet was it the hour for quaking or shrinking[1].'

Consequently, if anything happens, you will have been the death of me. And yet what was there dreadful in your laughing, if I were only out of danger? As with Epimetheus in the story—

'Forethought he would none, so had afterthought'—

so with me. I might have escaped then, but now encamped on a desert strand we sit lamenting, and turn our eyes as best we may to Alexandria and to our mother-land Cyrene—the one we had but we left it, the other we cannot reach, and we have seen and suffered what we should never have dreamed of.

"For, listen, so that you may not think it all fun either, and hear first what sort of a crew we had. The captain wished to die, he was so deep in debt. Of the crew who were twelve in all—the steersman made thirteen—more than half, and the steersman too,

---

[1] Homer, *Iliad* vii. 217, but not quite the usual text—οὔπω ἔτ' ἔσκεν for οὔπως ἔτι εἶχεν. People said Synesius had poor MSS.—a charge he admitted, pleading that they exercise the brain more than correct ones. Mr Halcomb, in his admirable article on Synesius in the *Dict. of Christian Biography*, has anticipated me in this apology for Migne's text of our author.

were Jews, a desperate race, firmly convinced it is piety to bring
about the deaths of as many Gentiles as possible. The rest—
herdsmen, ploughmen, who a year ago had never touched an oar.
And all of them, these as well as those, were crippled, every man
of them in one limb at least. As long as we were in no danger,
they joked, and called one another not by their names but by their
infirmities—Limper, Truss, Left-hander, Squint-eye. Each of them
had at least one distinction. All this gave us no slight amusement, but in the hour of need there was no more laughter about it
but wailing. We are more than fifty passengers—about a third of
us women; most of them young and pretty. But don't be jealous.
A curtain walled us off, and this of the stoutest,—a fragment of a
sail that tore a little while ago, to modest men a wall of Semiramis.
And perhaps even Priapus would have been modest, if he had been
sailing on Amarantus' ship—to such an extent did he never give
our fears of extreme peril a chance to rest.

"As soon as we were past your temple of Poseidon, he hoisted
all sail and made for Taphosiris[1] and tried for Scylla, which even
in pictures we abhor[2]. When we saw this and cried out, though
not before we were within a hair's-breadth of danger, at last and then
only under compulsion he reluctantly gave up the idea of a naval
engagement with the shoals. So turning the ship about, as if
repenting, he heads her for the open sea; and as long as he could
he battled with the waves. Then the south wind springs up fresh,
under which we soon lost sight of land, and by and by fell in with
some merchantmen with two masts, who had no concern with our
land of Libya but were on a different course. We protested and
made a fuss about being so far from shore, but Amarantus in the
rôle of a Titan stood on his deck and rolled out curses in the most
tragic style. 'We can't fly,' says he, 'and what is a man to do with
you people who are afraid of the land and afraid of the sea?' 'Not
a bit of it, my dear Amarantus,' said I, 'if a man were reasonable
with them. But we had nothing to do with Taphosiris—we only
wanted to live—and now what do we want with the open sea? But
let us sail straight for Pentapolis (said I) keeping a moderate
distance out from land, so that if any accident—the chances of the
sea, you know—I suppose it is always uncertain, as you sailors

[1] Not Taphosiris (Tomb of Osiris, Abusir) in Marmarica but a smaller one
in Egypt, Volkmann says. It is about thirty miles S.W. from Alexandria.
Strabo, c. 799, says the shore there is rocky.

[2] The reading, or the geography perhaps, is obscure. Failing to fathom
Migne's wonderful text, I have translated Petavius' Latin rendering.

say—there might be a haven near at hand to receive us.' My
words failed to convince him and the rascal was stone-deaf, until a
strong north wind came upon us, rolling the waves up, high and
rough. This fell on us quite suddenly, and took the sail on the
other quarter, making concave what had been convex[1]. We came
near being taken aback and it was with difficulty we came up to
the wind. And the groanful Amarantus says, 'There's scientific
sailing for you!' for he had been expecting, he said, a wind from
the sea for some time and that was why he was keeping out, and
now he could make a tack as the distance from the shore gave him
room. That would be our course now, but it could not have been
if we had hugged the shore, for we should have been driven on to
the land. Well, we accepted his story as long as it was day, and
there was as yet no danger, for that only began with the night, and
the waves kept mounting more and more.

"It was however the day which the Jews call the Preparation
[Friday] and they reckon the night to the next day, on which they
are not allowed to do any work, but they pay it especial honour and
rest on it. So the steersman let go the helm from his hands, when
he thought the sun would have set on the land, and threw himself
down, and

'What mariner should choose might trample him[2].'

We did not at first understand the real reason, but took it for
despair, and went to him and besought him not to give up all hope
yet. For in plain fact the big rollers still kept on and the sea was
at issue with itself. It does this when the wind falls and the waves
it has set going do not fall with it, but, still retaining in full force
the impulse that started them, meet the onset of the gale and to
its front oppose their own. (I *had* to use fine words, not to give a
mean description of mighty evils.) Well, when people are sailing
under such circumstances, life hangs as they say by a slender thread.
But if the steersman is a rabbi (νομοδιδάσκαλος) into the bargain,
what will your feelings be?

"When then we understood what he meant in leaving the helm
—for when we begged him to save the ship from danger, he went on
reading his book—we despaired of persuasion and tried force. And

---

[1] This phrase is one of several so very strongly suggestive of the landsman
as to give me confidence that if the translation contain blunders in navigation,
as it well may, it will at least give a fair impression of Synesius' seamanship.
[2] A memory of Sophocles, *Ajax* 1146.

a gallant soldier (for we have with us a good few Arabians, who belong to the cavalry) drew his sword and threatened to cut his head off, if he would not steer the ship. But in a moment he was a genuine Maccabee, and would stick to his dogma. Yet when it was now midnight he took his place of his own accord, 'for now,' says he, 'the law allows me, as we are clearly in danger of our lives.' At that, the tumult begins again, moaning of men and screaming of women. Everybody began calling on heaven, and wailing and remembering their dear ones. Amarantus alone was cheerful, thinking he was on the point of ruling out his creditors.

"For myself amidst the dangers, I swear to you by the God philosophy counts supreme, that line of Homer kept troubling me, for fear it were true after all that death by drowning involved the destruction of the soul too. For he says somewhere in the poems[1]

'Ajax drank of the salt sea wave and utterly perished,'

meaning that death in the sea is absolute destruction. For he says of no one else that he 'utterly perished,' but, as each dies

'so went he to Hades.'

Moreover in neither Nekyia is the lesser Ajax brought on the scene, as if his soul were not in Hades. Achilles too, bravest of men and most daring, plays the coward about death by water, which he calls 'baleful.'

"As I kept turning these thoughts over in my mind, I saw the soldiers all with their swords drawn, and on inquiry I was told by them it was better to breathe out one's soul in the air on deck, than into the waters gasping. So I counted them of the school of Homer by instinct, and I inclined to the dogma.

"Then someone bids all who had any gold hang it to their necks, and those did so who had any gold or its equivalent. The women did it for themselves and gave threads to any who needed them. This is an ancient practice and here is the reason of it. The dead washed up from a wreck must bring the price of his burial. For the man who lights on him and gets gain by him will be afraid of the laws of Nemesis, if he does not give a little back to him who has given him many times more. That was what they were doing. But I sat by and wept to think of the accursed purse,

---

[1] *Odyssey* iv. 511, but not exactly, for the editions at least read ἔνθ' ἀπόλωλε for the ἐξαπόλωλε Synesius had in his mind. Some bracket the line because (says Merry) "they fail to see the grim humour of it." Achilles in *Il.* xxi. 281.

the loan of my friend[1]. The God of strangers knows my fear was not of death but about the money, in case the Thracian should lose by me, for even in death I would be ashamed of that. In that case to 'perish utterly' and lose consciousness would be a gain.

"What made the danger so urgent was nothing but that the ship was under full sail. To reduce it was impossible. We tried the ropes again and again, but gave it up, as they were tight in the rings ; and the fear came on us (and it was not a lesser fear) that if we escaped the waves we might in such a plight run ashore in the dark.

"Day came and we saw the sun, I don't know if ever with more pleasure. The wind began to fall as the day grew warmer, and the dew rose and let us use the ropes and manage the sail. We could not shift it and put up the 'bastard'—it had been pawned—but we took in some of it, like girding up a tunic. And before four hours were over we, who had expected to die, disembarked on an utterly desolate shore without town or farm near by, and about a hundred and thirty stades down from a farm. The ship was tossing in the open, for the spot was not a harbour, and she was tossing on one anchor. The second had been sold, and Amarantus never had a third.

"As for us, as soon as we reached the land we longed for, we embraced it as if it had been a living mother. Offering as usual a hymn of gratitude to God, I added to it the recent misadventure from which we had unexpectedly been saved."

This was not the end of the adventures of the voyage, but for our purposes so much may suffice and we may turn to his pictures of country life in the Cyrenaica. Let us take as our starting-point *Letter* 148—"a gossiping letter" as he calls it. It will not be necessary to render it in full.

He is not a near neighbour of the sea, he says, for he lives up country toward the south wind, the last of all the Cyrenians, in a place where oars are as strange as to the people in the *Odyssey* who took the oar for a winnowing fan. His neighbours had no salt but "the salts of Ammon," and were very sceptical about lands over the sea and the sea itself. As to fish—how could salt water produce anything edible, when their fresh streams had nothing better than frogs and leeches? It is a plain country life they live, the sounds they

---

[1] *Ep.* 129 explains this. Proclus had lent him 60 gold pieces, which he entered as 70 and for which Synesius was to repay him 80. He paid it on his return to Cyrene, in spite of difficulties of communication.

hear are all of the farm, and if the products of their lands are not
severally the best of their kinds, yet collectively few countries can
rival them; they supply all their own wants with a little over for
the tax-gatherer. Their songs are simple strains of the countryside—"the praise of a good ram perhaps ; or a stump-tailed dog
gets a eulogy because he is not afraid of hyaenas and takes the
wolves by the throat. And not least, the huntsman is made into a
song, for he makes peace for the pastures and gives us good cheer
by bringing all kind of game...but nothing so often as certain
prayers, still in song, petitions for blessing on man and crop and
beast." "The Emperor and the court and the dance of fortune are
mere names, kindled like flames and quenched; here our ears get a
rest from such talk. That there is an Emperor always in existence,
I suppose they know quite well, but we are only reminded of him
once a year by the tax-gatherers. But who he is, is not so clear.
Some of us think Agamemnon is still king, the son of Atreus that
went against Troy, the brave and good[1]. For that is the king's
name we hear about from childhood. And there is a friend of his,
Odysseus, the good herdsmen talk of—a bald man but a rare hand
for doing things and finding a way in a scrape. Don't they laugh,
as they tell of him, thinking it only a year or so since the Cyclops
was blinded ; and how the old boy was dragged along under the
ram, and how the villain sat by the door and thought the leader of
the flock was in the rear, not because he was feeling the weight,
but because he was feeling for his master's bad luck. My
letter, you see, has let you be with us a little while in spirit.
You have seen the country, and the simplicity of our ways.
Life in Noah's age, you will call it, before law and order ended in
slavery."

Praise of country life and the joys and beauties of the field are
common themes of the later sophists, and wearisome and frosty
many of their eulogies and descriptions are. Except perhaps in
Daphnis and Chloe, even if there, it would be hard to find anything
as natural as Synesius' work, though his education is to be plainly
read in this as in everything he wrote[2].

[1] Compare Dio Chrysostom's *Borystheniticus* 9 and 14, on the popularity of
Homer among the Greek settlers on the Borysthenes (Dnieper)—their only poet.
He writes about 100 A.D.
[2] Dio Chrysostom's oration *Euboicus*, with its highly ideal picture of the
"settled low content" of the hunters in the desert country, may have given
Synesius a suggestion, but his description is independent and no doubt represents
a real life, though it omits the barbarians and the locusts and other drawbacks.

He says in the letter just quoted, "We have leisure to philo-sophize, but none to do wrong," and elsewhere (*Ep.* 57, 1388 c) speaking of these days he says, "I lived with good hopes, regarding the universe in which I was as a sacred precinct, and myself like a sacred animal free and unshackled in it, and I divided my life between prayer and book and chase; for that soul and body may be healthy, we need at once to work and pray to God." His brother came to live at the little port of Phycus, and we have letters that tell of their happy relations, of visits to each other and sometimes of business.

"So you are surprised," he writes (*Ep.* 114), "when you live in dirty Phycus, that you have shivering fits and have got your blood into a bad state? On the contrary you should be surprised if your system can endure the heat there. But if you come up to us, you may with God's blessing get better, once you are quit of the air corrupted by the marshy exhalations, quit of the water, brackish, warm and, generally, stagnant—which is to say, dead. What is there fine in lying on the sand of the beach—the only amusement you have? for where can you go? But up here! what a thing it is to come under the shadow of a tree! and if you aren't comfortable to change that tree for another—one grove for another. What a thing it is to cross the rivulet by the roadside! How pleasant the zephyr is, gently playing with the branches! and the various songs of the birds, and the colours of the flowers, and the bushes of the meadow—some the works of the farmer, some the gifts of nature, all fragrant, the output of a healthy earth. The cave of the Nymphs I won't praise, for it wants a Theocritus. And there's more too."

We hear a good deal about horses. His brother is raising a pair "for tribute" (*Ep.* 132). Now a soldier steals one of Synesius' own, "because, he says, a soldier should have a horse. He offers an absurdly small sum, and won't give it back when I refuse to sell" (*Ep.* 6). Now he sends one to a friend (*Ep.* 40)—"a horse excellent for every equine virtue; you can use him in racing, when you go hunting, in a cavalry battle or a procession, for I don't know which to call him—a hunter, a racehorse, a horse for parade, or a war-horse. And if he isn't as pretty as the Nisaean horses—being lumpish in the head and lean in the flank—perhaps not even to horses, any more than to men, does God give everything at once... Horses with you run to flesh, but ours to bone." And now we find him, like a good Cyrenian, importing an Italian stallion, who, it is

promised, will "leave good foals behind him," but who is left at
Seleucia "as the captain on account of the weather did not want
such freight" (*Ep.* 133). He also speaks of breeding dogs for the
chase (*Calv. Enc.* c. 4).

Now and again he went abroad. It seems he paid several visits
to Alexandria, on one of which (? 403) he married a Christian lady
to whose influence some have attributed a share in his conversion.
We do not hear much of her. Possibly Synesius held the view he
attributes to the virtuous Osiris in the book on Providence. "That
Osiris had women's apartments in his house, his child was the only
reminder, and he too was rarely seen. For Osiris thought it was
the one virtue of a woman that neither her person nor her name
should pass the curtain" (*de Prov.* i. 13). He has a severe letter
on the airs and graces of a lady married into his family, who was
annoyed at someone dying at the time of her marriage She
appeared at the funeral—an unusual thing for brides to do—but, to
avoid an unlucky omen for her husband, she came in red, wearing a
transparent veil, and gold and jewels in abundance (*Ep.* 3). On
the other hand, he had an intense admiration for Hypatia, who
transgressed his Periclean canon to good purpose.

Once he visited Athens. We have two letters, one written
beforehand, the other from the place. He gives his reason for going
(*Ep.* 54). "I shall gain not only this advantage from my journey
to Athens—to be rid of the present troubles—but also I shall no
longer have to adore those who come thence for their learning.
They don't differ from us mortals—at least not as regards understanding Aristotle and Plato—but move amongst us, like demi-gods
among demi-donkeys, because they have seen the Academy and the
Lyceum etc." Then he writes to his brother again after seeing the
sights (*Ep.* 136):

"I hope I may profit as much from Athens as you wish. Indeed
I seem more than a hand and a finger wiser already, and I can give
you a proof of my divine wisdom on the spot. I am actually
writing to you from Anagyrus, and I have been at Sphettos, Thria,
Cephisia and Phalerum. But ill befall the ill man who brought me
here, the captain. For the Athens of to-day has nothing splendid
to shew but the famous names of the places. And just as when a
sacrifice has been offered the skin is left to shew what the animal
once was; so, since philosophy has gone away from here, it is only
left one to go round and admire the Academy and the Lyceum, yes!
and the Painted Stoa, which gave its name to Chrysippus' philosophy

but is not painted (ποικίλη) any longer, for the proconsul has taken away the pictures in which Polygnotus of Thasos displayed his art[1]. But in our day it is Egypt that nourishes the seeds of wisdom, which it receives from Hypatia. As for Athens, the city was once the home of the wise, but nowadays it is the bee-keepers who make her famous. You can add the pair of Plutarchian sages, who gather the young men in the theatres, not by the fame of their discourses but with honeycombs from Hymettus."

Too much attention may be paid to this criticism of Athens and too little. There had been seven hundred years of rivalry between Athens and Alexandria, and Synesius belonged to the latter university, and had, as we have seen, a habit of taking humorous views of things. On the other hand, Dean Merivale describes Athens as already in Hadrian's time "a dirty city in decay" in spite of its monuments. Curtius and Rohde however do not think the case was as bad as Synesius says, though the city was going down[2]. The story about the proconsul should be noticed. Alaric had been ravaging Greece in 395 but he seems to have spared Athens, and now as often before (for Wachsmuth thinks the robbery was recent) it was the Roman official whom she had to dread. At any rate intellectually, in spite of Proclus, Athens' day was done and she had no longer anything to give to mankind.

The fruits of Synesius' "leisure to philosophize" are to be found in his three books the *Dio, Concerning Dreams* and *The Praise of Baldness*. They cannot be taken as a very serious contribution to thought. "A man of many and wandering thoughts" he was not really serious enough to do any very profound thinking. To understand this at once, it is only necessary to compare him with Augustine, who will be satisfied with nothing short of reality and certainty[3]. Manichaean science he tests and finds untrue to actual fact. Neo-Platonist theology fascinates him, but cannot hold him, because it fails in motive power, because it fails to meet the need of common people, and because when all is done it fails to bring God within reach. Synesius is different. Like Julian he is essentially a disciple, and he accepts without afterthought the "dogmata"

---

[1] Julian, *ad Themist.* 259 B, implies that the gardens of Epicurus, the myrtles and the little house of Socrates were among the "show-places" of Athens.

[2] Merivale, *Romans under Empire*, c. 66. See Curtius, *Stadtgesch. der Athen*, c. 8, and Wachsmuth, *Die Stadt Athen im Alterthum*, p. 717, who discounts Claudian's inclusion of Athens among the places ravaged by Alaric (*in Rufin.* ii. 191).

[3] Compare Augustine, *Conf.* iii. 6, 10 *O veritas, veritas, quam intime etiam tum medullae animi mei suspirabant tibi;* and v. 3, 3—6 on Manichaean science.

of the school which gave him his first quickening. True, he left
Neo-Platonism for Christianity, but his Christianity where it is at
all thought out is a superstructure on a Neo-Platonic base, though
in reality it is perhaps more a matter of feeling than of thought.
As a Christian he inquires as little as he did when a Neo-Platonist.
Whether his tenets correspond with reality is not his most vital
concern, as it was Augustine's, but whether they satisfy the
immediate spiritual craving of his own heart. He is content with
an easy solution if he can be rid of the question. There is nothing
approaching dishonesty about him, it is merely an unspeculative
habit of mind. Yet "the heart," Pascal says, "has its reasons as
well as the head," and Synesius' instincts and strong human
affections generally lead him to some sound working principle, even
though he does not realize in all its relations the truth underlying it.

The most important of the three books of this period is the
Dio. In a letter to Hypatia (*Ep.* 154), accompanying it and the
book on Dreams, he explains how he came to write it. He has been
criticized from two quarters, by the men in white, and the men in
black. The former were "philosophers," sophists and rhetoricians;
the latter, monks and clergy[1], were the more serious.

The philosophers, in effect, accused him of trifling, "of sinning
against philosophy, heeding charm and rhythm in diction, pretending
to opinions on Homer." "They attained to a view of the intelligible
world, but he might not, because he gave some of his leisure to
rhetoric and was only fit for amusement." A lost poem or two of
his had got abroad, he says, and were "eagerly received by some
young men, who cared for Hellenism and grace." So he holds
up Dio as an example of a rhetorician who turned philosopher
—a Stoic, not speculative but mainly practical—and yet retained
his charm of classic style. And indeed a partially educated man is
not educated, for the Muses all go together (Μούσας = ὁμοῦ οὔσας by
etymology), and the philosopher, worthy of the name, must fail in
no learning of the Graces nor lack knowledge of any notable literature, but must be a genuine "Hellen" able to associate with any
one. Knowledge of one thing makes a craftsman or a specialist,
but a philosopher is made by a harmony of all knowledge. These
stiff gentlemen, who despise rhetoric and poetry, are so, he expects,

[1] See the amusing account given by Socrates (vi. 22) of the Novatian bishop
Sisinnius, who preferred to wear white, and the scriptural reasons he playfully
gave for it (e.g. *Eccles.* ix. 8).

not of their own choice but by poverty of nature. Beauty of words is not an idle thing, it is a pure pleasure that looks away from matter to real existence. If you reject this pleasure, what will you take instead? for you must have some pleasure. A man may be well-equipped in speech and master of philosophy at the same time. But what do the grammarians do, these critics of syllables, the teachers? They are sterile. There is a child-birth of letters as of beings, and the man who gives forth habitually what is immature falls into a habit of miscarriage and never produces anything that is perfect, anything that can live. Your ready speaker has always a "cheap finish[1]." Synesius therefore feels justified in living his own life quietly among his books, developing his style and his mind together, as against the raw philosopher, and content to be called a trifler by the busy and didactic grammarian.

But he is more irritated by the gentlemen in black. Ignorance, he writes to Hypatia, gives them courage, and they are everlastingly ready to debate about God. Give them a chance and you are deluged. It pays them, for from their ranks come the city preachers, and to be that is to hold Amaltheia's horn (*cornu copiae*). "They want me to be their disciple and promise to make me in a twinkling a ready talker on the things of God, and able to harangue days and nights together." No doubt they did, for, as he says elsewhere (*Ep.* 57, 1389 B), "a philosopher's ordination attracts attention." Synesius' wife was a Christian, and he was doubtless kindly disposed to Christians as he was to everybody, though not inclined to be converted in a hurry. Neo-Platonism, we may perhaps say, had two wings, the Left composed of adherents who leant to theurgy, magic and enchantments, and were like Julian more or less bitterly opposed to Christians, and the Right consisting of the *animae candidiores*, who counted it "bad manners to hustle God (ὠθισμός)" by magic, piety to wait on him and the ideal life one of natural and willing communion with him[2]. These men, and Synesius with

---

[1] This phrase of Stevenson's ("Journalism," he said, "is the school of cheap finish") answers to ἀδύνατος σκέμμα παραλαβὼν ὥσπερ ἀνδριάντα ξέσας ἐς τὸ ἀκριβὲς ἀπεργάζεσθαι.

[2] Cf. Augustine's indignation, while he was yet a Manichaean, at an enchanter's overtures: *recolo...me autem foeda illa sacramenta detestatum et abominatum respondisse*, *Conf.* iv. 1, 3. The proposal had been to secure by sacrifice of some animals the aid of *daemonia*, and Augustine declared he would not sacrifice a fly for an eternal crown of gold. The poem *Lithica* of the so-called Orpheus, really a work of about the fourth century A.D. as its references to the unpopularity of religion and magic shew, deals with the qualities special stones possess of "compelling" the gods. See also *de Civ. Dei* x. 9 and 10, for Augustine's general criticism of Porphyry and the art *quam vel magiam, vel detestabiliore nomine goetiam, vel honorabiliore theurgiam vocant*.

them, would not wish to "hustle" others who differed from them, though they might pity and despise them.

The monks, then, according to Synesius, were on wrong lines. Disregarding pretenders among them, he says the rest do not realize man's nature. God can do without pleasure, the beasts have bodily pleasures. Man standing between cannot do without pleasure but need not choose the pleasures of matter. The monks try to be more than human; and "now they are in God and now in the world and the body," and from contemplation they have to seek relaxation in basket-making, while the Greek developes his mind and his perception in his very amusements—rhetoric and poetry. They aim, no doubt, at the same thing as the philosopher, the sight of God, but, though it may be granted that some few of them reach it by happy endowment, they do not travel thither by road but their progress is more like a Bacchic frenzy, a long jump taken in madness and excitement[1]. Nor do they understand very often what they are doing. They must be chaste, but why? They abstain from marriage as if such abstinence were an end in itself. The preparation they count the goal. But to the philosopher the virtues are stages toward philosophy, they are to it as the letters are to a book. They are not everything, but after all merely mean the removal of obstacles to attaining the real end. The monk receives a command to be virtuous, and he obeys, but it is external to him. He does not know *why* he should be so. His virtue is therefore unintelligent and in consequence unmeaning, and perhaps not even virtue at all in the highest sense. In other words, Synesius finds monastic virtue mechanical and uninspired, and Neander says he is right and finds his judgment remarkable for moderation and truth[2].

Synesius was in earnest about communion with God, but some of his ways of attaining it seem to us as strange as those of the monks. In his book *On Dreams* he pleads for intercourse with God in sleep. Chaste living and moderation in all things are the means to obtain good dreams of God, who will often communicate in this way warnings against threatening danger, guidance and so forth. This doctrine was one of the Neo-Platonists', of whose teaching at large the book is full. Julian communed so with heaven. Porphyry says good demons bring messages to the virtuous in their dreams.

---

[1] Curiously the author of *de vita contemplativa* c. 2 uses much the same expression of his Therapeutae; "seized by heavenly love καθάπερ οἱ βακχευόμενοι καὶ κορυβαντιῶντες ἐνθουσιάζουσι."

[2] *Church History*, vol. iii. p. 360, Bohn.

Macrobius classifies dreams from oracles down to nightmares and
Prudentius discusses the question in his poem for sleep-time.   Even
Ammianus pleads that divination by dreams is not more necessarily
futile because it blunders than medicine.   Augustine believed in his
mother's dreams, and says she told him "she could distinguish by
some strange savour, which she could not explain in words, between
a revelation from God and an idle dream of her own mind."
Synesius' own work was written at a divine command, which came
in a dream, and the whole of it in a single night or rather in the
remainder of that night on which he had the dream.   "Whenever
I take it up, I have a strange feeling, and a divine voice, as poetry
says, is shed about me."   Hypatia was to be the first reader.

The *Praise of Baldness* is frankly a humorous work, written
after the other two.   "Adoxography" was a recognized branch of
sophistic composition[1].   Unpromising, ugly or inglorious subjects
were chosen and the rhetorician did his best for them.   It was
"making the worse appear the better reason."   One of the most
accessible examples of the kind is Lucian's *Praise of a Fly*, which
adequately exhibits its possibilities of neatness and triviality.
Synesius wrote his piece in imitation of Dio's *Praise of Hair*, part
or all of which he quotes.   The work is not elsewhere preserved.

Synesius professes that he is growing bald, but reflects that hair
is the mark of the beast, while man is in the main bald, though
partially hairy to remind him of his midway position in the universe.
But with dogs, for example, the more hair, the less sense.   So the
balder a man is, the wiser and the more divine we may take him to
be.   Hair like the adornment of growing corn withers when the
fruit, here the brain, is ripe.   Of all shapes the sphere is most
perfect—and that is the shape of the bald head.   The soul naturally
aims at the imitation of God and yearns to inhabit a sphere, but
whether this be a star or a bald head is immaterial.   Our head is
our most heavenward part, and its baldness is heaven for us.
Though the vulgar admire hair, as they do everything external,

---

[1] Erwin Rohde, *Der Griechische Roman*, p. 308.   The author of the Clementine homilies sets an imaginary opponent of Christianity to compose a μοιχείας
ἐγκώμιον (Clem. *Hom.* v. 10—19) with abundant illustration from mythology—
a by no means extravagant performance for a rhetorician, which most adroitly
exhibits the bad side of Olympus.   Gellius, *N. A.* xvii. 12, speaks of these
themes and their uses, to rouse the wit, to practise cleverness, to overcome
difficulties, and says that they were favourite exercises of philosophers as well
as sophists, *e.g.* his teacher Favorinus praised Thersites and quartan fever.
There is another *Praise of Hair* in Philostratus (*Ep.* 16).   Claudian's poems on
the electric eel (or fish) of the Nile, the porcupine and the magnet may come
under this class.

the spheric is the blessed form. (So says Macrobius more gravely, *Comm.* i. 14. 8, 9.) Just as the moon waxes to the full, so does baldness, till it exhibits the head "shining back with full-orbed circle to the lights of heaven." Hair and the vices flourish and pass together. Even Achilles was bald in front—or at least Athene took him by the hair from behind. The best of men, priests and philosophers, are all painted as bald. This work is for philosophers and, if it be published, he hopes the "lovers of hair" (φιλόκομοι) will be ashamed and adopt the reasonable and honourable practice of shaving, but always pay special honour to those who do not need the barber. The fooling is exquisite but perhaps a little long. It should be noted that the ideas he parodies are Neo-Platonic.

But to this idyllic country life that only wanted a Theocritus there was another side. Cyrene was for the civilized world practically an island, but in reality it was unhappily not so. The barbarian tribes of the interior, Macetae and Ausurians, were in the habit of raiding the land, and in general little effective opposition was offered to them. There were troops to meet them, if only the governors and officials could be trusted, but they could not. They were as a rule not there because they were fit for their work. The barbarians, like the Iroquois in Canada, came and went as they would with suddenness and swiftness. Accordingly one responsible official sells the soldiers' horses and pockets the money, and nothing can be done with infantry. Another scatters the troops about in such a way that they are useless. Now and again a capable man is sent and the savages are taught a lesson. He is recalled and they return —actually to besiege fortresses and towns. Yet bad as this was, there was a worse symptom. The Cyrenians would do nothing for themselves, and when Synesius tried to rouse them and raise a troop of farm people, his brother wrote to warn him that such activity was dangerous in a private person. For centuries the Roman government had discouraged energy and initiative among the provincials, and they had acquired the habit of having everything done for them. Public spirit had been suspected and killed, and now an enemy, whose weakness was seen whenever any determined action was taken against him, plundered and burnt, drove off cattle and horses and camels and carried away children to bring them up to ravage as men the lands they played on in childhood—another Iroquois trait—all this for want of public spirit. The army itself was composed of foreigners—Synesius speaks of corps of Marcomanni, Arabians, Unnigardae—and the native-born Romans were kept in civil life to be taxed. He had not gone an inch beyond what he had warrant for, when in his speech on Kingship he had pled for citizen soldiers. And now neither the citizens nor the soldiers nor the officials were of any use. "The enemy are burning, slaying and kidnapping," he writes, "and not one of us is troubled; we sit and wait for the useless help of the soldiers. Shall we never stop talking nonsense? never come to our senses and gather the farmers and labourers and march out together against the enemy, for our children, for our wives, for our land—yes! and if you like for the soldiers too?" (*Ep.* 125).

A letter of Synesius to Hypatia, written apparently a short time after his return home from Constantinople, illustrates the situation and his own temper.

"'Yea though in Hades' realm the dead by the dead are forgotten,
Yet even there will I[1]'

remember my dear Hypatia. As for me, on all hands I am surrounded by the sufferings of my native land, and my heart is sad for her. For every day I see the foemen's arms and the butchery of men like beasts for sacrifice, and I breathe air tainted with corrupting corpses, and I look to suffer the like myself. For who could be of good hope surrounded by all that is humiliating and overshadowed by carnivorous birds[2]? Yet for all that I love my land. What should I else, who am a Libyan and was born here and still see the tombs of my ancestors held in honour? For you alone I think I can forget my land and return if I have the leisure" (*Ep.* 124).

This last was a mere compliment, Volkmann says, but it is not impossible that it is only a promise of a visit and not of a permanent change of abode. Visits, as we have seen, he did make to Alexandria, but he loved his land too well to quit it for ever. Letter 130 shews further stages of trouble.

"To Simplicius. Your greeting me through Cerealis gave him five days' grace; for so long we did not find him out for the knave he is. For the cities hoped for something good from a man whom Simplicius did not disdain to know. But he very quickly brought shame—not on you (for Heaven grant your reputation may never

---

[1] *Iliad* xxii. 389.
[2] See Lord Roberts, *Forty-one years in India*, c. 15, for 'the innumerable birds of prey which instinct had brought to Delhi from the remotest parts of India' in 1857.

depend on another) but on himself and his office, and, not to hesitate,
on the Roman empire—a man to be bought for a trifle, careless of
his fame, unwarlike and in peace oppressive—though he had not a
long enjoyment of peace. For as if there were a law that what is
the soldiers' is the general's, he took from everyone what they had
and in exchange released them from service and discipline and let
them go where they might think they could pick up a living. This
he did to the native troops, but as he could not get money out of
the mercenaries he did out of their towns, marching and moving
about, not where it was most profitable but where it was most
lucrative. The towns found their presence a burden and paid down
their gold. The Macetae soon saw this, and from the half-
barbarians to the barbarians the report spread.

'Thick as the leaves they came and thick as the flowers of spring-time.'

"Alas! for the youth that are lost to us! for the harvests we
hoped for in vain! We sowed for the enemy's fire. Most of us had
our wealth in beasts, in brood camels and horses out at grass. All
is gone, all driven off. I know it too well, as I am beside myself
with annoyance. But forgive me. For I am behind walls, and
I write under siege, seeing beacons often in the hour, lighting them
myself and passing on signals to others. The long hunting expeditions I once enjoyed securely and most of all for your sake—they
are all past. And I groan

'as I bethink me
Of that past youth, that temper and that mind.'

"But now everything swarms with horsemen and the enemy hold
the country. And I at my station between two towers am battling
with sleep.

'Under my spear I munch my barley-cake,
Under my spear a soldier's thirst I slake,
Drain the Ismaric, leaning on my spear.'

I don't know if Archilochus had any better right to say this. Evil
befall the evil Cerealis, if he has not anticipated my curse, for he
deserved to perish in the recent storm. For when he saw in what
plight the country was, he lost confidence at once in land, and put
his gold on some merchant schooners, and is tossing on the sea. A
skiff brings us his despatches, which bid us do what we are doing—
keep within the walls, not advance outside the trenches, not come
to close quarters with these invincible men, or else, he protests, he

washes his hands of us. He tells us to set four watches through the night, as if our hopes lay in not sleeping. For he seems skilled in such things, like a man born to disaster. Yet he did not want even a share in our misfortunes. For not by a battlement like me, Synesius the philosopher[1], but by an oar our general takes his stand.

"If you really like the poems for which you asked—though I am not aware of anything good about them except their subject—pray with the Cyrenians that they may have a little respite from arms. For as we are now, there is not leisure to take the books from the boxes."

There are other letters in like strain, which, with those describing the country and its people, give us a bright and living picture of the life of the province. The books and hymns reveal in some measure what was passing in Synesius' mind. The earlier hymns are frankly Neo-Platonic, but a change appears, for the fifth begins:

> "The offspring of the Virgin,
> The Virgin never wedded
> In human wedlock, sing we."

The remaining five are all more or less Christian. The eighth may be dated 405 or 406, and we may ask whether it is later or earlier than the three preceding. In any case, perhaps as much as three years before the bishopric is mentioned, Synesius was hymning the Virgin-born. This was an advance on Neo-Platonism. How had he reached this point?

He does not tell us what made him a Christian, his *apologia* about the bishopric turning on the reasons which led him to surrender the quiet life he loved for one of office and worry and business. Only a few hints occur from which we may gather some of his motives. In such matters it is always hard to be explicit. The reasons which a man will give for holding the deepest religious truths must generally seem more or less inadequate, because they can never be completely stated. Such truths are held by a man, or rather perhaps he would say, hold him, because they are to him a spiritual necessity, which he feels as the result of experience, and no one who has not had this or a similar experience can understand why he should so feel.

---

[1] Is he thinking of Dio, bidden by the Borysthenites to take arms and fight like Achilles against the barbarian raiders? (Dio, *Borysth.* 28).

Synesius under the stress of great danger had prayed in the churches of Constantinople, and this of itself shews a certain friendliness to Christianity. Julian, for example, would not have done so ; his visits to church were only dictated by policy. Synesius again had a Christian wife, who had been given to him by bishop Theophilus of Alexandria—a man who has not a good name in history[1]. However, Chrysostom had been in Constantinople when Synesius was there, and must have impressed him, as we find him speaking warmly of Chrysostom to Theophilus, the man who had hounded him to his death. We also see that the clergy and the monks tried to capture him, and while in the *Dio* he accuses them of being on wrong lines he admits that their aim is the right one. His own Neo-Platonic Trinity bears a close likeness to the Christian one. There were thus many things leading him to the Church. The difficulty was probably the Incarnation, the belief that God could stoop to contact with the material world.

To a belief in this he was helped, if my deductions are right, mainly by two things—a deepening sense of his own difficulty in keeping "clean from matter," and a growing feeling for the needs and sorrows of common people. Neo-Platonism was not clear as to how far a man, striving to be pure and godlike, received divine assistance. Did God leave man to work out his own salvation by himself, as Macrobius implies, or lend aid at every turn as Julian hopes (though Julian rested for this on magic), or intervene occasionally at great crises, as Synesius' book on Providence teaches ? The Christian account was much more explicit, even before Augustine developed the doctrine of grace. Synesius later on says incidentally that he cannot himself mingle with the material world and remain pure. "And if it had been possible even for an angel to become a man and for more than thirty years suffer nothing from contact with matter, why need the Son of God have descended?" (*Ep.* 57, 1396 c). Elsewhere he laments, "I have no strength ; what is within is not pure, and I cannot avail for what is without ; and I am far from being able to bear the pain of conscience" (*Ep.* 104, 1484 c). His case had been with differences like Augustine's, who says of his Neo-Platonist days:—"I thought continence a matter

---

[1] One example of outside opinion of Theophilus may suffice. In Sulpicius' *Dialogue* (i. 7) Postumian says of him *me quidem episcopus illius civitatis benigne admodum et* melius quam opinabar *excepit et secum tenere temptavit, sed non fuit animus ibi consistere ubi recens fraternae cladis fervebat invidia.* This was written even before the fall of Chrysostom.

of my own strength, which I did not really know, since I was so foolish as not to be aware (as it is written) that 'none can be continent unless Thou give it' (*Wisdom* viii. 21)" (*Conf.* vi. 11, 20). Experience had taught Synesius better. "It was necessary (ἔδει) that Christ should be crucified for the sins of all men" (*Ep.* 57, 1385 B).

Again, the suffering his country had to undergo fell on him no more than on his poorer neighbours. He had always been the poor man's friend, though as a Neo-Platonist he could not expect much philosophy from the poor and therefore must set them on a lower plane. But suffering seems to have put him and them on one level. They all suffered alike from savages and bad governors; alike they risked life and property, and together they fought and did sentry duty for their country. Though Synesius' own three children had not been carried off, he could as a father feel what such a loss was. What was to help these poor people, for whom Neo-Platonism was too fine and too hard? All this is, of course, inference, but it seems to me legitimate when I contrast a typical Neo-Platonic utterance with an expression wrung from Synesius, when bishop, by an outrage of the Governor Andronicus.

Hermes Trismegistus, voicing the pride that went with the magical wing of Neo-Platonism, the pride of being able to *force* the gods (ἀναγκάζειν is Iamblichus' word), writes thus:—"Marvellous beyond all marvels is it that man could discover the divine nature and *make* it....Calling forth the souls of demons and angels they have installed them in holy images and divine mysteries, whereby the idols have the power of doing good and doing harm" (*Ed. Bipont. Apul.* ii. p. 321)[1].

Synesius is humbler. "Precious among creatures is man; precious in that for him Christ was crucified" (*Ep.* 57, 1388 c). It is not an idle question of Augustine when he is writing of the Neo-Platonists. "Where," he demands, "where is that charity that edifieth on the foundation of humility, which is Christ Jesus?" (*Conf.* vii. 20, 26).

It is here that the Christian Church and the Neo-Platonists most fundamentally differ, and this must be realized if we are to appreciate Synesius. Otherwise we shall be liable to error, for his

---

[1] On this remarkable utterance, see Augustine, *C. D.* viii. 23, 24 *quasi quidquam sit infelicius homine, cui sua figmenta dominantur!* The confusion of the Bipontine text dates from the days of St Augustine, who avails himself of it to make a point one feels would have been impossible but for the Latin translator from Hermes' original Greek.

terminology is always Neo-Platonic, and many of his views too are not yet re-adjusted to the new position. Some have thought that because in an hour of trouble he sought comfort in "philosophy," he was harking back to Neo-Platonism, but this is a mistake. He merely means reflexion[1].

In 409 the bishopric of Ptolemais, now and for some time previously the chief town of the Cyrenaica, became vacant by the death of the bishop. In electing bishops the laity still had a voice which was often very effective They did not necessarily confine themselves to men already ordained, but looked about for some man of proved capability, who by wealth, birth, position, influence or experience would be likely to make a good administrator and a protector of the people. It was thus that in Milan Ambrose was most unexpectedly consecrated, and that in Constantinople Nectarius, Chrysostom's predecessor, was forcibly seized by the people and made bishop. Nothing need be said of Ambrose, but Nectarius was a worldly-minded man who liked to enjoy life. Ordination cannot have been regarded with much respect, when it was beginning already to be used as a method of punishing and reducing to obscurity men who had been politically troublesome. How secular might be the considerations which led to the choice of a bishop, we can see in Synesius' letters. In one see under his charge, the people revolted from a gentle old bishop because he was ineffectual, and set up a more drastic person, as they needed a man of energy and resource. But when the laity chose Synesius for Ptolemais, beside the reflexion that he was able, active and brilliant and had strong connexions in Constantinople and Egypt, we may surely credit them with some appreciation of his kindness, his honour and his piety.

The proposal was most unwelcome to him, but he had to consider it. A short abstract of a letter (*Ep.* 105) which he wrote to his brother will shew his feelings.

"The episcopate is a compliment, but am I fit for it? I think, very unfit. I will tell you, for I have no one else. I know you will be anxious for my good. Philosophy is all I am equal to. In serious things I go my own way, but I also like amusement. Now a bishop should be as able to do without amusement as God is. And in serious and sacred things he cannot go his own way and be independent, but must belong to everybody and teach what is

[1] It may be noted that in the earlier works written after his conversion, Augustine as a rule uses philosophic rather than Christian terminology.

recognized. He must be a man of affairs, able at once to undertake endless business and maintain his spiritual life. For myself, I feel it pollution even to go into the town[1]. A bishop should be stainless as he has to wash others of their sins, but my own sins are too much for me.

"As I know you will shew this letter to others, I will be explicit, that I may be clear of guilt before God and man, and before Theophilus. I am married. God and the law and the sacred hand of Theophilus gave me my wife, and I do not wish to part from her at all[2]. Further, philosophy is opposed to many current dogmata. (*a*) I do not think the soul is made after the body, (*b*) nor that the world and all its parts will be destroyed. (*c*) The resurrection as preached I count a sacred mystery and am far from accepting the general idea. (*d*) To conceal the truth is philosophically sound. Too much truth and too much light are dangerous at times[3]. I cannot obscure these opinions now, as I cannot be ordained to God's service and fail in truthfulness by concealing my real thoughts.

"I shall be sorry to give up sports. (My poor dogs!) But I will; and I will endure business, as a means of doing service to God. But my mind and my tongue must not be at variance. Theophilus must know all, so that he may either leave me in peace as a philosopher or, if he chooses to ordain me, may be unable to rule me out of the choir of bishops. If he accepts my terms, I will be bishop, for one must be ready to obey God with a good will."

The weight in this letter falls on the tenets which Synesius says are contrary to the usual faith of Christians. They certainly lean toward Neo-Platonism. The eternity of the universe is strongly insisted on by Macrobius, Hermes Trismegistus and Julian for example. The resurrection was repugnant to the school in consequence of their views on matter. If the essence of the higher life, the divine life, is to escape matter, how should matter be raised hereafter to be again a fetter on the soul? On the Neo-Platonist hypothesis the resurrection of the body was an absurdity. But

---

[1] Cf. Augustine, *Ep.* x. 2 *Nisi proveniat quaedam magna cessatio, sincerum illud bonum gustare atque amare non possum. Magna secessione a tumultu rerum labentium, mihi crede, opus est.* Like Synesius, Augustine had to surrender this life for that of activity.

[2] We are not told the decision about his wife, but it is thought she may have solved the difficulty by withdrawing from him voluntarily. This separation may have contributed to his depression when bishop.

[3] This line is taken by Augustine, *de Mor. Eccl. Cath.* vii. 11, who remedies the excessive light of divine things by the *opacitas auctoritatis*.

Volkmann brings out that these views, which Synesius professes, he does not emphasize so much because they were Neo-Platonic as because they were the views of Origen, against which Theophilus had started a terrible campaign involving the downfall and exile of Chrysostom. Synesius does not want that fate and does want to be open.

In the light of all this we must interpret the last of the four points reasonably. Ψεύδεσθαι "to lie" is a strong word—and is stronger in our English than in Synesius' Greek. With other Neo-Platonists he believed in retaining certain things, making mysteries and esoteric doctrines of them, and he lavishes a good deal of admiration on the Homeric Proteus[1], who put on any and every sort of form to evade all but the true philosopher, Menelaus, whose concern was to know the truth. Dr Hatch has shewn that this temper was not unknown in the Church, where the simple rites of the early Church were under its influence developed into awful mysteries.

The case was referred to Theophilus, and Synesius spent seven or eight months at Alexandria. What happened there we are not told. He mentions incidentally that "old men" told him "God would be his shepherd"; that "the Holy Spirit is joyous and gives joy to those who partake of Him[2]"; that "God and the demons fight for us, and that he by being consecrated would wound the demons"; and that "a philosopher's consecration meant much to the world[3]."

It is clear he did not wish to be a bishop and that he anticipated great trouble in the discharge of the office. His fears were amply realized. Cyrene received as Governor "a man from the tunny-fisheries," Andronicus by name, an extortionate, rapacious and vicious man. The people turned for help to their bishop. He had just lost a child and was crushed with sorrow. If he says "he could have done himself a mischief," we need not suppose he really contemplated suicide, as some have surprisingly concluded. Here as elsewhere he merely uses a rather vivid style of speech. He now

---

[1] Augustine similarly makes Proteus a parable of truth. *Contra Academicos*, iii. 6, 13 *Veritatis, inquam, Proteus in carminibus ostentat sustinetque personam, quam obtinere nemo potest, si falsis imaginibus deceptus comprehensionis nodos vel laxaverit vel dimiserit.*

[2] Cf. Augustine, *Conf.* viii. 11, 27, on the gladness of Christianity, *non dissolute hilaris.*

[3] Thus Augustine on the conversion of the great rhetorician Victorinus speaks of the importance of winning men of note, *quod multis noti multis sunt auctoritati ad salutem et multis praeeunt secuturis* (*Conf.* viii. 4, 9).

tried to do something to mitigate the Governor's violence, but only met insult. He found himself powerless and felt that others realized it and regretted their election of him. Overwhelmed with pain at his bereavement and mortification at his failure, he had recourse to prayer, but "here was the worst of his misfortunes which made his life seem hopeless; in the past he had always found God in prayer, but now he felt he prayed in vain." Once again, I think, his language has been forced to mean too much. He was essentially a man influenced by feelings, and whatever he feels he says freely— very much resembling Cicero in his sensibility and outspokenness— and it seems to me unfair to infer from such an utterance that his Christianity broke down. Andronicus went further. He nailed a notice to the church door that he would not recognize the asylum of the church, and when Synesius ran in the full heat of noon to sit by a man he was torturing, he raged at the sight of the bishop and crowned his madness with the boast, that none should escape Andronicus' hands though he clung to the feet of Christ Himself. Now Synesius called a synod together and excommunicated him, and in an address (printed among his letters as no. 57) makes an *apologia pro vita sua*, an honourable and affecting defence. To it he appended the sentence of excommunication to be forwarded to all bishops with an account of Andronicus' guilt. The villain gave way, begged for a second chance, received it and abused it, and the bolt was launched, and before long Synesius had to come forward to rescue him from injustice.

The barbarians, Macetae and Ausurians, continued their inroads. On two occasions effective generals were sent against them on short campaigns, but in the interval they grew so bold as to besiege Ptolemais.

Within two years Synesius lost his two remaining children. He writes to Hypatia about them in deep depression. "The memory of my departed children is wasting me away....Might I cease either to live or to remember my boys' grave!" (*Ep.* 16).

Yet I think the Cyrenians must have counted him a good and a wise bishop. As one reads his letters telling Theophilus of his procedure, one feels that R. L. Stevenson's praise of his missionary friend, Mr Clarke, might be applied to him—"a man I esteem and like to the soles of his boots; I prefer him to anyone in Samoa and to most people in the world; a real good missionary with the in-estimable advantage of having grown up a layman." Tact, courtesy, common sense and a remarkable absence of any feeling of his own importance mark his actions. It looks as if the sense of his own weakness and sinfulness made him more sympathetic with weak and tempted men, with wrong-doers and with men of doubtful opinions. One example may suffice. Two bishops had a quarrel about a little fort. It was the personal property of the one, and the other stole a march on him, consecrated it, and claimed it for his diocese. Some held that the consecration was irrevocable and nothing could be done. Synesius boldly upset it altogether. There was a proper balance to be kept between the sacred laws and the rights of the state. He drew a clear line between piety and superstition, the vice that aped it, and held it intolerable that by the most sacred things the most execrable wrong should be done and that the prayer, the table and the mystical curtain should be made the implements of violent aggression. It was no Christian teaching [as it was Neo-Platonic] that the Divine is subject to ritual word and substance, as if by some physical attraction. Where anger, passion and strife lead the way in an action, how can the Holy Spirit be there? He restored the fort, which he would not allow to be a church, to its owner, who, now that his own rights were maintained and his adversary had apologized, freely gave him the fort and the hill.

Synesius' ordination cost him some friendships, and what that meant we may read in one of his latest letters. He gently rebukes Auxentius for having dragged him into a quarrel in which he was not concerned. "Advancing years, I am glad to say, are dulling my quick temper; and the sacred laws, they say, forbid. At the same time I remember our common upbringing and education and the life in Cyrene. All this we must suppose to outweigh the suit of Sabbatius. Begin then the good work of friendship, and accept my good will; for I count the time of my silence as so much loss— and do you realize how even then I suffered? But I bore it as well as I could—such is the evil of having a quick temper" (*Ep.* 60).

And here our story ends. The 12th letter seems to imply that Theophilus is dead. He died in 412, and this is the latest date that can with any certainty be assigned to any work of Synesius'. Hence it has been plausibly conjectured his own death must have shortly followed. There is a wild theory that Euoptius, bishop of Ptolemais in 431, may have been his brother, in which case we gain the information that Synesius was dead before 431.

With his death darkness falls on the history of Cyrene.

I have so far only casually alluded to his hymns, with one of which, the 9th, in Mrs Browning's rendering, I close my essay. Volkmann says their poetic worth is slight, and this is certainly true of some of them, for their metre is very monotonous and their thought abstract.

Some of the hymns are little more than metrical expositions of the common doctrines of Neo-Platonism. There is a Trinity, which is a Unity, a Father and a Son, linked by the "mediating light of the Holy Spirit," through whom the Father is Father and the Son is Son. The Son is the Wisdom that made the world. Thence the choir of immortal rulers, the deathless army of angels, and all the descending succession of beings. The soul has come down to be on earth a servant, but enchanted by the magic arts of matter it has become a slave instead of a servant, yet is not without some gleam of hidden light, which even in its fallen state may help it to rise. His prayer is for divine aid, particularly against distraction and disturbance and the confusions of the material world—"let the winged snake go underground, the demon of matter, the cloud of the soul, that loves phantoms and hounds on its dogs against prayer"—"the demons that leap up from the abysses of earth and breathe into mortals godless impulses." Gradually he identifies the Son with the Virgin-born Christ, and finally calls him Jesus, still keeping the Spirit as the "centre" of the Trinity, and still praying for rest and quietness and salvation from matter and all that disorders the soul. At times he rises to flights that seem to justify the very high praise bestowed upon him by Mrs Browning, to whose brilliant essay on the Greek Christian poets I would refer the reader.

"He was a poet," she writes, "the chief poet, we do not hesitate to record our opinion—the chief, for all true and natural gifts, of all our Greek Christian poets....These odes have, in fact, a wonderful rapture and ecstasy. And if we find in them the phraseology of Plato or Plotinus, for he leant lovingly to the later Platonists,—nay, if we find in them oblique references to the out-worn mythology of paganism, even so have we beheld the mixed multitude of unconnected motes wheeling, rising in a great sunshine, as the sunshine were a motive energy,—and even so the burning, adoring poet-spirit sweeps upward the motes of world-fancies (as if, being in the world, their tendency was Godward), upward in a strong stream of sunny light, while she rushes into the presence of 'the Alone.' We say the *spirit* significantly in speaking of this poet's aspiration. His is an ecstasy of abstract intellect, of pure spirit, cold though impetuous; the heart does not beat in it, nor is the human voice heard; the poet is true to the ecclesiastic, and there is no resurrection of the body."

Well-beloved and glory-laden,
Born of Solyma's pure maiden!
I would hymn Thee, blessèd Warden,
Driving from thy Father's garden
Blinking serpent's crafty lust,
With his bruised head in the dust!
Down Thou camest, low as earth,
Bound to those of mortal birth;
Down Thou camest, low as hell,
Where shepherd-Death did tend and keep
A thousand nations like to sheep,
While weak with age old Hades fell
Shivering through his dark to view Thee,
And the Dog did backward yell
With jaws all gory to let through Thee!
So, redeeming from their pain
Choirs of disembodied ones,
Thou didst lead whom Thou didst gather,
Upward in ascent again,
With a great hymn to the Father,
Upward to the pure white thrones!
King, the daemon tribes of air
Shuddered back to feel Thee there!
And the holy stars stood breathless,
Trembling in their chorus deathless;
A low laughter fillèd aether—
Harmony's most subtle sire
From the seven strings of his lyre
Stroked a measured music hither—
Io paean! victory!
Smiled the star of morning—he
Who smileth to foreshow the day!
Smilèd Hesperus the golden,
Who smileth soft for Venus gay!
While that hornèd glory holden
Brimful from the fount of fire,
The white moon, was leading higher
In a gentle pastoral wise
All the nightly deities!
Yea, and Titan threw abroad
The far shining of his hair
'Neath Thy footsteps holy-fair,
Owning Thee the Son of God;
The Mind artificer of all,
And his own fire's original.

And THOU upon Thy wing of will
Mounting,—Thy God-foot uptill
The neck of the blue firmament,—
Soaring, didst alight content
Where the spirit-spheres were singing,
And the fount of good was springing,
In the silent heaven!
Where Time is not with his tide
Ever running, never weary,
Drawing earth-born things aside
Against the rocks : nor yet are given
The plagues death-bold that ride the dreary
Tost matter-depths.   Eternity
Assumes the places which they yield!
Not aged, howsoe'er she held
Her crown from everlastingly—
At once of youth, at once of eld,
While in that mansion which is hers
To God and gods she ministers![1]

---

[1] See Mrs Browning's poetical works, 1 vol. edition, 1898, pp. 602—605.
The work of Volkmann, which I have quoted, is *Synesius von Cyrene*, by
R. Volkmann, Berlin, 1869, an excellent and most useful book.

CHAPTER XV

GREEK AND EARLY CHRISTIAN NOVELS

ἀλλ' ἄγε μοι τόδε εἰπὲ καὶ ἀτρεκέως κατάλεξον
ὅππῃ ἀπεπλάγχθης τε καὶ ἅς τινας ἵκεο χώρας.

Odyssey viii. 572

No study of the fourth century would be complete which did not in some degree take account of its fiction. Yet to deal with it all and with precision would be an extremely difficult task. To begin, a good story—and every reader has his own idea of what is a good story—a story then that appeals to a large number of readers will probably be spread abroad not merely in abundance of copies but in various languages. It will be translated from one tongue to another, and as it travels it will undergo alterations. Passages will be added and others will be omitted. Eventually when criticism takes the much travelled story into consideration, widely differing recensions of it are found, and it is sometimes no easy matter to say which is the original form—has it been expanded by a Syrian translator or cut down by a Greek? Many of the tales with which we have to deal describe an almost entirely artificial world, and offer nothing beyond their style as a guide to the critic who will date them, and in some cases this is hardly any help at all, so that a novel like that of Longus is loosely dated as of the second to the fourth century. Others conceal the date of their creation of set purpose and flaunt a false one, and though the falsehood may be readily detected, the true date can often only be determined by long and tiresome critical processes, with the result that critics come to very different conclusions.

If however we bear in mind that, while the dates of the first appearances of the particular books to which we have to refer are in many cases highly conjectural, these works yet represent the popular taste for long after as well as before the period with which

we are dealing, and that their kind, if not themselves, has profoundly
influenced actual productions of our period, we may without material
error draw some real advantage from our study. We may begin
by a short survey of the general lines of development of Greek
fiction, for though a literary pedigree may be as hard to prove
as a canine, no work of art of any sort can help in some measure
betraying the environment in which it was produced, and something
of the processes by which that stage has been reached. At the
same time the author's individuality must be recognized. To take
a modern example, it is quite clear that *Paul and Virginia* owes
much to *Daphnis and Chloe*, and it is also clear that it owes a
good deal to *Robinson Crusoe*, the book which of all books most
influenced Bernardin de St Pierre from youth to age. Yet Paul
is agitated by questions that Daphnis never dreamt of, and which
he himself could hardly have dreamt of, if he had not been created
in the age of Rousseau, to say nothing of his creator's friendship
with Rousseau. Again, though the work has been pronounced to
be in some degree even anti-Christian in its quiet ignoring of such
matters as original sin and any necessity for redemption, and its
implication that man is born good, if only society will not corrupt
him, yet the difference between Paul and Daphnis, between Virginia
and Chloe, is not to be explained without Christianity. We thus
see that Longus, Defoe, Rousseau and the Catholic Church have
all contributed to this book, but perhaps after all we must recognize
that Bernardin de St Pierre contributed to it, or else we may have
to pronounce Shakespeare a second-hand dramatist.

We need not however write the history of literature to interpret
Xanthippe and Polyxena or the *Life of Antony* and their contemporary rivals. I would refer the reader to the admirable work
of Chassang, *Histoire du Roman*, which has been highly praised by
Sainte-Beuve but not too highly, and the more special monograph
of Erwin Rohde, *Der Griechische Roman*. At the same time
clearness will be gained by giving a very short sketch of the course
of development that Greek fiction has followed[1].

We may then classify our material very roughly in some five
groups, premising that in many cases it will be difficult to say
under which heading this or that work should more properly come,
as the same book may share the characteristics of more than one

[1] A. Chassang, *Histoire du Roman dans l'Antiquité Grecque et Latine*, Paris,
Didier, 1862; (Sainte-Beuve, *Nouveaux Lundis*, vol. ii.). Erwin Rohde, *Der
Griechische Roman u. seine Vorläufer*, Leipzig; Breitkopf and Härtel, 1876.

class. Our five classes may then be taken as (*a*) the tale of Troy
and cognate legends of early Greece, (*b*) the literary offspring of
Plato in two families—the descendants of Atlantis and of Er the
Armenian, (*c*) the history, degenerating into the romance, of
Alexander, with two great subdivisions, the tale of the hero, and
the tale of travel, (*d*) the avowed love-tale, and (*e*) the fiction
with an immediate national or religious purpose.

Our first group need not detain us long, important as it is.
The tale of Troy and the other tales of early Greece were first
worked over by the tragic poets; they were systematized by
collectors of mythology, and violently rationalized into history by
historians of the lower type, who "tortured mythology to the
detriment of poetry and without profit to history[1]"; they were
altered and abused by rhetoricians and sophists like Philostratus
(in his *Heroicus*) and the fabricators of Dares and Dictys; they
were turned into pantomimes and danced all over the Roman world
and perhaps even outside it; they recaptured Europe in the middle
ages, when Achilles and Hector disputed the popularity of Roland
and Arthur[2]: and finally at the revival of learning they took with
new life a still deeper hold on a wider world, which they yet retain.

Our second group we associate for convenience with the name
of Plato. While some took Atlantis for a real country, others saw
more clearly that, as Strabo wittily says, "its creator destroyed
it just as the poet did the wall of the Greeks" (c. 102). Real
or imaginary, it was a fruitful example, and the seas of the world,
or rather the parts outside the world, were dotted with ideal
communities on happy islands, which alas! fled further and further
away with the growth of Geography. As might be expected,
these lands appeared most often when the existing countries were
labouring under unhappy conditions. At a later day, and this is
more important for our present purpose, when the centre of gravity
in philosophy had shifted from the state to the individual, a new
type of Utopia displaces the old, the Utopia of happy thinkers who
live an ideal life of contemplation without any government at all,
without a state or social questions, and free from all disquieting
foreign or domestic policies. The book *On the Contemplative*

---

[1] Chassang's phrase. See Boissier, *Country of Horace and Virgil*, c. iii. § 1,
a good chapter dealing with the legend of Aeneas "falling into the hands of the
chroniclers and scholiasts. It had no reason to rejoice....The learned are not
light-handed."

[2] See Comparetti, *Vergil in the Middle Ages*, pt. ii. c. 1, who shews Virgil's
share in the popularity of the story of Troy.

Life, attributed, though wrongly, to Philo the Jew, is an example
of this. It describes the Therapeutae, who lived an ascetic
life together in large numbers a little way out of Alexandria, so
successfully avoiding attention that no geographer, traveller or
philosopher ever found them except in the novel.

The story of Er the Armenian was much derided by the
Epicureans, but it had a great influence. Cicero imitated it in
his dream of Scipio, which in its turn produced Macrobius' commentary, a book much used in the middle ages. Plutarch twice
copied it—in his vision of Timarchus (in the *de genio Socratis*)
and his story of the trance of Thespesius (*de sera numinum vin-
dicta*), the latter, according to Archbishop Trench, being not
altogether unworthy to stand beside Plato's Er[1]. How far these
and similar works may have influenced the authors of such Christian
apocalypses as those that bear the names of Peter and of Paul,
or whether their inspiration is to be found exclusively in the
Jewish thought that gave birth to such works as *The Secrets
of Enoch* and the apocalypse of Baruch, it is not for me to determine.

Our third group is perhaps more popular. The imagination
of the Greek world seized on Alexander and his wars and his travels,
embellished the tale with the marvels of mythology and the wonders
of India, and in the end left very little of the real Alexander.
Travellers' tales confused by far-away memories of the Mahabharata
and the Ramayana, by misunderstood monuments of Indian art or
worship, by Brahmanical fables of all sorts, attached themselves
to Alexander, and the marvellous tale grew with every generation[2].
The false Callisthenes' story of Alexander exists in some twenty
manuscripts with corruptions and additions of every age. Now it
was the Huns and now the Turks that the hero repelled. The
book was done into Latin, into Armenian, into Arabic and thence
into Syriac and Persian, into Hebrew from the Latin, into Turkish,
into Ethiopic from the Arabic version of the Greek, and so forth[3].
Elements were borrowed from it for other tales as freely as they
were added to it, and it has recently been pointed out that Scottish
history has been enriched from this source, for it seems that Bruce's
speech at Bannockburn and his slaying of Bohun are "practically

[1] Trench, *Plutarch*, p. 143.
[2] Chassang, *op. cit.* 140. Sainte-Beuve's comment on the influence of
Alexander on Greek letters deserves quotation: "Le goût attique avait été lui
aussi vaincu à Chéronée" (*Nouveaux Lundis*, ii. p. 423).
[3] E. A. Wallis Budge, Intr. to the Syriac *Hist. of Alexander the Great*.

identical, even in language, with portions of an early Scots translation of the old French romance of Alexander the Great." It is
comforting that this discovery has been made by a Scotsman[1].

The romance of the hero is of course older than Alexander.
Mankind did not wait till his day for tales of adventure, witness
the *Odyssey*, " die älteste Robinsonade." Again, the *Cyropaedia* is
a romance of a hero's education, and it is only in comparatively
modern times that it began to pass for history[2]. Romances por-
traying ideal types of character multiply with time. Cato was
hardly dead before his party began to canonize him. Brutus, Cicero
and Fadius Gallus at once wrote *Catos*, and Caesar had to reply
with an *anti-Cato* and set Hirtius to make another[3]. But it was
later and in philosophy that most of this work was done. Philostratus' *Life of Apollonius of Tyana* was undertaken at the
command of an Empress, Julia Augusta, because the *Life* which
she had wanted literary merit. Philostratus sends Apollonius
everywhere, with some errors of Geography, and sets him to perform
miracles and expose devils, with no regard for sense or fact. Now
he catches a satyr asleep[4], now he shews a young man that his
sweetheart is an Empusa intent on sucking his blood. It has been
supposed that this work was meant to counteract the gospels, but
it soars away from them into a rarefied atmosphere of New Pythagoreanism, of mystic asceticism. The real contrast is with Socrates,
Chassang says, and not with Christ. Porphyry in a somewhat
similar spirit wrote a life of Pythagoras, and even in the life of
his own master, Plotinus, sees fit, alongside of lists of his works,
to introduce interviews with demons and gods called up by magic[5].
This characteristic introduction of the magical into biography must
be remembered when we are dealing with the lives of the saints,
for it is not peculiar to them ; indeed it is often less noticeable
there than in pagan works. In some measure we may take Lucian's
story of the ingenious false prophet Alexander and his god re-
incarnated in a snake as a reaction at once against magic and
prophet.

---

[1] I owe the fact to Mr Andrew Lang's review of Mr Neilson's *John Barbour,
Poet and Translator.*
[2] See Chassang's excellent chapter on this work, pp. 45—70.
[3] Cicero, *ad Att.* xii. 45, *ad Fam.* vii. 24.
[4] St Jerome has a satyr awake in his *Life of Paul*—a surprisingly pious
one—and he declares that all the world knows another was exhibited alive
at Alexandria in Constantius' reign (c. 8).
[5] See St Augustine's criticism on Porphyry in this matter, *C. D.* x. 9—11.

The romance of travel was pushed beyond all reason till "things beyond Thule" (a reference to the romance of Antonius Diogenes) was a by-word for an impossible story. Ethiopians and Indians and especially Brahmans were the stock-in-trade of this kind of writing, along with big-eared men, dog-headed and one-eyed men, who reappear in Sir John Mandeville. Lucian in his *True History* parodies this class of fiction, naming as his great models Ctesias and Iambulus, and above all "Homer's Odysseus, who is their leader and teacher in this nonsense." Anticipating Jules Verne he goes from the earth to the moon, and travels probably ten thousand leagues under the sea, perhaps with more comfort than the Frenchman's heroes, for he finds a large island inside a big fish. Incidentally he reaches the Islands of the Blessed, and meets Homer who writes him a poem, and Odysseus who gives him a message for Calypso. There is not, as in Gulliver, any special satire against society in this piece, except the general satire against "the established practice of lying that marks philosophers"—no doubt a fling at the Utopia-makers.

Our fourth class is the love-tale. Rohde has traced its antecedents to local legends and popular tales, treated and modified by the writers of Alexandria, and preserving much of their style, not without traces of oriental influences. Such "tales of Miletus" were early popular and early won a bad name. It is notorious how many of them were found in the loot of Crassus' camp by the Parthians in 53 B.C. They continued to be written anew for many centuries, sometimes in the form of letters. One of them is readily accessible to the English reader in *Pericles, Prince of Tyre*. This was originally a Greek romance[1], written perhaps in the third century, worked over by a Latin, perhaps in the seventh, who confused it, adding the story of King Antiochus which has singularly little connexion with the rest, some more or less Christian reflexions and some Latin riddles. It passed into the *Gesta Romanorum*, and was done into English verse by Gower and incurred the censure of Chaucer:

> But certainly no word ne wryteth he
> Of thilke wikke ensample of Canace
> That lovede hir owne brother sinfully ;
> Of swiche cursed stories I sey "fy" ;

---

[1] See Rohde, *op. cit.* iv. 3, pp. 408—424.

Or elles of Tyro Apollonius...
Of swiche unkinde abominaciouns
Ne I wol noon reherse, if that I may[1].

Shakespeare turns Apollonius into Pericles, but holds fairly closely to the old tale's incidents.

It is a strange feature about this class of tale that, while the episodes are often extremely indecent, the character of the heroine, sometimes by accident only, but generally of her set design, is kept stainlessly pure. She is invariably a beautiful doll, who wakens the most unfortunate passions by her beauty. It may be that this preservation of her chastity survives from older days before the sophists and stylists took the romance in hand, days when it was a tale told among the common people, with a preference for *bourgeois* virtue, which was foreign to the goddesses and princesses of legend. None the less, serious people frowned on this class of books, and Julian forbade his priests to read them.

Our fifth class, while still fiction, is of rather a different character. I group here anecdotes, which swell into imaginary episodes of history for a purpose. Josephus quotes an old tale of a most friendly interview between Alexander the Great and the Jewish High Priest, invented as a document to support national claims. Such devices were not unknown to the Romans, and later on were revived with great effects in the Donation of Constantine and the False Decretals. Of course these are forgeries, but there are other productions surely meriting a less severe name. There is a great deal of Jewish apocalyptic writing, every book bearing the name of some great worthy of the past who did not write it. Their object was to justify the ways of God to men, and to explain why good and evil fall to men as it seems without distinction of vice and virtue, and above all why the nation, God's chosen people, the righteous people, fared so ill. Enoch is made to prophesy and see into things invisible in order to encourage the writer's contemporaries to faith and courage. Antiquity was not very severe as a rule in the domain of criticism, and saw nothing morally questionable in attributing a document to a great name to secure its reaching its goal. The book of Enoch had a wide influence not only on other similar literature but on some of the New Testament writers. Among the heathen, poems reputed to be by Orpheus were circulated at a late date, and abundance of oracles

---

[1] Prologue to the Man of Lawe's Tale.

were invented by Jew and Christian for the Sibyl, but as these are
in verse we perhaps need not further consider them.

These then are our five classes. They are not mutually exclusive,
for the Greek romance of love, as we have it to-day, has elements
of the romance of travel and perhaps even of the Utopia.
Nor are they quite comprehensive enough, for it would be hard
to set down in any one of them the Latin *Golden Ass* of Apuleius,
and still harder the book of Petronius Arbiter. But after all these
are both avowedly medleys, and parts of his work Apuleius drew,
he says, from Milesian tales. What of *Cupid and Psyche*? Where
does it come? Myth, parable or fairy tale, which is it?

Eventually Greek romance and literature generally fell into the
hands of sophists and rhetoricians. We may say, this happened
under Roman rule, recent discoveries shewing that the erotic novel
as we know it was already in full bloom in the first century.
Rhetoric pervaded everything. Romancers, poets, emperors and
fathers of the Church, all are tinged with it. The sermon of the
Christian preacher was called by the same name as the declamation
of the rhetorician (*homilia*, *logos*), and indeed was modelled after
it[1]. East and West, Roman and Greek, felt the effects of the
rhetorical school.

Synesius was a great admirer of Dio Chrysostom, the prince of
rhetorical sophists, but he draws a distinction between his rhetorical
and his political declamations. In the former, he says, Dio " holds
his head high and gives himself airs, *like the peacock turning round
to look at itself*; he seems delighted with the charms of his discourse,
as if this were his only aim, as if his end were grace of expression."
This attitude of the peacock, acute self-consciousness, tends to spoil
every production of the rhetorical schools, including the novels.
Style is the first thing and often the last, style so overdone that
in the end it is deplorable. Fine phrases are stolen, pretty words
hunted up, scraps of poetry culled from every age of poets, and
all are woven together into a patchwork of preciousness[2]. The

---

[1] See Hatch, *Hibbert Lectures*, no. iv. on Greek and Christian rhetoric.

[2] None of the Greeks is half so successful in this style as Apuleius. Here
genius has lifted a style of most doubtful antecedents into a region far above
anything of the kind in Greek. The *Golden Ass* is a triumph. Sainte-Beuve
is right on this against whatever odds, *Nouveaux Lundis*, vol. ii. p. 442. For
strange judgments on the school, cf. Monceaux (cited by Boissier, *L'Afrique
Romaine*, p. 246) who thinks Ap. has "the air of a Bedouin at a congress of
classics." Koziol, *der Stil des L. Apuleius*, may be consulted, especially the
section B (on figures). Socrates (vi. 22) says of Bp Sisinnius, λεξιθηρεῖ καὶ
ποιητικὰς παραμίγνυσι λέξεις—a good description of the school—and goes on to
say he was better to listen to than to read.

main thing is to display the author's cleverness, and he tries to do this by descriptions of every kind.

Yet while they were pilfering from Homer's vocabulary, the sophists never learnt why he did not describe Helen, for example, though her beauty was the base of his whole story[1]. Physical beauty is the outcome of a combination of a large number of elements all taking effect at once. The painter can therefore reproduce it but not the poet. The poet can make a list of some or all of these elements but he cannot coordinate them, nor can the rhetorician do more. His list can no more produce the effect of beauty, than a series of labelled and stoppered bottles, full of simple chemical substances, ranged along a laboratory shelf, can be said to represent some highly complicated compound of them all.

If it is not a human being, it is a scene, a landscape, that is described, or the picture of one. Thus Achilles Tatius begins his novel with a description of a picture of Europa and the bull. "Europa's the picture; the Phoenicians' the sea; Sidon's the land. On the land a meadow and a troop of maidens. In the sea a bull was swimming, and on his back a fair maiden sat, sailing to Crete on the bull. With many flowers bloomed the meadow; with them was mingled an array (phalanx) of trees and shrubs; close together the trees; intermingled their leaves; the branches joined their leaves, and thus the thickness of the leaves was to the flowers a roof. The artist had painted under the leaves the shade also; and the sun gently strayed down the meadow in patches, so far as the painter opened the over-arching of the leafy foliage. The whole meadow an enclosure walled about. The beds of flowers grew in rows under the leaves of the shrubs, narcissus and roses and myrtles. And water ran through the midst of the meadow in the picture, some springing up from the earth below, some poured about the flowers and the shrubs. And a field-waterer had been painted with a mattock in his hand, bending over one ditch and opening a way for the water." This figure is borrowed from Homer (*Iliad* xxi. 257) as a number of verbal coincidences plainly shew, and he adds the one touch of life to the picture. For the rest it is conventional, and so it always is. The criticism Bernardin de St Pierre passed on travellers' descriptions will do for those of the sophists—"they are as barren as a geographical map: Hindostan resembles Europe; there is no character in it[2]."

[1] See Lessing, *Laocoon*, c. 20.
[2] Arvède Barine, *Bernardin de St Pierre* (Engl. ed.), p. 51.

Compare Atalanta's cave in the Arcadian bush. There is of course ivy about it, and ivy in the trees ; crocuses in the soft and deep grass, and hyacinth and many other hues of flowers, not only as a feast for the vision, but their fragrance seized the air around, etc. Laurels there were many, and vines growing before the cave shewed the labour of Atalanta ; continuous and never-failing waters, fair to see and cold, to judge by touch and learn by taste, flowed plenteous and ungrudging, convenient for the watering of the trees ; and the spot was full of charms, making an austere and modest chamber for the maiden[1]. Compare again a livelier document, Synesius' letter to his brother (*Ep.* 114), for another scene of flower and tree[2].

Sometimes the novelists will adorn their stories with descriptions of natural marvels. Here is Achilles Tatius on the hippopotamus, a most appropriate animal for a love-tale, but it comes in very gracefully. Charmides, a military officer, invites hero and heroine, who have just been rescued by him, to inspect the beast newly killed by his men. "The horse of the Nile the Egyptians call it, and it is a horse (as its name implies) in regard to belly and feet, except that it splits the hoof: in size about the biggest ox ; its tail short and bare of hair, as the rest of its body is also : its head round, not small : its cheeks like a horse's ; its nostril gaping wide and breathing fiery smoke, as from a fount of fire ; its chin broad as its cheek ; its mouth opens back to its eyebrows. Its canine teeth are curved, in shape and place like a horse's but three times the size" (iv. 2). The reader should now have no difficulty in recognizing the beast. From the hippopotamus it is but a step to the elephant (cc. 4, 5) and not very far to the crocodile (c. 19). It will be seen that the luckless lovers are in Egypt, an almost inevitable country for lovers.

Sometimes the novelist prefers magic to nature. In the love-tales the magic is generally slight, an oracle perhaps at most, but in lives of holy men there is plenty of it—demons, enchantments, transportations and so forth. How far Apuleius' *Golden Ass* begins by being gently satirical only, I cannot say, but it does not so end. The whole basis of the tale is magic, and if in some of the episodes the author is making fun of it, he certainly had to stand his trial on a charge of using magic. The heathen revival of the second and third centuries was in fact largely based on

---

[1] Aelian, *V. H.* xiii. 1.   [2] Cited on p. 336.

magic—a point not always realized. If comment be needed, Lucian's amusing dialogue called *The Lover of Falsehood* may be read, a beautiful collection of ghost stories and enchantments. If Lucian scoffed, and the devout trembled, the rhetorician was cool, and added magic to his other themes for decoration.

Descriptions of emotions delight the school. Achilles in particular enjoys describing their psychology—explaining tears, or the effect of anger on the feelings. Longus is less clever, but more successful (if still rhetorical), and traces the gradual growth of love in Daphnis and Chloe with great delicacy according to Sainte-Beuve, but perhaps to say this one must be devoted to *Paul and Virginia*.

Summing up then we may say that the rhetorical novelist tries to capture us by his exhibitions of cleverness, his descriptions, his general brilliance, but he does not move us or convince us. The reason is that after all he is out of touch with life and reality. His scenes are unreal and conventional, never drawn from nature, but from books. His figures are unreal too—dolls, puppets, automata. The hero and the heroine, the gentlemanly brigand[1], the too susceptible captain, the pirate, are all lifeless, none realized. They have no individuality, no distinctive character. Their only motive is what their creator calls love, which is too good a name for it. With every newcomer to the scene, the heroine is in fresh danger. But even with this one motive or incentive, no legitimate action ever takes place. There are no real consequences of anything. Everything is chance. Sometimes an oracle, sometimes a dream starts things, and then begins a wild series of mechanical adventures, pirates, storms, robbers, slavery, separation, murder (never real murder) and everything to harass hero, heroine and reader. One thing is always certain—what will happen next is beyond conjecture, but in the end it will not matter, for nothing ever comes of threatening danger except delay. It should not be so, but "the fortuitous interference of Providence" (to quote Prof. Mahaffy's Irish judge) is invariable, and hero and heroine are rescued for the next mishap. "Once more," cries Xenophon's heroine, "once more pirates and sea! once more am I a captive!" Of course she is, and she may expect to lose her lover and follow him or be pursued by him over land and sea, coming within a

---

[1] One must however respect the best of all possible brigands—those of Apuleius in the *Golden Ass*, bk. iv. "C'est à donner envie de se faire brigand, si l'on a du cœur," says Sainte-Beuve of the story of Lamachus there told.

hair's-breadth of meeting him, but never achieving it till the last book, when, as Rohde says, one is glad to find them accidentally meeting, so that the marionettes can be laid back in the box[1].

One consequence in literature of this general failure to be true to reality is the decline of history. True, we have in Eusebius, Ammianus and Socrates three admirable historians, judicious, thoughtful and truthful, but perhaps the bad name of Rufinus is a better index of the feeling of the day. It is very interesting to see how Socrates from the first emphatically disclaims rhetoric— he will " give no thought to pomp of diction" (i. 1, 3)—and when by and by he finds out that Rufinus instead of consulting evidence has been guessing (καταστοχάζεσθαι), he goes back over his work and remodels his own first two books to bring them into harmony with truth (ii. 1, 3). Jerome himself accuses Rufinus of lying—of saying whatever comes into his mouth (*quidquid in buccam venerit*—a much better phrase). This is exactly the mark of rhetorical history, carelessness of everything but effect. The anecdote triumphs over everything but the speech, for every great man in history becomes a declaimer. The great defect of the rhetoricians, says Chassang, is to make their heroes in their own image[2]. Alexander the Great, Apollonius of Tyana, Pythagoras are drawn as the rhetorician thinks they should have been, very like himself. He inserts in their story anything that interests himself or that he thinks telling. I have already alluded to Porphyry's life of his teacher Plotinus, which shews history degenerating into romance. The effects of this style of writing are far-reaching.

That Christian writers should be influenced by their environment is not surprising. They are harshly judged sometimes in our days for faults they shared with heathen contemporaries : rather unjustly so, for the really remarkable thing is that they are on the whole so free comparatively from them, and after all they are known and read because they were so free. Everybody knows Tertullian's faults, and as they are not those of to-day they attract attention. How many critics of Tertullian could give as good an account of Philostratus or Porphyry or even Apuleius ? There is no comparison between the men. Tertullian has many faults of style which they have, but he is clean, he is serious and he is truthful. There is no one

---

[1] Rohde, *op. cit.* p. 400.
[2] Cf. Comparetti, *op. cit.* pt. II. c. 1, on the medieval transformation of Virgil into a magician.

so terribly in earnest as he with his seriousness born of penitence, but he flashes with assonance, antithesis and epigram to match the most flippant. But the writers with whom we are dealing are smaller men and more obscure. Yet they too, while reflecting their age, are marked by the seriousness of the new view of life.

In the first place the Christian novelists, if I may so call them, while they often shew the same faults as the heathen, do not shew them in such excess. Their pictures of life and society are still very apt to be conventional, and, if not conventional, at least unreal. Their characters are often wooden and their history is sadly to seek. But, whether the reader count this for better or for worse, they have less of the rhetorical style, they are less self-conscious in their writing, less clever. They have fewer arts and do not attempt to fly so high. Secondly, they are more alive and more serious. They are conscious of new motives in life, of new inspiration, and it is these that as a rule have led them to write, and their writing reflects the quickened spirit.

In almost every kind of literature they challenged the heathen world. They had no new story of Troy, but they had a new tale of truth, and Juvencus wrote about 330 his four books of Evangelic History—a marvellous feat. He made a harmony of the gospels in Latin hexameters, in a plain honest style, wonderfully faithful to the original and yet not without some poetic quality, though the metre is a little monotonous. Apollinaris tried the same in Greek but his work did not survive. But our theme is fiction.

The romance of the hero is represented by a long list of false gospels, some more or less dependent on the canonical four, but all tending to embellish and decorate them with fanciful incidents and other rhetorical devices. Acts of the apostles are perhaps even more numerous, and these permit the interweaving of the romance of travel. Not many of them but some have elements of the love-tale.

I do not know the date of "the wondrous and marvellous history of the glorious acts of Philip the Apostle and Evangelist." It is only extant in Syriac, and was probably first written in that tongue. It certainly deserves its name. Philip, in answer to his sea-captain's despair, prays for a wind that shall take them from Caesarea to Carthage in a day, and it comes and incidentally hangs head-downward from the mast a blaspheming Jewish passenger. "The ship was flying and going over the water like an eagle in the air," and the Jew hanging by his great toes was very uncomfortable. Philip inquires, "Now how dost thou view the matter?" and the Jew's confession is so extensive that we feel either he or the historian has read the apologists on the Old Testament. Philip rejoiced at this conversion, and the penitent is released. Arrived at Carthage Philip proceeds to find Satan, "an Indian man" (*i.e.* a black man) on a throne, with a belt of two snakes and a garland of vipers, with eyes like coals of fire, and belching flame from his mouth. He is overthrown by the sign of the cross, and Philip sets forth to preach.

The *Acts of Thomas* is a very different work, having a clear purpose in its insistence on virginity and asceticism—a Gnostic book also written by a Syrian and therefore perhaps outside our scope, though it is found in a Greek translation. We shall give more attention to an original composition in Greek on Greek models and of undisputed orthodoxy—the *Acts of Xanthippe and Polyxena.*

Another group of Christian romances, while connected with the tale of the hero, is perhaps rather to be classed with the Utopias. The romance of hermit life begins perhaps with Antony and goes on with Paul and others, and there is this distinction between it and an *Alexander the Great* that it exhibits an ideal life which all men may follow. We may all be Antonies, and the writer indicates that we should if we knew what is good for us, but Alexander lies beyond us.

Lastly, we may set down the apocalypses with their pictures of the other world in the same class with Er the Armenian, though, as I have indicated, their descent from him is very doubtful. Here too we often find a special purpose beside the general moral drift which marks such works.

Now that we have made our survey of Pagan and Christian fiction, it will be well to concentrate our attention on one or two examples of each class. The pagans will be represented by Achilles Tatius because he is like most of the pagan novelists, and Longus because he is unlike them. The *Acts of Xanthippe and Polyxena* is a clear imitation of these by a Christian hand. The latter part of the *Gospel of Nicodemus* will illustrate romance attaching itself to the Gospel. The *Apocalypse of Paul* will shew us a link in a great series of visions of hell and give us a hint of a great movement, which was not merely pictured in the *Life of Antony* but immensely promoted by it.

The story of Clitophon and Leucippe is told by Achilles Tatius in eight books. The date of its composition is uncertain. Rohde puts it after the beginning of the third century and before the middle of the fourth. The tale is told by the hero to the author whom he meets in front of the picture of Europa and the bull, part of the description of which I have quoted. Clitophon, a young man of Tyre, it was designed by his father, should marry his half-sister, but he did not want to, and instead fell in love with his cousin Leucippe from Byzantium. He wins her love by sighs and other pretty manœuvres, and a little chapter is devoted to their drinking from each other's cups turn about by way of signalling kisses. Ere long of course, for lovers must have adventures, they fly together and take ship at Berytus for Alexandria. They meet a storm, a rhetorician's storm, and are shipwrecked, reaching safety at Pelusium, where they see some works of art (carefully described) in a temple. They are caught by robbers and separated. Clitophon's rescue comes first, and he has to look on helplessly while Leucippe is made a human sacrifice, but he finds very soon it was a mere pantomime done with a collapsible dagger from a theatre. Then Charmides, the commander of the soldiers who rescued them, falls in love with Leucippe, who resists him, but is rendered dramatically insane by a potion given by another lover. After some fighting between soldiers and natives, Clitophon gets her safely away, cured by another charm. She is kidnapped again, and from the deck of his ship in pursuit Clitophon sees her head cut off—this time it is not a theatrical dagger, and a head is cut off, though of course not Leucippe's, as it turns out afterwards. He now returns to Alexandria and a rich widow falls in love with him, and carries him back to Ephesus. There he finds Leucippe a slave, and terrible complications follow. The widow's husband re-appears, for he had not after all been drowned, and he strongly disapproves of Clitophon. Melite (the lady no longer a widow) finds out about Leucippe, who is assailed first by a fellow-slave and then by Melite's husband but is saved from both. Prison and process, escapes and entanglements now jostle one another in quick succession for hero and heroine, but all characters are cleared by the ordeal of a miraculous fountain, which always drowns the perjurer. Melite distinctly gets the better of heaven by an ingeniously worded oath[1]. Clitophon and Leucippe go to Byzantium and are married, and the half-sister at Tyre is also married to a man who

---

[1] This is later on a favourite device of story-tellers. Cf. Comparetti, *Vergil in the Middle Ages*, p. 337.

early in the story had kidnapped her under the impression that she was Leucippe. What more?

Descriptions of nature, as we have seen, and discussions of psychology, excursions into mythology, geography and antiquarianism, an account of the Nile, a picture of Alexandria, speeches, letters and all sorts of things embellish the tale, but hardly save it from being tiresome. Achilles does not trouble heaven very much, but trusts to Fortune giving him all the confusion he wants. Yet at one time he has recourse to a dream to stop Clitophon's marriage. And after all, when once the half-sister was kidnapped, everything was clear and there need have been no elopement, but in that case there would have been no tale.

Suidas says this man Achilles became a Christian and was made a bishop, but critics find in this a mere imitation of the similar tale about Heliodorus. Socrates says, *people said* that Heliodorus, bishop of Tricca, was the author of the romance *Aethiopica*—it was a mere story which he quoted. Heliodorus says of himself that he was a Phoenician of Emesa, a descendant of the Sun, and Rohde rather associates him with the revival of Neo-Pythagoreanism and the Syrian dynasty in the early years of the third century. Neither he nor Achilles is to be credited with a bishopric.

The romance of Longus[1] depends for its charm on quiet country life with no foreign adventures. True there are one or two raids upon the peaceful scene, but heaven interposes some miracles and all is restored to be as it was. I do not know that the story would be affected, except perhaps in length, by the complete omission of these episodes.

It is a tale of two children, a boy and a girl, exposed as infants by their parents and miraculously preserved. This does not seem a very probable beginning for a tale, but it is more probable than it seems. One of the things that distinguished Christians from pagans was, according to the apologists, that they did not expose their children. Tertullian tells a horrible story of one actual case among heathens. The reason in Longus' case for using this artifice was to give a conclusion of wealth and splendour to his tale, and to introduce a momentary doubt as to whether Daphnis, recognized

---

[1] See Sainte-Beuve's essay in *Nouveaux Lundis*, vol. iv. He quotes Villemain and Goethe as types of the severe and the appreciative critics of Longus, leaning himself to admiration, as he is perhaps apt to do, but not failing to remark some necessary deductions.

as a rich man's son, would still care to marry Chloe. Dio Chrysostom, in his *Euboicus*, draws a picture of the happy life and contented poverty of two families of hunters in the wild lands of Euboea, but for a romance one wants a more triumphant ending than for a political or social parable.

The chief interest of Longus' novel lies in the idealization of the love of a boy and girl growing up together among goats and sheep in the happy worship of Pan and the nymphs. There are points that strike a modern reader oddly, as for instance Chloe's failure to remark the existence of such a thing as an echo till she was about fourteen. They both are too surprisingly innocent to be convincing, and here it is that Longus shews himself unmistakably of the family of Priapus by an exaggerated and impossible *naïveté*. Longus is at last disgusting, where Saint-Pierre is beautiful. But if we take episodes out of the story and concentrate attention on them as some of its admirers have done, we get a more happy impression. For like the other Greek novels this one breaks up easily into a series of more or less independent scenes, which could be rearranged, added to or lessened without material import. These better scenes then, taken by themselves, are pleasing, but they are not simple, and though nearer nature than anything else in Greek fiction, it is nature drawn by a rhetorician, a man of more taste than his class but still a rhetorician.

Chloe is first to fall in love, as is Virginia in the French novel. She sees Daphnis bathing. "What it was she suffered, she knew not, being but a young maid, bred in the country and one that had never heard tell of the name of love. Sickness seized her soul, and she was not mistress of her eyes, and much she talked of Daphnis. Her meat she neglected; by night she waked; her flock she despised; now she would laugh; now she would weep; then she would sleep; then she would start up; her face was pale, and again it flamed with a blush; nor would a cow stung by a gadfly behave as Chloe did."

Daphnis and a shepherd boy called Dorco dispute as to their comparative charms, and Chloe awards the prize, a kiss, to Daphnis, who falls in love with her and does not understand it. Here is his soliloquy.

"What can it be that Chloe's kiss does to me? Lips softer than roses and a mouth sweeter than honey-combs; but the kiss than the sting of a bee more painful. Oft have I kissed kids, oft have I kissed puppies newly born and the calf Dorco gave me.

But this kiss is strange; my breath leaps, my heart pants, my soul melts, and yet I would kiss again. O evil victory! O strange disease! whose very name I know not. Then did Chloe taste of drugs ere she kissed me? how then did she not die? How do the nightingales sing, and my pipe is silent! How do the kids leap, and I sit still! how do the flowers bloom, and I weave no garlands! but the violets and the hyacinth flower, and Daphnis withers. Then will Dorco seem more comely than I?"

All this is artificial in the highest degree, thoroughly rhetorical in every way. It is literary rather than spontaneous. The writer has read Theocritus and thinks of him, but his work is not Theocritean, for he has been infected with the arts of the school. Here is the series of little sentences, word by word exactly balancing; antithesis; apostrophe and abundance of echoes and false conceits. Let us try something better.

Winter came on and there was no more pasture in the open, but all the country folk were kept about their homes and farm buildings, so Daphnis and Chloe could not meet. Chloe was being taught to dress wool and use the spindle, but Daphnis had no such work to do and devised a plan to see her.

"Before the farmhouse of Dryas [her foster-father] and just under it were two tall myrtles and ivy upon them. The myrtles were near each other, the ivy between them, so that reaching its tendrils to both like a vine, it made an appearance of a cave with the alternating leaves; and clusters of ivy berries, many and big as grapes, hung from the branches. Round about them was a great swarm of winter birds, for food without failed—many a blackbird, many a thrush, and wood-pigeons, and starlings, and all other birds that eat ivy-berries. On pretence of catching these birds Daphnis set forth after filling his wallet with honey-cakes and taking bird-lime and snares as a pledge of his purpose. The distance was not more than ten stades, but the snow not yet melted gave him much trouble. But to love after all everything is an open way, fire and water and Scythian snow.

"He comes then at a run to the farm, and shaking the snow from his legs he set his snares, and the bird-lime he smeared on many twigs, and then sat down thinking of the birds and of Chloe. But birds came in large numbers and were caught in plenty, so that he had no end of trouble in gathering them, killing them and plucking their feathers. But from the farm no one came out, not man, not woman, not domestic fowl, but all abode lying by the fire

within, so that Daphnis was in sore straits, thinking they were
not lucky birds that gave him the omen to come (a pun, οὐκ ἐπ᾽
αἰσίοις ὄρνισι).   And he tried to gather courage to enter the doors
with some excuse and sought in himself what would be most
plausible.   'I came to get fire ; but were there not neighbours but
a stade away ?   I came to ask loaves ; but the wallet is full of
food.   I need wine ; but it was yesterday or the day before you
gathered the vintage.   A wolf was chasing me ; but where are the
wolf's footprints ?   I came to catch birds ; why then, when you
have caught them, do you not go away ?   I wish to see Chloe ;
but who confesses this to the father and mother of a maiden ?
Every approach is vain ; none of these but is suspicious.   Better
then be silent.   I shall see Chloe in the spring, since it is
not fated, so it seems, I should see her in the winter.'   With
some such thought in his mind he gathered up what he had
caught and started to go ; and, as if Love pitied him, this
befell.

"Dryas and his household were sitting at table ; meat had
been divided, loaves were set before them, wine was being mixed.
One of the sheep-dogs, watching for an unguarded moment, snatched
a piece of meat and fled through the doors.   In vexation Dryas
(for it was his portion) caught up a stick and ran after him,
tracking him like another dog ; and as he pursued and came to
the ivy, he sees Daphnis with his booty on his shoulders and ready
to depart.   Meat and dog at once he forgot, and with a great
shout, 'Welcome, my boy,' he began to embrace and kiss him
and took him by the hand and led him in.   When they saw each
other they all but fell to the earth, but making an effort to
stand upright they greeted and kissed each other, and this was
as it were a prop that they should not fall.

"So Daphnis, after giving up hope, had a kiss and had Chloe,
and sat near the fire and put from his shoulders on to the table
his burden of wood-pigeons and blackbirds, and told how he grew
weary of staying at home and went out to catch them, and how
he took some of them with snares and some with bird-lime in their
greed for the myrtles and the ivy.   And they praised his energy
and bade him eat of what the dog had left them.   And they
bade Chloe pour wine to drink.   And she in gladness gave to
the others and to Daphnis after the others ; for she pretended to
be angry, because he came and was about to go without seeing
her.   However before giving it to him she took a sip, and then

gave to him. And he though thirsty drank slowly, to have a longer pleasure by delay."

The author's failure is a moral one. At the end comes the general recognition and no one seems to attach much blame to the parents, who cast out their children because they had too many or were ill off for money. The general ignoring of evil of a gross kind shews how the rhetorician had fallen into that stage where evil results in insensibility.

Let us now turn to *Xanthippe and Polyxena*, a book I incline to attribute to the fourth century, though the first scholar to print it, Dr M. R. James, says it may belong to the third. The story of the victory by the cross' aid seems to suggest Constantine. It is the *insigne lignum* of triumph. The careful adhesion to "the straight and true faith" and the various theological expressions of it, though they do not refer to Arianism and its distinctive doctrines, yet suggest the great council. Some of the phrases describing other things also point to the later date

The tale, as Dr James shews, borrows hints from a number of others, but it hangs together very well, if we once grant that each of the heroines has her own story. We do not hear of Polyxena till chapter 22 and then we hear little more of Xanthippe. There is about both parts a bright air, a spirit of cheerfulness and faith. The author cannot forget the goodness of God, His mercy and His eagerness for the redemption of the sinful, His providence and care for those who serve Him. This last quite replaces the Fortune of the heathen novelists. At every stage the right man appears—not by accident but by divine instruction and guidance. The writer is like his heroine Xanthippe. "I wish to be silent, but I am compelled to speak, for one within me is fire and sweetness to me[1]." And now a short sketch of the book.

Probus is an official in Spain, a friend of Nero (though his name suggests the 4th century), an honourable man, very fond of his wife Xanthippe, though apt to be irritated by her abstraction and her sometimes rather hysterical piety. His wife, an *anima naturaliter Christiana*, hears of Paul's preaching in Rome and longs for more knowledge of the Gospel. She is much disturbed, to her husband's alarm, but after uttering some prayers, a little too nearly Christian for a heathen, she sees and hears Paul. The apostle is their guest and is heard joyfully by his hostess, who

---

[1] c. 14 φλέγει γάρ μέ τις ἔσωθεν καὶ γλυκαίνει.

has already "the sun of righteousness in her heart." The host after a while is worried by the crowds who come to hear Paul, and, indignant at "my house being made an inn," turns him out, and locks up his wife. She bribes the porter, visits Paul and is baptized, and on her return home has a vision of Christ preceded by a cross on the east wall of the room. But when she saw His face, she hid her own, crying, "Hide thyself, O Master, from my bodily eyes and enlighten my understanding." He vanishes, and overcome by a speechless gratitude she faints—the result of her fasting and watching and the vision. Meantime Probus has had a dream which turns him toward the faith, and he and his wife visit Paul, Probus being greatly impressed by her humility, which was rather a new virtue in her. He is baptized, and after a curious incident in which Xanthippe in a rage stabs a supposed dancer (really a devil) in the face, their story gives place to that of her sister Polyxena.

The story of Polyxena much more closely resembles those of the Greek novels. Probus' house is entered by a man by means of magical arts, and Polyxena is kidnapped. The captor puts her on shipboard to sail to Babylonia. On the way they pass a ship taking St Peter to Rome to overthrow Simon Magus (a fragment of an old story), and Peter by divine warning is bidden pray for a soul in distress on the ship from the west, *i.e.* Polyxena. They land in Greece and meet Philip the evangelist, who rescues Polyxena and entrusts her to a disciple. The kidnapper gets an army of 8000 men from a friend of his, a Count (κόμης), to recapture her. She flies, and her late host's thirty servants raising the sign of the cross slay 5000 of the Count's army and return hymning God. Polyxena takes refuge in a lioness' den—a hollow tree in a dense forest. The lioness however is friendly and guides her to a high road, where St Andrew finds her. She asks for baptism, and at the water they meet a Jewish girl Rebecca, and both maidens are at once baptized, for the lioness reappears and in a human voice bids instruct them in the true faith. Andrew leaves them, for it was not revealed to him that he should go with them. A man driving asses, who has sold his property and makes a mission of feeding the poor, of course a Christian, undertakes to bring the two girls to the sea-shore and aid them to escape to Spain. But they are carried off by a magistrate. The ass-driver tells Philip, who trusts that heaven will preserve them. Once more Rebecca is seized and laments, like Xenophon's heroine, "Again am I a captive." The magistrate's son is a Christian, converted by Paul and Thecla at Antioch, and he befriends Polyxena. In a rage his father exposes him and her to a lioness, who proves to be the old friend. This causes a great sensation and the magistrate is converted. Onesimus (the teller of the tale) appears and preaches, and everybody there is converted. Polyxena and Rebecca are sent safely back to Spain, where they are welcomed warmly by Xanthippe, Probus and Paul. The kidnapper reappears also, but he too is converted. So all ends happily.

It will be recognized that there is much here very like the Greek novel—kidnappings, surprising deliverances, magic and the wonderful lioness. The last suggests Androcles, but is probably a combination of the beasts that will not destroy Thecla (in the *Acts of Paul and Thecla*) and the speaking ass "descended from Balaam's" (in the *Acts of Thomas*). There is however a clear difference between this Christian work and the heathen models, for the heroine's virginity is the expression of a definite faith and service, and also there is nothing in the tale that could be called foul, as there is in every (or nearly every) Greek novel. In all probability the book was designed to supplant such stories. It was not the first Christian novel to borrow a framework from the enemy. The Clementine Homilies lie outside our present scope, but a word or two may be given them. They form one of the most interesting books of early Christianity, for they are in reality an early attack on Paulinism, and Baur and his school have tried to find in them a true presentation of Christianity properly so called. Peter is their hero and Clement is (one may say) his squire, and together they hunt down Simon Magus and other heathen antagonists. To give the story a flavour of life, Clement is represented as in search of his family, who are all scattered by a series of accidents recalling the Greek novel, and who are all found again by the help of Peter and Providence.

From *Xanthippe and Polyxena* we pass to a work of more importance—a work of genius. It is now embedded in the so-called *Gospel of Nicodemus*, a 13th century title for a combination of two much older books, the *Acts of Pilate* and the *Descent into Hell*. The former is a rather tiresome expansion of the Gospel narrative of the Crucifixion, resulting in the "whitewashing" of Pilate to some extent, and the latter is attached to it by a very simple device. Two of the dead, who were raised from their graves in the commotion following the Crucifixion, are called on to give an account of what happened. "They said to the chief priests, Give us paper and ink and pen. They brought them, and sitting down one of them wrote as follows." Here is given the second work, which I will quote in part, taking the Greek text of Thilo. This story is dated somewhere about or a little after the year 400; Maury, followed by Renan, placing it between 405 and 420. Tischendorf puts it a good deal earlier. Chassang compares its opening to Virgil's

Di quibus imperium est animarum umbraeque silentes,
et Chaos et Phlegethon, loca nocte tacentia late,
sit mihi fas audita loqui, sit numine vestro
pandere res alta terra et caligine mersas.

(*Aen.* vi. 264[1].)

"Lord Jesus Christ, the resurrection and the life of the world, give us grace that we may tell of thy resurrection and the marvels thou didst work in Hades. We then were in Hades with all that have slept from the beginning, and in the hour of midnight into that darkness dawned as it were the light of the sun and shone, and we were all enlightened and saw one another." Adam and Isaiah recognize the light as prophesied, and then comes John, "an ascetic from the desert," once more to be forerunner of Christ. Adam and Seth contribute their testimony, and "the patriarchs and the prophets rejoiced greatly."

"And while they thus rejoiced, came Satan, heir of darkness, and saith to Hades, 'All-devouring and insatiate, hear my words. A certain man of the race of the Jews, called Jesus, naming himself Son of God, he being in fact a man,—through my aid the Jews crucified him. And now that he is dead, be thou ready that we may hold him fast. For I know that he is a man, and I heard him say 'My soul is exceeding sorrowful unto death.' He did me much evil in the world above when he lived among men; for wherever he found my servants he drove them out, and as many men as I made maimed, blind, lame, leprous or any such thing, by a word alone he healed them. And when I had made many ready to be buried, these too he brought to life by a word.' Then Hades saith, 'And is he so mighty as to do all this by a word? And how canst thou resist him if he is such?'" Hades doubts the wisdom of

[1] An almost contemporary parallel would be Claudian's overture to his *Rape of Proserpine* (*R. P.* i. 20) *di quibus innumerum vacui famulatur Averni | vulgus iners......vos mihi sacrarum penetralia pandite rerum*, etc. His account of Proserpine's descent into hell (ii. 326 f.) has one or two coincidences with this book —*pallida laetatur regio—rumpunt insoliti tenebrosa silentia cantus—aeternam patitur rarescere noctem*, but with a few such phrases the likeness ends.

Satan's bringing him. "'And this I say to thee, by the darkness we have, that if thou bring him here, none of the dead will be left me.'

" As thus Satan and Hades talked one with the other, there was a great voice as thunder that said, 'Open your gates, ye rulers, and be ye lifted up, ye everlasting gates, and the king of glory shall come in.' And when Hades heard, he saith to Satan, 'Go forth, if thou canst, and withstand him.' So Satan went out. Then saith Hades to his demons, 'Make fast well and strongly the gates of brass and the bars of iron, and hold my barriers, and watch, standing all of you erect; for if he enter here, woe shall overtake us.' When they heard this the forefathers all began to mock him; 'All-devouring and insatiate Hades, open, that the king of glory may come in'...And when Hades heard the voice the second time, as if he knew not, he answered and said, 'Who is this king of glory?' The angels of the Lord say, 'A Lord strong and mighty, a Lord mighty in war.' And immediately at this word the gates of brass were broken, and the iron bars were shattered, and all the bounden dead were loosed from their bonds and we with them. And the king of glory came in, as it were a man, and all the dark places of Hades were enlightened."

Hades recognizes in the conqueror the Jesus who was nailed to the cross, and the arch-satrap Satan is bound in iron and delivered to Hades to be kept till the second coming—not without the taunts of Hades himself.

"The king of glory stretched forth his right hand, and laid hold of our forefather Adam, and raised him up. Then he turned and to the rest he said, 'Come ye with me, all ye who have been slain by the tree of wood this man touched, for behold! again by the wood of the cross I raise you all up.' And with this he put them forth. And our forefather Adam was filled with sweetness and he said, 'I give thanks unto thy majesty, O Lord, that thou hast brought me up from the lowest Hades.' So did all the prophets and the saints, and said, 'We give thee thanks, O Christ, the Saviour of the universe, that thou hast brought up our life from destruction.' While thus they spake, the Saviour blessed Adam on the brow with the sign of the cross, and this he did to the patriarchs and prophets and martyrs and forefathers, and he took them and leapt forth from Hades. And as he went, the holy fathers followed and sang, 'Blessed is he that cometh in the name of the Lord; Alleluia! this is the glory of all the saints.'

" And as he entered into Paradise, holding our forefather Adam

by the hand, he gave him and all the righteous to the archangel
Michael. As they entered in at the door of Paradise, there met them
two old men, to whom the holy fathers said, 'Who are ye, who saw
not death nor descended into Hades, but in your bodies and souls
inhabit Paradise?' And one of them answered and said, 'I am
Enoch, who pleased God and was translated by him, and this is
Elijah the Tishbite; and we shall live till the end of the world, and
then shall we be sent of God to resist Antichrist, and be slain by
him, and after three days rise and be caught up to the clouds to
meet the Lord.'

"And as thus they spake, there came another, a mean man,
bearing upon his shoulders a cross, to whom the holy fathers said,
'Who art thou, that hast the look of a thief, and what the cross thou
bearest on thy shoulders?' He answered, 'I was, as ye see, a thief
and a robber in the world, and therefore for this the Jews delivered
me to the death of the cross with our Lord Jesus Christ. As he
hung on the cross, I saw the signs that befell, and I cried to him and
said; Lord, when thou art king, forget not me. And immediately
he said to me; Verily, verily, to-day, I say unto thee, with me shalt
thou be in Paradise. So bearing my cross I came to Paradise and
found the archangel Michael and said to him; Our Lord Jesus the
crucified sent me hither; bring me in at the gate of Eden. And
when the fiery sword saw the sign of the cross, it opened to me, and
I came in. Then said the Archangel to me: Wait a little, for there
cometh Adam the forefather of the race with the just, that they too
may enter in. And when I saw you I came to meet you.' When
they heard this, the saints cried with a loud voice, 'Great is our
Lord and great is his might.'

" All this we two brothers saw and heard."

This story is not the creation of the fourth century, and perhaps
even this rendering of it is older, but that it was in the minds of
men is shewn by the hymns of Ephraem the Syrian, of Prudentius
and of Synesius[1], if by nothing else. There is a vigour about this
piece and an imagination, which rise to higher levels than the Greek
world dared now to attempt. And yet there is still to be felt in it
that quiet happiness, which Augustine recognized as the mark of the
Church[2]. There is no exaggeration, no rhetoric, but the work is as
simple as it is sublime.

[1] Prudentius, *Cath.* ix. 70—105; Synesius, *Hymn* ix. the translation of
which by Mrs Browning is quoted on p. 355; Ephraem, *Carmina Nisibena*,
xxxvi. 11, 12.
[2] *Conf.* viii. 11, 27 *non dissolute hilaris.*

We pass now to a book intrinsically of less interest but yet one which, Dr James says[1], has left traces of its influence in nearly all the medieval apocalypses and even in Dante's *Divina Commedia*. Its own account of itself is this. "A certain man of repute dwelt in Tarsus in the house of the holy Paul in the consulship of the pious king Theodosius and Gratian the clarissimus [in the Latin he is Cynegius], and to him an angel of the Lord appeared saying, 'Break down the foundation of this house and take up what thou shalt find.' And he thought it was a dream. But when the angel continued till a third vision, the man of repute was compelled to break down the foundation, and he dug and found a marble chest containing this apocalypse, etc."

The historian Sozomen (vii. 19, 34) can add to this. "The apocalypse of Paul the Apostle, as nowadays circulated, though none of the ancients ever saw it, a great many monks praise. Some maintain this book was found in the present reign. For they say that by divine revelation in Tarsus of Cilicia, at the house of Paul, a marble chest was found under the earth and the book was in it. When I asked about it, a Cilician priest of the church in Tarsus said it was a lie—he was an old man too as his white hair shewed, and he said he knew of nothing of the kind occurring among them, and he would be astonished if it were not the invention of heretics. So much about that."

Two things should be noted. A new discovery, especially if led to by some miracle, is a fairly safe index of a forgery. Sozomen's reference to the monks fits in well with the tone of the book. We may therefore conclude it was written in the reign of the younger Theodosius and one of its objects was to help monachism.

The feigned Paul then tells how sun, moon and sea appeal for leave to destroy sinful man, but God's patience protects the race, for which he is to be praised, and especially at sunset. For then the angels come before God to report the works of mankind, and of them all those are most joyful and most bright, who say, "We come from those who have renounced the world and the things of the world for thy holy name's sake who spend their lives in deserts and mountains and caves and dens of the earth, sleeping on the ground and fasting—Bid us be with them." Some come with sorrow "from those who are called by thy name and serve sinful matter." By

[1] Lecture on Apocalypse of Peter, Dec. 1892.

every man's death-bed stand angels, good and bad[1], and to the sinner the bad say "Unhappy soul, look to thy flesh; know whence thou comest out; for thou must return to thy flesh on the day of resurrection, to receive the reward of thy sins." An appalling picture of the soul's trial follows, when, after being confronted with the souls it has wronged, it is cast into outer darkness.

Paul is now taken to the city of the just, meeting Enoch and other patriarchs and prophets, and seeing rivers of honey, milk, oil and wine for the just who in this world abjured the use of them and humbled themselves for God's sake. David too is seen, his face shining as the sun, while he holds in his hand psaltery and harp and sweetly sings *Alleluia* till his voice fills the city. And what means *Alleluia*? In Hebrew it is *thebel marematha* [in the Latin version : *tecel cat marith macha*], 'let us glorify him together.'

Paul now visits hell, and sees the various torments of various sinners. There seems to be no descending scale of misery, but the tortures exist side by side. Let us only notice those who talked in church, and (for the sake of Longus) women who destroyed their children, and lastly the priest "who ate and drank and then served God," the bishop who judged unjustly and pitied neither widow nor orphan, and the deacon "who ate and drank and then ministered to God." Paul weeps, and then, in response to his entreaty and Gabriel's, respite on Sundays is granted to the wicked in hell.

Now Paul visits Paradise and receives the blessing of the Virgin and the lament of Moses for the people of Israel. He meets the three great prophets Isaiah, Jeremiah and Ezekiel, and Noah, who was a model of asceticism while he was building the ark. Then with the appearance of Elijah and Enoch the apocalypse abruptly ends in the middle of Elijah's address to Paul.

This apocalypse is modelled in part on the much earlier apocalypse of Peter, with which it shews some close coincidences. It no doubt impressed the minds of some of its readers, for this kind of revelation seems always to be more or less popular, succeeding better in its descriptions of hell than of heaven and thereby emphasizing some obvious morals. Dr James says indeed that we may owe some even of the present-day ideas of heaven and hell to the apocalypse of Peter, and in this case Paul has perhaps contributed too. But the

---

[1] A somewhat similar scene according to the Manichaeans, with a god of light and the devil of greed and lust, each with his attendants. See Flügel, *Mani, seine Lehre u. Leben*, p. 100.

book is in any case far inferior to the one we treated before it and to the one that follows. "So much about that."

It has been demonstrated in recent years that the *Life of Antony* is a work of fiction. I need not here go over Weingarten's arguments[1], but when once his result is accepted the book becomes much more intelligible. Of all books of the fourth century it had the most immediate and widespread influence, which, though outgrown by now, lasted on to the Renaissance. It was fiction as *Uncle Tom's Cabin* was fiction, and just as this American book, though perhaps not a work of the highest art and certainly denounced in no measured terms by people of the slave-holding States as a fabric of lies, yet swept America and England and, wakening the public conscience, contributed to the freedom of the negro, so the *Life of Antony* came at the right moment, and roused the hearts of good men and women to a sense of the possibilities of a life surrendered to God and dependent on His grace.

There was in the fourth century a great feeling of dissatisfaction with the world and even with the Church[2]. Life was difficult and the churches were not of the greatest possible aid. Then monachism began to suggest itself to the minds of Christians as a way of escape from an evil world and of approach to God. The movement was immensely helped by this *Life of Antony*, a book which displays the triumphs which a simple unlettered monk, trusting in the grace of God, wins over evil in every form. It is hardly a work of art, it is in some places a little tedious, it is often very impossible and sometimes even absurd. Yet it succeeded and deserved to succeed. It was constructed with some thought, if not of the finest. More than one Puritan movement had been unfortunately wrecked, because its leaders quarrelled with the authorities of the Church. Our author is careful to make Antony most respectful to bishop and presbyter (c. 67), yielding precedence to every cleric. Again, he wrote in the thick of the fight with Arianism, and between this heresy and monachism there was mutual hatred[3]. So Antony is exhibited to us as going to Alexandria and there, though an uneducated Copt who could not speak Greek, frustrating the Arian with tremendous effect. And more, the battle was not yet over and

[1] See Herzog's *Realencyklopädie*, vol. x. on Monasticism, A. § III., and Prof. Gwatkin, *Studies of Arianism*, Note B. p. 98.
[2] See Jerome, *Ep.* vii. 5, on his discontent with the bishop of his native place —*ut perforatam navem debilis gubernator regat*—, and above all the writings of Sulpicius Severus.
[3] See Hatch's Bampton Lectures, vi. p. 162.

Antony is represented as already dead, yet before he died he prophesied the troubles which the Church is even now enduring, and from which he foresaw her triumphant emergence.

The book is Puritan. Antony was a mere layman, and for long years he neither went to Church nor saw priest nor took sacrament, and yet lived in close contact with heaven. His ambition was, like that of Francis of Assisi, to follow the Saviour and live a life of evangelic poverty (Mt. xix. 21). Indeed to understand him one must understand Francis—the real Francis as M. Sabatier draws him. He had no need of books; to him as to Francis "it was given to know the mysteries of the kingdom of God, but unto others in parables."

Like nearly every one else our author believed in devils, but not as they did. For one great part of Antony's work is to prove finally that the devil is the most futile of beings. The troops of hell may play all their pranks as they please, but at the sign of the cross they vanish. "For the Lord worked with him, He who wore flesh for us and gave to the body the victory over the devil, so that of those who strive in deed every one may say 'Yet not I, but the grace of God that is in me'" (c. 5). Once the devils flogged him but he prayed. "After his prayer he said with a loud voice, 'Here am I, Antony; I fly not your blows. For though add ye more also, nothing shall separate me from the love of Christ.' And then he sang, 'Though an host should encamp against me, my heart will not fear.'" So the enemy for the time left him. Thus the effect of the book was distinctly to lessen and not to increase the attention paid to devils and demons. Antony is made to deliver a long homily (cc. 16—43) about them, explaining what they seem to do on the lines followed long ago by Apuleius and Tertullian, and emphasizing their insignificance.

Of course he wrought miracles and was generally benevolent and helpful. Not even the notice of the Emperor elated him. In fact every virtue the writer could think of he gave him. To one point I should like to call attention. The author gives Antony that peculiar and happy expression we associate to-day with a strong and active belief in the doctrine of grace. "From the joy of his soul, his face too was bright...he was never disturbed, for his soul was at peace; he was never gloomy, for his mind rejoiced" (c. 67)[1].

---

[1] Sulpicius says the same of St Martin—*caelestem quodammodo laetitiam vultu praeferens; v. Mart.* 27—and I have no doubt this expression did mark off many of the brighter spirits of monachism from a world, which the thought of the present must have made gloomy.

It should not be hard to understand the influence of the book. It was widely read and imitated. Jerome's *Life of Paul* is a copy of it—a wretched, rhetorical, soulless imitation of a great book. Very soon it was actually attributed to Athanasius, who had the credit of it till Weingarten reclaimed it for its anonymous author.

Of its effect on thoughtful people we have a striking illustration in St Augustine. He tells us he had reached a more or less satisfactory solution of his doubts, and now "desired to be not more certain about Thee, but more stable in Thee" (*Conf.* viii. 1, 1), and while he hesitated to commit himself to the Christian life as he now saw it should be, he heard the story of Antony for the first time. He was profoundly moved by the contrast between this ignorant man's achievement of holiness and the low level with which he himself for all his learning was content. Then resolving to try a *sors Biblica*, suggested by the episode of Antony hearing the text "If thou wilt be perfect, go and sell all that thou hast and give to the poor, and come, follow me," he opened at the text in *Romans* which struck home[1]. The great point to notice here is that the essence of the book is that doctrine which Augustine, by his own experience, was being led to make the centre of his faith and teaching—the doctrine of grace.

Here ends our study of the novels. In their own way they reflect their age, the over-elaboration and sterility of style, the failure of civic ideals, the growing individualism, and something of the new life still struggling for expression in the Church.

---

[1] *Conf.* viii. 6, 14 ff. and 12, 29.   See pp. 214—5.

INDEX

Abgar of Edessa, 23, 141, 142; his correspondence with our Lord, 24, 142 n. 1, 143.
Achilles in romance, 359, and Penthesilea, 87, and Polyxena, 100.
Achilles Tatius, 330, 365, 370–372.
Acts of Paul and Thecla, 378.
Acts of Philip, 369.
Acts of Pilate, 378.
Acts of Thomas, 142, 370, 378.
Acts of Xanthippe and Polyxena, 370, 376–8.
Addai, Doctrine of, 23, 141, 142.
Adeodatus, 199, 215.
Adoxography, 342.
Adrianople, battle of, 7, 37, 249, 327 n. 1.
Afrahat, 3, 236.
Agapetae, 299.
Ajax in Quintus, 87, 88; in Ovid, 88.
Alaric, 228, 238, 239.
Alexander the Great, effect of his conquests, 11; in novels, 360, 368, 370; his nose, 130 n. 4.
Alexander, an early pilgrim, 126.
Allegory, 75, 209.
Amarantus, Jewish sea-captain, 330–334.
Ambrose, 121, 153–155, 164, 208, 209, 215, 249, 253, 270, 271, 292, 293.
Amid, 25 n. 2; siege of, 25–28.
Ammianus, see chapter ii. *passim*.
  an Antiochene, 20, 71 n. 1, 72 n. 3;
  his character, 11, 45;
  his truthfulness, 32, 34;
  his birth, 20;
  his education, 32; admiration for Cicero, 32;
  in the army under Ursicinus, 21;
  in affair of Silvanus, 22;
  adventures in campaign of 359, 24, 25;
  at siege of Amid, 25-28;

Ammianus:
  his escape, 28;
  campaign with Julian in East, 28;
  with Julian at his death, 29;
  his indignation at Jovian, 29;
  his travels, 30;
  in Rome, 30, 43, 148;
  in Antioch, 30, 371;
  his views on treason, 31;
  his *History*, 31, 218; its excellence, 34; its variety, 35, 36;
  his death uncertain, 32;
  his style, 33;
  the danger of correcting him, 35 n. 1, n. 3;
  his attitude toward Empire, 31, 37;
  his sympathies, 38;
  his antipathies, 38 n. 3, 44;
  his religion, 38, 42 n. 4; he finds Julian religious overmuch, 56, n. 1;
  his view of Nemesis, 38, 39;
  his attitude toward Christianity, 40–42;
  his view of martyrs, 41; of bishops, 41; of theological controversy, 41, 42, 56;
  his preference for toleration, 42;
  his humour, 42, 43;
  on the murder of the Goths, 327 n. 1;
Andromeda, 133.
Andronicus, governor of Cyrenaica, 351, 352.
Anthology, Greek, 309.
Anthropomorphism, 202.
Antichrists, etc., 297, 298.
Antioch, 71.
Antiochus Epiphanes, 2.
Anti-pagan legislation, 69.
Antiquarianism, 177.
Antony, Life of, 18, 214, 370, 384–6.
Apocalypse of Gaul, 370.